Comunn na Feinne
1856-1946

MORE THAN A PUB NAME

(The History of the Geelong Highland Society and its activities 1856-1946)

Kerry Cardell

Cliff Cummin

Robert Bakker

First published in February 2018

This is a work of nonfiction. No names have been changed, no characters invented, no events fabricated. It depicts actual events as truthfully as recollection permits and/or can be verified by research.

This work is copyright. Apart from any use permitted under the Copyright Act 1968 (Australia), no part may be reproduced by any process, nor may any other exclusive right be exercised, without the permission of the publisher.

Kerry Cardell, Cliff Cummin and Robert Bakker assert their moral right to be identified as the authors of this work.

Published by Peter Diggins

E-Mail: outsider@eftel.com.au

Cover design by Peter Diggins.

Appendices, Spread Sheets (tables) and other references referred to in this work can be found online at:

https://comunnnafeinne.wordpress.com/

Copyright © 2018 Kerry Cardell, Cliff Cummin and Robert Bakker

All rights reserved.

ISBN-10: 0-9925152-6-2
ISBN: 978-0-9925152-6-3
ISBN: 978-0-9925152-7-0 (eBook)

Special thanks

Our thanks to Robert Bakker who wrestled the overwhelming amount of Comunn na Feinne statistical material into submission and tamely led it into a series of tables.

His proof-reading contribution and his brutally honest editing advice and suggestions have left the book a great deal lighter and the authors fully chastened and confirmed nervous wrecks.

CONTENTS

Acknowledgments		1
Introduction		3
Chapter 1	The Beginning 1856-1858	7
Chapter 2	The Gatherings 1859-1860	41
Chapter 3	Some Highs - Some Lows 1861-1870	66
Chapter 4	Gathering Steam 1871-1900	114
Chapter 5	"The Best of Times – The Worst of Times" 1901-1920	206
Chapter 6	Running out of Puff 1921-1929	325
Chapter 7	The Death of a Vision 1930-1946. A Drama in Three Acts	370
Conclusion		436

Acknowledgements

Without the extensive notes which had been kept by Mr Ronald Carmichael over a period of decades as a member of Comunn na Feinne, this book would probably never have been written. It is a great sadness to the authors that Mr Carmichael, who died some years ago, did not live to see the publication of the history of Comunn na Feinne.

We are grateful, too, to Mr D. Henderson who, since the death of Mr Carmichael, has kept the notes safe and sound, and for his generosity in allowing us to work on them for a period of several years, and to retain them.

Our special thanks to Peter Diggins for his assistance with the 'black arts', more commonly known as IT, and for his encouragement. His advice regarding style and his artistic talents, especially employed to effect in producing the covers, and his handling of the necessary red tape requirements were invaluable. In addition, his ability to take selfies while bush-walking backwards up a mountainside fill us with awe and show us that we are in the presence of a master!

Thanks, too, to all those who offered advice, who bullied us and who gave us help. You know who you are Evelyn, so we won't embarrass you by mentioning your name.

Conversion Table

Currency

£1 = $2.00

10/- = $1.00

5/- = 50c

Length

1 mile = 1.61 km

1 Yard = 0.914 m

1 foot = 300mm

1 inch = 25.4mm

Weight

1lb = 0.454kg

1 ounce = 28.3 grams

[Editor's note: All appendices and tables referenced in this work can be found online at https://comunnnafeinne.wordpress.com/]

Introduction

Comunn na Feinne, Geelong, began its life in December, 1856 and continued to entertain, educate and support the Geelong district for almost ninety years. For the great majority of that time, its 'headline act' was it's annual Highland Games, staged to mark the beginning of each year. From its very beginning the Society also had charitable work as one of its major goals and in that regard, it came to function much as service clubs of today, such as Rotary, Apex and the Lions. However, its Charter traced a more comprehensive aim than simply that of a service organization. During its lifetime Comunn na Feinne provided the community with many cultural diversions – concerts, dances, balls, haggis suppers and the like. For many years, it also conducted a very successful annual Eisteddfod which gave many singers and musicians, some of whom later became famous worldwide, their first platform, as well as financial support. Additionally, it fostered education in a variety of ways and, in its early years, supported local militias, the volunteer fire brigade, local brass bands, and, later, its own pipe band.

The Gaelic name Comunn na Feinne translates into English as "Band of Fingalians". Fingal was the hero of a work which bore his name, 'Fingal' - An Ancient Epic Poem' published by James Macpherson in 1762. It, and its companion piece, 'Temora' (1763), gave to Scottish readers a legendary history pertaining to a band of warriors from the heroic age – something akin to the revered age of King Arthur of English lore, or the Saga era in the Scandinavian countries. In the eighteenth century, great interest had emerged in the distant history and folklore of European nations and this movement was fuelled by the popular 'historical' novels and ballads of Sir Walter Scott, and the 'national' folk tales of Germany and the Norse countries.

The name, Comunn na Feinne, was to last for the lifetime of the Society, defying several attempts to replace it with an English one. It even saw off an early misreading that the Society bearing this name was a communist one endangering the youth of the colony! It was also alleged – wrongly - that only Gaels were welcome in the Society. Only in the present century did the hotel in South Geelong which bore its title, shorten its name to 'The Commo'.

Nevertheless, it is reasonable to ask why Gaelic legend and the Gaelic tongue were used to name and identify the fledgling group? Answering these questions sheds a good deal of light on the background against which the Society arose, and on the path it would follow throughout its almost ninety-year history. In taking the name, Comunn na Feinne, the Society was revealing both that its founding members were familiar with Gaelic language and culture and that they admired the deeds of the ancient Fingalians, going so far as to adopt certain militaristic trappings. Its badge, and its letterhead consisted of a figure of a fully armed Highlander flanked by a similarly armed Aboriginal warrior. Ancient Gaelic mottoes such as standing 'Shoulder to Shoulder' in facing adversity, and 'Behaving nobly', even towards one's enemies, were also cited. The Aboriginal warrior on the Society's logo represented not only an old and living tradition, it was also a reminder to the latter-day Fingalians to support and encourage the Aboriginal populace of the district and to behave towards them in a manner reflecting the spirit of Comunn na Feinne.

The Society was undoubtedly aspiring to create a 'band of brothers' who would behave 'nobly' and support others in a just and equitable manner. Just as Freemasonry invokes the assumed organization, training and practice of masons, who supposedly built the pyramids and the great cathedrals, in order to exemplify the moral behaviour it wishes to inculcate in its members, so Fingal and his band of legendary Celtic heroes were invoked to suggest the virtues of solidarity, selflessness, courage and dedication to each other from which contemporary members of the Society would draw inspiration and put into practice as members of the local community.

The Gaelic name of the Society was to remain until its demise, in 1946, seeing off early criticisms that members must be a band of communists, and that it implied that only Gaels could join the group. But as time passed the name became 'naturalised'; accepted and used without comment by the local community. By 1856, when the Society began, the Gaelic tongue had some sort of base in Geelong. Its founders and many early members were Gaelic-speakers. The Presbyterian minister James Forbes estimated that among the many thousand or so Scots in Geelong and district there was a substantial sub-set of Gaels. In the 1850s Highland and Island Immigration Society ships landed in Geelong discharging many Gaels whose only language was the Gaelic tongue. Many of these immigrants had been displaced by famine and Clearances from their homeland, and they were objects for Comunn na Feinne's initial benevolent impulses. Many of these new arrivals needed a helping hand in finding accommodation, employment and friendship in their new home.

The Gaelic 'flavour' of the new Society was initially very strong. Some of its founding members had been involved in establishing, in Geelong, a Gaelic church in 1854 and a Gaelic school. Electioneering advertisements in Gaelic, as well as Gaelic church intimations, were carried in the local newspaper, the *Geelong Advertiser*. For a number of years, the Society ran a Gaelic essay contest, and Gaelic Orthography examinations, for young school students, as well as Gaelic poetry contests for adults. Unsurprisingly, then, programmes for the first Comunn na Feinne Highland Gathering on 1st January, 1857, were handwritten in Gaelic.

As you follow the activities of the Comunn na Feinne recorded in this book, one interesting issue to ponder is whether the highly public activities of the Society were attempts to keep a tradition alive, or were they part of a wider movement to manufacture a tradition? In promoting Highland sports, encouraging the use of the kilt, holding Burns' nights and the like, did these emigres, having witnessed the assaults upon their culture in Scotland itself, see these activities as a way of 'saving' and 'preserving' their national identity? Or, since modern tartans, pipe bands, and highly organized Highland games are claimed by some to have no real part in Highland culture until the nineteenth century, were they helping to invent, and perhaps even commercialize a culture? Grant Jarvie in his *History of the Highland Games* presents the former case, Eric Hobsbawn and Terence Ranger in *The Invention of Tradition* argue the latter one.

The Society was seeking to preserve elements of Highland – and later a more generalized Scottish – identity through many of its 'symbolic' public events such as the annual Highland Games. Other parts of the identity its founders sought to preserve were subsumed into a more universal humanitarianism; like the heroes of old, the Society was to promote justice, equality and community. Like most organizations, its members did not always "stand shoulder to shoulder" in the strife – there were divisions and defections at times – but behind the Scottish national trappings the impulse toward community-building in the new homeland remained strong for most of the Society's history.

It will become clear in the following pages that while the symbols and slogans which the Comunn na Feinne chose for itself suggested a group of men bonding together to uphold certain traditions, and to behave charitably toward distressed fellow-countrymen cast adrift on a foreign shore, and towards Aborigines, similarly dispossessed in their own land. In fact, the Society's actual social remit was extended to fostering the well-being of the wider local community. Over the decades of its existence it was to garner much affection and support for so doing.

[Editor's note: All appendices and tables referenced in this work can be found online at https://comunnnafeinne.wordpress.com/]

Chapter 1

Comunn na Feinne -The Beginning 1856-1858

Although the actual formation of Comunn na Feinne was signalled by a notice in the *Geelong Advertiser* on 1st December 1856, calling for a meeting of Scots, it seems that a certain amount of pre-planning had already taken place several months earlier. For example, the *Geelong Advertiser* on 16th February, 1917, in a retrospective article looking back over fifty years, referred to a Gaelic communication it had received in October 1856 detailing a meeting which had been held to discuss the formation of a Gaelic Society of sorts. Apparently, this earlier meeting had mapped out the setting up of such a Society, as well as listing its proposed charter aims and choosing Comunn na Feinne as its name. The *Advertiser* stated that, "it had the following translation supplied of the report of the meeting of Highlanders held in October, 1856, to form a Society."

> A short time ago a number of Scottish Highlanders in Geelong held a meeting in the Gaelic School House for the purpose of establishing a Gaelic Society, to be known under the title of Comunn na Feinne.

This earlier meeting is detailed in the Gaelic paper, *An Teachdaire Gaidhealteachd (The Gaelic Messenger)*, Issue No 10, November, 1857, p8, and can be found in Appendix 2 in its original Gaelic form. Archibald Douglas was one of this paper's Victorian Agents.

The actual formation of Comunn na Feinne, however, was signalled by a notice in the *Geelong Advertiser* on 1st December 1856. At that meeting, James Rankin called for a committee to draw up a set of appropriate rules and regulations. It was also proposed to hold a social gathering in the form of a Caledonian Games on the forthcoming New Year's Day to bring together all who might wish to join the nascent society. Other meetings followed, on 11th December 1856 and 21st December 1856, at the National and then the Argyle hotels. The well-attended meeting on 11th of December, 1856 was reported in the *Geelong Advertiser* the next day.

> A spirited public meeting last evening was held in the National Hotel, Moorabool Street, Geelong, when a large number of members were enrolled. Office-Bearers were appointed for the First Annual Highland Gathering, competitions of which due notice will be given by advertisement.

It was at this more numerously attended meeting that the first office bearers were elected. These were; Archibald Douglas (President), Alexander McKenzie (Vice-President), John Clark (Treasurer) and James Rankin (Secretary). A committee of six was chosen to support these officials. A programme was drawn up for the inaugural Highland games to be held on New Year's Day, 1857 and this was ratified at another public meeting of the Society at William Rae's Argyll Hotel on 21st December, 1856. There was an influx of new members at this meeting and £60 was raised in subscriptions.

The charter approved at these early meetings was printed in the Gaelic paper *An Teachdaire Gaidhealtachd* (Hobart, 10th November, 1857, p.8):

1. To cultivate and preserve the Gaelic Language and Highland Nationality. To encompass Gaelic and kindred dialects, and to engender respect for the patriotism and customs of their ancestors.

2. To practice morality by which all members were expected to display honourable principles and magnanimity in their own conduct and to encourage the same in those with whom they associated.

3. To engage in the study of every department of antiquarian research, particularly the origins and history and archaeology of the Celtic nation.

4. To engender in oneself a spirit of philanthropy.

James Rankin put these into plain English: the aims were to promote Highland and general athletic games, as well as the intellectual and practical improvement of the whole community, from the children at school to the general public in whatever role they filled in society. In this summation Rankin placed stress on the Society's ambition to serve the wider community, as well as the aims of fostering the Gaelic language and preserving Highland traditions. In the immediate short term these aims were not to be the easiest of bedfellows.

With the 21st December, 1856 meeting having ratified the charter, attention was then turned to the Games themselves. The events which were to take place at the New Year's Day Gathering reflected what would have occurred at similar gatherings in Scotland itself, with physical field activities, such as tossing the Caber, throwing the hammer and putting the heavy stone, dominating the list of sports. Foot Racing together with High Jumping were also included in these inaugural Games. Solo Piping and Highland Dancing, too, featured as competition events. A prize for the best original Gaelic poetry was also offered. This initial gathering, a chance for Highlanders to meet and socialize, was open to the general public, and traditional Highland sports were joined by general athletic contests. The programme was hand-written by John Clark of Teesdale, treasurer of the Society, in both Gaelic and English

Initially, the desire to avoid ethnic exclusiveness was to cause some confusion. Practically on the eve of the first of Comunn na Feinne's New Year's Day Gatherings, the issue of exclusivity reared its head. A notice in the *Geelong Advertiser* of 22nd December, 1856, setting out the intended programme for the upcoming Games, mistakenly intimated that the Games were open to Highlanders only. The advertisement stated that competitions for the prizes were, "to be open to the Highlanders in all the Australian colonies."

> Comunn na Feinne - There is to be a Highland gathering on New Year's Day, 1858, near to the town of Geelong, Victoria. We hope that all of our countrymen who are able will come to this large meeting which is faithful to the language and games of the Highlander. Among the prizes which will be

awarded at the Gathering is a special one separately for reading and spelling Gaelic. This is very useful because many of the Gaels in Australia so far away are backward in reading and writing their native language.*
*[See Appendix 2 (b)]

The Comunn na Feinne secretary quickly responded, in the next issue of the *Advertiser*, pointing out that, ambiguity aside, the notice was not meant to indicate that the competitions were exclusively for Highland or Scottish competitors in general, and the *Advertiser* should not have assumed that it was. The Society's rules (which, of course, the public had not yet seen), made this clear, and the upcoming Games were open to all.

> A mistake has crept into your notice of our proceedings in Saturday's paper. We do not exclude competitors whatever their nation. Our rules distinctly state that our games are open to all the colonists and not exclusively to Highlanders.

In fact, it was mainly for the sake of colour that those competing in the traditional Heavy events (tossing the Caber, throwing the heavy hammer and throwing the light hammer), were for many years required to be kilted, but kilts would be supplied for strong men of any nationality who needed them! Participants in the Games, if wearing tartan, were excused from paying the competitor fee!

One reason why this constitution was able to be presented for adoption so quickly was that a draft had already been prepared in October, 1856. Another lay in the political skills and community service record of very early members. Dougal Rankin, Archibald Douglas and Robert McInnes had been active in the movements which brought about a Gaelic Free Presbyterian Church, and a Gaelic school in Geelong, as well as social reforms in the town. Pioneer Squatter Alexander Thompson had, on several occasions, served as Geelong's mayor and had served in parliaments in Sydney and Melbourne and assisted the Buntingdale Aboriginal mission (1839-51). Alexander Fyfe* was also a state parliamentarian who had supported the Eureka rebels. Both men espoused somewhat radical and reformist politics. Dr William Hingston Baylie*, the Society's first medical officer, was also an ex-mayor who had campaigned for improved sanitation, advocated for a volunteer fire brigade and a local militia, and had experience in aboriginal welfare in two States. Men like these were joined by local businessmen in founding and shaping the early Comunn na Feinne.

*[See short biographies, Appendix 3(b).]

The leading figures initiating this new Society were, therefore, already experienced in a whole range of social reform activities aimed at promoting the well-being of the Geelong community.

With a pool of such men already experienced in working for social causes, many of which the fledgling Comunn na Feinne was soon to adopt and interpret as being suited to the outworking of their own aims, the Society had a ready-made platform from which it was able, quickly, to establish itself and to immediately launch into action. The movement initially gained its impetus from Scots and others who were living in and around the town and who were engaged in small businesses, trades and in the professions, and who were committed to improving their community. These men were, of course, joined by others from working class backgrounds as well as those from the landed 'class'**.

**[A list of some early members and their occupations, can be found in Appendix 3 (a)]

Ossian Macpherson was a local resident who had already published two books of Poetry in Britain before emigrating to Australia. He became the Society's 'bard' and also its 'special reporter', and general 'warm up' public relations officer. Macpherson, in the *Geelong Advertiser* 10th December, 1856, launched the forthcoming Highland Gathering with a suitably framed call to the children of Fion, entitled, 'The Battle Song of Gaul', which he gave in Gaelic and English. This was taken from the ancient poem, Fingal, Book IV, allegedly composed by the C3rd AD warrior poet, Ossian, after whom Macpherson was named. This was prefaced by some remarks from Macpherson about the poem's source and also about his translation which he regarded as being better than the one which had originally been published in 1760! Public relations people are not known for being over-endowed with modesty!

The epic verse sang of an older race of ancestors, the Fingalians, and contained allusions to doing battle and fighting bravely and nobly, and spoke of the exploits of its hero, Gaul. The call, therefore, was to the contestants at the 1857 Games, these modern-day Fingalians, to emulate the 'spirit' of the warriors of the poem. They were to be 'fair' and 'just' in the mock trials before them in the various contests to be 'fought' out on the South Geelong arena. The call to arms was, of course, a metaphorical one in order to encourage sporting prowess on the Games arena.

The Battle Song of Gaul*

Offspring of the Chief
King of Spears!
Strong arm in every trial;
Ambitious heart without dismay.
Chief of the host of severe sharp
Pointed weapons
Cut down to death.
So that no white sailed bark
May float round dark Innistore.
Like the destroying thunder
Be thy stroke, O hero!
The forward eye like the flaming bolt,
As firm rock
unwavering be thy heart.
As the flame of night be thy sword
uplift thy shield
Of snorting steeds, high bounding
Like the flame of death,
Offspring of the Chiefs
Of snorting steeds,
Cut down the foes to earth.

*[The *Geelong Advertiser*, on information provided by the Comunn na Feinne, offered the following explanation of this song. "A war song of the ancient Celts probably nearly 2,000 years old, holds no uncommon interest. It is taken from the copy which the Rev Alexander Gallie (sic) of Kincardine, in Ross-shire communicated to the Highland Society from memory. It may be found in the 4th Book of Fingal, as translated by James McPherson; however, the present translation by Comunn na Feinne's own bard [Ossian Macpherson], seemed to them to be preferable." The original Gaelic version can be found in Appendix 2.
[Ossian Macpherson's poems can be found in Appendix 5 (a).]

This poem, among other things, drew comment that 'national' divisions were seemingly to be encouraged by the forthcoming Games.

At this time, a measure of anti-Scottish sentiment was evident in the British press and the emergence of Comunn na Feinne in Geelong, together with its intended nationalistic display, was enough to provoke a similar outburst of this sentiment from one indignant Geelong Anglophile whose letter appeared in the *Geelong Advertiser* 8th December, 1856.

> Is it not, sir, the height of impudence in these proud highlanders of Geelong at this time of day, to begin to assert their obsolete nationality, if ever they had any. When will they have the sense to recognize Anglo-Saxonism as the only nationality to be tolerated in this land! Indeed, the few among them who possess a spark of common sense are so ashamed of their origins that they have long ago amalgamated with the all-absorbing mass of universal Anglo-Saxonism compared with which all other races are but as a drop in the bucket. I would seriously recommend these 'children of the mist' to learn to forget their past renown, and to accept the popular title, whether right or wrong, the boast of every Englishman.

Insensitive, yes; but such perceived busybodies did not warrant going unchallenged, and a broadside quickly appeared in the following day's *Advertiser*.

> I will briefly allude to the Anglo-Saxon's [letter] whose ill-judged attempt to thwart a good cause will, I trust, prove ineffectual. I for one would not join or recommend the society if it engendered any feelings prejudicial to the interest of our adopted country. ... It is the first time that ever I have seen it asserted that Highland men were ashamed of their origins, get me one to acknowledge it and I'll get a thousand to spit on that one.
> Does Anglo-Saxon for a moment think that a despot's power shall rule over and chastise us with a rod of iron? His language implies such when he says that Anglo-Saxonism will be the only nationality to be tolerated in this land. Short-sighted mortal! How does he or I or anyone but know that this country is destined to become the exclusive property of pig-tailed Tartars, who know as much about Anglo-Saxonism as I do about Chinamen ... The children of the mist will not forget their past renown; but they will never cherish any national feelings that can possibly offend their fellow-colonists; they will mind their affairs which is more than 'Anglo-Saxon' has done.

It is unclear how many ruffled English feathers would have been soothed by reading such pugnacious lines as the foregoing!

As 1856 quickly slipped into 1857, the Society had set itself a mammoth task. From its first tentative steps in the early days of December, 1856, it had affirmed a constitution, recruited members, announced its first Games for New Year's Day 1857, and had hastily drawn up a programme of events for these Games. As might be expected, the first Gathering did not have an extensive list of competitions, although the total prize money was approximately £44.

The track and field events were:

Field Sports*	**Highland Dancing Events**
Tossing the Caber	Gille Calum (Sword Dance)
Throwing the Heavy Hammer	Reel of Tulloch
Throwing the Light Hammer	Highland Reel
Putting the Heavy Stone	
Putting the Light Stone	Solo Piping
Running High Leap	
Standing Leap	
Long Leap	
Footrace - Men (300 yards); Boys (100 yards)	

*[The results of each of the competitions at the Games, over the life of the Society, are to be found in the tables provided at the site shown.]

The town newspaper, the *Geelong Advertiser*, although it was to blow hot and cold in its coverage of the Society over the years gave, for this the first Gathering, good space to the various meetings of the founding committee as well as to descriptions of the games, the lists of competitors and the results. It became the custom for the *Geelong Advertiser* to report the various activities of Comunn na Feinne, and especially the annual New Year's Day Gatherings. Here, on the occasion of its first Highland Games, the *Advertiser* went out of its way to be supportive and encouraging to the Society and its leaders.

Comunn na Feinne was formally launched on 1st January, 1857, with great noise, colour and excitement, and even a summary of the *Advertiser*'s report, from the following day, captures the paper's enthusiasm. The Society's first Highland Games took place on open ground in South Geelong on 1st January, 1857. The *Geelong Advertiser* in 1860 explained this choice of day:

> To Scotsmen, generally, Christmas Day is not associated with ideas of festivity so intimately as New Year's Day which, throughout North Britain, is emphatically the festival of the year. Unless we err greatly, the observance of Christmas beyond any other day at all events as a religious festival would, by strict disciplinarians, be looked upon as something wrong, and for all sportive purposes New Year's Day in Scotland is the counterpart to Christmas Day in England.

A procession to the sportsground was headed by some pipers in full Highland dress, Comunn na Feinne's President, Archibald Douglas, its Committee and a sturdy bodyguard brandishing a Lochaber Axe, all of whom were joined by ordinary members, many in Highland costume, and townsfolk of all nationalities. The route of the Procession taken by members and supporters, and anyone else who cared to tag along, stretched from the centre of the town to the South Geelong ground and was a long trek. This first march started what was to be an almost unbroken tradition throughout the life of the Society.

There was such a brandishing of weapons, such a triumphant anthem, such a display of tartans of every clan (and none!), such regalia, such pomp and such noise as to make the whole town aware that the Games were here!

The Society's bard and public relations man, Ossian Macpherson, quoted in the *Carmichael Notes*, found grandiloquence in the occasion. If his poem, printed in the *Geelong Advertiser* 10th December, 1856, drew forth a measure of arrogant pride from 'Anglo-Saxon', his description of the inaugural Highland games in the *Advertiser* 2nd January, 1857 was not, in any sense conciliatory!

> The first Highland Gathering was held on an area of land generally described as the plain at South Geelong near the Barwon River, the New Year's Day, 1st of January, 1857. And a memorable day it was, a real Highland Gathering. The historical and traditional associations by which the Highlander is enveloped, give him a supremacy at such gatherings, which he has proudly and self-sacrificially earned in the past. It is an unquenchable spirit and on the particular

day of the year it infects the whole populace, for few can be so lamentably warped in their appreciation of the chivalry and bravery of the Scottish [as not] to rise to a full and generous appraisement of the Scottish trait.

The heavy games, the focus of many of the spectators in the early Geelong Gatherings, were to frequently throw up public 'heroes' whose exploits drew admiration from those acquainted with such games. In 1857 Duncan McIntyre was one such competitor and he was successful in all of the heavy events except the Caber tossing. Track events, too, produced 'stars', a colourful early one being an imported "Yankee" Cobb and Coach driver, Elbridge Gerry Emery*. He was a talented athlete who figured prominently in the Games in the early years of Comunn na Feinne. Emery went on to work the athletic circuit which developed, competing at Ballarat, Castlemaine, Buninyong and elsewhere.

*[See details in Appendix 3(b) Short Biographies]

As the yearly games went by, 'fan' clubs emerged around certain outstanding contestants, especially those competing in the Heavy events. Whether it was for prowess in the tossing of the Caber or in dancing up a storm in the Irish Reel, certain names began to emerge as 'stars' destined, of course, to be the subject of wagers!

Less physical, but no less important, was the competition for the best poem in Gaelic descriptive of the aims of Comunn na Feinne. The prize was a set of books, *The Lives of Eminent Scotsmen.*

The close of the first Highland Games was accompanied by a sense of satisfaction and self-congratulation among the office-bearers and members of Comunn na Feinne. They marched, elated, back into town, led by a "sturdy and venerable Highlander" bearing the Society's standard and a mean-looking Lochaber Axe, and gathered at the National Hotel where, "they sat down to an elegant and substantial supper …" A prize for an impromptu Gaelic poem was offered at the dinner and, it was the treasurer of the Society, John Clarke, who carried the evening with his lines, translated as follows.

> Sons of the North come boldly forth
> And join our chosen Band.
> Be not dismayed but lend your aid

> With willing heart and hand.
> Can we forget we owe a debt
> To mem'ries past and gone?
> For if we do we can't be true
> To selves and Calidon.

Along with self-congratulatory verse, the supper produced an early sign of Comunn na Feinne's willingness to cultivate the friendship of those with power and influence to further the Society's cause. The *Carmichael Notes* quote the response of Alexander Fyfe, a state politician, who was toasted.

> Many toasts were proposed and downed with Highland Honours and cheering. The constitution and the local member of the State Parliament, Mr Alexander Fyfe MLA, were also toasted with Fyfe responding suitably in an elated speech in which he expressed a hope that the Comunn na Feinne would flourish. He regretted that he was not a Highlander although he said he had the spirit of a true one and would do all he could to forward the Society called the Comunn na Feinne.

That offer was soon to be taken up!

Fyfe's position as an MLA., was used to secure a meeting with the State Governor, Sir Henry Barkly, on behalf of the Society. Early in 1857, Seeking a Chief for their Society, the executive, through the offices of Alexander Fyfe MLA., obtained an appointment with Sir Henry Barkly, the new Governor of Victoria, a Scot who had arrived in Victoria on 26th December, 1856, after service as Governor of British Guiana and then of Jamaica. He was the son of a sugar merchant and he had been born in Ross-shire, Scotland. Fyfe explained to Sir Henry the nature and objects of the Society and added that, "he need scarcely remark that Comunn na Feinne was founded with a most liberal and humanitarian Charter."

> His Excellency, with much feeling, expressed his delight in accepting from Comunn na Feinne the Ticket of Membership. He was the son of a Scotsman, and had it in his power to say that the blood of the Ross and McKenzie flowed in his veins. He was an active member of the Highland Society of London. He loved to look at the national costume and encourage national sports and national gatherings, and he felt honoured in being appointed "The Patron and Chief" of the Society in Victoria

Fyfe also arranged the right contacts when the Society sought legal rights to the land it was using for its sports-days. Thus, within a year of its inception, Comunn na Feinne had not only conducted its first successful Gathering but had also recruited the highest political figure in the colony as its patron! The first quarterly meeting of the Society, held on 3rd February, 1857, was thus a buoyant one. It was decided that the Society would donate an annual amount of £10 to the Geelong Hospital, thus beginning a connection which lasted the life of the Society. Comunn na Feinne remained a generous patron of the Hospital to which it eventually donated and supported a bed.

The infant Society next turned its attention to an international matter: the raising of funds to erect a monument in Scotland to the great Scottish hero, Sir William Wallace (c1270-1305), the renowned Scottish patriot and martyr in the struggle for Scottish independence. In the mid-nineteenth-century appeals began in Scotland, and worldwide, to raise funds for such a monument. An interim 'Wallace' Committee was set up to prepare for a "grand meeting" at Geelong to be held on 20th February, 1857. This proved to be a large gathering the core of which came from Comunn na Feinne itself. Archibald Douglas was called to be secretary, and Alexander Fyfe MLA, was called to take the chair. The *Geelong Advertiser* of 12th February carried a notice that Comunn na Feinne members, "were urged to appear … in Highland dress."

This notice calling for a public meeting drew some unflattering comments through the letters column, one coming from 'Civis', regarding "Crotchety Scots" and their national sensitivities. In answer, a correspondent retorted that although it was true that Wallace was considered a hero to Scots:

> [M]any also from that country against which he so often stood and fought … now highly regard him as a Patriot, and I have no doubt they would be willing to unite in helping onward (sic) the cause …

Wallace's name, and his example as an opponent of tyranny, had been invoked by Scots in campaigns for political independence for the Port Phillip District and, again, in the struggle to keep that colony free from convict settlement in the 1840s and again in the 1850s. Thus, like the example of the Fingalian warriors, adopted by Comunn na Feinne, Wallace was seen as an example of bravery and chivalry to be emulated (metaphorically of course!) by its members. Despite some Anglophone letters to the local newspaper, the wider community recognized that Wallace was being used as a symbol for liberty and freedom and not as a nationalist figurehead promoting Scots. Wallace was held up as the exemplar of selfless behaviour on behalf of those who were oppressed. Scots in general were, therefore, not slow to identify Wallace as the archetypal 'freedom fighter' when it came to political freedom and liberties for all in their new colonial society. In Victoria, for example, Wallace was one of the names which had been invoked in the struggle to keep the new colonial homeland free of convicts.

> Let Britons and Irishmen rise from their slumbers,
> Combined with the lovers of freedom and Bruce;
> Shew England what advocates liberty numbers,
> Before she has turned her criminals loose;
> The genius of Wallace, of Hampden, and Grattan,
> Will smile when you rise in your might as you should,
> To crush every knave who desires to fatten
> On labour extorted by torture and blood.

Journalist, and Scot, William Kerr, asserted that the spirit of Wallace was not unique to any single race but, rather, it was a yearning which drove every people to assert their freedom. Scots could be proud of their hero, but the masses of oppressed people everywhere, struggling for political freedom were, by adoption, sons of Wallace, aspiring for the day of Robert Burns' 'radical hope':

> When man to man the warl' o'er,
> Shall brithers be, an' a' that.

Comunn na Feinne played a large part in the Victorian Wallace Monument campaign. The *Advertiser*'s report of 21st February, recognized that the Society was seeking to assist raising a monument, not to a person, nor to a single country's people, but to the 'ideals' of liberty and freedom from oppression and to the belief in the equality and brotherhood of all men; ideals for which Wallace fought and died.

As if to amplify such sentiments as the foregoing, relating to equality, justice and universal brotherhood, Comunn na Feinne's membership cards were distributed during the week following the Wallace Monument Rally. The card represented visually the credo Comunn na Feinne had taken for itself. It showed a Highlander and Aborigine as equals in stature and might, and with a common commitment to fair play and mutual respect. This was issued on 28th February, 1857 and it was described by the *Advertiser* the following day.

> [It] … is most elaborately engraved having in the centre an entablature representing a well-known incident from Ossian's Poems, the 3rd Book of Fingal, surrounded with a wreath of Scotch Thistles, and supported on the left hand by a Highlander in full Costume, and on the right by an Aboriginal in the attitude of throwing his Boomerang, on which is enscribed (sic) the word "Merambie"** or 'Belonging to me.' … Besides these there are Emu and Kangaroo …

*[By the mid-nineteenth century, the initial contact and harsh treatment of local Aboriginal tribes by some settlers had more or less passed in the Geelong district.]
** [This, presumably, was an Aboriginal term.]

The Comunn na Feinne logo used on all of its medals.

Given that the Society was barely two months old, the fact that membership cards had already been designed, printed and delivered, further confirms that considerable pre-planning had taken place before Comunn na Feinne's formal launch. The card had been designed by the Society President, Archibald Douglas, and J.M. Tulloch, a committee-man, and, "included the motto of the Society engraved ... in Celtic characters". The inscription, 'Lean gu dlù ri cliù do shinnsre', 'Follow steadfastly the fame of your Fathers' was an old and well-known Gaelic saying. At the bottom of the card there were two lines written in Gaelic quoting another ancient proverb: "Search not thou for Battle, nor shun it when it comes."

The remainder of 1857 passed with meetings of the Society being concerned with raising funds for future sports-days. The total prize money for the 1858 Games was £24/14/6 but there would be 12 silver medals* to accompany certain of the monetary prizes. In addition, the attention of Comunn na Feinne was soon directed to the improvement of education in the district.

Before 1872, there was no compulsory education and many schools (which could be set up by virtually anyone) had no settled curriculum and were of dubious quality. In Victoria at the time 'private' colleges and home tutoring existed alongside [the] government (national) schools and denominational schools. Comunn na Feinne, true to its Charter, quickly took up the task of seeking to improve both the quality of teaching in local schools and the quality of the curriculum being offered, by awarding prizes at competitive examinations.*

*[See Appendix 11 for outline of the areas covered in Comunn na Feinne Examinations. The subject relating to Gaelic in schools was dropped after 1861. Open Competitions in Gaelic Poetry and Prose, however, continued into the twentieth century.]

The quality of instruction being offered could vary widely between the 'private' schools, the government (i.e. national schools) and denominational (i.e. church) schools. A good description of the existing situation in Victoria, as far as education was concerned, before 1872, can be found in Appendix 14 (a).

At a meeting held on the 10th December, 1857, the Society established that fostering education lay within its charter. The *Geelong Advertiser* of 11th December, 1857, quickly summarized this aspect of the Society's goals.

> One of the objects of Comunn na Feinne is the promotion of education. Annual educational examinations, the scope and object of this extension of the Society's usefulness are, by this time, well understood under its auspices. Open to all classes and denominations of the rising generation, attending the schools or otherwise, in the County of Grant. Prizes are to be offered for proficiency in the subjects of plain English, Reading, Writing, English History, Grammar, Dictation, Composition, Arithmetic, Geography, Natural Science and Gaelic Orthography.

Having determined upon this course, Comunn na Feinne lost no time in organizing its members as fund-raisers to meet the expense of conducting these examinations and funding the appropriate prizes. Donations and subscription lists were to be submitted at the Monthly Meeting on 20th December, 1857.

The first examinations took place in the Mechanics' Institute Hall on Friday morning the 1st January, 1858. The assumption was that over time competition among pupils would result in improved teaching and in a fuller curriculum, with teachers at the various schools more diligently preparing their students in areas covered by the Comunn na Feinne examinations.* The initial examiners were the two Government inspectors of schools; representing both the National School System (Mr A.B. Orlebar) and the Denominational system (Mr J.S. Millar). Silver medals, specially minted in London and bearing the crest of the Society, were to be awarded for the best scholar in each of the areas of examination.

> [A]bout 40 boys, pupils of various educational establishments in the town, responded to the invitation of Comunn na Feinne and presented themselves yesterday for examination at the Mechanics' Institute …

*[See Appendix 11 for examples of Comunn na Feinne's Exam curricula.]

On the same day as the education examinations, the second New Year's Day

Highland Gathering took place, and this was eulogized by the Society's bard, Ossian Macpherson. His poem, from the *Advertiser* 2nd January, 1858, led off the Games' report.

> The Gathering of Comunn na Feinne.*
>
> Shade of the mighty dead! Sire of the bard
> Whose name will but perish when mountain is glen,
> Come from thy mist – as our patron, our guard-
> Fingal, our sire, mighty Chieftain of men!
>
> Barkly!** The ghosts of thy ancestors rise,-
> Those heroes whose backs from the foe were ne'er seen,
> They point ye to join us – their beck ne'er despise.
> Remember your past, Chief of Comunn na Feinne!
>
> ……………………………………………………
>
> Come with the hammer, the camac***, the stone,-
> Nimble as deer, bring your muscles of steel:
> The strength of the children of Feinne must be shewn
> In glorious strife, by the might ye reveal,
>
> Join ye the dance on the green, grassy brae,
> Heedless of care be your boisterous mirth;
> Strathspey, Gillie Callum, or wild Caber Feidh-
> Foot it with pride for the land of your birth.
>
> ……………………………………………………
>
> Clann nan Gael! Up with ye! Shoulder to shoulder
> Albannach summons her children today;
> And memory must die, and the heart must grow colder,
>
> Before that the summons we cease to obey.

*[Macpherson's full poems can be found in Appendix 5 (a).]
** This was a reference to Sir Henry Barkly (1815-1898), who was Governor of Victoria, 1856-63, and first Chief of Comunn na Feinne, Geelong.
*** A camac is the stick used in the game of Shinty (camanac in Gaelic). It is shaped something like a crude curved cricket bat.]

Macpherson also waxed lyrical about the crowd scenes the day would bring, using the words of one of "old Scotia's bards" - John Mayne (1759-1836) - from his poem 'The Siller Gun', which described a scene from a bye-gone market day in Scotland. These were lines, wrote Macpherson, which were "remarkably apt" for the present-day attendance at the Gathering.

> "Hech, sirs! What crowds cam' into town,
> To see them mustering up and down!
> Lasses, and lads, sunburnt and brown-
> Women and weans*,
> Gentle and simple, mingling, crown
> The gladsome scenes!
> *weans - infants

The possession of 'an eye for the main chance', famously (and infamously!) attributed to Scots, was evidenced in the *Geelong Advertiser* at the time of this celebration by a classified advertisement from the 'Scotch Clan Tartan House', Market Square Geelong, Prop. A. MacCallum, which advertised 'Clan Tartans in Stock'. Listed were the tartans for the clans Macpherson, MacLean, Campbell, Cameron, MacDonald (two branches) as well as about a dozen others.

While local enthusiasm for the new Society was palpable, the Melbourne *Age*, on 1st December, 1858, may have been a little carried away in its promotion of Comunn na Feinne when it alluded to it possibly setting up an early form of an Institute of Sport!

> Comunn na Feinne is rapidly assuming an important position, prospering in funds, and increasing in membership. Some of the more enthusiastic belonging to the body are devising a public school for athletic purposes, and tuition in the use of arms, more especially in fencing, small sword, and broadsword drill, a course of education much desiderated and too much neglected.

This paper also wrote a spoof on the militaristic accompaniments carried and worn by Scots on Geelong's New Year's Day. The brandishing of Lochaber Axes, Claymores and Dirks, and the wearing of the Sgian Dubh, all of which would appear in the procession to the arena, as well as around the ground, according to the *Age*, were no grounds of apprehension on the part of Geelong folks. For those inclined to take the presence of warrior- clad Highlanders as some sort of threat, the *Age*, in its report on 1st December, 1858, with tongue very firmly planted in its cheek, assured those of a nervous disposition that, despite appearances to the contrary, they could sleep peacefully in their beds without any fear of some latter-day Jacobite rebellion!

> [Any apprehensiveness] to this intent is probably owing to the extraordinary display made in the windows of Mr McCallum, where, for the last day or two, peaceful brocades, silks, satins, bareges, and other sorts of pacific draperies, have given place to warlike equipments, and Highland outfits in particular. Double hilted claymores flash in the light, half-sheathed skean dhubhs (sic) threaten, with cairnghorm (sic) luster (sic) over lowland feelings. Clan tartans flout before the distracted eye - imagination pictures gigantic highland-men, and conjures up ideas of the "slogan." Were there any descendants of "Bonnie Prince Charlie" amongst us, it might give rise to the suspicion that our quiet friend in the Market square was acting as an army agent in the interest of some scion of the "Young Pretender" … Geelong is prepared, however, to meet any descent of the mountain chieftains, with their retainers, from the fastnesses of the Barrabools. District business engagements interfere with military duties; and our rifle corps, though somewhat inefficient as marksmen, could line the river at very long intervals from the Montpelier Punt to the Barwon Bridge, and when the Macs, the Campbells, the Camerons, the Argyles (sic), and Duffs, headed by Copperfaicht* (sic) No. 1, rushed from the gorges, the Victorian Geelong Rifle Corps could retreat to their respective strongholds, their places of business, and sell out the enemy. This view, founded on mature reflection, will set at rest any misgivings that might arise about the "Comunn na Feinne" and the warlike exhibition of Highland accoutrements displayed in the peaceable precincts of the Market square.

* [This probably should read 'Caber Feidh' – meaning The Stag's Antlers. It was a motto of the McKenzies and of The Seaforth Highlanders, a Scottish Regiment, which lost its separate identity when it was amalgamated with the Queen's Own Highland Camerons in 1961.]

If any such fears, real or imaginary, existed, they were not sufficiently terrifying as to dissuade the general public from flocking to the Gathering. The numbers attending the 1858 Games were far greater than those that had gathered the previous year and the picture was made more colourful by the increased number of men in their kilts (many, no doubt, hired from the various Geelong Clan and Tartan Shops now advertising such wares).

At this, the second Highland Gathering, there was a notable addition – the participation of local Aborigines in some events, including those which allowed them to demonstrate their own skills.

> The event of the day will of course be the Highland Gathering at South Geelong ... The gathering is expected to be much more brilliant than that of last year. All nations, including Aborigines of Victoria, are invited to compete for the prizes offered by the Comunn na Feinne.

The Aborigines, from 1858, took their place in the yearly procession to the sports ground at South Geelong. They were identified as a distinct 'national' presence, along with the other 'national' group taking part. Aborigines, who had been invited to take part in the Procession and the Games, were appropriately dressed in plaid donated by the Society, and their presence along with the other variously dressed organizations and individuals who took part in the march, duly added to the festival air of the day. They attended not only as spectators and some of them joined in certain of the sporting contests held on the day, as well as in competitions involving their own native skills.

Although it is possible to ascribe Comunn na Feinne's willingness to embrace the local Aborigines simply to notions of nineteenth century Victorian paternalism, the length to which the Society went in order to be involved with the Aboriginal people seems to suggest that a deeper concern motivated it. As already noted, the Society's membership card displayed on one side a representation of a Highlander and that of an Aborigine. The medals awarded to prize winners also contained a representation of a Highlander and an Aborigine. The presence of Gaelic slogans, when translated, denoted that here was a representation of the two peoples' traditions - warriors, equally worthy, equally matched and equally respected.

One of the most popular sports in which the Aborigines participated was foot-racing and these events were to attract Aboriginal athletes from throughout Victoria and also from interstate. However, it was in their own traditional skills that they excelled and for which they often won great applause.

> The spear-throwing by Aborigines was perhaps more interesting to many spectators than any other of the sports. A painted kangaroo was the mark and

the distance forty-five yards. Six competitors presented themselves for this trial of native skill. As they stood, kilted and turbaned, poising, the spears in one hand, and holding the boomerang in the other, they formed one of the most picturesque groups of the day. The spear throwing was not good … and only two displayed anything approaching to a dangerously skilled aim. Both of these were thrown by the same man, our old friend 'king' Jerry* … One of his spears was of Iron Bark; the other of Mallee-timber.

*[It was common practice to give English names, often just the first name, to Aborigines. It was probably the case, as much as any other explanation, that this was due to the inability of the colonists to anglicize certain Aboriginal names, words or terms. The *Advertiser*, for example, reported that 'Jerry's' Aboriginal name was the "typographical absurdity", Coighcoighquhohoaghm. However, whether this was his actual name or just an attempt to render his Aboriginal name into an English form is not known.]

'Jerry' Dan-Dan-Nook (Barrabool Tribe, Geelong).

Unfortunately, at the foregoing Games, the wind was too strong to allow the Boomerang to be thrown safely, "in the midst of so large a crowd." This portion of the programme was therefore "relinquished." Aboriginal foot-racing (200 yards) also took place with 'Jerry' taking winner's honours. As well as competing in their own events, some of the Aborigines also took part in the general athletics. In the Society's

Handicap Foot Race (400 yards) 'Jerry' took second place. Something of an all-rounder, he also entered for the High Jump event and the Running Long Leap. He was unplaced in the high jump, but took out second prize in the latter event.

The accounts of these early annual Highland Gatherings confirm the active part which Aborigines took in the celebrations, suggesting that there was a positive response from them to the welcome extended to them. The demonstration of other aspects of Aboriginal culture also took their place alongside that of the Scots. In a reciprocal act of cultural sharing a corroboree (a festive celebration or warlike meeting of a group of Aborigines), held near the Comunn na Feinne grounds on the eve of the Highland Gathering, was open to Scots and other townsfolk. This became a regular feature of the Society's annual activities, with the Aborigines, in turn, regularly attending and participating in the Highland Games the next day. Accounts of this are given in the *Geelong Advertiser* 4th January, 1858, and also in *Bell's Life* 9th January, 1858. According to *Bell's Life*, the Aborigines also held a corroboree at the close of the Gathering in 1858.

Their inclusion in the annual Highland Gathering was just the public face of concern for the welfare of local Aborigines shown by certain Comunn na Feinne members in particular and the Society in general. Further examples of this goodwill extended by the Society towards the local Aborigines was their specific inclusion in the offer by the Society's medical officer and committeeman, Dr William Hingston Baylie, to provide free medical and hospital aid for any members "in distress." Years later when the last of the Aborigines residing in the town of Geelong passed away, Comunn na Feinne officers, Robert de Bruce Johnstone and Robert Shirra, arranged memorial graves for them which can still be seen in the Geelong West Cemetery.

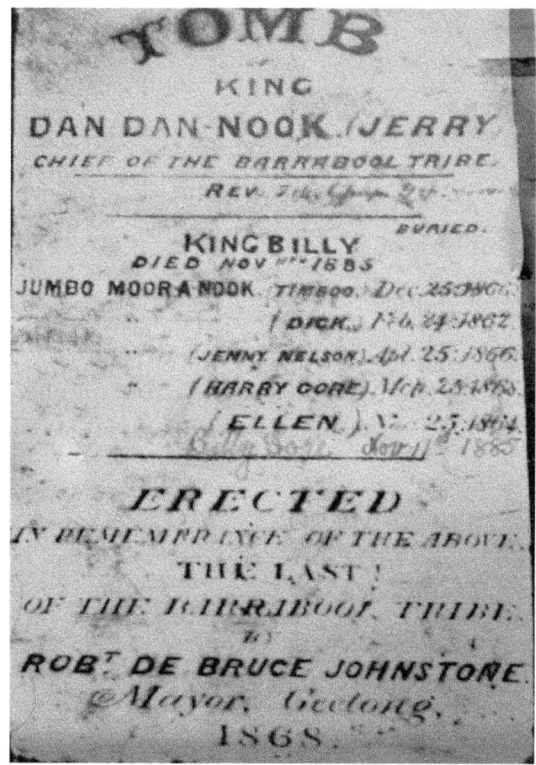

Aboriginal grave site in the Western Cemetery, West Geelong.

After only twelve months, Comunn na Feinne's New Year's Day Gathering had progressed from a seemingly *ad hoc* arrangement to one assuming the trappings of organization and permanence. The Games took place on the same grounds at South Geelong, but the site had been much improved from the previous year. According to the *Advertiser* of 10th December, 1857, the Society had used the services of botanist Daniel Bunce*, Director of Geelong's Botanical Gardens, in landscaping and in generally improving the grounds. In order to have the bare, empty paddock look more like a sporting arena, the Committee had arranged for a temporary grandstand to form one end, with refreshment booths below it. A fence had also been erected encircling about three acres of the ground and it was within this area that the field games were carried out.

*[See Appendix 3 (b) – Short Biographies.]

Where the Society's bard and reporter, Ossian Macpherson, wrote poetically about the Gathering, the *Geelong Advertiser*, on 2nd January, 1858, was somewhat more prosaic in its account of the day and less demonstrative in its descriptions of the Gathering which it termed an "annual fete." It found fault with the proceedings, pointing out that the Gathering's overwhelming success at these second Games had led to problems resulting from an underestimation by the Society of the numbers who would be attending the Games.

> The programme of amusements was sufficiently attractive to bring together a concourse of not less than five thousand people. An arrangement for the accommodation of a large number of persons were (sic) perfected on the meeting ground situated a short distance from the Barwon River on the flat below South Geelong, but they fell far short of requirements.

Despite the Society's improvements, the *Advertiser* reported that these had proved inadequate to cope with such a crowd as had gathered at the Games. Many more found their own ways of gaining a view - without an entrance fee!

> A charge being levied for admission within the enclosure, of course the great majority of the people assembled outside; while many enjoyed a commanding view from the numerous vehicles that were brought into requisition [in order to see over the perimeter fence] on this occasion as the day wore on, however, the vigilance of the Police was affected by the relaxing influence of the meridian sun, troops of unscrupulous persons jumped the fence and crowded around the platform to the great inconvenience of the orderly disposed, and these disorders in some measure interrupted the regular plan of proceeding.

As already noted, the *Geelong Advertiser* was not the only paper covering the 1858 Games and a lively account of this Gathering appeared in *Bell's Life in Victoria and Sporting Chronicle* (hereafter *Bell's Life*), This weekly sports newspaper gave the attendance figure as seven thousand and provided a report reminiscent of Macpherson himself. Its prose was generally purple:

> The thrilling sounds of the great highland bagpipes were heard in the distance, and presently the procession was beheld approaching the ground, headed by the pipers and followed by the Chief* with his band of Highlanders, the whole being "Plaided and plumed in their tartan array." **

*[In the absence of its Chief, Sir Henry Barkly, the Society chose its President, Archibald Douglas, to fill the role of 'acting Chief' for the day.

** Although quoted often by Scott, and often attributed to him, this line actually comes from Thomas Campbell (1777-1844). The line 'All plaided and plumed in their tartan array', appears in 'Lochiel's Warning' (1804), a poem about the impending disaster of Culloden and the warning given by a wizard to Lochiel not to join with Bonnie Prince Charlie. A warning, unfortunately, which Lochiel did not heed.]

A platform, in front of the grand stand, [also] had been erected for the purpose of the dancing and piping competitions and it was on this stage that the Chief stood to welcome the spectators, and the image painted by *Bell's Life* demonstrates the liveliness of the scene. With the Band of the Volunteer Geelong Rifle Unit to the left of the Grand Stand and, on the platform, the Chief with his guard of Lochaber Axemen, the scene was impressive. It became more-so when the main body of the procession burst into the arena. This gave rise to spontaneous applause from those already gathered, with the colour of the procession, the fluttering Scottish Lion Emblem, and other flags, all complementing each other.

> [S]uddenly emerging on the left, was a body of aborigines, marching two and two preceded ... by the pipers. Their appearance was the signal for general plaudits, and added materially to the poetic character of the whole ... Conspicuous in the midst was seen the spotless blue flag of "Comunn na Feinne". The committeemen, with their ribbons of various colours, and members of the Society formed the main body, the rear being composed of an enthusiastic crowd of both sexes. The whole appearance was highly picturesque ... a huge thistle proudly rearing its purple crest upon the summit of the Grand Stand and, as if conscious of the treasure of beauty committed to its protecting care,* appeared fully to express its paraphrased but defiant motto, "Touch me who dares."

* [The Grand Stand was usually occupied by the ladies.]

The "yankee pirate", Elbridge Gerry Emery, was again successful in the foot-racing but it was the heavy games which attracted most attention and hero-worship. Missing from the prize-winning ranks was the previous year's 'star' Duncan McIntyre. The Cameron brothers, Angus and Donald, cleaned up at the heavy events by winning medals in the Putting and the Hammer events. The Caber event was postponed owing the unsuitability of the tree trunk which had been provided for it, and this competition was rescheduled for Saturday 27th February, 1858. As well as the music provided by the competition pipers, the Brass Band of the Geelong Volunteer Rifle Corps played throughout the day.

Bell's Life provided a fitting postlude to the arena events when it wrote, "A grand corroboree by the natives, with a display of fireworks, concluded a well-spent day, which will be ever memorable in the annals of the colony."

In a demonstration of the enduring stamina of its members, beginning on the evening of New Year's Day, 1858, following what had been a long day at the Games, Comunn na Feinne entered into the world of theatrical entertainment. Disproving the caricature of Scots in general as a race of sour-faced killjoys, averse to the 'lighter' pleasures of life, there appeared an advertisement for a variety concert at the Theatre Royal, under the auspices of the Society. Among the other items on the Bill, there was mentioned a "Great Scottish Festival – Come and see the Comunn na Feinne Sports of Turning the Caber etc., in the Pantomime."

The committee, at the Annual Meeting of Comunn na Feinne, on 8th February, 1858, must have felt themselves well gratified by their roving reporter's coverage when, "the sum of £10/10/0 was voted to Ossian Macpherson for his services as special reporter for the gathering." Macpherson was shrewd enough to know what the Society wanted to see in a description of its Gathering. The treasurer's report announced that, "the balance sheet showed a considerable sum in hand." Members were informed that a copy of the report, along with a poem by Ossian Macpherson, the Society's bard, would be distributed to them. The Society did not lose sight of its welfare role, and it was reiterated that this welfare extended to the care and concern of the sick and needy within the Society and in the wider community itself.

The buoyant mood continued when the President, Archibald Douglas, was asked to vacate the chair while a resolution was passed presenting him with "a Gold medal as a token of the esteem in which his service in the promotion of the Society was held by the members." Gratitude was expressed, too, to Mr A.B. Orlebar Esq., MA., for his contribution to the Society's Educational Examination. And, while in this generous frame of mind, the Society spread its largesse even further, albeit leaving the recipients, the nine constables on duty at the grounds, with the problem of dividing, evenly, £10 between the nine of them!

At the Directors' meeting, held on the same evening (8th February, 1858), and following the annual meeting, Alexander Fyfe MLA., officially moved that the Government should be petitioned for the grant of the South Geelong grounds. Fyfe was a member of the State Parliament and used his political contacts to set up a meeting between a deputation from Comunn na Feinne and C. Gavin Duffy, President of the Board of Land and Works. This semi-formal meeting was followed up, on 14th October, 1858, by an official application from the Society setting out their case for a grant of that land currently being used for its Gatherings. [The land containing the sports' arena was bordered by Balliang street, Bellerine street, Fyans street and Swanston Street. Comunn na Feinne's case for this land can be found in Appendix 4 (a).]

The Caber event, which had been undecided at the New Year's Day Games due to the unsuitability of the Caber, was duly re-staged on 27th February, 1858. The rules*, as used by Comunn na Feinne, were quite explicit regarding what constituted a successful 'turn' of the Caber. To understand how the event was judged it is helpful to consider some of the main points which the Society adopted. These were included in the *Advertiser* on 2nd January, 1858.

> In turning the Caber, the competitor shall erect it on the small end; then, stooping, shall grasp it near the ground with both hands, then raise it off the ground, supporting it in its erect position with the shoulder, then run forward and tilt it from the starting line in a perpendicular direction. The judges shall decide the best throw in the following manner. The Caber will not be reckoned as turned until the grasped end shall have fallen beyond an angle of forty-five degrees with the parallel of the standing line. In the event of the best throw having equal angle [with one or more others] preference is to be given to that whose furthest point would describe the widest circle, having its centre in its

angle with the standing line.

*[Common rules governing sports at the Highland Games did not exist until the late nineteenth century. The standards followed at Geelong, for example, need not have been the same as those laid down by other Caledonian Societies throughout Victoria, and elsewhere.]

This delayed event was to be contested between Duncan McIntyre, the champion of the heavy events at the January 1857 Games, but who failed with the Caber, and a newcomer, Denis Powell. McIntyre again failed at this event with Denis Powell triumphing when he managed to turn the Caber 19' 7". Powell was an Irishman and a novice concerning Highland Sports, but he was obviously a quick learner!

On the same day as the postponed Caber event a competition of another sort was taking place. This was the Society's inaugural educational competitions for Gaelic, subsequently announced by the *Advertiser*.

> [The examination for] Scholars under 16 years of age in Gaelic Orthography [who are] willing to compete for the Society's Silver Medal will be examined in the class-rooms of the Mechanics' Institute at 3 o'clock, the same day as the Tossing the Caber event, the 27th February, 1858.

The role of Comunn na Feinne in providing educational competitions* was considered by the Society as coming under the fourth aim of its Charter regarding 'philanthropy'. The goal of improving educational standards and thereby equipping the individual to be of service to the wider community, was to be a prominent feature of Comunn na Feinne, especially in the early years of its existence.

*[The role which Comunn na Feinne had in Education is dealt with more fully in Appendix 14 (a).]

Many similar societies were a part of early colonial life. Some were ostensibly "national associations", others cast themselves, more generally, as "friendly societies." These associations, including Comunn na Feinne, acted as employment agencies, charitable agencies and as general welfare providers. Comunn na Feinne also carried, within the aims stated in its charter, the desire to provide and improve education in the widest possible sense, fostering its availability, providing for it and raising its standards and, thereby, better serving the whole community.

However, not everyone in the community was trusting of the Society's motives regarding its work in the area of Education. In fact, the accusation from an anonymous correspondent to the local press was that Comunn na Feinne, rather than seeking to improve educational standards purely out of selfless motives, was resorting to the 'brainwashing' of the malleable minds of the youth of the district.

> Sir, The Comunn Na Feinne must change its name. I am told it is pure Gaelic for 'Communistic Society'. I deeply grieve also that, true to its title, it is assisting in the spread of the obnoxious doctrines, and, in the most insidious way, training up disciples from amongst our youths. What else can I think when I see this theme on one of their examination papers. It bears the number of 8, in the third division of the Grammar Class: Analyse the following: 'That form of Government is most useful to its subjects and most honourable to itself, which provides for the well-being of all classes of the community.' Why, Higginbotham* (sic) himself could say nothing more levelling than this. (quoted in Carmichael's Notes)

*[George Higinbotham (1826-1892) was an Irish lawyer and journalist who emigrated to Victoria in 1854 and was admitted to the Victorian bar in the same year. He entered politics, was deeply involved in journalism and he eventually became Chief Justice of the State. He was considered a political 'radical' at the time, a 'liberal' as he might be called today, but accepted that compromise was inevitable at times to allow things to get done. See Appendix 3 (b) – Short biographies.]

If this were not conspiracy enough, the suspiciously-minded correspondent was also able to rope in the band, the music and even the military, as conspiring in some dastardly revolutionary plot.

> Another thing I would draw your attention to. In the band performance at the Botanical gardens last Saturday, was played a tune compounded of Mourie pour La Patrie and the Marsellaise. It was not on the programme; of course not. But it was artfully shoved in just before the Helter Skelter gallop. If this does not mean revolution first, and then a stampede of friends of law and order, I don't know what it can mean. I suppose we must conclude that the Artillerymen generally, are in the plot. (quoted in *Carmichael's Notes*)

Surely one of the most bizarre criticisms appearing in the *Advertiser's* Correspondence column, was that signed 'Caution', who saw in the society's name, in its educational programme and even in its music, hidden references to communism, the seduction of the youth and the overthrow of the existing social and political system.

Again, Comunn na Feinne showed that it had no intention of being dictated to by those whose only qualification for criticising its name and purpose was that of ignorance.

> SIR, Referring to a letter in to-day's issue, signed "Caution", wherein the writer suggests that Comunn Na Feinne must change its name," he having been told "that it is pure Gaelic for Communistic Society." I have no doubt that, notwithstanding his large amount of caution, had he been told that it was pure Dutch, he would in his simplicity have believed it.
>
> A little enquiry would, however, have convinced him that Comunn Na Feinne is true to its title, and that it does not, as he says, "in the most insidious way train up disciples from amongst our youth to obnoxious doctrines. (quoted in *Carmichael's Notes*)

[The *Advertiser's* editor responded, "Caution" will, we trust, have a sound night's sleep after this assurance.]

During 1858, Comunn na Feinne was also to organize several functions, and take part in a number of others, in addition to its annual Gathering, thereby broadening the scope of its involvement with the wider community. For example, it inspired a 'Discussion Class' held at the Mechanics' Institute under the secretary-ship of Comunn na Feinne member, James Campbell Jun. The initial topic, "Was Queen Elizabeth justified in signing the warrant for the execution of Mary Queen of Scots?", had probably been inspired by the Society's own bard, Ossian Macpherson, whose poem on the death of Mary Queen of Scots, for which he had won a medal at Melbourne literary competitions, had been published in the *Geelong Advertiser*.

There was also a practical reason behind such extra functions as organized by Comunn na Feinne. Partly they were to provide entertainment but they also had the purpose of raising funds for the Society's charitable activities and its welfare role. The cost of running the Games, together with prizes and other expenses, meant that Comunn na Feinne had to commit some of its time and manpower towards bringing in funds. A series of popular concerts was begun and the Society hired the entertainer, John R. Black for one such Concert, "A Night wi' Robert Burns", for 28th November, 1860. The *Advertiser*'s report of 2nd December, was full of praise for the man and his talents.

> It is superfluous to add another word to what has been already written in praise of John R. Black's varied talents; they are well known and appreciated by the musical public …

Indeed, so popular was this concert, that the Committee, on 6th December, 1858, requested, "before his departure from the Colony", that Black provide Comunn na Feinne with, "another evening's entertainment." The singer replied on the 13th December saying that he would return to stage another concert titled, "The Wreath" on 28th December, 1858. The items for this entertainment certainly demonstrated Black's great versatility, with the programme stating that he would introduce, "English, Irish, Scottish, French, German and Italian songs [with] appropriate narrative [as well as] other songs not yet hitherto sung in public."

The Society had also been busy preparing for its second Educational Examinations which were held on the 15th December, 1858. The date had been shifted from 1st January, 1859, the intended date of the examinations, as the examiners had stated that they would have found it too much of a rush to have the papers marked so that the medal winners could be presented with their awards at the same time as those who had been successful in the athletic, piping and dancing competitions at the New Year's Day Games.

The *Geelong Advertiser* of 15th December, 1858, wholeheartedly endorsed the Society's efforts at improving the educational standards within Geelong and district.

> Today the Highland Society, Comunn na Feinne, offers, for competitions to the young of our town and country, a number of silver medals as prizes for proficiency in the various branches of scholastic learning. The idea is a happy one, and it is to be carried out on a broad and liberal scale that does honour to the originators of the plan. Highly as we prize cricket and other athletics and many other sports, we think this movement in advance of such awards to manual dexterity. The need is, more justly, due (sic) to intellectual superiority, and we cordially hope that our schools, public as well as private, will unite in

friendly strife, all party and partisanship being thrown aside. Qualified umpires have been appointed who will do justice to the youthful candidates and it is anticipated that there will be such a gathering in the Mechanics' Institute Hall on this occasion, girls being eligible as well as boys, as will cheer the hearts of those … striving to advance the moral culture of the young and who are anxious that the rising generation should be wiser and better than the men and women of the present age.

Doubtless it was a sign of the times that the newspaper could remark, with a hint of surprise, "Several of the competitors were girls and remarkably clever." In fact, as detailed in the tables of results, girls prominently figured as 'high achievers' in the educational competitions. [See Tables in Appendices for fuller information.]

The remainder of the year was mainly taken up with 'housekeeping' business relating to the upcoming New Year's Day 1859 Annual Gathering. Further improvements were necessary at the grounds and Tenders were sought for new fencing.

An important source of income for Comunn na Feinne arose from the licence fees paid by those who conducted the 'refreshment' areas at the grounds. The *Advertiser* announced on 23rd December, 1858, that an auction was to be held for the right to operate one or more of the three 'refreshment' booths which were to feature at the arena, with the Society informing would-be bidders that the crowds expected at the Gathering meant the potential transaction of a great deal of business! These rooms had been erected at [a] considerable expense and intending lessees were reminded that the previous year, from, "5,000 to 7,000 visitors were on the ground."

Looking back at the close of 1858, with the experience of two Gatherings now behind it, the Society was well satisfied with what it had achieved. Not the least of these achievements was its ability to appeal to a diverse public, often going far beyond what might have been expected. Part of the Gathering's appeal through the years, as we will see, lay with its ability to devise activities which went beyond any appeal narrowly based upon a single ethnic group. Scottish national games, national music and national dancing continued at the Games, but the Society was not slow to add innovative contests and entertainments to its annual programmes and these additions were soon to swamp the Scottish activities at the Games.

In the space of just two years, a Scottish organization had thus begun the process of morphing into a general community organization. As part of this process of change it had established a service link with the Geelong Hospital and the town Orphanages, and it had extended a hand to the Aborigines. With the scarcity of good general educational institutions in Geelong and district, the Society had begun a community service of providing annual educational competitive examinations aimed at improving the educational standards of Geelong district's schools and furthering education more broadly. Its arena competitions, apart from Scottish games, involved volunteer fire brigades and volunteer military groups competing in such areas as rifle-shooting, sword and lance skills and horsemanship. All of these contests were designed to improve the capabilities of those civic institutions whose functions were to protect the citizenry. Comunn na Feinne, in these and many other areas, continued to identify with the whole community and, even before the professionalization of various municipal services, it provided some of the man-power and training for volunteer groups. Many of these latter activities are dealt with in Appendix 14(b).

By the end of 1858, therefore, Comunn na Feinne had begun to consolidate its place as part of the Geelong community. It had set about turning the bare grounds at South Geelong into something more resembling a sports arena, and had petitioned the State government seeking tenure over the ground it was using for its annual Games. It demonstrated that it was capable of generating crowds of up to ten thousand to watch its Gatherings. Its initial membership of 30 had grown to 239 by October, 1858, and the amount of its prizes had risen to £139.

Comunn na Feinne, despite the initial charge of it being a 'Scots only' organization, was actively engaged in community work which transcended any narrow ethnic bias. In these first two years, what had emerged beyond the tartans, the Caber, the Bagpipes and the Sword Dance, and beyond the fenced sportsground, was the genesis of a 'blueprint' for the advancement, not of a particular national group, but, rather, of a whole community.

Chapter 2

Comunn na Feinne Games – 1859-1860

As with most outdoor sporting events, the weather frequently had a large bearing on the success, or otherwise, of Comunn na Feinne's annual Highland Gathering. According to the *Advertiser*'s report on the 1859 Games, the dawn of New Year's Day revealed weather conditions which were most unpromising for those intending to venture out of doors.

> With a violent north wind, and, ever and anon, a hurricane of dust, begritting the teeth and parching the throat, and whisking off your hat *eodem flatu*, people were justified in ruminating – while looking at their bibulous neighbours – upon the question, 'if such things are done in the green morn, what would be done in the dry noon?' It was all dust and thirst at that early hour.
>
> A few persons in the early part of the morning, struggled across that local dust bin, yclept* Chilwell Flat, towards the grounds; the weather was such that it boded ill for the success of the Society's Annual Gathering … the strong southerly buster … blew clouds of impalpable powder into the eyes, noses, and the mouths of the inveterate pleasure-seekers, during the forepart of the day …

*yclept – called, named.

The *Advertiser*, over the years, made frequent references to this terrible dust which was raised on windy days. The Society's ground was situated on what was called the Plains and on certain days it was easy to see the reason for this title. It was flat, hardly grassed and possessed no shade of any kind. Thankfully, for the numbers attending in

1859, there was a change in the conditions from mid-day onwards, and the report continued that the strong gusts, "dropped down about twelve o'clock to occasional mild sneezers, when the Flat began to be alive with people, and the grand-stand very shortly presented an array fully equal to that of previous years." The dust was to be a recurring problem facing the Society's Gatherings at South Geelong. Although steps were taken, by planting bushes, flowers and shrubs, and damping down the ground, to alleviate the dust problem, it continued to plague spectators. However, it is 'an ill wind,' as the saying goes, and, "as might be expected, the necessity of 'washing down' the dust, was frequently demonstrated on all hands," much to the pleasure, added the *Advertiser's* report on 2nd January, of the refreshment booth licence holders!

But no matter what the conditions, those born and raised in 'Caledonia, stern and wild', were hardly daunted by the prospect of such an unpromising start to the day, and the supporters were "true to their tryst", gathering at the starting point of the Mechanics' Institute for the march to the sports ground. Among the marchers in 1859 were Archibald Douglas, the President of the Society, the Comunn na Feinne committee and members, all of whom were joined by a contingent from the Caledonian Society of Melbourne headed by its President, John McGregor. Adam Robertson of 'Struan', Lismore, John Gordon McMillan, and other Patrons of the Society, were also in the van of the procession which was headed by some pipers playing the old Highland air 'The Gathering of the Clans'. A man, wearing the McDonald Tartan, with all the bearing of an army veteran, and who seemed to appear from nowhere that morning, claimed the honour of carrying the Society's standard to the grounds.

Thus, the noise and excitement, encouraged by the waving of banners and by the presence of the 140 children who had taken part in the December educational competition, signalled the arrival of the special day. Other groups in the procession included the Geelong Volunteer Brass Band, Members of Fraternal Lodges, the Volunteer Rifles, the Volunteer Fire Brigade, and Geelong's St Patrick's Society. Aborigines, too, joined the march, the males dressed in Black Watch kilt and plaid, the females in their bright new attire, all in rank, and provided a colourful and 'holiday-cheerful' procession to the ground. Upon arrival, the marchers finished with a parade around the arena where a fluttering flag bearing the identification, "Talla nam Fiann" (literally; Fingal's Hall), welcomed the large numbers already within the spectators' areas and who, despite the "intensely oppressive weather", came "trooping in from far and near, mounted or afoot, determined to enjoy the day." The end of the circuit of the arena by the processionists signalled the commencement of the proceedings with the scene, commented the *Advertiser* on 3rd January, needing, "the pen of a Walter Scott" adequately to describe the various clan tartans on display.

The Society's press officer, Ossian Macpherson, although certainly no Sir Walter Scott, did his best to give a word picture of all that was on show, and it is in his accounts that we find the most colourful descriptions of these scenes. But even Macpherson was to be upstaged by events more dramatic than he could have anticipated. In these initial years of the Gatherings, every event on the programme had been vetted although unplanned and sudden spectacular incidents could upstage even the most thrilling of the orchestrated Games' event. The 1859 Games boasted three such examples which generated surprise, scares and even danger. As an added attraction before the start of the Games, and one which would bring a measure of excitement to the opening ceremonies, it was arranged that a Cobb & Co coach, one which had brought spectators down from Ballarat to visit the Gathering, would, at full pelt, enter the arena, do a circuit, and charge back out again. Unfortunately, what took place did not follow 'the script'. This touch of a wild-west rodeo event produced unexpected results, as reported in the *Advertiser*.

> William Sheppard, the well-known coach driver to Ballarat, on New Year's Day, took the reins in hand and drove ten spirited young horses attached to Cobb and Co's (sic) large coach, freighted with upwards of forty persons from the Western and Union Hotels, to the Comunn na Feinne Gathering at South Geelong. We regret, however, to state that on leaving the ground the tackling or the hook at the end of the second pole gave way, the driver with great difficulty retained his seat and only by allowing the reins to slip through his fingers was he enabled to do so. That the matter terminated otherwise, the consequences would have been, in all probability, most disastrous; as it was, it

> resulted seriously for one individual; for the six leading horses, finding themselves at liberty, galloped off at a most terrifying rate, partially concealed by a cloud of dust. They had not, however, proceeded more than a few hundred yards when two, getting at liberty, each took different directions, whilst the other four made towards a row of houses. Here, several persons on horseback, who had watched the affair, attempted to stop the troop, but without success. One person, bolder than the rest, galloped in front, was knocked down, with man and horse rolling over each other. A child of some three or four years old, was next, in turn, knocked down and run over. The child, when picked up, was conveyed to the Hospital, crying and bleeding. The horses were soon afterwards stopped without further mishap, with the exception of one which made off for the bush. The affair was purely accidental, and might, and would, have occurred in any ordinary matter of the kind. The driver, William Sheppard, showed coolness and determination at the time of the occurrence.

The next day, the 4th January, 1859, a bulletin stated the child had not been seriously injured. Mr Irving, the child's father, grateful for the care given to his son, even made a donation to the hospital! They bred the children tough, and the parents more charitable, and less litigious, in those days!

Secondly, the loss of the grandstand roof to strong gusts of wind was too good a story to pass up and it constituted a further example that not everything, "would be alright on the night."

> The 'grand stand,' just unroofed by a whirlwind and nakedly occupied as it was by a thousand people (for the most part, ladies), conveyed to the Fahrenheitish mind a notion of caloric not to be ventured upon on any account. That idea was not all weakened upon view of sundry gauze veils freely gyrating in a whirlwind of dust, while sundry parasols were at the same time appearing in the new character of parachutes. In spite of all, however, the immense concourse of people … seemed bent upon making the best of it.

After a reprise by the band of 'The Gathering of the Clans', the New Year's Day Games were officially launched. But a third mishap was to follow, and the *Advertiser*, rightly taking a serious view of what occurred, took the Society to task for its lack of crowd control.

> While a number of people, many of them women and girls, were crowding close to the platform looking up at the Highlanders Dancing the Highland Reel, some of the visitors amused themselves with trying their want of skill at

throwing the heavy and light hammer and stone. One of the inepts, losing his grasp of the hammer, before taking aim let it fly right into the midst of the crowd. Fortunately, it hit no one; making a deep indentation in the ground, close to two girls, who were looking at the dancing.

The Highland Dancing contests, together with the piping competitions and the prizes offered for original Gaelic and English poems, show that Comunn na Feinne had not forgotten that one of its Charter aims related to the maintenance of tradition, physical or artistic. For 1859, for example, the Society had set a competition for the best poem in Gaelic* and the best poem in English. Neither was well supported. The prizes consisted of a Gaelic dictionary for the winner of the Gaelic poem category and, for the winner of the English language poem, *a History of the Highlands*.

*[It is unfortunate that, with the destruction, or disappearance, of the Society's records, material relating to its various written contests cannot now be located. The few examples which were able to be tracked down, were those which had been published in Highland newspapers such as the *Oban Times*. The *Geelong Advertiser* did print a couple of prize-winning poems but only the ones in English. The shifting of Ossian Macpherson to the country may have denied the Society further Gaelic compositions by him.]

The *Advertiser* referred to the unexciting prizes on offer as a possible explanation for the low number of entries. Up to the day of the Gathering, only one poem, in Gaelic, had been submitted, with a similar number of entries for the Poem in English. The Gaelic entry was, reported the *Advertiser* on the 4th January, 1859, regarded by the Gaelic experts, "to possess neither rhyme nor metre." Likewise, the single English entry was judged as being one, "which would scarcely warrant its perpetrator a tomb in the Abbey."

Some Comunn na Feinne members had expressed their disappointment that Ossian Macpherson had not submitted an entry given that his previous work "had displayed considerable skill in composition and a perfect appreciation of the subject treated, namely, the objects of Comunn na Feinne." Following the failure of any of the poems submitted to warrant a prize, a second Gaelic poem, on the Objects of Comunn na Feinne, "appeared in the afternoon yesterday, and received the prize." The winning poet hid under the pen-name of "Gaidheal."*

*[See Appendix 10 (c) on Gaelic Competitions with some examples.]

The sheer cross-section of people and formal societies taking part in the march to the grounds demonstrate how, by the time of the third gathering, there had already been a considerable widening in the type of events making up the programme of the Gathering. To the athletic contests and the traditional and colourful events, such as the heavy games and the piping and dancing, competitions for rifle marksmanship and for fire-fighting drills had also been introduced. Competition was being used by the Society to advance the physical and mental skills of such volunteer groups whose purpose was the protection and defence of the wider community. By 1859 the Society was, therefore, using its signature day to foster both literary and practical skills. By including these competitions, the Society promoted, too, its belief that 'education' was a far wider process than the 3Rs; it went beyond any narrow definition and it was applied to all areas of life, the practical as well as the cultural. Education was believed to improve social cohesion and to foster talents. This vision also included the ambitious aim to make the individual workplace more connected to the wider community. In later years, for example, when the Society was running an Eisteddford, it actively encouraged the formation of choirs in factories, schools and churches.

For 1859 there was to be only one prize for tossing the Caber: a silver cup and two guineas. The heavy games, in the inaugural Gathering in 1857, had been dominated by Duncan McIntyre. The competition events, Throwing the Heavy Hammer, Throwing the Light Hammer, Putting the Heavy Stone and Putting the Light Stone, had all been won by him, but the prize for Tossing the Caber had eluded him. At the 1859 Games, McIntyre's desire to capture the Caber crown, after his previous failures, added a keen edge to that particular contest. It also engendered no little interest from the punters in the crowd! There was also some needle between the champions carried over from the previous year's competition. Thus, to say that the competition was keen and that egos were to the fore, would be to understate the tension surrounding the event. There was also fair amount of rivalry, with personal pride on the line.

The Caber event was a sport which gave the chronicler of the Games in the *Advertiser* free rein to indulge his imagination, and his humour, and the 1859 contest in this event was no exception. The measurement of the Caber was thirteen feet six inches in length and of a proportional thickness. The length and girth of this tree trunk seemed to have defeated all of the competitors and it seemed to those watching, as well as those competing, that the Caber had a mind of its own!

> The Caber would do everything but turn. It would overbalance itself behind its holder's shoulder, and threaten the heads of persons standing too near; it would allow itself to be thrown and then recoil and make a feint of striking the thrower playfully in the ribs; it would twirl mirthfully on end, and then make a lunge at all the corns, bunions and shins in its vicinity. Now and then it would be vicious, and strain the loins, or sprain the wrists or twist the arms of those who handled it.

But it was not only the 'eccentric' behaviour of the Caber which provided the amusement of the occasion. It defied every effort to 'properly' turn it and the athletes' frustrations seemed to be heading towards outright belligerence. The President of Comunn na Feinne then stepped in and quickly deflated the warring egos by confiscating the offending length of timber. There were protests from Denis Powell and Duncan McIntyre both of whom claimed to have turned the Caber, though no one apparently saw either do so. Others, too, made similar boasts and what followed was a babble of claims and counter-claims all directed at the President. Competitiveness and good sportsmanship then, as now, do not always make good bedfellows!

> Then [Duncan McIntyre] was said to have turned it sometime previous in the day, and to have been turned off the ground himself because he had no right to do so. Then Dennis Powell doubted the story about Duncan McIntyre. Then William Fraser would bet £10, and pulled it out of his pocket, that Duncan McIntyre existed, and could be found and had turned the Caber, and could do much better than Dennis Powell. Then Dennis Powell would take the bet himself, and it was he who would turn the Caber better than any Duncan McIntyre. Then Duncan McIntyre was found and brought to turn the Caber. Then, however, the President, Archibald Douglas, would not allow the games to be interrupted. However, the loan of the Caber should be permitted on Monday, for the convenience of betting competitors, but Duncan McIntyre must not, just then, turn the Caber.

And so, like a parent in charge of his squabbling children arguing over a toy, Douglas had the Caber "carried off in custody" on the understanding that a separate competition would be carried out and that Powell and McIntyre should meet the following Monday, "to turn a Caber, at noon, for ten pounds a side." But tempers flared further, and wilder and more extravagant claims were made for the relative prowess of the two competitors. But then, with tempers getting hotter and fuses getting shorter, and with an outbreak of testosterone-driven warfare between contestants and their respective backers becoming more and more likely, suddenly, in a scene which could have come out of the unlimited store of celtic fairy lore, from somewhere came the infectious, magical sound of a fiddle turning thoughts, which a few seconds before were working out ways and means by which to inflict bodily harm on persons of both sides, to gentler things; and bewitching everyone's feet to obey Macpherson's call to:

> Join ye the dance on the green, grassy brae,
> Heedless of care be your boisterous mirth;
> Strathspey, Gillie Callum, or wild Caber Feidh-
> Foot it with pride for the land of your birth.

And such was the fiddle's enchantment that the command was spontaneously obeyed:

> [For now] John Gordon McMillan must dance a reel, [and] everybody must dance a reel with John Gordon McMillan. Then the President, Archibald Douglas, must dance, and the Pipers must dance, and such a reel was danced as had not been danced that day; and the arena was no longer a sacred place [and] the crowd rushed in to join the reel, and the games were over, and three cheers, three strong ones, and have done with it, were given for Comunn na Feinne; and everybody was very hot and very grimy; and everybody found out that it was seven o'clock, and felt for the first time during the day that Highland sports had the one drawback – [that] of fatigue.

A week later a notice duly appeared in the *Advertiser* on Saturday 8th January, 1859, announcing that the Caber challenge between Duncan McIntyre and Dennis Powell would be taking place on Monday 10th January, 1859. The *Advertiser*, the day after the re-match, reported that Duncan McIntyre, his supporters, some Comunn na Feinne committeemen with "Lochaber axes" (presumably only for decoration!), and the Caber, were all present. Absent, however, was Dennis Powell, his supporters and, presumably, his money backers! Those of McIntyre's camp decided to give an extra half hour's grace to the Powell camp to see if they would appear. This deadline having expired, those present, including a large number of general spectators, decided to proceed, with Duncan McIntyre setting out to "redeem his part of the engagement."

> The Caber was no sooner in his hands then, running forward two or three paces, he tilted it clear over at an angle equal to that of Dennis Powell's turning on the Saturday. Not satisfied with this measure of success, [he] stated that that was not his best throw. He again tilted the Caber and this time turned it clear over in the direct perpendicular. Thereupon, of course, were there great congratulations on the part of the Highlanders. McIntyre was hoisted on the shoulders of admiring friends, his name, Duncan McIntyre of Lochaber, was proclaimed; and his father and grandfather's names were also soon in the mouths of many of those present, who showed pride at the claim of having come from, or heard of the place of the champion's birth.

Sensing a champion worthy of myth-making Macpherson, the event's official chronicler, described McIntyre as a true athlete:

> [He is] of very superior build to that of any of the [other] competitors on Saturday. Prodigiously muscular he is, withal, well-set and nicely poised in all his movements. He appeared to hold the Caber like a toy, and the manner in which he advanced with it, and [then] delivered it, was as graceful as that of the most accomplished professional acrobat.

This was not to be the last time the Caber contributed problems for the athletes. Before standardization, a sporting event involving a tree trunk of variable length, shape, and weight, was likely to behave unpredictably, and would always draw eager interest from spectators on the look-out for fun as well as athleticism. Such was the case on 1st January, 1862, when the athletes were presented with a veritable 'giant' of a timber, with a length of over 24 feet. In the practice sessions, with a field of only 6 entrants, and without Duncan McIntyre and Dennis Powell, it was found that none of the entrants could turn the Caber. The saw was produced and the trunk was "shortened" to 23 feet 9 inches. It was only after a series of unsuccessful attempts by the contestants, reported the *Advertiser* on 2nd January, that one, E. Anderson, eventually made a turn good enough to bring him the prize.

Some events proved, each year, the truth of 'Murphy's Law', and Caber tossing was often one of these. This particular contest became an annual certainty for things going wrong and it proved to be a storehouse of comment and excuse, as well as the occasional aesthetic opinion on the Caber's appearance! The *Advertiser*'s report on the 1863 Games, for example, described the Caber that year as, "one of the ugliest pieces of wood" that ever could have been chosen and it doubted that, "such a dog's leg" piece of timber" could ever be made to turn. But despite the *Advertiser*'s skepticism, turn it did and Thomas McKenzie won with a length of 35 feet 3 inches along a good line. Longmore took second with an equal length but a line that was completely out of plumb. How anyone could have judged what was and what was not plumb, when the Caber was said more to resemble a fiddler's elbow than a straight piece of timber, was anyone's guess!

Off the sporting field, contention and controversy were absent from the Society meeting which took place on 5th February, 1859. The *Geelong Advertiser*, the following day, reported that, on a turnover of £852.13.8 the Society achieved a surplus of £22.13.5. The 1859 New Year's Day Gathering, the financial position of Comunn na Feinne, the election of office-bearers and the admission of new members, all featured at this annual meeting of the Society. The reports were generally very encouraging with the financial situation showing a profit, small though it was, and there was a general attitude of self-congratulation arising out of the positive reports on various aspects of the Society's activities over the past year.

Already by 1859 Comunn na Feinne had branched into conducting competitive examinations for schoolchildren, was supporting several Geelong volunteer utilities and held fund-raising efforts on behalf of the erection of a memorial in Scotland to the hero Sir William Wallace. In 1859 a grand dinner was held to mark the centenary of the birth of Scotland's national poet, Robert Burns. As with Wallace, so too with

Burns, the emphasis was on what these respective 'heroes' represented in the minds of the people attending. Burns, it was stated, was not only the poet of Scotland, but poet-philosopher to the world. Wallace stood for freedom, Burns for the spirit of humanism. Freedom and equality were hailed as components of 'the brotherhood of man' and Comunn na Feinne saw itself as upholding and promoting these universal values.

Another social function, held 30th March, 1859, and recorded in the *Advertiser* the next day, was a complimentary dinner given to two office-bearers of the Society, Robert Shirra (secretary) and Robert de Bruce Johnstone (treasurer). They were being honoured for their voluntary contributions to 'good works' in Geelong. It was the 'spirit' of Comunn na Feinne, as well as the men themselves, which was being honoured and such men, it was stated, exemplified the very essence of the Society. The chairman, Archibald Douglas, said that, "In a country like this, it was pleasing to find men willing to undertake onerous and arduous duties in their devotion to promote philanthropic objects."

Evidence of the wider community spirit which Comunn na Feinne was seeking to foster can be seen in the presence of the local St Patrick's Society representatives at the function. This was particularly noted, and especially included, in a toast to other local national Societies made during the function. The St Patrick's Society was given permission to use the Comunn na Feinne grounds and facilities for its own St Patrick's Day celebrations. The *Advertiser* of 27th May, 1863 revealed that the Society also permitted the Irish Hurling Club the use of its South Geelong grounds. Considering the violent history of Roman Catholic-Protestant relations in Melbourne, especially between the 1840s and the 1860s, the amity between these two groups in Geelong stands out as remarkable, and credit must be given to the liberal views adopted by both of these Societies.

'All are welcome', was the attitude which the Society brought to its relationship with other groups in the community. Its educational competitions invited all Schools to participate irrespective of denomination or type. The Games were open to all competitors irrespective of their national background. The procession through Geelong to the sports' arena, held before the opening of the competitions, featured Aborigines and marchers from Irish Roman Catholic institutions, various types of Lodges, civic authorities, Brass Bands, Pipers, 'Uncle Tom Cobbly and all'. Here, for its time, was a genuinely multicultural celebration.

Despite these efforts by the Society to demonstrate its non-discriminatory policy, it obviously was still smarting a little from some earlier unfair and misleading charges against it on the grounds of it being exclusive. Some committeemen and general members thought, therefore, that the Society would have to go even further in its efforts to prevent charges of 'ethnic' exclusivity. A discussion took place at a special general meeting called for the 30th June, 1859, to consider a change of name for the Society to ensure that the public at large could not regard it solely as a Highland/Scottish association. A change of name, it was argued, would prevent the recurrence of such unfair criticism. It was pointed out by some that membership already included not only Scots but also Irish and English settlers. If the Society was made up of these different nationalities, it was reasoned, it seemed incongruous to keep the present title which seemed to indicate that it was just a Highland organization. Archibald Douglas, the President, agreed but added that it just so happened that those who founded the Society had come from the Scottish Highlands and, although it was far wider than this, both in its membership and in its activities, he thought that it would be a pity to lose this original link with its beginning and the 'romantic' past contained in the name, Comunn na Feinne. Moreover, the Society wanted itself identified with the ideals represented by the aims as summed up in many of the slogans of the ancient Fingalians which were the inspiration behind the Society's charter.

After considerable discussion, a vote to change the name failed on the Chairman's casting vote. The Gaelic name remained, and the Society continued to grow and develop as an institution seeking to serve the wider community. The Society managed to avoid being a focus of any one section of the Geelong community and, in fact, continually widened its appeal. This characteristic partly explains its longevity and popularity even when the ethnic composition of Geelong and district had changed considerably after the 1850s. The expanding nature of the Games themselves, and the multiplicity of other activities which the Society initiated, was to keep Comunn na Feinne in the forefront of community life, work and entertainment well into the twentieth century, and to prevent it being regarded as an anachronism. As we will see, however, this was not to be the last of the challenges to the Society's name.

At the last Comunn na Feinne meeting for 1859, held on 30th December, the final touches were made for the upcoming Highland Games to be held on Monday 2nd January, 1860. The directors were pleased to announce that a completely new Grandstand had been erected which would be capable of seating 1,000 spectators. Wings to the stand would accommodate at least a further 800. Altogether, therefore, covered seating was available for about two thousand spectators. It also corrected a misunderstanding which had been abroad that the entrance ticket to the general grounds would not be enough, and that a further charge would be made for entrance into the actual arena. The payment of the ordinary entrance ticket, it was made clear, would not only get the payer through the gates but also into the spectators' section around the fenced-in arena.

In the initial years of Comunn na Feinne, there was an attempt made to maintain a freshness in the annual Gatherings. This was a deliberate policy which remained the Society's aim for its whole life. At the Directors' meeting on 30th December, 1859, for example, in preparation for the 1860 games, several additions and improvements were adopted. Spectator comfort, spectator safety, and spectator interest were also on-going concerns. While Comunn na Feinne maintained the traditional contests, it also sought to be novel and utilitarian in its choice of events for the New Year's Day Gatherings.

Archery, for example, introduced in 1860, not only added to the interest of spectators, but it also was the first of the events in which ladies were able to compete for the prize. A special day was advertised by the Comunn na Feinne as being set aside to practice for this new event. Whether it was because of being open to ladies, or just as a natural precaution, the event was sited away from the main arena. This decision, as with the Rifle Shooting, thereby avoiding the chances of novice contestants 'bagging' a spectator or two, and it demonstrated the wisdom of the Games organizers! This safety precaution proved not to be a complete success, initially, for at the 1861 Games, a policeman was wounded in the leg from what was, presumably, a misdirected arrow! This led to the apparently impatient remark by the *Advertiser* that, "the circumstance gave rise to a slight interruption of the match by the interference of his comrades!"

Other competitions such as Tilting at the Ring, Broadsword exercises, High Jumping and Vaulting were also added. Given the scope for "accidents" at some of these events, the *Advertiser* suggested that some solid practice before the events were staged might not be such a bad idea, especially for Tilting at the Rings which, helpfully, it went on to describe.

> One of the new features in the Highland games this year will be a species of exercise on horseback, under the style and title of Tilting. The game will consist of riding at top speed, with a spear in vest, and piercing a ring descending from some woodwork rigged up ... Judging from the frequent practice, we may reasonably expect that some of our drivers will have attained to considerable proficiency in accuracy of aim combined with plucky horsemanship, against the 2nd of January, 1860. The practice on the grounds of the Comunn na Feinne yesterday afternoon was carried on with spirit and considerable fun was created by the left handedness of some of the horsemen, and the harmless mishaps of others.

But the keenness of intending participants in the games did not stop at the practice for 'Tilting'. Many of the competitors took seriously their events and entered into strenuous sessions in preparation for the 1860 games which were held on Monday 2nd January, 1860, following the practice of the Society not staging the Gatherings on a Sunday.

For those who may have 'come in late', the *Advertiser,* on 2nd January, 1860, obliged with an explanation of the Games and why they were held annually on the New Year's Day.

To Scotsmen, generally, Christmas Day is not associated with ideas of festivity so intimately as New Year's Day which, throughout North Britain, is emphatically the festival of the year. Unless we err greatly, the observance of Christmas beyond any other day at all events as a religious festival would, by strict disciplinarians, be looked upon as something wrong, and for all sportive purposes New Year's Day in Scotland is the counterpart to Christmas Day in England. Thus, the Scotsmen of Geelong banded together in friendly brotherhood in the society yclept 'Comunn na Feinne', which may be freely translated the 'Society of Fingalians', and selected New Year's Day for their annual festival … The camp is fixed in South Geelong where will float in the breeze a flag which will recall the days of auld to many a son of Caledon. Sir Walter Scott, in his poem, 'Lady of the Lake',* has sketched a gathering somewhat similar, but in far other circumstances to that of today and, as our readers will prefer the spirit-stirring strain of Scott to our dull prose, with his description we conclude:

> When bent beneath the standard's weight,
> When e'er the western wind unrolled
> With toil, the huge and cumbrous fold,
> And give to view the dazzling field
> Where, in proud Scotland's royal shield,
> The ruddy Lion ramp'd in gold.

[*The *Advertiser* reporter correctly identified the poet as Sir Walter Scott but misidentified, and slightly misquoted, the poem. These lines, in fact, are from Scott's 'Marmion' (Canto 1V, Stanza XXV111), and not 'Lady of the Lake' and Line one should read "Yet bent beneath …" and line four should read, "And gave to view …" instead of the reporter's miss-quotations.]

And so, in 1860, the usual Procession of the Society, 'aborigines and a', wound its way from Geelong town to the sports ground led by pipers playing 'Gathering of the Clans'. The weather which was unfavourable from the start, unfortunately became worse as the day wore on. However, such grim forecast did not deter general spectators nor 'the sons of the heather, undaunted and true.'

The arena, with its new furnishings, despite the dull and overcast skies, was a blaze of colour, and it was not long before the new grandstand and its wings were full. There were two other circles of spectators. The inner one, separated from the competition arena by a fence of rails, was "densely packed with eager throngs of sightseers." Behind this concourse of spectators, and beyond the perimeter fence, there was another crowd. This was composed of unpaying visitors overlooking the proceedings, from beyond the boundary of the official grounds, and standing on "vehicles, which formed an outer circle."

The *Advertiser*, in its report on 3rd January, 1860, described the crowd as the greatest so far in Comunn na Feinne's history and this was reflected in the gate-takings although, with the numbers who watched from outside the boundary fence, the takings, added the paper, did not reflect the actual numbers of spectators. The sum of £387/10/0 was taken at the gate. Overall it was estimated that there were 4,800 people present within the fenced area of the grounds, and between 2,000 and 3,000 persons on the outside of the grounds. As there was nothing blocking the view of those outside the grounds proper, many spectators watched the proceedings without having to pay the fee for entrance to the grounds. Overall, the paper estimated that there would have been something like 12,000 people who witnessed the Games. This was a very large crowd for its day at any outdoor spectacle. Considering the population of Geelong at the time (approximately 20,000), it demonstrates the enormous pulling power of these annual Games and, perhaps, not a little exaggeration on the part of the newspaper!

Great interest was taken, as usual, in the 'he-man' events. The buzz in the crowd was that a new man on the scene, John Cameron, was set to shine in the heavy events. But many of his backers were destined to lose their shirt when, and not for the first time, a sure thing turned out not to be so! At first, the competitors in the Hammer Throw seemed to find difficulty in not fouling on their first effort.

> Duncan McIntyre led off and delivered a fine throw, but overstepped the mark in the delivery. Ronald McDonald followed suit, and threw foul. James Cameron, as a light weight, was perhaps the best competitor of all. His first throw was 56 feet 9 ½ inches. Donald Cameron's throw was fair as regards distance, but the delivery was declared foul. The first, second and third throw of each competitor determined the placings, with Duncan McIntyre winning clearly ahead of James Cameron who came second with a throw almost eleven feet shorter than the winning distance!

As if to put his stamp on the Heavy Games, after some disappointments from the previous years, Duncan McIntyre took first prize in 'Throwing the Heavy Hammer', 'Throwing the Light Hammer', 'Putting the Heavy Stone', and 'Putting the Light Stone'. Having seen off Dennis Powell, his 'thorn in the flesh' at previous competitions, as well as the new 'champion on the block', John Cameron, McIntyre might have thought to make a clean sweep of these traditional sports when the event, Tossing the Caber came up. As in previous years, it was this event which attracted, and held the most interest for the devotees of Highland Heavy Games. The main problems with the Caber always involved its size, shape and weight which, before standardization, could, as already noted, vary widely from year to year. Problems with the size and weight of the 'muckle stick' were also to challenge the 'big' men competing at the 1860 Games. The first action, therefore, was to cut off 6 inches at one end and 11 inches at the other. Even with these 'amputations', the Caber was still 14' long!

> The next feat of strength consisted in turning the Caber, the dimensions and weight of which seemed rather to stagger those whose business it was to toss it over. Even John Bell [a judge of the event and, himself, one of the strongest men in Geelong] did not scruple to condescend so far as to call it a 'big stick'.

Cameron and McDonald each failed in their attempts to turn the Caber. Powell did turn it but neither the toss nor the angle satisfied him. The judges then decided that, to make a contest of the event, it would be necessary to shorten the Caber by another foot or so. Powell, however, objected to this and at another attempt he turned it with the Caber falling "scarcely a degree from the perfect angle." To accommodate the other contestants, the Caber was shortened by nearly a foot, but again Cameron and McDonald each failed to turn it. Denis Powell, therefore, remained alone as master of the Caber event for 1860. As for the man of the moment, Duncan McIntyre, he was nowhere to be found!

The *Geelong Advertiser* had carried several notices regarding the 1860 Comunn na Feinne Gathering. The Society had obviously tried to play on the Powell/McIntyre rivalry of the previous Games to work up some added interest for the 1860 Heavy events. For example, apart from its usual general advertisement for its annual Gathering, the Society singled out a few items which it hoped would draw particular attention. It advertised:

> A match between Powell and McIntyre, throwing the stone for £10 a side.
> A prize of £3 for turning the Caber. (Powell excluded)
> A prize of £3 for the hop, step and jump.
> A prize of £3 for three standing jumps.

It would seem that these latter contests were privately sponsored and that they took place apart from the normal programmed events. Similarly, although not having been included in its original programme for 1860, it was further advertised that following its usual field sports, "a football match" would take place with sides to be chosen at the close of the general sports.

The new events at the 1860 Games provided a lively and, at times, too realistic a contest among participants. The report of the "single Stick" [Broadsword] event began tamely enough, all very gentlemanly and proper as befitted some of the 'officer-class' competing. The first bout was between Lieutenant Wright and Thomas Hosking. Considerable amusement was caused by the free and easy manner in which both competitors exchanged hits. Lieutenant Major Varcoe, who counted the hits, gave the palm to Lieutenant Wright.

However, any element of gentlemanly courtesy in the next bout was signally absent as a seasoned sailor, definitely not of the 'officer class', showed himself to be no respecter of rank. This "jolly jack tar", Edward Matthews, had unceremoniously thrown out his challenge to anyone who would take it, and was obliged in this by Mr Thomas Hosking, who had just finished his polite and gentlemanly duel with Lieut. Wright. The display which ensued was not for the squeamish, as the sailor's style was certainly not learned at any officer's knee!

Each received his sticks and, given the look and the ungainly stance of the old mariner, the "spectators anticipated some fun." Whatever Mr Hosking expected was not what took place. He scored first point with "a slight tap" on the old mariner. The 'jack tar', not being familiar with the gentlemanly "etiquette" after receiving a hit, light though it was, retaliated immediately with a heavy slash on Hosking's sword arm which "made the dust fly in a cloud." He followed this with "another thwack" which echoed all over the arena. The gentleman contestant had his blood somewhat raised by these blows and, "after one or two cuts and thrusts, distinguished rather for strength than skill, one of his sticks broke and the contestants were separated."

This ending of the bout was much to the spectators' disappointment, "as they thought the other portion of the sports tame in comparison." However, Mr Hosking lost what was left of his genteel composure and, "wished to finish the combat with the naked fist." It was the 'uncouth' old "man o' war" who had the last word, however, muttering, "A pretty swordsman to want to finish with his fist." The old mariner, having vanquished one gentleman then put out the challenge that he would, "have a turn with the sticks with anyone for £10." Given what they had just seen, however, there were no takers for the challenge! The managers of the field Games, rather than risk blood, if not a corpse, quickly ended the event and rushed the contestants for the next event, the high leap, onto the arena!

The 'yankee pirate,' Elbridge Gerry Emery, again took off the main prizes for foot-racing. The Aboriginal events were watched with much appreciation, the interest of the spectators being taken with their skill and abilities with their traditional weaponry.

> Eight aborigines entered the lists to contend at spear-throwing. … The target was placed nearly forty yards from the natives who, in turn, hurled their weapons at the butt with great force and considerable precision. This portion of the games, from its great volatility, caused much interest among the spectators.

Dick Alexander, who was from a local Aboriginal tribe, took out the first prize in the foregoing event. In the Aborigines' Handicap, the winner was a competitor who had travelled from Sydney to enter the games. The boomerang throwing by eight Aboriginals was also a wonder, "enjoyed by the spectators."

Dennis Powell, the champion of the 'muckle stick', and John Riddoch, Vice-President, of Comunn na Feinne (and later a celebrated winegrower in South Australia), were just two of the notable contestants, ten in all, in the Tilting event. *Bell's*

Life gave its report on 8th January, 1860.

> The gentlemen entered for the Tilting at the Ring. Three wooden stands were placed at intervals of about 20 yards in the circle of the enclosure from each of which was dependent an iron spring holding a small brass ring. This ring is held so lightly that a very slight touch will disengage it. The competitor, at a hard gallop on horseback, endeavours, in passing, to take the ring with his lance; if he succeeds a man, stationed at each of the stands, instantly places another ring on the spring. Each of the competitors was allowed five minutes.

It was definitely not the day for 'Gentleman and Officers': Lieutenant Wright, highly favoured to win the event, failed to gain a place in the first three. Riddoch took off a dozen rings while his nearest competitor could manage only five. Riddoch also proved himself the better man in another way too, by donating his prize to the Geelong Hospital.

The rest of the games had proceeded efficiently and with decorum although a slight hiccup appeared in the dancing when a Mr Erskine, who gained second place, was supposed by some "to be a wee bit fou'." Whether that was his state when he was dancing or when receiving his prize is not recorded! Perhaps it was as well that it was the Seann Triubhas and not the Sword Dance that he was dancing at the time!

The *Advertiser*, in a short essay appearing a day after the Games, expressed its opinion that Comunn na Feinne's activities, especially its Highland Gathering, had a significance which went beyond providing mere entertainment for the masses. Comunn na Feinne saw its own role in the community as one of promoting harmony, looking to realize Burns' vision of an eventual 'brotherhood of man'.

> It seems likely that we in this colony shall have to thank the Scotch among us for something very much more valuable than an annual spectacle however brilliant—and yesterdays was certainly without exception the most brilliant that Geelong, and we believe we may add to that, the colony, has ever seen—something which will tend towards bringing Victorian social life into a completer harmony ... To the careless on-looker yesterday's sports were good, anti-dyspeptic, invigorating tom-foolery, and nothing more; but, in reality they had a much higher importance. There was seed sown by the spectacle which must - and will probably do so far more widely and vigorously than many would be sanguine enough to conceive at the present moment - spring up and branch out and bear fruit in thousands of human lives not only in this corner

of the colony but in every place where any of the right sort who were present at yesterday's gathering may hereafter sojourn.

The inauguration by Comunn na Feinne of what was to become a major feature of the Geelong social year, an Annual Highland Ball, reported in the *Advertiser* 26th January, 1860, proved to be very popular. These events were ostensibly for the purposes of raising funds for charitable causes with which the Society was engaged. Tickets at 30/- each would have confined the nights to middle-class business men, local government officials and wealthy pastoralists, together with their ladies. However, these Balls were always well oversubscribed and, as the *Advertiser* reported, the first Ball achieved the type of success, "with which the Society has so frequently distinguished itself." With many of the gentlemen in Highland costume and the ladies with tartan sashes, all eager to dance up a storm, both the piper and the Stoneham Band were kept to, "an advanced hour" providing for the dancers.

Social events such as the Annual Ball became a regular feature of the Comunn na Feinne's year and it steadily increased its areas of activity. Its growing list of charitable causes and its involvement with the competitive educational examinations meant that it was going far beyond its defining annual New Year's Day Highland Gathering as its main presence in the community. Income, from membership fees, from gate takings at the Games, and from admission charges and rental of booths, however, was barely covering costs. Comunn na Feinne sought, therefore, to include in its annual calendar of activities more and more general fund-raising social functions which would also foster sociability and community spirit. These included the annual Burns' anniversary dinner, a Scottish Concert on New Year's night, its St Andrew's Day socials and its sponsoring of theatrical performances. The Society also founded a variety of social and sporting clubs including ones devoted to quoits, cricket, football and fishing, and it was closely involved with volunteer bodies such as the various brass bands of the town, the fire brigade, the various military bodies and the Rifle unit. [The subject of Comunn na Feinne and volunteerism is more fully explored in Appendix 14(b).]

Financial difficulties were to dog the Society throughout most of its history and this issue is explored more fully in Chapter 7. Comunn na Feinne was, of course, a 'not-for-profit' organization and, for the present, after meeting its operational expenses, it was content to function as a benevolent society. Its costs consistently exceeded its income and its increased activity in income-generating ventures often did little to improve the situation. The first monthly meeting of the year, held 3rd February, 1860, demonstrated how the success of its events often bore little relationship to its profitability. The financial statement was hardly encouraging, despite the consistently well-attended annual Gatherings and the generally large attendances at the extra events throughout the year. The *Advertiser* reported, on 4th February, 1860, that:

> It did not appear quite clear whether the Coffers of the Society would or would not be much enriched after all the recent and popular exertions. A special meeting will be held tomorrow evening to take into consideration some matters of importance connected therewith.

Comunn na Feinne's founder, and first President, Archibald Douglas, left Geelong to go to Queensland during 1860 and this was a blow to the still infant Society. The loss of his organizational skills, his 'hands on' approach to overseeing the Annual Gathering, his quiet authority and his leadership, were acknowledged by the Society. His departure necessitated the appointment of a new President, and at a meeting of members on 1st June, 1860, John Riddoch, who was Comunn na Feinne's Vice-President, was elected President in Douglas's place.

The Chief of the Society, Sir Henry Barkly, paid his first visit to Geelong and a day of welcome was held on 6th November, 1860, for the Governor and his lady. Sir Henry Barkly, was, of course, the Chief of the Society and members of the executive of the Society, including Dr Alexander Thomson MLA., entertained the vice-regal couple as they visited Comunn na Feinne's grounds at South Geelong. The Governor complimented the Society on its setup and, at the invitation of Dr Thomson, "he expressed his determination to be present at the next gathering."

At a Special Meeting on 12th October, 1860, the members heard news regarding its request for formal control of the land on which the Society held its sports meetings. This land had been used, on an *ad hoc* basis, as Comunn na Feinne's games' arena from its first Gathering, and the Society had sought permanent title to it. Another meeting on 16th October, 1860, was held to appoint trustees, "to whom will be conveyed the Land Granted to the Society by the Crown." However, the government decision re the Society's request for title to the land was far less than the Society sought, for it did not, in fact, grant to the Society permanent title to it, but only use of the area until the government sought to use it themselves. The report in the *Government Gazette*, on Monday 14th January, 1861, clearly stated, "that a temporary grant of land at South Geelong, has been made by the Government to the Society, until it is required by them for other purposes."*

*[A full transcript of this *Government Gazette* announcement can be found in Appendix 4 (b).]

The Society held a 'Night with Robert Burns' on 28th November, 1860. John Black, a well-known Scottish singer of the day, whose visits to Geelong had always been enthusiastically received, responded to the Society's invitation to stage a Robert Burns concert at Geelong under Comunn na Feinne patronage. His entertainment was greatly enjoyed by the sell-out crowd who attended.

Comunn na Feinne's competitive activities soon spilled beyond staging the annual Games on the designated tract of land at South Geelong. Before the birth of the Society some of its future members and office-bearers, such as John Riddoch, Dr William Higston Baylie, James Harrison, George Wright and Archibald Douglas, motivated by the Crimean War in 1853, had taken part in a public meeting on 3rd February, 1854, to petition the government authority to establish a Rifle Corps for civic protection. Consequently, a Rifle Corps was established 13th May, 1854 and, according to the *Advertiser*, this was the first volunteer military body formed in Victoria.

The Society took pride in announcing, on 29th November, 1860, that it would include competitions involving the Rifle Volunteers and that it would stage a Grand

Rifle Match, "open to all Volunteers in the Colony". The Comunn na Feinne Grand Rifle Match, and the Highland Games Rifle Competitions, for safety reasons, were not conducted at the Comunn na Feinne grounds, but on a vacant piece of land "in the vicinity of the butts at the rear of the Botanical Gardens". A local jeweller, L. Kitty of Moorabool Street, Geelong, was commissioned to design and make three special silver cups to be awarded as prizes for the Rifle competitions to be held at the 1861 Annual Highland Gathering.

The Comunn na Feinne could be well satisfied at the reception of the event and the performance of some of the local shooters. The *Advertiser*, reflected this pride:

> The results of the rifle match have not only afforded much satisfaction but have proved that, with a little more practice, we may reasonably expect the Geelong Corps to turn out some marksmen equal to any in the Colony.

The local Colour-sergeant, John Zimmer, was beaten into second place by a competitor, William Thompson, from the Carlton Corps. It was a close contest with both men shooting 18 points but Thompson won on a count-back. Geelong men were far from disgraced and were placed in the next five out of six places. Zimmer, the runner-up, wrote to the Society:

> I beg to thank you and Comunn na Feinne for this valuable cup, and for their kind and patriotic interest in the Volunteers. Although I am a German by birth, and have borne arms in my own country, I am proud to be a Victorian Volunteer. I feel very grateful for the honour you confer, and am certain that whatever skill we may acquire in the use of the rifle will be used only for the defence of our adopted country against all invaders, and for the honour of the well-renowned British Flag 'God Save the Queen.

Such sentiments, demonstrating both national integration and the improving of skills, would have pleased Comunn na Feinne as these were some of its main aims. The part played by the Society in promoting this form of Volunteerism was central to the realization of one of its core goals.

Having now successfully staged four annual Highland Gatherings, the next decade was to be a testing time for the Society with rapid changes in its Chiefs and its Presidents. Further, it had to inculcate its grand 'vision' in the minds of its members and supporters alike, showing them that Comunn na Feinne was more than just a social club. The challenge also was to be able to consolidate with so much movement among its executive, and to avoid the fate of the Caledonian Society of Melbourne which started with overwhelming enthusiasm and confidence in 1858 only to fade away following 1861.

It was also clear that a more sound monetary base would have to be consolidated. In 1860, Comunn na Feinne was still a fledgling Society: could the momentum of its early years be maintained? It would be the decade of the 1860s which would determine whether or not it was to survive and see any of its long-term goals realized.

Chapter 3

Comunn na Feinne 1861-1870. Some Highs! Some Lows!

The great excitement and the initial noise of the launch and the first few years of Comunn na Feinne's activities had generally subsided by the beginning of the 1860s. The Society had gained government approval for the use of the grounds at South Geelong, where it had held its first four Highland Gatherings, and it had also attracted a good deal of community interest, not only through its Highland Games, but also through its wider involvement in local affairs including its competitive educational examinations and its involvement with various community volunteer movements and charities.

The Gatherings had fallen, more or less, into a pattern which included the Procession to the grounds, the staging of the heavy events, Highland dancing and solo piping and the track and field sports. This is not to say that Comunn na Feinne fell into a regular and predictable format, for it was at pains constantly to add new sporting events to the competition. and to drop those which seemed to have grown stale or unpopular. One of the motives which led the Society continually to introduce different events was its desire to appeal to all sections of the community, not just the Scottish element. As certain 'core' features of the day followed the pattern noted earlier, these will no longer be detailed year by year unless the unusual, the unexpected or the amusing added novelty to the occasion.

With the passage of time changes took place not only in the Society's annual

Highland Gatherings, but also in the range and number of Comunn na Feinne social activities relating to education, to charity, and to communal harmony. Whatever the Society undertook, at whatever time of the year and within whatever context, all was part of the outworking of its founding charter, and indeed it appeared to 'word up' the *Advertiser* to this effect in order to appropriately frame its reportage of the annual Highland Games. A positive newspaper coverage was important for Comunn na Feinne as it expanded its activities throughout the community. Comunn na Feinne members, therefore, would have been gratified with the *Geelong Advertiser*'s opinion on 1st January, 1861, that its Games had enriched New Year's Day for the entire Geelong community.

> To Comunn na Feinne must be accorded the praise of giving a character to the holiday on the first day of each year. The festival of Christmas has a character and significance everywhere and the attractions of the domestic circle are sufficient to make the day pass pleasantly without external adjuncts, but not so the *jour de l'an*,* which we call all Geelongites to witness, was never observed as a thorough holiday until the annual Gathering was inaugurated under the auspices of Comunn na Feinne. Apart from the Games altogether, the sight of so many people enjoying themselves on the Society grounds at South Geelong forms a point of attraction and interest to crowds of people who otherwise would spend the day in moody retirement, instead of sharing with their fellow townsmen the gaieties of the hour.

*[French for 'New Year's Day']

The *Geelong Advertiser* reporting on the January, 1861 Games may have been resorting to hyperbole when it said that the effect the Gathering had was that of emptying Geelong of its people and of its means of transport, other than by foot, to the grounds, but its point was well made.

> Geelong appeared to be deserted, and after one o'clock neither cab nor any other conveyance could be procured at any price and, up to very nearly the close of the day's sports, parties of two's and three's might be met straggling from town southward, despite every foreboding of a coming storm.

The *Geelong Advertiser*'s attitude towards Comunn na Feinne and to its Highland Gatherings could be somewhat ambivalent at times. For example, with some understatement, the *Advertiser*, commented on the apparent drawbacks of the traditional hockey-like game of shinty, played at the 1863 Gathering. This game was played with a similarly shaped stick as used in hockey, but the *Advertiser*'s report, on 2nd January 1863, commented bemusedly that shinty could not be played within a confined arena, there was no restriction on the number of players, and that there was no limit to the duration of the Game! Otherwise, one presumes, it was a worthwhile event! At other times, however, there could be detected a definite warming in the newspaper's attitude which was reflected in its favourable coverage of the Games.

Although the *Advertiser* could be quite severe in its description of Geelong's annual Gatherings, it could also be quite protective of them if someone from 'outside' Geelong dared criticize one of Geelong's 'offspring.' For example, in a year where the *Advertiser* itself was less than generous in its opinion of the New Year's Day Highland Gathering, describing it as being "inferior to the real thing," it took a Melbourne paper (the *Argus*) to task for its critical report in its issue of 2nd January, 1868, of these same Games.

> Our contemporary, the *Argus*, appears to be misinformed as to the Highland Gathering at Geelong ... not having been a success ... Several circumstances occurred to make it not so successful as usual ... [but] on the whole it may be certainly classed as a success.

The Band of the Volunteer Rifles' Regiment, which had provided some early selections of appropriate music as the procession was completing its march to the grounds, once the formalities were out of the way, gave way to the Highland Pipers who took over opening the Games proper with a rendering of "The Gathering of the Clans."

Tilting at the Ring was proving to be a popular event but, as with other sports, it could lead to less than sportsmanlike attitudes on the part of contestants. However much the Games were pictured as being set in a warm and cozy 'Brigadoon' background, for the contestants there was a deadly seriousness which was not always so cheerfully obliging. Challenges by contestants to their placings in events could bring strains to sportsmanship. William Stoneham of the Geelong Rifles had been declared winner of the broad sword exercise only to be challenged unsuccessfully by Mr Mason. The 300 yards' race attracted eight runners and it was won by Samuel Holms, but

David Duffy entered a protest, claiming that he had been fouled by Holms and that, but for this, he would have won the race. Holms won the re-match and took the winner's prize. Sportsmen, unfortunately, do not always prove to be 'good' sports.

The *Advertiser* commented on the role athletic competition could play in fitting the athletes for challenges which might emerge in life, sentiments which, from its beginning, the Society would approve as being part of its central aims and beliefs.

> The manly exercises of to-day have a significance beyond the mere enjoyment inseparable from the friendly contention in which they will be conducted. They are a valuable adjunct to the great Volunteer movement; a feature not only local to the time and the place but wherever an English heart throbs in unison with the aspirations, the hopes and the—fears we were going to write, but there are no fears—sense of danger to the mother country from the machinations of her jealous enemies. The manly fellows who to-day toss the Caber, throw the hammer, leap, run, and dance Gille Callum, are just the men to do prodigal acts of valour should an invading foe, endowed with more temerity than prudence, ever put foot on the soil, sacred to our hearths and homes.

The Rifle Shooting competitions had actually taken place on the 26th and 27th December, 1860, but were regarded as being part of the 1861 Annual New Year's Day Games. Before presenting the prizes, "three very elegant cups, the largest of the value of £60, the next £30, and the third £15" (indicative of the value then being placed on marksmanship), John Riddoch addressed the crowd reiterating Comunn na Feinne's aim, through its Games, of raising the skill levels of participants in order to better serve the wider community. The *Advertiser* provided, its usual cover of the Games, and also reported John Riddoch's speech containing the Comunn na Feinne's vision regarding its educative role.

> Ladies and gentlemen, this Society fully appreciating the value and importance of the Volunteer movement in the colony, determined recently to encourage, by every means in their power, efficiency in the use of the rifle; for this purpose they offered three silver cups as prizes, which were competed for on the 26th and 27th of December, 1860, and from the excellent practice obtained at that competition we have good reason to believe that the Volunteers in [this district] will, ere long, number amongst their ranks marksmen equal to any in the colony; and seeing the result likely to be obtained by these rifle matches, this Society feels proud at having taken the initiatory part for the

> encouragement of so laudable an object.

The *Geelong Advertiser* was deservedly proud of the way in which the Geelong Riflemen had conducted themselves at the competition.

> When we reflect that the majority of the competitors had had their rifles for a very brief period and that a great many of them had never until very recently tried any range beyond 200 yards, there is every reason to be well satisfied with the results – more especially as a few of the picked shots from some of the Melbourne Corps came down to compete with our men.

On the 5th January, 1861, the paper, in territorial mood, was also quick to defend the local shooters against a slur that had been cast on them!

> We have been requested to contradict a rumour prevalent at the Pivot, that the five competitors from Melbourne had been hissed by some of the Geelongese. We are informed that there is not the slightest foundation for the report. and it is one that we can scarcely believe could have been credited by any one acquainted with the good feeling that animated the whole of the members of the volunteer force throughout the Colony.

In a general summing up of the 1861 Highland Gathering the *Advertiser*, although generous in its coverage, made the point that not enough 'good' competitors were being attracted to the competitions at the Geelong Games and thus the spectacle was not as grand as it could be, the crowds not as big as they should be and "the skill and dexterity" of the competitors, lower than usual. The *Advertiser*'s report on 2nd January, 1861, said that:

> A great deal of this, no doubt, arises from the migratory habits of the population, which has the effect of removing sometimes an important corner stone in affairs like these; but notwithstanding this, we believe there would have been many entries by competitors from more distant parts of the country had the society judiciously given the affair a somewhat longer and more extended publicity.

The *Advertiser* stated that other large-scale Highland Gatherings in the State had been great successes and that the Castlemaine Gathering in particular, "from the extensive publicity given to it, drew a great number of persons to the ground from very long distances."

The Geelong Games offered smaller cash prizes than could be won by athletes at some of these other venues and, reported the *Advertiser*, for this reason good competitors were by-passing the Geelong Gathering. For example, while Geelong, in 1861, offered a first prize for solo piping (Pìobaireachd) of £5/5/0 and a second prize of £3/3/0, Maryborough awarded a £7/7/0 first prize with £5/5/0 for second, and Bendigo and Castlemaine similarly offered twice as much as Geelong. The first prize for Throwing the Heavy Hammer at Geelong was £2/2/0 while at Maryborough it was more than double that at £5/5/0. This was the case, too, with Throwing the Light Hammer where Maryborough's first prize of £4/4/0 was double that offered by Geelong. Bendigo followed suit with even higher prizes for some events. The Heavy Hammer drew a first prize of £6/0/0 and the Light Hammer £5/0/0. Castlemaine's prize list showed that 1st Prize in the Heavy Hammer event was £10/0/0!

The Caber event, in all of the places mentioned, advertised a Money-Prize far bigger than the Geelong Games offered. Geelong advertised a first prize only for Tossing the Caber, and this was £2/2/0, while Maryborough, Bendigo, and Castlemaine each offered £5/5/0 with £2/2/0, for the runner-up. These differentials were true also for the track events with Geelong at the bottom of the table in terms of 'prize purses'.

The Geelong Society placed more stress on the 'honour' of winning or being a place-getter than it did on monetary reward. It thus placed greater emphasis on its cups, its certificates and medals, as appropriate rewards. However, a class of 'professional' athletes was emerging, men who followed the various Gatherings and Athletic competitions around the State, and even interstate, some of them making a living from their winnings. Elbridge Gerry Emery, prominent at Geelong's first

Gathering in 1857, won over £600 in just two races in the racing circuit! The presence of 'professional athletes', *Bell's Life* had pointed out as early as 1858, would ruin the innocence of such occasions as Geelong's annual Highland Gathering. Certainly, by century's end, Bell's prediction had come to pass. It was also suggested by the *Advertiser* that 'dirty tricks'- in the form of financial inducements-may have been used to divert competitors away from Geelong's Gathering. If nothing else was learned by the Society through the exercise of the 1861 Games, three issues were brought to the fore which were having an impact on the Geelong Gatherings. These were disputatiousness, competition from other Highland Gatherings and the meagre prize monies being offered by Comunn na Feinne.

One thing which the Geelong Gatherings did not lack, however, was the number of new competitions being introduced each year. In the five years from 1857, by way of innovation, the Society had already added 15 new events to its original programme.

Additional events, however, meant larger overall costs and a greater need for volunteer officials and judges, as well as creating overcrowded programmes. An attempt at solving this latter problem was to hold the Gathering over more than one day. Comunn na Feinne was not doing anything revolutionary in staging its Games over two days. Melbourne, as well as Castlemaine, and some of the other country Caledonian Games, had actually stretched over three days on occasions, and this without any public criticism.

In the case of the Geelong Games, however, the *Advertiser* was quite scathing. The activities of the second day were not, the newspaper reported, of any special interest, with most of the low turnout of spectators coming from the "young unwashed". Had entry to the grounds not been free, it continued, it is doubtful if the Games would have attracted any spectators at all. With the programme consisting of a little tilting and throwing the hammer, and being, generally, of a "very desultory character", the *Advertiser* wrote that had it not been labelled by the Society as the second day of its Highland Games, "we question if anyone would have troubled to walk over there."

The actual programme on the second day would seem to render the *Advertiser*'s remarks somewhat severe and misleading. In fact, some of the events held on the second day included foot-racing, Broadsword and Cavalry Exercises and Aboriginal spear-throwing, as well as Highland dancing. A Shinty Match, "was got up outside the grounds and some found amusement", with "five or six hundred people remaining until dusk." In addition, the Band of the Geelong Volunteer Rifle Regiment, "provided a varied concert of band music" including a "Grand selection of Scottish Melodies," throughout the second day.

When Ossian Macpherson moved from Geelong to Hamilton in 1860, the Society lost its best PR man, and its 'bard', so there was no poem calling out the people to the grand gathering of 1861. Poems welcoming the New Year's Day Games became less frequent in the *Advertiser* although it occasionally featured contributions from several local poetasters. But, for 1862, the public was informed, not by original verse but with lines from earlier Scottish poets, John Mayne and Allan Ramsay. New Year's Day 1862 was said to dawn auspiciously for the grand Highland Gathering at South Geelong and John Mayne's words, from his poem 'Siller Gun', were considered apt for the occasion.

> "The lif* was clear, the morn serene,
> The sun just glintin' ow're the scene.
> *'lif' - sky.

Allowing the joy of the verse to bear along its report, the *Advertiser* continued:

> And the heart of man and woman was roused at the bright prospect, thus afforded, of pleasure and pastime with Comunn na Feinne. For all that has been said and written 'time out o' mind' about the canniness of the Scots, it strikes us that they are as fond of amusement, and willing to pay for it, as any other nation.
> "Let reist* day come as it thinks fit,
> On pleasure let us employ our wit,
> And laugh at fortune's feckless powers. (Allan Ramsay)
> *reist – rest

Further proof of the Society's attempt to do everything in its power to make its Gatherings an attractive experience, was to be seen in the improvements which had been undertaken on the sporting grounds. The *Advertiser* reported that the programme of events was skillfully managed and entertained the six thousand spectators who were in attendance and that it had been one of the most successful Gatherings to date. Attendees were drawn from all social classes, and many had made a very early start in order to achieve a good vantage point and, quoting Mayne again:

> "Mony a beau and belle were there,
> Doited* wi' dozing in a chair;
> For lest they'd sleeping, spoil their hair,
> Or miss the sight,
> The gawks**, like bairns*** before a fair,
> Sat up a' night!"
>
> * stupified, bewildered.
> ** fools, idiots.
> *** infants, children.

But this was no example of the working class at their simple entertainments. The 'gawks' who lost sleep in order to get a good position at the grounds represented no one single class of society. If the work-a-day world separated the people of Geelong into classes, there was little doubt of the levelling effect of the Highland Games. Here was an opinion which would have been pleasing to the founders of Comunn na Feinne. At these Games, the *Advertiser*, again in Mayne's words, noted that it was almost impossible, among the crowds gathered, "to distinguish the man of high from low degree."

> To see them mustering up and down
> Lasses and lads, sun-burnt and brown-
> Women and weans,
> Gentle and simple, mingling crown'd
> The Gladsome scenes.

Much colour was added to the day by the ladies with their colourful dresses and hats, and with their "blithe up-cast and merry countenance." The stand was decorated with "flags of all nations" and, fluttering from a staff over everything flew "the Red Lion Rampant."

Overall, the newspaper felt the 1862 Gathering had been a successful day, even though events did not always run to time:

> All who were in the gathering on the present occasion will acknowledge that it

was one of the most successful that has taken place. The arrangements were, on the whole, satisfactory; and, in the cases where the sports did not come off in the advertised order and punctual to time, they were delayed rather by the difficulty of bringing the competitors together in such a large variety of events than by any want of preparedness and efficiency on the part of the managers.

Extending the Games to a second day had not entirely been successful, as the Society had also attempted to cope with its expanding programme by reducing the time allotted to each event. This had led to some unintended consequences!

Tilting at the Ring had proved to be a popular, skilful and exciting demonstration of horse control, requiring, from the competitor, a steady hand and a good eye. It had the excitement of charging horses, lowered lances and a demonstration of eye and hand coordination, all combined with superb animal control.

The idea, as we have seen, was to scoop a ring, hanging from a device at one end of the course, with the tip of a lance while moving on horseback. Originally each rider was allowed 5 minutes for each Tilt at the Ring. In order to save time, however, the duration of each charge was reduced to 3 minutes. This did not allow the rider time to compose himself, achieve the necessary balance of rider and lance, nor to get any fractious horse under control. The *Advertiser*, for example, reported that the horses supplied for 1862 were the most, "unmanageable brutes as could well have been found for such a purpose, and as success chiefly depends upon the control over, and steady pace of, the animals, the results were, perhaps, not so surprising." The *Advertiser* went on to record consequent low scores; the winning tally of 19 rings in 1861 dropping to just 4 rings in 1862. There also was a diminution of the spectacle offered by shortening the time allowed for each run at the rings. There was, however, an increase in bumps and bruises from riders falling from their mounts because of the haste involved!

Extending the length of the Games day could also result in a late finish to some contests. In 1862, the *Advertiser* reported that the Games had to call it a day at 7.30pm, "when it was getting too dark to see anything." It was to be hoped, for the safety of the competitors, the judges and the spectators, that events such as the Archery contest, Aboriginal spear-throwing, Tossing the Caber and the Sword dance were not still in action in the gathering gloom of the evening!

The usual humour and interest sparked by the Heavy events was shared, in the 1863 games, by a new item, the Steeple Chase. The *Advertiser* reported this new contest on 2nd January, 1863, and anticipated that it had been included to provide some light entertainment:

> The fun of the day ... in regard to foot-racing was centred in the Steeple Chase, for a piece of water fourteen feet wide and about five feet deep was situated opposite the grand stand, and it was no doubt wickedly hoped that some of the competitors would get a ducking.

There were only three entries in its initial appearance, and the crowd's expectancy of seeing mass 'drookins', although slightly dampened, was met at least with two of the contestants taking the plunge with good humour. The third, however, gave up before the first hurdle rather than run the risk of getting himself wet.

In summing up the Games on 2nd January, 1863, the *Advertiser* pointed to the exciting finishes of several of the races, the brawn and muscle on show during the Heavy events, the fun of the Steeple Chase and the thrill of the bayonet and cutlass exercises, as some reasons for the success of the New Year's Day Gathering, despite the discouragingly bad weather.

While the forgoing reasons for the day's success would have been sufficient, the *Advertiser* delved a little deeper into explaining what made the Games attractive to the diverse peoples of Geelong and to those who came from other districts to attend the spectacle.

Although the annual Games were called "Highland," the *Geelong Advertiser* pointed out that at least half of the 1863 programme was devoted to the sports of, "the three kingdoms," and were familiar to all spectators. Such sports were played in England, Ireland and Wales, as well as Scotland, and were all represented. The paper clearly saw that the Gathering was intended to represent the interests of all of the community, but the instance it cited contained humour of which the reporter was not fully aware.

> No more apt illustration could be offered than the fact that yesterday an old

Scotchman,* of Seventy-five, carried the prize for an Irish jig, while archery, foot-racing, leaping, Sword and bayonet exercises, sailors' hornpipes, and tilting, together with bag piping and the Gillie Callum, formed a medley so comprehensively national that he must have been a " prick my dainty' indeed, who could not find something to gladden his heart, and stir up old and pleasant remembrances of youthful days.

*[In fact, Mr Martin was an Irishman!]

Yet another change of President of Comunn na Feinne took place during the year, as John Riddoch tendered his resignation pending his move to South Australia. This was three Presidents in two years and would have been unsettling for the Society, and Riddoch was persuaded to remain as President until the year's end. John Bell*, of Bell Post Hill, a large property owner and grazier, was unanimously elected to fill the role, and this was confirmed by the members at Comunn na Feinne's General Meeting on 2nd February, 1863.

*[See short biographies Appendix 3(b).]

A further issue facing this meeting, was a motion, "that it was desirable to change the name of the society", not because of ethnic exclusivity or fearful political connotations, as had been mooted in 1859, but because the name seemed to allude to a 'barbaric' past. A long and animated discussion followed, during which it was pointed out that the "Fingalianism" to which the title pointed was not an allusion to bloodlust but to the fraternalism, honesty equality, justice and civic mindedness evoked by the Society's charter. John McGregor, a Gaelic scholar and an ex Vice-President of the Caledonian Society of Melbourne, and a member and friend of Comunn na Feinne, gave his opinion as a Gaelic scholar, which was reported first in the *Geelong Advertiser* Supplement, 4th February, 1863 and, later, in the *Age* on 30th December, 1863.

> The phrase as a whole then means rigid justice, the unbiased impartiality and the magnanimous love of fair play always maintained by the Fingalians among themselves and towards all others … and it always signifies the clannish, or rather fraternal attachment, unswerving fidelity, and the unconquerable energy which they invariably displayed in vindicating the honour, in maintaining the interests,

and in avenging the injuries of the individual and of the community against the whole world.

Furthermore, it was submitted that, "as the Society had prospered under the title Comunn na Feinne ... the members deemed it undesirable that any change of name should take place." The meeting overwhelmingly decided that the name would remain unchanged. In the following year, the Society devoted one of its regular public discussion evenings, held at the Mechanics' Institute, to the subject of the meaning of its Gaelic name, Comunn na Feinne, and to its suitability or otherwise as a name for a Society in the nineteenth century. The role of Comunn na Feinne in building social harmony, improving the standards of school-teaching, widening the school curriculum, and ensuring a challenging education for pupils, as well as its welfare role and its zeal in promoting and improving all branches of the Arts still was not, apparently, grasped by all of its members. Its 'philosophy' only gradually became understood throughout the community and, as we have seen above, even within part its own membership.

But the Society in general decided that it had had enough of 'naval gazing' and identified again, in its 1864 annual report, "the various objects for which the Society was formed," and its determination not to lose sight of these aims. Comunn na Feinne's role in providing care and protection for the local Aborigines, one of its self-appointed responsibilities, was also re-affirmed. Unfortunately, in this regard, the decade of the 1860s was one of the 'low' periods in the Society's history. Its well-meant nineteenth century paternalism was being applied to a dispossessed race in numerical decline. The annual report expressed regret that the participation of Aborigines at the last Gathering was quite small in contrast to the numbers at the earlier Games.

> This society having from its origin taken great interest in the welfare of the Aborigines, on every occasion invited their attendance at the annual gathering, and supplied them with suitable clothing; they have competed in the athletic sports and obtained silver and other medals as prizes for proficiency. Your directors regret that only six were at the sports on New Year's Day, being all that are left of the once numerous Corio Tribe; only three years ago as many

as 20 having been present.

This sentiment continued throughout the 1860s. For example, the *Advertiser* on 2nd January, 1866, reported that the Society had sounded a sad note regarding the absence of all but a few of the local Aborigines whose presence and marching had once been a popular part of the day. As well as being absent from the procession, there was also a noticeable absence from the main sports arena of the group of local Aborigines who normally competed and displayed their skill with traditional weapons.

> There were a few Aborigines on the ground, decked out in fashionable attire, their new year's gift from Comunn na Feinne. If five were present that was as many as there were of the Barrabool Tribe; a few years ago, five times that number took part in the festival. [Their] spear-throwing and foot-racing [did not take place] as there were few of the Aboriginals to display their skills … and there were no competitions for these prizes.

More bad news had come when Comunn na Feinne sadly announced the death of 'Jumbo', Moor-A-Nook (affectionately known as 'Timboo'), on 22nd December, 1866. The *Advertiser* reported his death on 29th December, 1866, stating that he had been buried at the Western Cemetery in the Aboriginal area established by Comunn na Feinne.

The Aboriginal Grave site, Western Cemetery, Geelong West.

At the inquest held into the death of 'Timboo' the role of Comunn na Feinne and its caring attitude towards the Aborigines was evident. 'Timboo' had apparently been attacked by another Aboriginal man about six weeks prior to his death. Dr Baylie, the Society's medical officer, had had a long history of caring involvement with Aborigines and their health, was called in to examine and prescribe for the injured man.

'Timboo', although severely ill, had left Geelong and upon enquiry by the Society President, Robert de Bruce Johnstone, of his whereabouts, he and another member, Mr James M. Garratt (local Geelong carer of the Aborigines), tracked down the injured man at Moolap and found him in "a deplorable condition". 'Timboo' was so ill that he could barely crawl to the cab which they had hired to take him back to Geelong Hospital. Unfortunately, his injuries were so bad that he died on Saturday 22nd December, 1866. The *Advertiser*, on the 26th December, carried the *post mortem* results which concluded that 'Timboo's' death was the result of having been kicked in the chest. Comunn na Feinne announced on 28th December that it would be staging a concert at a later date, (6th June, 1867), in aid of the Aboriginal woman who, "notwithstanding the illness of herself and children, so affectionately attended upon the poor dying 'Timboo' with such motherly care." This concert, the *Advertiser* later reported, consisted of a well-received, "Scottish Night of Reading, Recitation and Song."

Despite its sense of elation in describing the 1867 Games, the *Advertiser*, on 2nd January, 1867, expressed sadness that there were no Aborigines present, "to display their skills in their native amusements …" although several took part in the usual Procession. The *Advertiser*, on 2nd January, 1867, provided another witness to the declining number of Aborigines, remarking that 'King' Jerry, [and] "Billy and Harry …[who] … were the sole representatives of the once numerous Barrabool Tribe", were present but none took part in the Games.

Further 'low points' in the Society's decade of the 1860s included the sad news that

Dr Baylie, whose example of community service and reformist politics had an influence upon the Society's community affairs, had died on 14th September, 1867. There was also the announcement of the serious illness of its President, Major John Bell, necessitating his leaving for Europe in August for health reasons.

Comunn na Feinne's material concerns for the local Aborigines, and their inclusion in its annual Gatherings, was again brought sharply into focus when the *Geelong Advertiser* on 11th May, 1870, related the sad story of the decline and death of one of the few remaining Aborigines who had frequented the Society's annual Gatherings. This was ('King') Jerry of the Dan-dan-noc (sic) (Barrabool) Tribe, who had regularly competed and had been among prize-getters in some of the events at the Society's early New Year's Day annual Games.

> Having been supplied with provisions [he] departed on one of his short tours through the district. He made his way to Queenscliffe, (sic) but had not been long there when he was taken ill. Dr Williams attended upon him, but finding that he could not live long, thought it best that he should be forwarded to the hospital ... Hearing of this while he was waiting at J.M. Garratt's [the local protector] office, poor Jerry resolutely declined to be sent there, saying he did not wish to die in the hospital. Poor fellow, broken down as he was, he would doubtless have liked to have breathed his last in his own native bush. One would have thought, he having so long associated with white men, and so often participated in the comfort of having a roof over his head, that he would have preferred the hospital to exposure; but it was not so, a wild man he was born, and so a wild man did he wish to die.

Comunn na Feinne office-bearers, J. M. Garratt and Robert de Bruce Johnstone, were both at a Town Council meeting, but when apprised of the situation regarding 'Jerry', they immediately excused themselves, and rushed to his side.

> Both of these gentlemen are great favourites of the unfortunate Aborigine, but it was not without a good deal of kindly pressure that he would allow himself to be placed in a cab, and conveyed to the hospital [where it was found] that there was very little hope that he would long survive. We have, now and again, had to record the death of a member of his tribe, but the illness of 'King' Jerry has caused more sympathy than all previous occurrences of the kind ... 'King' Jerry used to be a great attraction at the gatherings of Comunn na Feinne and at all the athletic sports meetings.

The *Advertiser* reported on 19th May, 1870, that the doctor at the hospital had explained that there was little which could be done for the patient and that he was merely "patched up" and this would not greatly prolong his life. Unfortunately, the patient's death was not so mercifully swift as the Doctor assumed, and Dan-dan-nook, "of the Barrabool Tribe" lingered painfully until his death at the Geelong Hospital on 21st October, 1870. He was 45 years of age. The Aborigine known as 'Billy Gore', the President of Comunn na Feinne, along with other office-bearers and members of the Society, were among those who attended the funeral. Dan-dan-nook was buried in the special burial area, "created and maintained by Comunn na Feinne" at the Western Cemetery, where other members of the Dan-dan-noc (sic) Tribe already lay.

It was realized, both by the public and Comunn na Feinne alike, that the total absence of Aborigines from the Games might be imminent, and the presence of only one Aborigine at the 1871 Gathering signalled, wrote the *Advertiser* on 3rd January, 1871, what had been expected for some time.

> The almost total absence of the Aboriginals from Comunn na Feinne's Gathering on Monday told a sorrowful tale. Fourteen years ago, the [Tribe] of Dan-Dan-Nook, under the command of their 'King' Jerry, who has but recently died in the Geelong Hospital, used to be one of the leading features in the Procession to the Society's grounds. There used to be thirty or forty of them and their spear-throwing at the target created no little amount of interest. On Monday, only one Aboriginal represented the natives of this district, and he, the last of this race, will not, it is to be feared, live to represent them at the next Highland Gathering.

Of course, the indigenous presence in the district did not cease with the passing of the foregoing Comunn na Feinne favourites. The *Advertiser* declared, for example, that there would be, at the 1871 Games, an Aboriginal performance called, "an Exhibition of their Majesties - Woormi-Banip, of Connewarree and Col-Co-Co-Coich in, 'King of the Warriors'." It is difficult to know what this advertisement meant however, because the event did not take place.

One of the problems which occurred year after year at the Games arose from the absence of fixed standards relating to such things as equipment, tracks, and rules. As early as the 1863 annual meeting, it was reported in the *Geelong Advertiser* (Supplement, p1) 4th February, 1863, that, in the interest of fairness in its competitions, that Comunn na Feinne had already contacted Caledonian, and other such Societies throughout the colony suggesting that the standards used at its own Gatherings at Geelong, become the accepted standard throughout Victoria. Unfortunately, it reported that, "To this request only one reply has been received, and your directors would recommend that this subject be again attended to." The standardization of weights, track quality and regulations had to wait until the emergence of Regulatory Associations later in the nineteenth century.

The decline in Aboriginal numbers, a name challenge, programme management, the events' standardization issue and the illness, and consequent absence overseas, of the Society President, Major John Bell, constituted just some of the 'lows' in the 1860s; but Comunn na Feinne also was to enjoy several 'highs' during this decade. Among these was an indication that its work had been acknowledged overseas, though perhaps it had generated this interest itself. A member, A.E. Kempson of Clunes, Victoria, presented the Society with a cutting from *The Illustrated London News* dated 11th April, 1863. The cutting contained an engraving of the Gathering at the Comunn na Feinne Grounds at South Geelong held on 1st January, 1863. It also contained remarks relating to its community work. It said, for example, that, "A very prominent feature of the Association is the encouragement of education, for which purpose it holds regular examinations, and offers prizes and gold and silver medals."

Lithograph of Highland Gathering at South Geelong grounds.

The magazine acknowledged that the engraving had been done by Robert Shirra, vice-president of the Society, and in its description of the scene, which it had taken from the Melbourne newspaper, the *Argus* of 2nd January, 1863, it reported that, "the Gathering was patronized by a large number of elites of our society."

Equally cheering to the Society was the letter appearing in the *Argus* on 9th December, 1863, praising Comunn na Feinne's efforts in promoting education. The newspaper, impressed with what the Geelong Society had achieved in this area, encouraged the formation of a similar organization in Melbourne (though the author felt that the athletics, "throwing the hammer etc., might be dispensed with!"), to emulate this community work of Geelong's Comunn na Feinne. The letter went on to claim that schools within Geelong and district, "will be the most efficient in the Colony … [and] … why cannot Melbourne, Ballarat, Bendigo and Castlemaine join in this movement and thereby give a great stimulus to education?"

The *Carmichael Notes, (1861-70)*, record another of the special events in the life of Comunn na Feinne in 1863. This involved the passing of the flag as Chief, with the conclusion of Sir Henry Barkly's term as Governor in 1863, to Sir Charles H. Darling, his successor. Darling was invited to become Comunn na Feinne's second Chief by a special deputation, "consisting of Captain John Bell, Robert Shirra, William Weddell and James Bertram". Darling assented and intimated "his wish to give his connection with the Society an enduring character by becoming a life-member [and] also presenting them with a very substantial cheque." Although the new Governor had advised the Society that he would be unable to attend its annual New Year's Day Gathering for 1864, he did visit Geelong on the 8th December, 1863, when he was taken on a tour of the district by Town officials and spent some time in the Barrabool Hills. As a sign of his interest in the Society he requested his *aide-de-camp* to arrange a meeting for him with Captain John Bell, Robert Shirra, William Weddell and John Bertram, the President and office-bearers of Comunn na Feinne during this visit. This he did when he personally was able to convey his appreciation of the Society.

Darling was replaced by John Henry Sutton as Victoria's new Governor on 15th August, 1866, and on Sutton's first visit to Geelong, on 10th October, 1866, he was approached by a Comunn na Feinne delegation and invited to become the new Chief of that Society. His formal assent was received on 12th October, 1866. Thus, in the space of three years, the Chieftain of the Society had changed three times!

The December 1863 monthly meeting presented the draft programme for the 1864 Highland Gathering for members to approve. There was to be a 'surprise event' in the 'heavy games' one added to the programme by Captain John Bell, the President, an event of which the *Advertiser* said, "We are not at liberty to anticipate the publication of the programme by describing the nature of the feat."

The 2nd January, 1864, reported the *Advertiser*, "broke with splendid promise, not with an Australian summer sky, glaring heat, and clouds of dust, with which for several years past our annual Scottish Games has been associated, but mild and beautiful ...". The usual New Year's Day Highland Gathering procession completed, the *Advertiser* reported more lyrically than usual about the Games, inviting comparison with those of ancient Greece, despite the 50,000 spectators claimed for the latter!

But the annual Society Gathering was more than people, events and results, the paper said. 'Waxing classical', it drew a picture of the Greek Athenians who held their ancient games at a spot giving access to all would-be spectators. Such Games drew up to 50,000 people and were open to all. But, both in ancient Greece, and in present-time Geelong, the *Advertiser* pointed out that it was not the number of spectators which gave meaning to the event.

> By comparison with so gigantic a scheme as this [ie Greece] the annual Olympiad of a small town in a far-off dependency of the British empire, must apparently sink into insignificance. But it is not altogether so for, after all, the grandeur of the idea is in the national spirit of a people which can create a demonstration in full proportion to its numerical strength and importance.

With this assessment Comunn na Feinne would have whole-heartedly agreed. It was not any narrow ethnic 'spirit', Scottish, Highland, English or Irish, which motivated the Society or which drew so large a proportion of the local population (5,000 out of Geelong's population of 20,000 with, it was claimed, as many more viewing from outside the official perimeter). While such large numbers were gratifying, not least because they helped balance the books, Comunn na Feinne hoped that its activities throughout the rest of the year would similarly attract such attention and demonstrate the breadth of its involvement with the community.

As the 1864 Games progressed, the "surprise" event was revealed as an addition to the traditional heavy sports. For those who knew Captain John Bell as having held the title as the strongest man in Europe, his "surprise" event, involving tossing, "a Cannon Ball (32lbs)", for which he had donated a silver cup as first prize, would have 'surprised' no one! Bell gave a demonstration throw of 24 feet. The actual prize winner, Donald Cameron, a youth of 17 years, threw 22 feet, drawing Bell's admiration.

Already, even by the time of only the eighth annual Highland Games, exaggerated memories of the deeds of past athletes had emerged! The 14' 7" Caber for the present Games was dubbed a mere "twig", and was compared condescendingly with the tree trunks of over 24' presented to aspiring champions at earlier Games. But even this "short stick" defied the efforts of the contestants to turn it and, not for the first time, this Caber, too, was sent for a surgical amputation. It was eventually tossed by John

Clinnick, of the Barrabool Hills, who finally emerged the winner.

Amusing incidents during the Games always caught the eye of the newspaper reporter when looking for something to lighten his coverage of yet another Scottish dance or yet another solo piping contest. The Steeple Chase, with its water jumps provided such amusement, and fresh 'copy'! Two spectators, according to *Bell's Life* on 9th January, 1864, while having an altercation near the track, also managed to tumble into the water jump, hopefully the experience cooling their tempers! In January, 1869, Sam Holmes, in the Handicap Steeplechase (twice around the course over hurdles 3 feet, 9 inches high with water leaps), beat Robert Grange, "a strong man from Bellarine" who was favoured to win, into second place." Grange, perhaps angry at himself in his disappointment at losing, went "souse"* into the water jump to cool his frustration!

*[Souse means going into water with a sudden splash. However, Souse can also mean a thump or a hit and it is in this latter sense that it is used with the Quintain event as explained below]

To inexperienced (and uninitiated) entrants of the 1864 water jump event, some unintended farce was also created, as the *Advertiser*'s report revealed, when two of the judges volunteered their services to show the 'green' competitors just how the hurdles should be taken. The judges, perhaps past their prime as athletes, unfortunately taught them nothing and both ended in the water, "up to their necks, and came out like drowned rats, much to their discomfort, no doubt, but vastly to the amusement of the spectators." The Steeplechase, with water jumps, earned such a reputation over the years for providing competitors with an unplanned bath, that it was difficult in some years to attract sufficient contestants.

The lack of an Ossian Macpherson to welcome each new year and issue a call to 'sporting arms' was corrected for the 1865 Gathering when a local versifier, William Stitt Jenkins, took over Macpherson's role. Unfortunately, as a sample of his verse demonstrates, he could not quite match the quality or the excitement of Macpherson's contributions. Stitt Jenkins was Anglo-Welsh, and an ardent Temperance man and moralist, so the intrusion into his 'heroic' verse of moral preaching sometimes tended to dampen the excitement or fun expected of mock-heroic verse. He greeted *Geelong Advertiser* readers on the morning of 3rd January, 1865 with 'The sports Begin', a few verses of which are shown below. [The complete poem can be found in Appendix 5 (b), Poems of William Stitt Jenkins*]

> 'The Sports Begin'
>
> Come, Donald, first at feast or fray,
> And still the last to run away,
> Come on my man!
> Feel ye the Caber's mighty weight,
> And leap ye over the five-barred gate,
> And rap with single stick each pate,
> As best ye can.
> ....
>
> Ye sons of Scotland far away,
> March as of yore, in close array-
> Remember this is New Year's Day,
> Come one, come all.
> ....
>
> The Celt and Saxon, hand in hand,
> Together meet in this fair land,
> In love and joy.
> Of ancient feuds they dream no more,
> On their adopted austral shore,
> They dwell in peace for evermore,
> Without alloy.
> The sports begin!

*[See information of his life in Appendix 3 (b) Short Biographies.]

And come the spectators did:
> All went merry as a marriage bell ... and there was nothing to mar the enjoyment of the thousands of pleasure seekers who from an early hour in the morning thronged to Comunn na Feinne grounds at South Geelong. The grandstand creaked beneath the weight of its fair burthen*.

* burthen – archaic spelling of burden.

Nothing, apparently, could spoil the merry mood of the crowds and the *Advertiser*'s eye was quick to point out some amusing incident or other. While outside the ground, the paper also found some fun to be poked at:

> Very amusing it was to watch these picturesque groups outside, chiefly of country people who make a family holiday perhaps once a year. It was a great day for the young Gumsucker who will imbibe such *outre* Scotch notions, it is to be feared, as will never be eradicated.

There was amazement, too, expressed at the first meeting of an Aboriginal girl with a kilted Scot. The *Advertiser* waxed philosophical over this. With hindsight, we might say far better, indeed, it was to only be amazed at a harmless kilted man than to suffer the fate of many of her forebears whose first sight of a European sometimes had a far more tragic outcome! "There was merriment, too, in the sight of a Chinaman who thinks "Tullochgorum"* (sic), 'belly good', "but profanely enough applies the feminine gender to the man in the kilt." Indeed, continued the *Advertiser*, the outside of the grounds yielded up as much amusement as did the inside.

* [Tullochgorm is a Scottish Reel and a favourite dance at competitions.]

The Heavy Games had drawn the usual attention but while many of the familiar faces of past competitions were missing, others stepped up to fill their places and, "there were plenty of brawny arms to tackle the Caber, the stone, and the hammer." Although falling far short of the distances, real or exaggerated, achieved by some of the early stalwarts of the Games, the events seemed to satisfy the spectators. When the same athlete, J. McDonough, carried off the 'light' and the 'heavy' Hammer events, the 'light' stone event, tossing the Caber, as well as the Hop, Step and Jump, it would have seemed to many of those present that a new 'hero' had arrived. He was denied a 'clean sweep', however, when James Smith of Ballarat threw to victory in the heavy stone event. Smith also won the special event, throwing the heavy (32 lbs) Cannon Ball a distance of 26 feet.

It was difficult, in the early years, for anyone to upstage the 'heavy games' performers but, one competitor, Peter Martin, on more than one occasion, managed to do so. The fact that it was in the dancing competitions that this took place, and that the competitor was 84* years of age, made it all the more remarkable. Peter Martin had, reported the *Advertiser*, won the Irish Jig competition three years in a row. Now he carried off the Irish Jig again, and was second in the Sailor's Hornpipe dancing competitions. His appearance and success at earlier games had already drawn comment from those who knew of his age, and his stamina! For a few years, the exploits in the dancing, arena of this agile and determined veteran almost overshadowed the exploits of the 'giants' of the heavy games. It may have been, however, that age (or loss of hearing!) was eventually having an effect. Both the Irish Jig and the Sailor's Hornpipe require speed, grace and dexterity in stepping, but the tempo of the music had to be adjusted somewhat as the years slowed down this 'ancient mariner' of dance! Thus, the Piper had to resort to drastic measures such as playing a slow air to accompany the Irish Jig!

> The old Terpsichorean could on no account, however, step to the bagpipes, and he and the Highlander were in a quandary till the latter happily hit on a lively Celtic dirge that had probably done duty for the old man on some festive occasion sixty summers ago.

Dancing a Jig and a Hornpipe to a slow air must have been something to behold! Yet again in 1865 Mr Peter Martin, took out the double - Irish Jig and Sailor's Hornpipe.

*[This may be a mistake by the *Advertiser* which gave Mr Martin's age in 1863 as 75.]

In 1865, some additional excitement was provided in the Lancers' exercise (Tilting the Ring) where, "there was some fair sport, and at one time a prospect of broken necks." On this occasion, it was the horses rather than the competitors who were given the spotlight. The first contestant, "who ventured outside [on] a horse appeared to have no control over the animal, for it twice threw him; another quadruped showed an evident disinclination for such sport by galloping now and then outside the ring, and going full tilt at the crowd."

The Society continued its recently established practice of prolonging the New

Year's Day entertainments into the evening. Moving beyond holding the post Highland Games dinner for a few members and officials in a Geelong Hotel, the Society began holding social gatherings at a variety of hotels. A series of these began in 1863, with local hotels joining the action. In 1864 The Retreat Hotel at South Geelong, opposite Comunn na Feinne's grounds, offered, after the Games proper, the following sports which it advertised as being under Comunn na Feinne patronage.

> Sports of various kinds at the Retreat Hotel, South Geelong.
> A Match at skittles, open to all-comers, Prize, silver watch and gold chain.
> Also, a Grand Match at Quoits for Ten Pounds a side.
> Cutting the Cock's Head off*, Prize £1/5/0
> To conclude with a Grand Masquerade Ball.

*[For the squeamish, there is no evidence that the 'sport' of beheading a cock ever made the official programme of events at Comunn na Feinne's Highland Gatherings!]

'Gents' tickets were 2/6d each, Ladies free! In some way, this may have been an attempt to provide a cheaper 'down market' form of dancing and entertainment for those who might not have been able to afford Comunn na Feinne's official evening Concert; free entrance for ladies added some respectability to the venture. It is of course difficult to know whether the Society had anything to do with choosing or vetting these kinds of Hotel entertainments offered in its name.

The Society itself was not above using entertainments, which some would now see as being in questionable taste, such as the black-face American minstrels who performed at the official post-Games concert. On New Year's Day 1865, the Society's concert featured the popular American troupe of entertainers, the Christy Minstrels. Their show highlighted music, dance and humour from the American South, but performed by white Americans whose faces were blacked up. The *Advertiser* was full of praise for the entertainers and for Comunn na Feinne, its contemporary sensibility finding no disparity between the Society's professed liberalism and what would now be seen as "racist" entertainment. However, 'political correctness' was still many years away from this period of Australia's social history.

> A splendid house rewarded the appearance of the Christy's Minstrels at the Mechanics' Institute last night, the hall of the building being full to the door. Somehow or other fortune seems to favour Comunn na Feinne, and most

deservedly so, too, we think, [this] excellent Society [is] founded on a broad and liberal basis. The Christy's were in excellent form and humour last night, and amused the audience no less with their drolleries than they charmed them with their melody. In their singing and dancing, the Christys seemed as much at home as if they were real darkies in their native plantations in Louisiana, or any other state; and the dancing was also exceedingly well rendered. We feel sure they will have no cause to regret the Comunn na Feinne night at the Mechanics' Institute.

After a successful Gathering, and a well-attended evening concert, it was on a 'high' that the Society's annual meeting, took place on 7th February, 1865. Members heard a financial report, "showing the Society to be in a very favourable position", and an equally positive report on the competitive educational examinations conducted by the Society. The educational committee reported on a satisfactory number of students taking part, although it was looking to extend the number of schools involved. The important part which volunteers played in making possible such societies as Comunn na Feinne, and the services it rendered in the community, was acknowledged in a motion of appreciation. Thanked, too, were donors such as Major John Bell, John Riddoch and Captain William McLean, whose contributions made possible the conducting of these examinations and also the medals and books which were awarded as prizes. Expressions of gratitude were again meted out at a meeting in October, 1865 where members were informed that a letter of thanks had been sent to Daniel Bunce, curator of the Botanic Gardens, for the gift of trees and for the planting of them around the Society's grounds at South Geelong. It was reported that an earlier effort at planting trees at the grounds, which had been carried out by the Geelong Council, had not been a success as a great many of these trees had died.

The 1866 New Year's Day Gathering, marking the Society's tenth anniversary, proved to be as popular as ever, with an attendance, reported the *Advertiser* on 2nd January, 1866, "of not less than six thousand." There were those, continued the paper, who thought that the popularity of this event was waning, but the present Gathering would have been enough, "to convince even the most sceptical" that this was not the case. As exciting as the running and the heavy Games could be, it was not in the

Hammer throwing or in Putting the stone or even the Caber tossing (although one competitor managed to drop the Caber, "on the heel of Mr M.S. Levy one of the judges"), nor in the Steeple Chase with its water jumps, nor even with the octogenarian Irish dancer, where the most attention was generated on the day. The *Advertiser*'s report noted that horses rather than the human competitors, won the crowd's interest and were, overall, the 'champions' on the day. In Tilting at the Ring, the winners, according to the *Advertiser*, should have been the horses over the humans as it was the beasts which turned in the best performances!

Perhaps, too, demonstrating the truth of the injunction never to work with animals or children, stampeding horses again gained the headlines when, during the Tilting events, some children ran on to the arena and were knocked down. None was hurt to any extent. At the same Games, an out of control crowd of 'feral' youngsters also caused some confusion when, about half way around the foot race for boys under 13 they, *en masse*, decided to join in the race making it difficult for the judges to identify the legitimate contestants, winner and place-getters!

From the earliest years, there had been some concern regarding 'professional' athletes who competed at the different Highland Games throughout Victoria, and even interstate, and who effectively denied the prospect of success to the casual, especially the local, entrant. Eldbridge Gerry Emery would fall into this category of 'professional' sportsman. The concern, as we have noted, was raised as early as 9th January, 1858 by the sporting newspaper, *Bell's Life*, when it considered the Comunn na Feinne annual New Year's Day Games and pondered:

> [W]hether professional parties, who devote all their time to the study of Scottish pastimes as a means of livelihood, should be allowed equal privileges with those who have only the cessation from everyday labour to practise for the competitions. While it is desirable that every encouragement should be given to professional teachers, it may be that some arrangements may be made, either by competition among themselves, or by any other mode, whereby the performance of the professional will not clash with that of the simple amateur.

The issue arose again at the 1865 Games when the *Advertiser* reported that E. Nichols, who had won several of the racing events, and who was a regular on the

Games circuit, was: "becoming too dangerous a competitor for such novices as enter for mere holiday sport."

Another 'famous' speedster of the day was James Joshua whose circuit of the various Gatherings around Victoria netted him some substantial purses. In other centres, such as Bendigo and Maryborough, *Bell's Life* wrote that the policy adopted at their respective Highland Games, of having separate races for 'amateurs', was already in place. It was many years before the Geelong Gathering caught up and held competitions which were reserved for the week-end, 'non-professional' competitor, and even then, only in selected events.

As well as maintaining the traditional Highland Games' heavy events, the Society was faithful in fulfilling another of its Charter aims. This related to the preservation of Highland culture as represented in traditional music and dancing and, taken up elsewhere in this story, the Gaelic language. Piping, Highland Dancing and Step Dancing thus formed part of the Gatherings each year. Highland Dancing and Solo Piping had been included from the first Gathering in 1857. Pipe Bands, as we know them today, outside of British military regiments, did not exist in Victoria until the early years of the twentieth century; thus, the majority of the local piping musical entertainment at such events as Comunn na Feinne's annual gathering was provided by individual pipers. On occasions, a group of pipers would come together on an *ad hoc* basis and march together during the Procession to the grounds. Comunn na Feinne did not have its own Pipe Band until 1907, although individual pipers, competed in the solo Piping contests and accompanied the Highland dancing competitions. There were solo piping competitions for Pìobaireachd, the 'classical' music of the pipes, as well as for the lighter music such as marches, reels and strathspeys, but Pipe Band competitions did not exist in Victoria before 1905.

The Charter aim, as it related to Bagpipe music, was to preserve, and to pass on, the main styles of traditional Piping. In this, Victoria was fortunate indeed to have Peter Bruce* and Simon Fraser**, as well as a few others, who were master pipers and teachers. Simon Fraser received teaching from Peter Bruce and passed on the traditional methods to his sons, one of whom was Hugh Fraser, champion player and, later, pipe major to several pipe bands (including the Comunn na Feinne Pipe Band).

[For * and ** See Appendix 14(b).]

Fraser was taught Pìobaireachd in the traditional manner of the classical pipers of Scotland, by Peter Bruce, hence maintaining the style of interpretation and execution of the classical music of the pipes which had come down through the various teachers since the C16th days of the MacCrimmons who were the hereditary pipers to the McLeods of Skye. The MacCrimmons had opened a 'school' of piping at Boreraig on Skye which lasted for several centuries.

H. FRASER, Winner of Piping Contest; R. FRASER, 2nd; and Two Other Competitors

Competing solo Pipers. Left to Right - Hugh Fraser, Ralph Fraser, Rex Paterson, unknown.

The bulk of the music for entertaining the spectators at the Geelong Gatherings was Brass Band Music. Many of the municipalities had their own Brass Bands and volunteer military groups, as well as Fire Brigades, also had their own Brass Bands. Despite its popularity at outdoor events such as the Highland Gathering, the Geelong Regimental Volunteer Artillery Brass Band's financial state was always bordering on the precarious. Such volunteer groups were not officially funded by local councils or by any type of government aid. Private and public donations enabled volunteer organizations, such as this Band, to survive.

The *Geelong Advertiser* was keen to promote the 1866 New Year's Day Gathering, and assured its readers that they need not fear resorting to the grandstand in order to view the Games.

> As the preparations for the approaching gathering of Comunn na Feinne draw towards completion, it becomes evident that, weather permitting, the occasion will attract as large a concourse as ever assembled on any former occasion to witness the national games and feats that annually come off under the auspices of this Society. Anticipating the extra pressure, the directors have had their grand stand professionally examined as to its capabilities, and have been assured that the building is fully equal to any amount of strain.

On the great day itself, the public was surprised by another summons* – this time from Ossian Macpherson himself. Whether by request or not, Ossian Macpherson had sent down from Hamilton some rousing verse invitations to Geelong's grand event, one of which must have reminded Geelong people of earlier New Year's Day Gatherings. The first was addressed to "Sons of Fion", and although not up to Macpherson's best, it carried the familiar call to gather and to celebrate.

*[See Appendix 5 (a) for the complete poems.]

> Sons of old Fion! Good morrow! Hogmanay!
> A brother greets ye with the opening day.
> A new born year has heard the latest chime;-
> And bursts to life to fill the Throne of Time.
> Forth from the distant hills proceeds a voice,
> And bids on this hallowed day, rejoice;-
> The voice that cheers amid the battle's roar,
> It calls today on you in gentle strain,
> To join in harmless strife upon the plain:
> 'Tis Scotia's summons from the mountain side-
> Bursting o'er oceans which her sons divide-
> Up then! And gather to the welcome sound,
> And let her spirit mid your ranks be found,
> Up then! And gather here in fair Geelong,
> And join in Caledonia's muster song.

As a bonus, the *Advertiser* included yet another Ossian Macpherson poem which, it claimed, was an 'exclusive' not having been in print before.

> Air—" McGregor's Gathering."
> The Pibroch is sounding o'er mountain and dale,
> And the Slogan of Scotland is heard on the gale!
> Then proud let each bonnet be raised to the brow,
> For the shades of the mighty are watching us now
> Then gather! Gather! Gather!
> Gather! Gather! Gather!
> ....
>
> For the day of our fathers, whose Mem'ry we cherish,
> In the hearts of the Children of Fion shall not perish.
> There's the struggle of life, with its storms and its cares;
> And its course ever changing with hopes and despair,
> To the wind with them all! for no sorrow to-day
> Shall chase from our thoughts bonny Albion away.
> ....
>
> Then haste to the fray! To the battle field gather.
> Undaunted and true! gallant Sons of the Heather.
> Then Gather! Gather! Gather!
> Gather! Gather! Gather!

Perhaps inspired by Macpherson, large numbers of marchers in the usual procession set off in perfect Games weather. Perfect, that is, for those in the kilts, "but rather warm to those who had to walk in fashionable attire," wrote the *Advertiser*.

The Geelong Volunteer Artillery Band had obviously survived the year since its financial crisis and the *Advertiser* was fulsome in its praise: not only had it led the traditional procession to the Grounds but its performance overshadowed the other events of the day.

> In justice to them it must be admitted that although many had their friends in various events in the sports, the music was 'the attraction,' and [the Volunteer Artillery Brass Band] always compensated for what would otherwise have been a dreary gap.

Summing up the day, the *Advertiser* was full of praise for the events, the athletes and the overall organization of the Gathering. Even the judges had been touched with whatever 'spirit of *bonhomie*' had influenced the *Advertiser*. "The judges played their part well, and none was heard to rail against their decisions. This was proof that the management was complete", remarked the *Advertiser*. Some of the judges wrote to Comunn na Feinne commending the Society for the part it was playing in maintaining and improving Scotland's traditional music and dance. The Society would have been gratified to have this accolade addressed to its upholding of this Charter aim.

> Gentlemen, in acknowledging the honour conferred on us by your committee as judges of pipe music and Highland dancing, we have the honour to report that we consider the music and dancing of this year to be a great improvement on former years in that both the pipe music and dancing are year by year improving, and are well worthy of the countenance of your praise-worthy exertions in promoting the music and pastimes of our old mother country. The competitions in dancing, especially in the Gille Calum* and the Highland Fling, was as good as to commend our special admiration.
> We have the honour to be, gentlemen:
> John McGregor of Melbourne
> Alexander McKenzie of Geelong
> John McGillivray of Colac.
>
> *[The traditional Sword Dance.]

Another successful New Year's Day Highland Gathering was followed by a familiar calendar of events for Comunn na Feinne in 1867. It was with a sense of elation, too, that the news of a royal visit to Australia of Queen Victoria's second son, Prince Alfred, the Duke of Edinburgh, was received by the Society. Following his visits to Adelaide and to Melbourne, the Prince was then to visit Geelong on 3rd December, 1867.* There was much in this announcement to raise the spirits not only of Comunn na Feinne, but of Geelong's townspeople generally.

*[A full account of the Prince's visit to Melbourne and Geelong is contained in Appendix 6.]

A high degree of excitement ensued, together with the bustle involved in setting up planning committees and the headaches of establishing the 'pecking order' of those who would actually meet the Duke. The enthusiasm among the people was palpable.

But what had this, specifically, to do with Comunn na Feinne? The Society was well represented in the Prince's visit indirectly, through its President, Robert de Bruce

Johnstone, for example. He was also the Mayor of Geelong, had served on several State government committees and was soon to enter Parliament as one of Geelong's representatives. As Mayor of Geelong during the Prince's visit, he was involved in leading his town in the arrangements for the royal visitor and, as Comunn na Feinne President, his was the responsibility of determining the Society's role.

A Special Meeting of Comunn na Feinne had been held as early as the 24th September, 1867, to deal with various pieces of correspondence relating to the pending royal visit. The *Advertiser* of 25th September reported that this meeting agreed that when the Prince arrived in Melbourne some members should be there, "appearing either in kilts or wearing some badge of nationality." Requests to Comunn na Feinne had also been received from the Ballarat and the Buninyong Caledonian societies seeking information regarding Comunn na Feinne's plans for the Prince's Geelong visit and asking assistance in staging their own local celebrations when the Prince visited their respective towns.

More directly, Comunn na Feinne was involved in various committees which were set up to handle different parts of the visitation arrangements. For example, William Clarkson, a director of the Society, headed up the catering committee and had several members assisting him with this job. Robert Shirra, a vice-President of Comunn na Feinne, represented the Volunteer Fire Brigade demonstrating the Society's commitment to this community utility. Comunn na Feinne's influence can also be seen, for example, in the fact that one of the dances listed for the Ball was the Highland Reel, reportedly favoured by the Duke himself. Disappointingly, the Duke, on the occasion itself, weakly excused himself on the night on the grounds that his official piper had forgotten to bring his bagpipes!

More broadly, Comunn na Feinne members who had businesses in town, set up displays in their premises, some featuring expensive gas lighting.* In a number of these the Scottish theme was very much to the fore, but there were also many representations of Aborigines, demonstrating Comunn na Feinne's relationship with the indigenous people in and around Geelong, with some showing Aborigines in poses of familiarity with Queen Victoria.

*[See Appendix 6 for details of these illuminations.]

In Melbourne, a "Free Banquet" held on the banks of the River Yarra to honour the Prince's visit had ended in a melee. A combination of factors was to contribute to the descent of the people into an out-of-control rabble. A very hot day, a delayed opening of the event, news that the Prince would not, after all, be attending, and the presence of a free wine fountain, constituted some of the main factors which combined to bring disaster to the event. Added to this list was the fact that a "free banquet" prepared for a maximum of ten thousand people was faced with handling a crowd of between 70,000 and 100,00 who turned up!

Notwithstanding the Melbourne *debacle,* a similar event was held in Geelong, organized by Comunn na Feinne committeeman William Clarkson who, when faced with a similar crisis in the making, was sufficiently adroit to take decisions which avoided absolute mayhem. It was due to his efforts alone that the Geelong 'free banquet' did not descend to the depths of "a frightful Saturnalia" revealing "the natural baseness of the masses," as the *Argus* of 28th November, 1867, described the Melbourne event. Unfortunately, not one of the other members of his committee, appointed to carry out the catering arrangements at Geelong, was present to lend a helping hand. Clarkson was already there when the young folks began to arrive, and he distributed among them a number of bats and balls, skipping ropes and other articles, with which to amuse themselves and while away the time until the food was put out. From nine o'clock in the morning, the people began to gather in such numbers that by eleven o'clock there was not less than three thousand on the ground and this quickly rose to at least five thousand by 1pm.

Given the increasing size of the crowd, Clarkson thought it wise to start serving the food and drink an hour before the due time of starting. The *Advertiser*'s editorial of 4th

December, 1867, dealt with the picnic with an even hand stating that the 'working class' may have seemed like "wild beasts feeding", but the 'respectable' class was worse, having made off with the cutlery! The free alcohol produced a predictable and widespread result which would have been much worse except for Clarkson's deliberately spilling of the wines onto the ground.

Interestingly then, it was without any note of irony that, to commemorate the Prince's visit, it was decided to erect a Lunacy Reception Ward at the Geelong Hospital!*

*[See Appendix 6 for a longer account of the Duke's visit and a description of some of the various window illustrations illuminated by gas all welcoming the Duke to Geelong. It was estimated that, in Melbourne, it could have cost a householder £50 for gas illuminations in the windows of the house.]

Comunn na Feinne had played a large part in the organization, administration, and celebration of the Prince's visit. Members were exhausted and some much out of pocket. It was probably inevitable that the Society would be financially unable to stage its 1868 New Year's Day Highland Gathering. Having had much of its time taken up with arrangements for the Duke's visit, preparations for the New Year's Day Gathering for 1868 had been laid aside until it was too late. Towards the close of December of that year, therefore, the Society decided to make other arrangements regarding the holding of the Highland Games on 1st January, 1868. The *Advertiser*, on 30th December, 1867, reported the shock news that the 1868 Games had been cancelled and, "There would be no fun at all to be seen on the reserve. The Society's grounds at South Geelong would be silent."

Not for the first, or the last, time, the *Advertiser's* announcement was not quite accurate. There would, indeed, be Highland Games but they were to be under the auspices of the Geelong Volunteer Fire Brigade with whom Comunn na Feinne had a long and close connection. Many Comunn na Feinne members were volunteers with the unit, and the Society had long supported them financially, as well as with manpower. This was thus no desperate, unplanned decision by the Society, and its call on the Brigade to shoulder the burden of these Games in January 1868, made good practical sense. The Society could not bear the responsibility of the arrangements nor the costs involved, and the Volunteer Fire Brigade desperately needed funds which, hopefully, would derive from the profits on the day. A special meeting of the Brigade was held on 28th December, 1867, and the Brigade's foreman, Mr Knight, expressed his misgivings, writing that Comunn na Feinne, "with all their efforts had never at their demonstrations succeeded in making a profit." While this was not literally true, any profit derived from the annual Games was usually a small one. Any profits accruing from the 1868 Games were to be devoted to the Volunteer Brigade which, itself, also supported a range of charitable works. A letter from Comunn na Feinne was read to the meeting giving the Fire Brigade full use of the Grounds at South Geelong as well as a sample programme of events which it had prepared.

Following a discussion by Brigade members, it was moved and accepted, despite the opposition of the Chief, that the Fire Brigade would proceed with taking over the 1868 New Year's Day Gathering, "and many of the members present announced their intention of attending the ground to contribute to the success of the movement."

To emphasize the importance of volunteers, the *Advertiser*, in its report of the Games on 2nd January, 1868, recognized that the utility of volunteer community bodies was rendered more effective through engagement in the exercises and competitive displays which were staged by Comunn na Feinne. This included not only the Volunteer Fire Brigade but also other bodies such as Volunteer military forces which benefited from such competitions in bayonet and sword exercises as well as rifle marksmanship and horsemanship.

The *Geelong Advertiser* duly reported the arrangements on 30th December, 1867, and encouraged the public to get behind the venture.

> For the first time for a long series of years, Comunn na Feinne will allow this New Year's Day to pass over without holding their usual Highland Gathering. We are glad, however, the Geelong Volunteer Fire Brigade have (sic) determined not to allow the day to pass without a Gathering and we trust their efforts to please will be rewarded with a crowded attendance ... judging from

the number of Scottish bonnets, worn by a number of Highland visitors on the streets of Geelong last evening, there will be no lack of competitors. The proceeds are to be devoted to the reserve fund of the Brigade which has ever been foremost in giving its support to any entertainment having for its object the benefit of our charitable institutions, and therefore merit all the support that can be given them.

The *Advertiser*, on 1st January, 1868, praised the Fire Brigade again and went further in identifying what voluntary organizations meant to a community. The fact that they were voluntary bodies made their survival all the more precarious and their service all the more precious to a citizenry.

> [A]n active Volunteer Fire Brigade is one of the most useful public bodies that a town could possibly possess, and that our brigade is an active one the many valuable services they have rendered to the rich and poor fully proves.

Members of the Geelong Volunteer Fire Brigade featured prominently on the day of the 1868 parade, but active service called some away from the procession as the *Advertiser* reported, on 2nd January, 1868.

> Yesterday, during the procession through the town, the fire bell rang out the alarm, and it was ascertained that the back portion of the premises in Malop street, occupied by Messrs Shirra and Moodie, [both members of Comunn na Feinne and the Volunteer Fire Brigade] were on fire. A number of volunteers, however, were soon on the spot; and the Fire Brigade, with their (sic) usual dispatch, were (sic) soon in readiness, and succeeded in arresting the progress of the conflagration which, at one time, threatened the destruction of the whole premises. By an advertisement in another column, it will be seen that Messrs Shirra and Moodie return their thanks for the assistance rendered them during the fire.

Shop fire aside, the 1868 Procession, with not a single piper to lead it, lacked the public excitement of other years, continued the *Advertiser*'s report. It added that the usual pre-Games Procession had always been able, "to draw a thousand or two over the sandy plain which existed between Geelong and the ground." Despite the absence of the drawing power of the marches of old, the *Advertiser* reported that the number of spectators at the ground was still commendable. The numbers amounted to several thousand, but the ill-mannered behaviour of certain sections of the crowd spoiled the spectacle for others. The *Advertiser*, however, was generous in laying no blame for the poor crowd control at the feet of the Fire Brigade whose members, it said, worked hard, "to make the meeting a success". The Fire Brigade, it explained, was not used to handling such a large undertaking. Rather, the newspaper continued, the blame lay with Comunn na Feinne which, too late, gave notice that it would not be able to manage its usual annual New Year's Day Gathering. As bad as this was, the news that the Games would be proceeding under the supervision of the Volunteer Fire Brigade was also late in being made known. As a consequence, although there was a decent crowd of not less than 3,000, many potential competitors and spectators, believing the earlier announcement that Comunn na Feinne would not be holding a Gathering on New Year's Day, did not bother coming to Geelong. Notwithstanding these, and other, criticisms, the *Advertiser* pronounced the Games a financial success.

Perhaps, with the *Advertiser*'s criticisms still ringing in its ears, the Society, in the lead up to the 1869 Gathering, went all out in its publicity campaign on behalf of the upcoming Games. As well as the usual favourite events, the newspaper proclaimed that "several novelties" had been introduced into the Programme. These included, "the Quintain, the tilting at the target which requires consummate skill on the part of the cavalier – one second too slow and 'souse' comes a sandbag against his unfortunate back." The *Advertiser*, on 24th December, 1868, reported that the Society was confident that this new event would be an attraction greeted with great interest. To enable spectators to better understand the new event, it offered a brief explanation, while pointing out the need for practice sessions for would-be entrants.

> Quintain is an object to be tilted at. It was sometimes the figure of a man and often an upright post on the top of which turned a cross-piece on one end of which was fixed a broad board and on the other a sand bag. The player was to tilt or ride against the broad end with a lance and pass without being struck by the sand bag behind. To get away without being struck requires no small amount of skill, and we would therefore recommend players to avail themselves of the opportunity offered them in practicing.

Tartans galore would be on display among the crowd. Special guests would be coming from the Royal Caledonian Society of Melbourne* including its President, "who would be clad in the 'Garb of Auld Gaul. There would be dancers and reels aplenty, and many a 'Braw Laddie' will doubtless try his skill with the 'muckle stick' and the 'big stane'. Quoit matches will be fought out, and the Volunteer Brass Band, will discourse sweet music throughout the day."

*[The history of the Royal Caledonian Society of Melbourne suggests that the Society had lapsed between 1861 and 1884 at which time it was revived. However, the presence of its President at the Geelong Comunn na Feinne's Highland Gathering, along with other members, would suggest that it was still operating, at least in some form, in 1869.]

New Year's Day 1869 thus saw Comunn na Feinne back at the helm of its annual Gathering and, at least as far as the *Advertiser* was concerned, order had been restored to the universe! In its excitement, the paper predicted a crowd of thousands, a fact which in past years, "has made the words 'Comunn na Feinne' familiar to every man, woman and child throughout the Colony." Failing a contribution from Ossian Macpherson, the newspaper itself seems to have taken over the role as cheerleader of the Games commending to its readers the Gathering at the South Geelong grounds where the Pipers, "will blaw a skirl, enough to mak' the rafters (o' the new grandstand) dirl." The newspaper did, noisily, if not poetically, occasionly bang the drum on behalf of Comunn na Feinne's New Year's Day Gathering!

The wet start to the day seemed to have dampened any hope for a crowd of "thousands" at the Games. Only a few of the members joined up behind the Geelong Volunteer Artillery Band to march in procession down to the Grounds. Weather notwithstanding, the *Advertiser*'s report on 2nd January, hailed the Gathering as, "a great success." Doubts about attracting a crowd were soon dispelled and come the public did, "in chaise carts, in one or two-horse cabs, and on foot, they could be seen making their way across the plains towards the flag of 'Auld Scotia' which floated merrily in the breeze." The Procession on reaching the South Geelong arena was greeted with the sight of a crowd of a thousand people present and by early afternoon, this had grown, and, "Counting the cheap and easy customers who looked over the boundary fence, there could not have been less than three or four thousand people present …".

The inevitable bit of humour continued to emerge out of the annual Games, although sometimes it came from an unexpected quarter. On this occasion, one entrant, a Frenchman, obviously unfamiliar with the language, or the rules, or common sense (or all three!), competed in the foot-racing and, "persisted in running twice as far as he ought to do, and winning nothing!"

Less humorous was controversy, never far away in some events, and when Dougal Rankin's effort in putting the light stone a record distance of 36 feet was disallowed, there was a decided murmuring among his supporters. But, as he accomplished this record throw at his fourth attempt, when only three were allowed by the rules, his throw was disallowed. As it was, he did earn second prize with a legitimate throw of 33 feet, 8 inches.

In Caber tossing John Clinnick, a new champion in the making, was brought to public notice. Clinnick had already featured among the prizewinners at the heavy games for the last three Highland Gatherings, especially in the Caber event. At the 1868 Games, he took the prize for the Caber and at the 1869 Gathering he came into his own, taking not only the Caber prize but also that for putting the cannon ball (32lbs), as well as coming third in the heavy hammer event. It is noteworthy, too, that joining Clinnick in the prizes at the previous three games had been John McLennan, who was to emerge as the long-time rival of Clinnick at these events.

As foreshadowed in the *Geelong Advertiser* on the 30th December, 1868, there was also to be a return to the evening Concert following the Games on New Year's Day. A Grand Concert, was held at the Mechanics' Institute with the takings devoted to the funds, "of our really efficient Volunteer Fire Brigade and the Volunteer Brass Band", each of which body, "fully deserve all the support that can be given them." A torchlight procession, with the Geelong Volunteer Artillery Band leading, took place and the Hall, "was filled to over-flowing with an enthusiastic and delighted audience." The entertainers included several professional, "celebrated vocalists" from Melbourne along with 'specialist' Highland dancers and a comic, all also from Melbourne, to lend support to local performers. The singing and the Highland Dancing and Piping, "was all that could be desired, and the managers of the entertainment were to be congratulated on the excellence of the concert." At a committee meeting of the Society, held on 11th January, 1869, and reported in the *Advertiser* the next day, it was announced that the sum of £24 from the Concert would be handed over to the bodies mentioned. This may seem a small amount given the large audience attending the concert but having to pay for entertainers from Melbourne would have been expensive.

Despite the success of the 1869 Games the *Advertiser*, non-plussed, announced for the second time in three years, that Comunn na Feinne was pulling out of conducting the 1870 Highland Gathering! In the *Advertiser* of 15th December, 1869, on the same day as the foregoing decision had been announced, the Fire Brigade had inserted a prominent advertisement which suggests, at the very least, that Comunn na Feinne must have already discussed with it the matter of running the Games once again.

> Grand Highland Gathering
> At the Comunn na Feinne's Grounds, South Geelong
> On Saturday 1 January, 1870
> Under the Auspices of The Geelong Volunteer Fire Brigade.

It is not clear whether Comunn na Feinne felt unable to stage the 1870 Games or whether it had acquiesced to a request from the Geelong Volunteer Fire Brigade to stage them. In any event, according to the *Advertiser* of 17th December, 1869, the Society had agreed to, "granting the use of the Comunn na Feinne Grounds on New Year's Day, the Brigade to pay £10 for the use of the reserve." The close relationship between the two organizations has already been mentioned and the Society would have regarded its decision as financially assisting the Volunteer utility. However, the *Geelong Advertiser* read into Comunn na Feinne's decision something a little more sinister. There were persistent rumours, it hinted, of a disruption within the Society likely to lead to its imminent collapse. The newspaper asserted that it based this analysis on the view, "of several gentlemen, who were formerly members of Comunn na Feinne, who do not know whether the Society is still in existence and is to hold a Highland Gathering ..."

If this was more than just 'gossip,' it would suggest that there had been some sort of break-away group of ex-members, and that this disrupted the Society so much that it could not organize the 1870 Highland Games. However, in the absence of any evidence beyond the *Advertiser*'s 'rumoured news', the decision of the Society not to head the Gathering for 1870, could just as easily be explained as Comunn na Feinne's generous action on behalf of the Geelong Volunteer Fire Brigade. The *Advertiser* supported the day, irrespective of its sponsor and, on 1st January, 1870, it wrote: "It is hardly necessary to call attention to the sports in aid of the Geelong Volunteer Fire Brigade on the Comunn na Feinne grounds today. The claims of the Brigade are so great that we are sure that there will be a large attendance."

The Fire Brigade chief proudly announced that three pipers had promised to play for the 1870 Procession and at the Gathering itself. But, as in 1868, there were some within the Geelong Volunteer Fire Brigade itself who were opposed to it conducting the Games, and it became necessary for the Brigade to use a little bit of 'bribery' to win them over. The *Advertiser* on 31st December, 1869 revealed this arrangement:

> A special meeting of the Geelong Volunteer Fire Brigade was held last evening at the station. Mr J. Miller, the foreman, was in the chair. The business was not of general interest, being almost entirely confined to the appointment of money-takers, check-collectors, &s. for the sports and concert on Saturday. There being opposition, it was decided that the secretary should issue free tickets to those members who are present at the procession in the morning, and the meeting then terminated.

The *Advertiser*'s report of the Gathering, which appeared on 3rd January, 1870, began with little to be cheerful about. The weather was discouraging and the traditional Procession from the town to the sporting grounds was not well attended by members of the public.

> The Fire Brigade, headed by the Geelong Artillery Band, marched from the brigade-station … down to the grounds where they arrived shortly after 11 o'clock. At that time, there were not more than a hundred persons present and an hour later matters had not improved in this respect. Added to this there was a great difficulty in obtaining entries, and the consequence was that it was afternoon before the first event could be started.

Just when things looked like they could not get any worse, it was announced that neither the pipers nor the dancers would take part in the day's proceedings unless they were "paid heavily." The effect of a growing professionalism, which was now common at Sports gatherings such as the Society's Games, can be seen in this incident which shook the spirit of Comunn na Feinne somewhat. As a result, the piping and dancing events were immediately cancelled. However, bowing to the inevitable, and not wishing to disappoint the spectators, "who now at that time numbered fully two thousand", the organizers "came to terms" with the 'striking' performers and the cancelled events went ahead as usual later in the afternoon. The agreement promised that, "all Pipers in Highland Dress who will consent to play when required, will each receive £1/0/0 irrespective of prizes." Comunn na Feinne was also to honour this agreement at future events and, in fact, for the 1871 Games, it raised this payment to £2, irrespective of any other sums gained as prizes.

Several certainties had emerged over the annual Games in recent years, and these included John Clinnick's consistency in gaining prizes at most of the heavy events in which he took part. The Caber crown again went to him together with a first in Throwing the Heavy Hammer and second place in Putting the Light Stone. One of the other consistencies was seeing a Mr Martin in the prize winners list for the Irish Jig. However, on this occasion the victor was Mr B. Martin, the veteran's son! The *Advertiser*'s overall judgment of the day was not fully damning and, in fact, it could even be considered a charitable one.

> As to the sports themselves, they were certainly not quite up to what was expected, but, bearing in mind the excellent purpose to which the proceeds were to be devoted, any little shortcomings were generously overlooked.

The newspaper was also gratified to be able to report that the Volunteer Fire Brigade would have a decent return on the day with the net profit from the Games and the evening Concert being about £50.

While it devoted space regularly to the annual Highland Games, the *Advertiser* was also gracious enough to publicize some of Comunn na Feinne's charitable endeavours and to relate some of the other welfare interests which engaged the Society's attention and support. One of these was its association with the 'Industrial School' children*. During the 1870 sports day, the Fire Brigade honoured a pre-arranged Comunn na Feinne undertaking to entertain and 'fete' some eighty children from the Geelong Industrial School.

> Among the visitors were 80 children from the Ryrie-street Industrial Schools, in charge of Miss Drowley and Miss Cowin. The youngsters appeared thoroughly healthy and enjoyed the sports well, while those who were in charge of them showed themselves most solicitous for their welfare. Thanks to the liberality of Mr Miller, they were all well regaled with sandwiches and other refreshments.

*[In 1864, the Victorian government introduced a system of Industrial Schools and Reformatories through its Neglected and Criminal Children's Act (1864). Those children who were considered "neglected" were sent to Industrial Schools one of which was established at Geelong. These came in for much criticism and a Royal Commission set up in 1872 to investigate the system recommended that Industrial Schools be shut down. A more detailed explanation of Industrial Schools can be found in Appendix 7.]

This relationship between Comunn na Feinne and the Industrial School at Geelong was a continuing one, and the *Advertiser* reported, on 3rd January, 1871, that the Society, having once more assumed control of the annual Games, had again treated a large number of the children at the Gathering.

> There were some two hundred Industrial School children who, thanks to the kindness of Robert de Bruce Johnstone MLA., and Robert Shirra, were accommodated with seats in the arena, which they nearly half surrounded, and were treated, too, to some of the good things children eat and drink.

The introduction of the Velocipede into the 1870 Games, agreed at an earlier meeting of the Society in 1869, demonstrated Comunn na Feinne's continued willingness to progressively add new events to the list of competitions at the annual Gatherings. Although the long running equestrian event, Tilting the Ring, with the rider on horseback, was continued, a new novelty event, which combined a new form of transport (the Velocipede), was introduced at these Games and, instead of riding a horse, the competitors rode on Velocipedes. These machines, basically like a bicycle, were propelled by the rider using his feet pushing along the ground for propulsion (there were no pedals, crankshafts or chains by which to provide motive power). In the initial appearance of these machines at Comunn na Feinne's New Year's Day Gathering in 1870, there were only two competitors W. Richardson and T. Ball. Richardson, in the five minutes allowed, snared 5 rings whereas Ball, who entered "merely to make up the event" gave up after going only halfway down the course!

As transport technologies changed the Velocipede gave way to the bicycle and this, in turn, led on to motor-cycles and then to motorbikes. Each of these innovations was incorporated into the programme of races, and other events such as stunts with side-cars. Likewise, Fire Brigade competitions altered as new and better equipment and techniques were introduced. Some of the contests introduced by the Society were to move on to wider arenas. The inclusion of the ancient Highland game of Iron Quoits in the Society's annual Gathering, for example, led to the formation of a Quoits Society and the construction, by Comunn na Feinne, of a permanent Rink at Geelong which was used for inter-Quoits Club fixtures throughout the whole year.

Not all of the new events turned out to be successful, however, and the Society had no hesitation in dropping those when it became obvious that they were not popular with the public. These included the Eglinton-styled tournament which was to re-enact the jousting matches of past centuries, and Maypole Dancing, each of which was to be introduced at the 1871 Games, only to sink without trace thereafter!

Innovation covered more than the actual events in the Society's programme. For example, night lighting was introduced to allow outdoor evening events. In 1910, large Lux Lamps were used to light-up Kardinia Park (a century before the Cats stadium achieved this), allowing the Pipe Bands to perform, as well as for Highland dancing and other entertainments to take place in the evening. Lux Lights were kerosene lamps made especially for outdoor use by the Lux AB Company, Zurich, Switzerland, from 1901. These Lights largely went out of use by 1912 when generated electricity became available. The use of generated electricity to light up Kardinia Park for Comunn na Feinne purposes followed in 1913, and again in 1918 and 1919 and then, thereafter.

The night concerts in Johnstone Park similarly, from this time on, also used electricity for lighting.

On the eve of the 1871 Highland Gathering, it appeared that the Society had managed to restore some stability within its organization. Normalcy was seen to return to the promotion and preparation of its New Year's Day Gathering. At its Annual Meeting held on 11th November, 1870, Comunn na Feinne announced that it would be holding its New Year's Day Highland Gathering on January 2nd 1871. The *Advertiser*, the next day, welcomed this news and cited the return from Queensland of the former President, and newly elected Secretary, Archibald Douglas, as a guarantee of the day's success. It was also announced the staging of a medieval tournament with 'armour-clad knights' in jousting matches:

> Another novel event to be held during the 1871 Highland Games was a tournament, "in which knights, we presume, will appear in armour cup-a'-pie,* lance in hand to maintain the beauty of their lady-loves against all-comers. ... The combatants, in full armour and mounted, will be appointed and equipped a-la-Eglinton** The champion will be dubbed by the Chief a Curri-nam-Fiann, and invested with the decoration of that dignity by a young lady.

*[This derives from the Latin, caput – head, and pes – foot. Here it is shown in the form of an expression in the French, cap-a'pie – meaning head to toe. Combined with the word 'armour,' it simply meant clad head to toe in armour.]

** [Archibald William Montgomerie (1811-1861), was the 13th Earl of Eglinton whose family seat was near Kilwinning, Ayreshire, Scotland. He was an admirer of medieval chivalry, popularized in Walter Scott's novels, and decided to stage a re-enactment of a medieval Tournament.]

By making reference to Eglinton, the *Advertiser* must have been well aware of that nobleman's disastrous attempt to stage such a Tournament on his property in Ayrshire, Scotland, in 1839. Eglinton's effort in Scotland took place over a period of a few days in 1839. Unfortunately, atrocious weather and overwhelming crowds (admission was free) turned the spectacle into a disaster!

The death of the last of the Aborigines, who had taken part in Comunn na Feinne

Games, had been announced earlier by the *Advertiser*. Nevertheless, there was also a special announcement by the newspaper relating to an Aboriginal performance to take place at the 1871 Gathering. The Society obviously had requested Aborigines from another local district and tribe to participate at the Gathering. It thus declared that there would be, at the 1871 Games, an Aboriginal performance called, "an Exhibition of their Majesties - Woormi-Banip, of Connewarree and Col-Co-Co-Coich in, 'King of the Warriors'." It is difficult to know what this advertisement meant as the event did not take place and no details were given.

A final attraction, the newspaper recorded, would be the playing of the, "Geelong Volunteer Artillery Brass Band, with twenty performers," which would constitute, "one of the exciting prospects at the [1871] Games." The evening Concert following the Games was to be in aid of that Band.

Comunn na Feinne having experienced a mixed decade of 'highs' and 'lows', emerged at the end of it full of enthusiasm and was enjoying much encouragement from the *Geelong Advertiser*. It had welcomed back into its fold its first President, Archibald Douglas, who was now the enthusiastic Secretary, and with its practice of continually adding new events (although not all were received with equal enthusiasm), it demonstrated its determination that the Games not become stale or boring. The Society looked forward with confidence that it had acquired the expertise, and the attitude, to avoid any further obstacles to its success. It looked forward, then, to a period of growing in strength.

Chapter 4

Gathering Steam 1871-1900

The weather was, unlike that of many previous hot New Year's Day Gatherings, exactly the opposite of what might have been expected for January 1871. The *Advertiser* of 3rd January, 1871 reported that it was initially thought that low temperatures and the presence of a cold wind, would deter many from attending the Games, and that the 'gentle sex' would find little joy seated in the stand, "facing the south when such a breeze prevails from that quarter."

> However, close to midday the weather brightened and, "as piper after piper marched across the plain playing … a stream set in, and hundreds could be seen wending their way to the scene of action.

On some occasions, the *Advertiser*'s reporting could be magnanimous to the nth degree, and 1871 was one such occasion.

> The annual Highland Gathering which took place at the reserve of Comunn na Feinne was in every point of view an unprecedented success. It was estimated that at least 5,000 spectators were present within the arena, and not a few well-packed wagons surrounding the enclosure, enabling their occupants a sight 'on the cheap'. [The admission of carriages to the Grounds, it claimed, would have produced more paying customers.] The Red Lion Rampant, the Scottish Flag, surmounted a vigorous and profuse display of bunting. Nor were the dresses of the competitors less interesting. Pipers and Dancers in Highland Costume … made an admirable show of Tartans and decorations.

The Heavy Games featured familiar names in the winning lists. John Clinnick won the Caber event from a field of eight competitors, albeit only after a little tree 'surgery.'

The Caber, being made of "stringy bark timber was too heavy to toss, and had to be cut shorter three or four times before it was thrown." What the early champions would have made of the 'softer' athletes now competing can only be guessed at!

John McLennan, who usually was runner up to Clinnick in the heavy events, missed out on the Heavy Hammer prize, a matter that "was generally regretted." The event was actually won by the phenomenal John Clinnick with a distance of 71 feet. But there was a 'what might have been' moment when McLennan threw 80 feet, "a distance that would have blitzed all other competitors' throws," except that his throw was "disqualified" as being off line, although it was "only a few inches outside the line of demarcation", sympathized the *Advertiser*. McLennan did have some compensation in running second to David Smith in the Putting the Heavy Stone event and winning the Standing High Leap.

There were laughs, too, at the 1871 Games, when the Handicap Steeplechase, as usual, provided some fun for the spectators, and a cold bath for the runners, with one contestant introducing a new style over the hurdles! Hilarity followed each of the contestants as they took the inevitable bath while Mr Carr, just to be different, "actually turned a back somersault into the water". The Walking Race, over a distance of one mile, was now in its third year, and was starting to attract an increasing number of competitors with seven entering for the event which was won by J. Wheeler, a regular-prize winner in these races.

Despite its impatience, on occasions, with what it regarded as the seemingly never-ending stream of dancers and their accompanying pipe music, the *Advertiser* freely acknowledged the opinion of experts, noting that the judges, as they had following the 1867 Gathering, praised Comunn na Feinne for its role in maintaining and raising the standard of Scottish traditional Bagpipe music and Highland Dancing.* As in earlier years, the *Advertiser*'s references to "men" in the Dancing, as well as the Solo Piping contests, at the Highland Games, were literally true. At the 1871 Games neither ladies, nor children, could compete in the dancing or piping events. Later, from 1873, juveniles were eligible consisting of Boys under 15, Girls under 12.

Only men were allowed to compete at Highland Dancing.

*[Such competitions, together with prizes for poems and essays, were deliberate attempts by the Society to foster traditional Highland culture, and it was meeting with some success in this regard. As noted previously, the Society conducted competitions in traditional piping, Highland dancing and singing, as well as in step-dancing and in harp playing. It was often commented upon, by the specialist judges, that the standard in these events was exceedingly high. Comunn na Feinne's Highland Gathering, as with many of the great Gatherings throughout Victoria and in other States, helped keep the music and dance traditions alive. Step-dancing, for example, was in steep decline in Scotland at this time and was revived there only because it had been kept alive in Australia and other locations where the Scottish diaspora settled.]

The Cliadheamh-Mor (two-handed broad sword or Claymore) sword fight in relation to the Eglinton Tournament, as advertised in the *Advertiser* on 24th and 28th December, 1870, did not eventuate. The Velocipede Tilting at the Rings event had also been dropped for 1871, and no reference was made of the advertised Connewarre Aboriginal exhibition having taken place. While praising the Heavy Games and Dancing and Musical events, the reporter said he saw nothing in the so-called Tournament to warrant a good word: "the whole affair was a great farce! … which, it was hoped, would never be repeated." It wasn't! No one could understand the rules, the wooden lances too easily snapped and there was such a confusion that, "even

Ivanhoe would have objected to it." But, with the exception of the Eglinton-style Tournament, the reporter acknowledged that nothing could have been done to make the day and the events more memorable! High praise, indeed, from the *Geelong Advertiser*!

A Directors' Meeting of Comunn na Feinne on 2nd December, 1871 was held in the office of Archibald Douglas, secretary of the Society. The decision to hold a Gathering on New Year's Day, 1872, was confirmed and a committee was formed to draw up a programme. The meeting re-iterated the earlier promise regarding payment to pipers and dancers who were "engaged by the committee to play when required [and who would] each receive £2 irrespective of prizes they may win." It was also intimated that some new sports would be introduced and that the prize money had been increased to £107. Of this increase the *Advertiser* approved, saying that it was all very well to hold to a more noble view that contestants should be satisfied with the honour which came with winning, but that wouldn't pay the bills or attract top athletes! The Melbourne newspaper, the *Argus*, on 1st January, 1872, wholeheartedly agreed with this decision, making the point that "honour should be conjoined with profit." The stage was set, therefore, for what was anticipated would be an excellent day of sports and music at the New Year's Day Gathering on 1st January, 1872.

The *Advertiser* declared the 1872 Games a great success, numbering the crowd (those actually paying for entry), at more than 5,000, with the Society taking £200 at the Gate. The *Argus* pointed out, however, that once all the expenses were paid, any profit would be greatly decreased. The numbers who watched from the periphery and did not pay for entry, and those who simply leapt over the fences, continued to take away needful revenue. Although the Society had declared itself satisfied with the day, it was planning, for the next Games, to have new fencing erected and also to enlarge the actual enclosure to allow even bigger crowds to attend. This was one of the early signs that Comunn na Feinne was aware of its need for a bigger ground which would accommodate larger crowds, thereby generating more income at the 'box office'.

It was not all business, however, and the *Advertiser* picked out some individual colour from the day commenting that the "octogenarian chief of the clan McGregor", who was on the official platform, was, "dressed in the garb of auld Gaul ... with the fire of old Rome still burning in his breast." That Methuselah of dancing, Mr P. Martin, now well into his 80s, "with an agility and grace that would have cast many of his younger rivals in the shade", took second place in both the Irish Jig and the Sailor's Hornpipe, and he was also the recipient of a special award. Unfortunately, Mr W. Hazeldine, a competitor in the one-mile race, obviously did not possess the same stamina and fainted from exhaustion and, reported the *Age* on 2nd January, 1872, "was for some time in an insensible state."

The heavy games produced a mixture of old and new names in the various events. John Clinnick continued to own the Caber-tossing prize, while a relatively new name was now cropping up among prize-winners and place-getters. This was Peter Fleming who finished second to Clinnick in the Caber event and beat him into second place in Putting the Stone.

In every way, the *Advertiser* heaped praise upon the 1872 Games and was lyrical in its description of the scene at the Grounds. How many Gatherings could have been typified thus!

> To many of the spectators, music and dancing were the principal features ... The games were announced subsequently (sic) to the opening of the gates, by the sound-stirring notes of the Bagpipes playing that Scottish air familiar to every Highlander and Lowlander, 'Lochiel's Gathering'. When the well-dressed Chief of the arena and [his retinue] did gather, there was a scene such as the eye might delight to linger upon. It was a sight that must have called forth time treasured memories ... in the breast of many a hoary Caledonian; for old men mixed with the young, and even joined in their games.

Towards the end of 1872, the *Geelong Advertiser* wrote a further affectionate and encouraging piece on Comunn na Feinne which appeared on the 14th December.

> One of the oldest, most popular, and hitherto most successful institutions of Geelong, is its annual Highland Gathering. For seventeen years past, New Year's Day has been celebrated by this special festivity, held under the patronage and direction of the Comunn na Feinne Society. The games of the Gael of past days were reproduced under circumstances that could scarcely fail

to revive the sympathy and veneration of their descendants. The sound of the pibroch, which gave energy to the heroes of Alma, Balaclava, and Lucknow, which now have (sic) fallen into disrepute with modern taste, could not fail to find its admirers, for the loud wild notes of the bagpipes brought with them the traditions and recollections of the heroic and chivalrous deeds of bye-gone times. So far as attendance was concerned, last year's gathering was notably one of the most successful ever held since the arena at South Geelong was constructed. The present, it is anticipated, will be equally so.

The *Advertiser*, referring to previous troubles (perhaps to the 1870 Gathering which had to be staged by the Volunteer Fire Brigade), and criticizing some of the Society's former members, praised Comunn na Feinne for fighting back and overcoming these "adverse circumstances". It showed, the paper continued, that, "sufficient fire and energy has been left in the trusty few who adhere with tenacity to their time-honoured sports, to stimulate them to increased exertion."

Perhaps encouraged by the *Advertiser*'s comments, the Society held a meeting on 16th December, 1872, designed to keep up the renewed enthusiasm for the New Year's Day Gathering and, "it was unanimously resolved" to make the next Games an outstanding success. No doubt, towards this end, the Society met on 30th December, 1872, and announced the feast of piping that would be delivered at the next Games where the largest number of pipers playing as a group should prove to be a magnet by which many will be drawn to the Gathering. "Those who delight in hearing the Bagpipes played – and what Scot does not?", said the newspaper, will be well satisfied by this event. The pipers were to include 12 young men, the sons of members of the St Andrew's Society in Melbourne, who had formed themselves into an *ad hoc* "pipe band", together with 6 locals, making it the largest assembly of pipers ever at the Games. New events were also mentioned including a Harp playing competition and Irish Pìob-h'ionnach*(sic) events.

* [*Pìob shìonnach*, Irish bellows pipes, are played by filling the pipe bag by means of bellows worked under the arm. The normal Scottish bagpipes (*pìob mhòr*) operate by inflating the pipe bag by blowing through a blow stick. *Pìob shìonnaich* has a gentler sound which is more suitable for playing in a domestic context, and can have a range of several octaves.]

It was also decided to enlist the members of the Geelong St Andrew's Lodge, to take part, in full regalia, in the traditional procession to the Society's Grounds, joining Comunn na Feinne office-bearers and members, the usual assortment of Bands and other community service organizations. It was also mentioned that Comunn na Feinne was giving its patronage to the usual concert, a "dramatic performance", to be held in the evening following the Gathering, on behalf of the Geelong Volunteer Fire Brigade.

David Hughes, the latest rhymester to contribute verse to advertise the annual New Year's Day Highland Gathering - not to mention his shoe shop - contributed his offering to the last issue of the *Advertiser* for the old year.
[The full poem can be found in Appendix 5 (c) Poems of David Hughes.]

COMUNN NA FEINNE, 1873

Air: "THE CAMPBELLS ARE COMIN'
(Composed by David Hughes)

Let us meet brither Scots
At the Comunn na Feinne,
And we'll hae a day's sport
Such as never was seen;
There the pipers shall play
On the stage in the ring,
While the Macs, in their tartan
Dance the Hielan' Fling.
....
And if for the New Year
You want tae buy shin,
Ye ken whaur my shop is,
So please tae step in;
I have got some braw boots
That you never hae seen—
They will suit young or old
For the Comunn na Feinne.

The attendance at the 1st January, 1873 Gathering was a large one and, given the fine weather and the attractions of beaches and other picnic destinations, the Society's Games stood up well in the face of such competing attractions. The organizers were to be commended for the preparations which they had made. "As usual the arena was beautifully decorated with flags, [with] the 'Scottish Ensign' floating high above the others."

> Before the time for assembling, the town resounded with one of the most demonstrative musical processions ever witnessed in the district. William Kingsbury, dressed in full fireman uniform was the leader, followed by the Town's Brass Band, and then came a dozen young pipers, dressed in Highland costume … the music naturally attracted a large crowd of followers.

The grand stand was filled and, among the crowd generally, the presence of the kilt, "was very conspicuous" with the sound of the pipes recalling, "historic events on the flood and field" such as the British race are proud to acknowledge." The *Advertiser* on 2nd January, 1873 reported the presence of young lads "as pipers and dancers" who, for the first time were able to compete in the Juveniles' Dancing and Piping events (boys 15 years and under, girls under 12 years only), and commended the Society for this innovation. With the advent of solo piping competitions for juveniles, the *Advertiser* further recommended that Comunn na Feinne should begin teaching, "young boys in the art of playing the pipes." This, certain members were already doing in their efforts to maintain Scottish cultural traditions such as piping and dancing.

It was also sadly noticed that generational change was taking place with the absence of "weel kent faces", as age and death removed many of the original members, judges, spectators and participants. Perpetual crowd favourites, John Clinnick and John McLennan, so often winner and runner-up in the Caber event, were relegated to second and third places respectively when they had to defer to a new competitor, Donald Cameron, in Throwing the Heavy Hammer. Six competitors fought out the Caber event although, by the *Advertiser*'s report, not all did so with equal skill with some demonstrating, "by the manner they tumbled over the walking stick", although "highly amusing", a lack of experience in this event. Clinnick, had no such trouble, continued the *Advertiser*, "but this is what might be expected from previous performances." In fact, Clinnick was setting something of a record for holding the Caber tossing crown, and McLennan likewise for coming second! The Heavy Stone event caused something of a stir among the spectators when the relatively new competitor, Peter Fleming, entered the lists and took first prize. He was a local man, formerly of Inverleigh, and impressed the long-time Games watchers by his "graceful manner", and he had already been stamped by them, even before the first event, and despite his less than athletic build, as a natural winner.

Although the Games were open to all, the *Advertiser*, with a sharp focus, described also the unusual and the touching moments which occurred throughout the day, demonstrating that the Gaelic background to the Games still had some relevancy for some. There was a special 'magic' abroad touching everyone - whether Gael or not!

> A Gaelic expression was quite sufficient to gather a group together and the hearty congratulations and seasonable compliments that ensued might have occasioned surprise and pleasure could the words have been understood by the listeners generally. Hands were firmly grasped, friendship linked and good feelings expressed in all directions. New Year's Day has seldom or never been better celebrated than [it was] at this Gathering.

The Walking Race in 1873 also provided the local journal with some grist for its mill. The judges awarded 1st prize for walking to a boy named W. Riley who had, however, broken the rules by being a late entrant. The Judge's decision, continued the report, was obviously influenced by the boy's "plucky behaviour." In singling out this ten-year old boy as a contestant who should have been disqualified, the reporter conveniently overlooked the infringement of the rules by other 'walkers'. Apparently, all of the competitors had difficulty following the rules regarding correct style, and all had been delivered warnings about breaching them. One comment overheard at the event was, "the less said about the event the better", and others agreed that whatever it was, "it was no *Walking* match." The favourite, based upon his previous performances, was J. Wheeler who disappointed his many backers by not contesting the race. Wheeler did, however, enter and win the Handicap Flat Race over half a mile, and pocketed first prize of £4 which was more than the £3 prize money for the mile walk. He obviously knew what he was doing by saving himself for the more gruelling half mile Handicap. His 'backers', no doubt, would have appreciated being 'let in' on his tactics for the day!

Harp competitions, and *Piob-shionnaich* contests, also enlivened the day's proceedings and there was always the unexpected event outside the sports arena itself, such as a grass fire, to bring its own bit of spectator interest and excitement.

> Quite an exciting scene, and one not included in the Programme, was witnessed at the Highland Games on New Year's Day. Some one of the numerous visitors happened to throw a lighted match carelessly on the ground, and the grass took fire and the flames spread with alarming rapidity in the direction of a drinking booth superintended by Mrs Fairly. The landlady could be seen running about in all directions in a state of frantic excitement, while a crowd assembled, and with the aid of some tall weeds growing near the spot, managed to beat out the flames.

To add jam to his already 'well-buttered' story, the report added, "About half an hour afterwards a mounted constable and a water-cart put in an appearance but, of course, their services were not required." Did the speedy action on the part of the nearby men have anything to do with the fact that the fire was heading for a 'refreshment' booth?

Archibald Douglas, one of the founders of Comunn na Feinne at Geelong, and its first President, had moved to Queensland in 1860 and, as already noted, he had returned to Geelong in 1871, and was elected Secretary of the Society. However, after having overseen three Gatherings, he resigned at a meeting of Comunn na Feinne on 12th November, 1873 to move again interstate and thence to New Zealand where he spent the rest of his life. His guiding hand was missed. James Shillinglaw McKay was elected to fill Douglas's position and, wrote the *Geelong Advertiser*, "as his colleagues are known to be energetic men, there is little doubt the Gathering of the Clans on 1st January, 1874, will be a sight worth seeing." The Society held a meeting on 3rd December, 1873, at which, "there was a very strong muster of the Society's committee," for the purpose of re-affirming that a Gathering on New Year's Day, 1874 would definitely be staged. As if to dispel any doubts which may have been in people's minds, the *Advertiser* on 4th December, 1873, reported that:

> There was to be a gathering of the McDonald's, the McGregors, the McDuffs, the Campbells, the Rankins, the McLeods, the McKays, the Chief of Glenlivet and all the other Clans at the Comunn na Feinne Reserve, on New Year's Day. There was a very strong muster of the Society's Committee … when the Hon. Robert de Bruce Johnstone MP, the Chief of the Celtic Brotherhood in this district, occupied the Chair and it was decided to hold the usual Grand Highland Gathering [in 1874].

Several new members were inducted into the Society and, "several energetic Directors were elected." The programme for the 1874 Games was, "revised and unanimously adopted" at the Society's meeting on 8th December, 1873. A new event was announced, "the introduction of a foot race, open only to the members of the Geelong Volunteer Fire Brigade." The *Advertiser* sensed a new enthusiasm within the Society:

> [A]nd from the spirit manifested by the members present and reports from various parts of the district, confident hopes were expressed that when the wild note of the Pibroch resounds on 1st January, 1874, there will be such a gathering of the 'Sons of the Heather', and their Saxon friends, and members of the Emerald Isle, as was never before witnessed even in the palmiest days of the Society.

Commenting upon the Programme approved for New Year's Day 1874, the *Advertiser* wrote, in its issue on 9th December, 1873:

> The prizes are liberal and will undoubtedly induce a good muster of musical competitors. Pipe music forms a special feature, and the war signal of feudal times, Lochiel's Gathering, will be an appropriate prelude to the Games. A numerous and well selected committee has been appointed, and under their (sic) direction, the Games can hardly fail to turn out as great a success as they have proved in the past.

On occasions, Comunn na Feinne's own prizes were supplemented by gifts, such as trophies or cash donations, from individuals both within and outwith the Society. At a further meeting on 30th December, 1873, for example, it was intimated that Major John Bell, Chief of Comunn na Feinne, had supplemented the prizes in the Heavy events at the 1874 Games by donating four "very handsome" silver cups. They were to be awarded for the Hammer Throw, Tossing the Caber and Putting the Stone events and for the 440 yards Steeplechase. The *Advertiser* regretted that the announcement had not been made earlier, "as the cups are of sufficient value and beauty to have attracted competitors from all parts of the Colony, who will not now have time to enter." However, the Society did decide to hold entries for the Steeplechase event open until the day of the Games to try and encourage more competitors for that particular event.

At this last meeting before the 1874 Gathering the Society ensured that the Procession from the town to the grounds would be a large and colourful one. It invited the Order of St Andrew, the St Patrick's Society members - "in regalia and uniforms" - and the Geelong Volunteer Fire Brigade members, also in their bright red uniforms, "to assist the Procession by their presence." Comunn na Feinne also joined with the Town Council to present a Moonlight Promenade Concert at Johnstone Park on the evening following the end of the Games. In the pages of the *Advertiser*, too, was another of David Hughes's offerings encouraging the people of Geelong to demonstrate a New Year's Day spirit.

[The full poem can be read in Appendix 5 (c) Poems of David Hughes.]

> How Auld Freens Meet at Ne'ar (sic) Day Time.
> Gude day, auld freen, I'm glad we met,
> And pleased tae see ye look sae weel;
> Just come wi' me and hae a wet-
> Ye dinna ken the joy I feel.
>
> Yes, Donald, freen' depend on me,
> Ye'll see me there, if spared, that day;
> It cheers my heart the lads tae see
> Them dancing reels, jigs, and strathspey.

The 1874 Gathering was considered, by the *Advertiser* of 3rd January, 1874, to have been both successful and colourful:

> [W]hat with the Brass Band playing, the pipe music skirling, the Highlanders' dancing, the Caber tossing, the hammer throwing, the foot running and jumping ... and the scarlet-coated Firemen, the kilted Highlanders knocking about, the Cairngorm Brooches of the latter and the Topaz-headed Dirks sparkling in the sunshine ... it was a day to remember.

The crowd continued to swell and, as the afternoon wore on, it was reported that, "there were fully four thousand persons present." The *Advertiser* continued: "Few things were more admired than that of the veteran Martin [in the dancing], and the pipe playing of two little boys named Grant."

But, together with its praise for the day, the *Advertiser* also noted that change was hovering over the Society. Death had removed two well-known judges of Highland dancing, Mr A. MacDonald and Mr Forbes, "whose usual seats were filled by younger men, *sic transit mundi*, their places knew them no more. But long will the two enthusiastic Highlanders be remembered by the Celts in Geelong." Further, the number of Piping and Dancing competitors was down on previous years with, "so many having been drawn to Bendigo by the prizes offered there." This was no lame excuse. The *Advertiser* had earlier reported that the Highland Games at Sandhurst (Bendigo) had offered prizes for piping that none of the other districts could or would match. The promoters of the Bendigo Gathering were offering £20 for the best piper and, "to induce competitors from distant localities the committee undertake to defray their travelling expenses." These were inducements Comunn na Feinne was not prepared, or not able, to match!

However, many of the stalwart competitors were present at South Geelong as usual although changes in the prize-winners' list caused some surprise. It was in the 1874 Caber tossing that the biggest shock occurred. In that year the seemingly evergreen John Clinnick surrendered the Caber tossing crown to a new champion, Peter Fleming who, as well as the prize money, also was awarded one of Major Bell's donated Cups.* It was not entirely a complete changing of the old guard, though, as the well-experienced John McLennan kept up the 'veterans' side' by capturing first place in throwing the Hammer (18lbs) and Putting the Stone (23 lbs) - thereby winning two of Mr Bell's donated cups. The reporter commented that the heavy competitions, involving seasoned champions, such as Clinnick and McLennan, "reminded one of the palmiest days of the Society."

*[The Chief, Major John Bell, was absent due to illness that was later to cause his death. However, his presence was there through his donation of generous prizes. On this occasion he had donated four 'very handsome cups' which, "were much admired, and it is worthy of note that in every instance they were preferred to the money prizes." Such was the generosity of the donor, Major John Bell, that each of these Cups was to be inscribed with the winner's name, the costs being covered by Major Bell.]

The Steeplechase lived up to its name of providing amusement for the spectators, and unwelcome baths for the contestants, with the four competitors falling into, "the fifteen feet of water", not once, but "on every possible occasion." The winner (Mr W. Bolton) also gained one of Major Bell's Cups, wetter but happier than when he began!

Following the Games, Comunn na Feinne held the promised Moonlight Promenade Concert at Johnstone Park. This event was to raise funds for the Geelong Artillery Band Fund and it was this band that provided the music for the evening. Chinese lanterns lighted up the various glades. A pleasant breeze provided some relief from what had been a very hot day and the many visitors enjoyed the coolness and the music and appreciated the fireworks display.

> The fireworks were the great attraction. Such rockets as manufactured and sent up by Mr Johnson, of the Ordnance department, have never been seen in Geelong; they shot up fully 400 yards, and their long fiery tales (sic) were at the finish of their aerial flight surmounted by scores of beautifully coloureds stars. The bombs were even a greater success than the rockets as they were fired out of the small iron mortars and were heard miles away, and the vivid constellations they produced when bursting at a height of something like three hundred yards must have been seen and admired by many residents in the country districts around the town. Then, again, there were some very brilliant hand lights, which lighted up the Park very distinctly, and the colours of which changed in rapid succession, these were perhaps more admired than any portion of the pyrotechnic display.

Towards the end of 1874, Comunn na Feinne engaged in a flurry of activity with three meetings all within five days. The first seemed innocuous enough with the New Year's Day Programme Committee looking at how the Society might best carry out its goals of benevolence and those of maintaining Scotland's traditional music and dance. By holding an evening concert, following the New Year's Day Gathering, the

Society, reported the *Advertiser* on 12th December, 1874, could cater for those unable to attend the Games because of age or physical problems. However, this same Committee, meeting a few days later, went a lot further in terms of the direction it wanted to take the Society.

At one of these December planning meetings to arrange the 1875 Games, there was an apparent attempt to leave behind the Society's traditional 'cultural' events by modernizing and adding variety to the whole programme. There was a decided effort to re-make the Society's annual New Year's Day Gathering altogether, thus showing the early roots of the 'spirit' of reform, and of latent problems, within Comunn na Feinne, which were to emerge more fully developed in later years.

> At a meeting of the programme committee of the Comunn na Feinne, held last evening, a very full and interesting programme of sports was arranged. Unusual pains were bestowed upon the preparation of the details, with the view of securing an entire change in the music, and also introducing a variety in the dancing and character of the sports, so as to render them as distinct as possible from those of previous years.

It seemed, however, that the Games Committee was out of step with the majority of members and office-bearers as, once the suggestions of the fore-mentioned Committee meeting were more widely known, a full general meeting of the Society was called shortly after. The result was a revised Programme for the Games which followed the more familiar pattern of events. In fact, the number of music and dancing competitions had increased, partly due to the introduction of juvenile categories, but adult dancing, as with piping, was still confined to males. Gaelic singing and Irish Pipe competitions also continued, as did many of the favourites such as the Heavy Games events. By the tone of the *Advertiser*'s report, the full Committee of the Society wanted to get its message out that it was, 'business as usual' for the upcoming Games. The 'radicals' had lost - for now. And, just in case there was still some doubt as to its intentions regarding the 1875 Gathering, the *Advertiser* reported, on 15th December, 1874, that the decision of the later meeting clearly indicated that nothing of substance had been changed from previous Gatherings.

> Those who delight in seeing old associations and sports maintained in their

integrity, and the games of centuries gone celebrated as they used to be or, if possible, with still greater *èclat* than in the days of our forefathers, will be glad to learn that at a meeting of Comunn na Feinne last evening, it was decided unanimously to carry out the annual Highland demonstration this year on a scale of magnificence that (sic) has ever yet been attempted.

The *Advertiser* reporter, like many of the spectators, braved the elements to attend the 1875 Games. The paper noted, in its report on 2nd January, 1875, that the St Patrick's Society and the Saint Andrew's Society had both assembled for the pre-games procession commenting that, "Probably on no occasion have the Scotch and the Irish been so united as they were on this occasion." If the *Geelong Advertiser* had, at times, been somewhat equivocal in its attitude to the annual Highland Gathering, it showed no such equivocation in its opinion of the 1875 Games. In the spirit of the occasion everyone is a Scot!

> Let Comunn na Feinne for ever perpetuate the sports common to this season, and we will make it our duty to assist in making the effort a success. It is only once a year that the Highland Gathering takes place, and there is no patriotic Scotsman, or British subject, who can ignore the appeal which such a grand gathering makes to their national instincts. Long may the first day of the New Year reign supreme as a day of pleasure and not of work.

The harmony between the different immigrant groups was a matter of pride and was testimony to the Society's success in working towards a united community. The *Advertiser* commended the spectators, too, for braving the elements and, despite the atrocious weather, it concluded, "suffice it to say, that no man on the ground failed to enjoy himself if he took the slightest interest in athletic amusements."

The popular competitor John McLennan, so often the runner-up to John Clinnick in the heavy contests, emerged in 1875 achieving a 'clean sweep'. He won the Caber event as well as the Hammer Throw and Putting the Stone, with the 'new' man, Peter Fleming runner up in all of these except Tossing the Caber where Clinnick beat him into third place.

As usual, a Grand Caledonian Concert under the auspices of Comunn na Feinne was held in the evening, at the Town Hall, and this, "concluded the day's rejoicings, which, notwithstanding the unfavourable weather, never flagged." Nor did the weather affect the takings. The secretary reported that the amount taken at the gate was £135/0/0 which, despite the atrocious weather, was only four shillings less than had been taken at the gate the previous year. Entry fees from competitors added another £20 to the day's total income. A general feeling of *bonhomie* carried over into the next day when Comunn na Feinne office-bearers farewelled Melbourne supporters who had attended the games. All those who had gathered, seemingly unwilling to break the 'spirit' which had inhabited the Gathering on New Year's Day, sought to hang on to the traditional sounds and sights of the Games Day.

> The Geelong Railway Station presented quite a lively scene on Saturday when Angus F. Cameron of Melbourne, Hon. Robert de Bruce Johnstone, James Shillinglaw McKay, and Robert Shirra, officers of the Comunn na Feinne Society, attended on the platform to wish God Speed" to their Scottish friends, who had been patronising the Highland Gathering on the previous day. The pipers played a number of Scottish Melodies and long after the train had left the station, the stirring strains of 'Scot's wha hae', could be heard dying away in the distance.

It has been noted earlier that Celtic diasporas in Australia, and elsewhere, responded sympathetically and generously to homeland causes and their appeals. The Wallace Monument Fund drew support and funding, as did Highland Distress especially between the 1840s and the 1850s. A similar appeal to establish a Chair in Gaelic at Edinburgh University was no less successful in attracting large crowds at public meetings and in eliciting donations. This was as true in Australia as it was in other areas of the world, such as Canada and America, where large numbers of Highlanders, and Scots in general, had settled.

The *Geelong Advertiser* carried an announcement from James Shillinglaw McKay, Comunn na Feinne secretary, to the effect that a public meeting for "Highlanders and others" was to be held on 8th September, 1875. This well-attended meeting, to discuss the appeal, was arranged by Society office-bearers.

> Some enthusiastic Celts in Geelong, animated by a desire to perpetuate their mother tongue, and to show that Australian associations have not diminished the warmth of their patriotism have convened a meeting … for the purpose of expressing their sympathy with the movement. It is intended to form a committee who will take charge

of contributions and remit them to the proper quarters.

The *Advertiser*, in its report the next day, sympathetically elaborated on some of the main issues raised by the public meeting which had led to this proposal to help establish Gaelic as a serious subject of study and as a discipline at Edinburgh university.

> The perpetuation of the Gaelic Language as a classic accomplishment, and one of the features of a modern Anglo-Saxon University, is a matter that, for a number of years has engrossed the attention of the scions of the Celtic race. Scotsmen throughout the world are said to be invariably apathetic in things not pertaining to their immediate welfare, but the decadence of a tongue, even the ancient tongue whose traditionary (sic) lore inspired an Ossian, and gave a world-wide appreciation to the author of *Waverley*, has evidently sent a keen thrill throughout their veins, otherwise the movement for the establishment of a Celtic Chair at Edinburgh University, would not have elicited the warm response which it did … last evening.

At this public meeting at Geelong, a committee was set up to show support for the movement by soliciting subscriptions. This large committee contained many Comunn na Feinne officers such as its Chief, Major John Bell, its President, Robert de Bruce Johnstone, its Secretary, James Shillinglaw McKay, and its Treasurer, Dougal Rankin. Chaired by Mr Alex Davidson, and supported by James Shillinglaw McKay, the chairman said that he was well acquainted with the matter and he traced, "the history of the movement." It was shown that the scheme had the support of many influential people, including Queen Victoria who had given a substantial donation. Several resolutions were passed supporting the movement in general and an interim committee was set up to show support in a more practical way by soliciting subscriptions.

This interim committee, which was elected, was basically made up of those Comunn na Feinne officers mentioned above and they were called to fill much the same positions. Also forming part of this Committee as members were representatives such as George Morrison, Principal of Geelong College, John Clark of Teesdale and representatives from Inverleigh, Modewarre, Connewarre, Colac, Winchelsea, Horsham, and the Wimmera along with many others from Comunn na Feinne. Although many of those on this Committee were Gaelic-speakers, the movement was not confined to Highlanders and the appeal was to Scots in general and other interested parties. The meeting reconvened on 16th September, 1875, with the *Advertiser* reporting on the outcome the next day.

The gathering heard that circulars had been drawn up and sent out. It was also decided, "that a number of clergy of Victoria" should be contacted with the aim of, "enlisting their sympathy." It was also agreed that the support of the "Irish Celts" in Geelong and district be obtained. The *Advertiser* added that, "Those present contributed very liberally towards the fund, a great amount of enthusiasm being shown; and it is confidently anticipated £100 will be raised in the Geelong district.

The work of the Gaelic Chair committee was ongoing but it did not interrupt the normal activities of the Society. Shortly after this meeting Comunn na Feinne returned to its core business, convening a Games Committee on 14th October, 1875, to arrange the 1876 Gathering. A follow-up meeting on 12th December, 1875 was reported in the *Advertiser* the following day, to the effect that the programme had been drawn up for the Games and that the Chief, Major John Bell, had again bolstered the monetary prizes by donating three silver cups for the January, 1876 competitions. Another valuable trophy was also donated by Dr Crooks with the committee left to decide in which event it should be contested.

At a final meeting for the year, held 30th December, 1875, it was announced that preparations had been made for the watering of the reserve in order, "to lay the dust, which has often lessened the pleasure of visitors to the reserve." It was also announced that a Grand Caledonian Concert was to be held on New Year's Night, at the Mechanics' Institute Hall. The *Advertiser* noted, too, that David Hughes's poem for "Ne'ar Day", as Hughes termed it, welcomed the 1876 Gathering in his usual eccentric manner. It was the same mixture of lament for now dead friends, together with the encouragement to enjoy the fun that was Comunn na Feinne. One of those whose absence the poem laments was Mr Peter Martin* that dancer *extraordinaire*, who had finally hung up his dancing shoes. He had died, aged 91 in 1875.**

*[This is a reference to the amazing Mr Peter Martin who, well into old age, continued to win Highland Dancing events at the Comunn na Feinne Games.]

**[This age is based upon *Geelong Advertiser* reports and may not be accurate. The official death records show him as dying in 1874, aged 92.]

[The full poem is included in Appendix 5 (c) Poems of David Hughes.]

>Rhymes for Ne'ar (sic) Day and Comunn na Feinne, 1876.
>
>Anither year, anither rhyme,
>Tae mind ye here o' "Auld Langsyne."
>Auld Scotia's sons ken what I mean—
>On Ne'ar (sic) Day meet at Comunn na Feinne.
>...
>Wha noo the reel or jig will dance,
>What ne'er yet could be learned in France,
>Noo puir auld Martin's** gone tae rest,
>At dancing jigs was aye the best!
>
>And brither Scots I needna name—
>Cauld noo they lay (sic) beneath the stane;
>Year after year, doun on the green,
>There's freens we miss frae Comunn na Feinne.
>
>Still, what's the gude o' being sad?
>At Comunn na Feinne each heart be glad,
>Like brither Scots, let's wat oor whistle
>In honor o' auld Scotland's thistle.

And, on the eve of Comunn na Feinne's annual New Year's Day Gathering for 1876, the *Advertiser* contributed its own bit of light-hearted puff.

>Let not our Anglo-Saxon readers feel alarmed tomorrow morning should their slumbers be disturbed by the shrill bagpipes announcing that 'The Campbells are Coming' or by playing 'March of the Cameron Men,' … The war cry of Clan Alpine, and the Slogan of Lochiel may be heard tomorrow morning but there will be nothing to fear [because] … No longer do these scions of old warlike families seek to wield the claymore against their English and Irish friends. They say to them, "Your fates and ours, have 'shoulder to shoulder', in hot countries and cold, fought against and conquered the foreign foe, come join us then in our annual merry-making at Comunn na Feinne. We will run with you, or dance with you; at turning the Caber or throwing the hammer and

stone, we will compete with you or, should you prefer it, we will tilt against you. Come one, come all!

Of course, "Anglo-Saxon" competitors were not restricted to a "Scottish" agenda in 1876 or any other year. The *Advertiser*, for several years, had been emphasizing the broad nature of the Games. As evidence of this 'inclusiveness', which Comunn na Feinne had engendered through its sports programme, four styles of wrestling (Cumberland, Welsh, Scottish and English), were featured regularly at its Games, as was the case in 1877. This 'multicultural' Community offering was a common pattern in the Society's programme, with solo piping contests, for example, involving Irish pìob shìonnaich (bellows pipes), as well as pìob mhòr, (the great Highland bagpipes). Comunn na Feinne, concluded the *Advertiser*, was a 'broad church' admitting all who would come to its services as, "along with traditional Scottish sports, there are many events in which other Britons love to compete. The bill of fare is a very liberal one indeed."

The Society, as we have noted, had the harmony of the community as one of its main goals, and the inclusion of other national societies and community service groups, and sports of all nationalities, was just some of the evidence of the Society's desire to be seen as all-inclusive - in its membership, in its Games and in its service to the local community - and beyond. The Procession was, in every way, evidence of the multi-cultural composition of those involved with the Gathering. Here, marching together, would be found members of the St Andrew's Society and the St Patrick's Society. Here would be found the Geelong Volunteer Fire Brigade parading together with the, "Gentlemen in the Garb of Auld Gaul." Here, playing together, were the Bands of the Geelong St Patrick's Society and those of Protestant organizations. As mentioned earlier, this harmony, given the strained relationships which existed between the two national groups, as represented by the Irish Roman Catholic Church and the Protestant Orange Lodge, in Melbourne, is quite remarkable. So fragile were the links between these groups in that city, that riots were a feature of the Melbourne streets, especially in the period of the 1840s and 1850s, where enmity between bigoted groups on either side continued to cause social problems.

The 1876 Procession to the grounds was awash with 'green' as the Geelong St Patrick's Society Brass Band as well as the members of the St Patrick's Society of Geelong turned out in force. The *Advertiser*'s report of 3rd January, 1876, was as colourful as the scene it described. Multi-coloured tartans, too, added to the scene with the Order of St Andrew's Society, various pipers and the kilted Comunn na Feinne office-bearers and members, as well as "visiting Gentlemen in Highland Garb", all gathered at the assembly point. Added to this were the uniformed Geelong Artillery Brass Band and the Geelong Salvage Corps, and the march through the "main streets of the town", and to the grounds, was a scene of sound and colour. With bagpipe music alternating "with the really excellent playing" of the Volunteer Artillery Band, the march had gathered, "hundreds of pleasure seekers" along the way and down to the arena where, "the yellow and red ensign of old Scotland was waving proudly in the breeze" and where, "there could not have been fewer than five to six thousand gaily dressed [spectators] within the enclosure."

The *Advertiser*, continuing its reminiscent mood when discussing the 1876 New Year's Day Gathering, made the inevitable comparison of the present crop of athletes with the 'giants of yore'. It was plainly concluded, by the paper, that although the present generation of athletes were competent enough, they could not compare with those of former years.

> In the contests of strength there was a noticeable falling-off in comparison with former years. Certainly, those who did contend performed their work creditably, but in the number of competitors and the general vigour displayed, the Caber-tossing, stone-throwing etc., of this year were not on a par with those of a few years back.

There was dismay, at times, over the defeat of a local hero, such as James Smith who had been the Pole Vaulting champion for the previous four years. He missed out on a fifth straight year when he was beaten by a vault which was two inches greater than his own. But, although spectators could be disappointed when their old favourites were defeated, they could still generously applaud the new talent which was emerging.

True, old-fashioned sportsmanship, such as was occasioned in the case of the tie in the Running High Leap, where J. Smith and another competitor, J. Riley, each achieved a height of 5ft. 4½ inches, was appreciated by the spectators. This event, while carrying a money prize, also earned the winner a valuable cup donated by the Chief, Major John Bell. Riley graciously allowed Smith to receive the cup. Contrary to the *Advertiser*'s contention regarding older competitors, another local favourite, John Clinnick, was back in the winning list with a first in the Caber tossing event, albeit with a Caber "lighter than of yore" and, "tossed with the greatest apparent ease by that powerful, burly fellow, Clinnick."

The cups donated by Major John Bell, who was absent due to his prolonged illness, were presented by the President, Robert de Bruce Johnstone. The first cup was awarded to John Clinnick, winner of the Caber event, and the second to Owen Shirley, victor from a field of twelve in the Comunn na Feinne Hurdle Race, and the third cup was received by J. Smith, for the running high jump. Dr Crooks presented the trophy which he had donated, to William Pearson, winner of the St Andrew's Society foot race. The *Advertiser* reported that the Games were never more ably conducted and, with such a large number of events to be performed, it was essential that "the greatest punctuality" be maintained; and it was:

> Not the slightest confusion prevailed at any period; not a hitch occurred during the long day to mar the harmony of the proceedings. When the pipes were not playing, the Artillery Band took over, so that there was ever music to soothe the most savage breast – had any of the happy crowd possessed so undesirable a member.

The now customary Grand Concert in aid of charity followed in the evening, at the Mechanics' Hall, and served, "as an appropriate finale to the Comunn na Feinne Gathering of New Year's Day." Many of the competitors from the earlier Games appeared in Highland costume and gave exhibitions of Highland Dancing and Piping. Solo and duet singing was also appreciated by the audience.

The *Geelong Advertiser*'s surfeit of goodwill spilled over into the 1877 Highland

Gathering. It announced the Games at length encouraging those who were able to attend and, again, stressing the community nature of the Gathering. The *Advertiser*, on 30th December, 1876, also talked up the Games as likely to be one of the best ever staged. The newspaper could be, on occasions, an enthusiastic champion of the Games, leaving no adjective unturned in its promotion of the day, and the programme!

> The usual Scottish games and pastimes will be indulged in, whilst foot-racing, dancing, etc., will feature in the programme. Bands of musicians have been engaged to discourse pleasant music to all, whilst the best pipers in the land will play, to the delight of the Highland and Lowland men.
> The gathering of 1877 is expected to be the best that has taken place for some years and from the interest already taken in the affair by almost everybody in the community, there is little doubt that the anticipation of the Comunn na Feinne Society will be fully realized. It is tended to make the procession to the Ground as imposing as possible.

Very late in the year, almost on the eve of the Games, the Committee for the Celtic Chair at Edinburgh University, which was headed principally by the Comunn na Feinne hierarchy, promoted a fund-raising concert on the evening of 29th December, 1876, on behalf of the Celtic Chair Fund.

> This evening the [Carandini] company have been engaged to give a grand concert in aid of the fund for the establishment of a Celtic Chair, at Edinburgh University. A programme of popular songs and ballads has been prepared, and bagpipe playing, Scotch and American dancing, and other novelties will be introduced by several amateurs.

> MECHANICS' INSTITUTE, GEELONG,
> THE CARANDINI OPERATIC and BALLAD COMPANY*
> Will give a GRAND SCOTCH NIGHT
> In Aid of the 'CELTIC CHAIR,'EDINBURGH,
> ON THIS (FRIDAY) EVENING, 29th DEC.,
> When, in addition to a splendid selection of
> Operatic Music, English, Irish, and
> Scotch Songs, Duets, Trios, etc.,
> Numerous Performers will intersperse with
> "Pipe Music," "Pibroch Marches,"
> Scotch Dances—" Gillie Callum," bagpipes (accompaniment),
> Irish & Rattlesnake Jigs, Highland Flings, etc.,
> forming a splendid evening's amusement.
> Doors open at. half-past 7, to commence at 8 o'clock.

Admission—Dress Circle, 3s; Stalls, 2s; Body of the Hall, 1s.

*["The Carandini Company was composed mainly of the Carandini family several of whom were classically trained singers. Maria Carandini the matriarch of the family achieved some fame as an Opera singer. Her daughters also had trained voices and sang in the various performances staged by the Carandinis. The Carandini group travelled giving concerts in towns large and small both within Australia and overseas. See Appendix 3 (b) Short Biographies, for more details.]

The *Advertiser* reported that the performance drew a "larger audience" than the Carandini Company normally attracted, and it attributed this to the fact that the proceeds, "were in aid of the Edinburgh Celtic Chair Fund." A wide selection, from opera to popular Scottish song, was received enthusiastically and, "During the evening Mr Finlayson played the bagpipes, whilst Mr Aikman executed the necessary Scotch flings (sic) and reels, to the delight of the audience."

David Hughes welcomed the festive season and, of course, the upcoming 1877 Comunn na Feinne New Year's Day Gathering with yet another 'poem'. Hughes did not take himself seriously as a poet and he was amazed that anyone else would do so and then criticize his work. As usual, he did not forget to squeeze into his verse, reference to his Shoe Business!

[The full poem can be found in Appendix 5 (c) – Poems of David Hughes.]

A MERRY CHRISTMAS AND A HAPPY NEW YEAR.

> Critics they sneer at what I write,
> And would-be poets show their spite;
> "What more expect of any man,
> Than try to do the best they can."
> Myself I wish them for to know it,
> I don't profess to be a poet;
> But merely for to pass my time,
> I try my hand at writing rhyme.
>
> Still this is not the time to write—
> And Christmas here—on spleen and spite;
> When friends do meet, been long apart,
> Then love should be in every heart
> ....

> Christmas when gone, comes the New Year,
> Clansmen in tartans then appear;
> With pibrochs march down on the green,
> To play or dance at Comunn na Feinne.
> ....
>
> Adieu that day to Boots and Shoes,
> Open who likes for David Hughes.
> Until that day please give a call,
> I've Boots and Shoes to suit you all,
> All kinds for Christmas for to choose,
> And cheap they're sold by David Hughes.

The *Advertiser*'s 2nd January, 1877 coverage of the twentieth anniversary annual New Year's Day Highland Gathering lingered longer than usual in its musings on the meaning of the Gathering for the peoples assembled. When life expectancy was a great less than it is today, the twenty years which had passed since the first Gathering, meant more in terms of aging, the loss of friends and family and the declining powers of body and mind, to the audience being addressed, than it might mean today. The message, appropriately, therefore, was an extended mixture of nostalgia, melancholy, joyous reflection, and praise, with a high 'maudlin' rating!

Once the ground was reached, the marching numbers of the public joined spectators who had already arrived at the ground earlier and, together, they formed a respectable number watching the spectacle from within the enclosure. However, the weather threatened to spoil what was anticipated as being a fine day of sports and amusements. That it did not do so is testimony to the 'pull' of the Highland Games, together with the superb organization which allowed everything, despite the rain, to run smoothly.

> Taking the weather into consideration the Gathering was an unqualified success, a fact due in a great measure to the liberal programme issued, and the untiring exertions of the secretary, the committee and others interested in the Gathering....there must have been, in round figures, fully 2,500 people [ie those who paid through the gates] present during the day.

John Clinnick was absent from the heavy events at the 1877 Gathering because of an injury to his hand, but this did not prevent him entering a different event altogether – Tilting at the Ring. He made his presence felt straight away in this contest coming second to J. Pywell. Although only two prizes were awarded for this event, Clinnick tied for second with Hinchcliffe. On a play-off for second place Clinnick won with a tally well ahead of Hinchcliffe, who promptly blamed his horse for his poor showing! Clinnick had, for so many years, dominated the heavy games, and his absence allowed some who had played second fiddle for so long to achieve their 'place in the sun'. One of these was Peter Fleming who first came to notice at the 1872 Gathering. Now he was a seasoned competitor and he demonstrated it, winning the Caber event and the Heavy Hammer throw, to which he added a second in the Heavy Stone event and a second in putting the 32lb Cannon Ball, which had made a welcome return as an event. His performances at these Games were much appreciated and he was, "loudly applauded."

The close of the Games saw the official organizers happy, and tired. As usual, they then adjourned to the Black Bull Hotel where, "sundry toasts were drunk and congratulations offered all round" while a sense of satisfaction settled on the company. But there was hardly time to savour such feelings as the Moonlight Concert, taking place later that evening at Johnstone Park, required the same committee, and the same members, along with many others, to be present and actively sharing the organizational duties. Among the attractions was to be an enactment of a house fire, with the fire brigade going through its paces, as well as a fireworks' display and other entertainments suitable to the open air. Highland piping and dancing exhibitions were also given and there was the opportunity of taking, "the various walks in the park", which seemed to be much appreciated. The evening was, declared the *Advertiser*, "a great success."

> MOONLIGHT CONCERT
> Although the night air was cold, promenaders, dressed almost in winter clothing, mustered in full force, and within the enclosure there was rather a brilliant assemblage. The rotunda in the centre of the park was, of course, lit up with gas, and here the artillery band played at intervals during the evening … and the treat in this direction was worth the small charge made for

admission.

What took place next shows how far our present 'nanny State' prohibitions are from the attitudes in the late nineteenth century regarding things such as outdoor fires and fireworks, and just having a good time!

> Below the rotunda, a number of energetic firemen were engaged as busily as possible in firing off rockets, squibs, rainbow wheels, &c., and the pyrotechnical display was the best that has yet taken place during the summer evenings. ... A fire-balloon was successfully sent up, and the highflyer could be seen far away in the distance for nearly twenty minutes, the direction taken being apparently across the Bay towards the You Yangs. The performances concluded with a sensational incident, viz., a house on fire, the ringing of the fire bell, the saving of a couple of children from the burning building, and the leap for life taken by two firemen, who threw themselves from the roof of the tenement in flames, and safely landed in the useful jumping sheet. The effect was very good, the park being illuminated in almost every part.

The Society met on 3rd December, 1877 to update its preparations for the New Year's Day Gathering, 1878. It considered the programme of races and revised them in accordance with the money it had available for prizes. Because of the uncertainty of the level of funds at the Society's disposal, the Games Committee decided to postpone finalizing the rest of the programme until the next meeting. However, it did conclude that, "from present appearances a most successful gathering is expected to take place."

At year's end, on 29th December, 1877, another concert was held to raise funds for the projected Chair of Gaelic at Edinburgh University. This one had a more pronounced 'Scottish' flavor. The Committee had again hired a professional group of entertainers, the Carandini family, as well as some from its own ranks, to stage another 'Grand Scottish Concert'.

> MECHANICS' INSTITUTE.
> GRAND SCOTTISH CONCERT
> In Aid of the:
> CELTIC CHAIR, EDINBURGH,
> On FRIDAY EVENING, 29th DECEMBER, 1877.
> The Celtic Chair Committee have (sic) arranged with the highly popular Carandini Troupe to give an entertainment consisting of Scotch, English, and Irish songs, Duets, Trios, etc., on the above date.
> Numerous Performers will intersperse with "Pipe Music,"

"Pibroch and Marches,"
Scotch Dances—" Gillie Callum,"[with] bagpipe accompaniment, Irish & Rattlesnake Jigs, Highland Flings, etc., forming a splendid evening's amusement.
The Entertainment will he interspersed with Pipe Music, by one of Comunn Na Feinne's Pipers, also dancing by Champion Performers.

Comunn na Feinne Games Committee met again on 27th December, 1877 when final touches were made to the programme for the 1878 Highland Gathering which, the Committee believed, would be popular with the public. A 'novelty' event at these Games was the Manx Race, a three-legged race, which promised some fun. The Society also received news of the presence of the war ship, *Cerberus*,* which had docked at Geelong, and it was subsequently announced on 30th December, 1877, that at the 1878 New Year's Day Gathering, "the brass band of the *Cerberus* will, by the kindness of Captain Mandeville, perform selections of music."

The 1850's 'scare', deriving from the Crimean War, that Victoria was vulnerable to enemy attack from the sea, led the Victorian Government, in 1866, to appeal to the British authorities to provide a war ship for protection against such attack. This was acceded to and an armoured war ship was designed and later built at English dock yards, and after an incredible amount of bureaucratic delay, it left for Australia in October, 1870. During the voyage, *Cerberus* suffered storm, engine breakdown and desertions among the crew, to say nothing of additional 'red-tapeism', eventually reaching Melbourne on 9th April, 1871.

*[A full and interesting account of *Cerberus* from the laying of its keel in 1868 to its ignominious end, in 1926, as a breakwater for the Black Rock Yacht Club, can be found in Appendix 8.]

Greeting both the New Year, and Comunn na Feinne, David Hughes contributed his usual brand of verse and self-promotion for 1878. The full poem can be found in Appendix 5 (c) Poems of David Hughes.]

Comunn na Feinne, 1878
Air—"The Campbells are Coming."

Ye Clansmen get ready
For Comunn na Feinne,
When Ne'ar (sic) Day is here
Let us meet on the green;
And pipers be ready
Your pibrochs (sic) to play,
While Clansmen's (sic) competing
In reels or strathspey.
....
While young chaps they leap
And run round the ring,
While some at the water-leap
Tumble right in.
....
So come, Adam's sons,
To the Comunn na Feinne,
For you will be welcome
That day on the green.
....

The *Advertiser*, on 31st December, 1877, also gave the approaching New Year's Day Games a last-minute promotion.

> On the 1st January, 1878, the HIGHLAND SPORTS in the Comunn na Feinne reserve take place, and there can be no doubt that much interest will be centred in them. On every occasion hitherto they have attracted a deal of attention, and the programme for to-morrow is certainly a very attractive one. There are a large number of races for pedestrians, whilst tilting in the ring, vaulting, jumping, dancing, and other amusements are to be provided for the public. There will be the usual procession in the morning, in which the members of the St. Patrick's Society are expected to take part.

This "usual Procession" to the ground saw the street outside the Mechanics' Institute Hall, "alive with people" to watch and join in the march, and the *Geelong Advertiser* of 2nd January, 1878, gave it good coverage. However, the newspaper account was not totally complimentary when, describing the presence of seven pipers in the march, "their bagpipes giving full vent to their weird music", it seems to have lost all objectivity! On the other hand, it felt that the *Cerberus'* Band, which had begun playing quite early on Games Day, had given much delight, and had contributed to the success of the Gathering. The St Patrick's Band, along with forty members of the St Patrick's Society, had taken part in the procession, indicative of the continuing special relationship between the two Societies. Financial support towards the St Patrick's Society was given by Comunn na Feinne, a fact acknowledged at the Geelong St Patrick's Society annual meeting, held on 15th January, 1878.

The heavy hammer throwing took place with great spirit. Peter Fleming was proving himself a worthy champion taking first prize. Once again, in the absence of that long-time champion, James Clinnick, Fleming also carried off the Caber tossing prize and came a close second to the winner, Duncan Cameron, in putting the Stone. Cameron also won the Throwing the Cannon Ball (32lb) event, narrowly outdistancing Fleming by a mere two inches!

In the foot races, the *Advertiser* reported that, "a blackman' (sic), E. McKinnon, who resides in the Barrabool Hills, won the Handicap 300 yards Flat Race. In his stature, and also in his style of running, he resembles very much the well-known Pompey, but is, if anything, of heavier build." McKinnon showed this win was no fluke when he then went on to take the Hurdle prize with comparative ease, even though penalized one yard for a false start.

The Dancing competitions provided a few surprises, and the occasional protest. Donald 'Dosh' McLennan, later to become the Society's official piper, also demonstrated his all-round abilities in piping, dancing and heavy games. McLennan was second in the Strathspey and Reel piping contest, he won second place in Tossing the Caber, second place in Throwing the Heavy Hammer, third place in Throwing the Stone and fourth in Throwing the Cannon Ball. No one would be calling this piper a 'sissie' to his face! He also demonstrated his grace in dancing the Reel of Tulloch and The Highland Fling, and gained a third place in the Gillie Callum (the Sword Dance). The veteran dance competitor, Johnny Walsh, won the prize for the Irish Jig. His opponent, W. Holden, however, lodged a protest on the grounds that the piper had played a reel instead of a jig. It was, reported the *Advertiser*, one for the Directors to sort out! In the piping, some competitors had more difficulty in competing than just getting to Geelong, showing that the 'Master-Servant Act was not quite dead!

> We had almost omitted to mention that among the pipers was a Mr Bruce* who was allowed by his employer, Mr Angus Cameron, of Dunkeld, to be at the sports.
> His playing was much admired by those who understand piping.

* [Peter Bruce was a master piper and teacher. Hugh Fraser's father, Simon Fraser, received teaching from Bruce. Hugh Fraser, also taught in the traditional manner of the classical pipers of Scotland, and later was to become involved with Comunn na Feinne's Pipe Band. He was an award-winning piper and was taught Piobaireachd by Peter Bruce, hence maintaining the style of interpretation and execution of the classical music of the pipes which had come down through the various teachers since the days of the C16th McCrimmons of Skye.]

Although Step Dancing was not on the programme of competitions for 1878, one of the crew from the *Cerberus* gave an exhibition of it. So well was it executed, and so well was it appreciated by the spectators that, "the directors decided to award the man, named Samuel Maddings, a prize." One way or another, the crew of *Cerberus* made its presence felt that day when another of their number witnessed an incident at the Gathering, "when a cowardly fellow, under the influence of drink, struck a young girl." The crewman grabbed hold of the man and held him tight until, "the police arrived."

The *Advertiser*, on 2nd January, 1878, reported that the Sports, overall, were well conducted. It might well have added that its earlier complaint about the declining prowess shown in the heavy games was being belied by the emerging champions of whom it was currently writing. In the initial years of the Games, Mr John Clarke of Teesdale had produced handwritten programmes, in both Gaelic and English, though this had lapsed after a short while. The *Advertiser* now suggested that a printed Programme would be of great benefit to the spectators, and this could be sold at the grounds. This would give the names and the colours worn by the competitors, making it easier for the spectators to identify them. Colour-coding, however, might not have sufficed to solve "problems" seen in the boys' races!

Without doubt the events in which boys were engaged were the most amusing portions of the day's sport. In one of these races a dozen, and in another nearly a score, started, and to see them scamper round, the looks of earnestness which they wore on their faces … were worth going a long way to see. There was undoubtedly some decided swindling in these events, as the winners in the races in each case were several years above the prescribed age.

The presence of the *Cerberus* throughout the year led Comunn na Feinne to involve the ship's Brass Band again in the 1879 Gathering. The list of events for these Games was a wide-ranging one and it was agreed, "to offer about £120 in prizes for the Games." Among the novelties in the racing events, was to be a Flat Race for the members of the Mopoke Troupe.*

*[The Mopoke Troupe was a popular Geelong amateur group which entertained for local charities and provided fun and song at their concerts. Their presence at a Comunn na Feinne Gathering, it was hoped, would prove a great hit with the spectators.]

Comunn na Feinne also decided to revive the Essay competition which had been part of the Society's original Schools educational examinations and which largely had been phased out in the 1870s with the advent of the Education Act which had made primary education compulsory in the State. The essay subject set was, "The State of Scotland in the days of William Wallace and Robert Burns." Prizes of £5/5/0 and £3/3/0, respectively, were offered for first and second place-getters. This was aimed at school students and was limited to boys and girls under the age of 16 years.

The *Advertiser*, on 31st December, 1878, announced the 1879 New Year's Day Gathering events, highlighting the Irish Piping competition which was again included in the programme. The reporter, however, perhaps unfamiliar with the language, managed to translate the term "piob h-ionnaich" (sic) as a dance instead of what it was i.e. Irish bellows pipes!

> The Highland Gathering [is] an annual event which creates a deal of interest both for the Scotch (sic) and other residents of the town and district. The Comunn na Feinne Sports are expected to be superior to those of last year, so that visitors will

find sufficient to gratify them in the way of excitement. In addition to the pedestrian events on the programme there are dances which include Highland Flings (sic) and Irish Pìob h-ionnaich (sic) … and a host of other sports which should prove of interest to all.

Hughes was on hand to contribute his latest poetic offering extolling the Games and his shameless self-promotion. Repetition also played a large part in his compositions and if he fancied a line from earlier poems, he was not afraid to use it again, and again, and again!

[The full poem can be read in Appendix 5 (c) Poems of David Hughes.]

COMUNN NA FEINNE, 1879

> Auld Scotia's sons both far and near,
> Mind Comunn na Feinne again is here,
> Come bring your pibrochs (sic) on that day,
> And play us reels, jigs, and strathspey.
> ……………………………………
> All nations come, you're welcome there,
> With Scotia's sons their joys to share,
> There's room for all down on the green,
> On New Year's Day at Comunn na Feinne
> ……………………………………
> And let them do the patriots' part,
> Each have their country's good at heart,
> And meet like brothers on the green,
> On New Year's Day at Comunn na Feinne.
>
> Ye ken the line that I am in,
> I keep in stock a' kinds o' shin,
> I am selling cheap, please gie a ca',
> I've boots and shoes to suit ye a'.

The *Geelong Advertiser* was again generous in its praise of Comunn na Feinne and its object of creating community harmony which it revisited in its Games report on 2nd January, 1879. This object, it wrote, was again nowhere better displayed than in the annual Procession to the grounds. The 1879 march was, as usual, a lively one and included a large number of the town's utilities and many of their associated bands. Thus, along with the pipers in Highland Costume, there marched the St Patrick's

Society Brass Band, Mulder's Brass Band, the different Fire Brigade Bands and many members of the various societies with their different costumes and tartans all making a colourful, if noisy, display. By the time the marchers reached the Grounds, there were, according to the *Advertiser*, already nearly 4,000 spectators present and the grand stand, "was filled with spectators who thus comfortably looked into the sports arena." The ground was draped with flags and pennants and "the grand stand decorated with evergreens." The programme was an extensive one and, "competitors from all parts of the colony – as far as the Upper Maffra in Gippsland – were induced to take part. Taking the gathering altogether, it must be considered to have been a very successful one."

The visiting competitor from Upper Maffra in Gippsland (Thomas Cromb) was a notable presence at the 1879 Games. He won the Heavy Hammer event with the *Advertiser* commenting that so great was his winning margin of seven feet over the next best, that no one could get near him. Cromb's victories in putting the Heavy Stone and in putting the Cannonball, were equally decisive. Added to this, was his success in the Running High Leap and, taken together with his other successes, the *Advertiser*, with some understatement, felt he had "quite a successful day."

John Clinnick, having missed the Heavy Games for a couple of years through injury, in this, his last appearance at the Caber-tossing event, came a creditable third in what was a strong field of competitors including Thomas Cromb, Peter Fleming and John McLennan. Cromb, who had gained firsts in the other Heavy Games events, had to settle for second place to Peter Fleming in Tossing the Caber, and was thus denied the 'grand slam' in the Heavy Events. Clinnick, easing himself out of the Heavy games, continued competing in one other event, Tilting at the Ring, in which, at the 1879 Gathering, he came second.

As noted earlier, some of the athletes and the pipers did the circuit of Highland Gatherings and, if good enough, could pick up a number of monetary prizes to make their effort worthwhile. However, a new kind of competitor was beginning to appear at the various contests, not only around the State but from even further afield. This was the fully professional competitor. The rise of Athletic, Cycling, Pipe Band and Highland Dancing Associations were to establish certain common standards relating to their respective areas of competition. In the case of field sports, uniform standards were laid down regarding the athletic tracks, the judging, the handicapping and so on. It was the emergence of professionals, and their complaints about the 'amateurism' of judges and the various track officials, and their desire to be able to compete on well-made and accurately regulated athletic surfaces and under proper supervision, which brought about the need for professional bodies to be formed to oversee these issues. As the century wore on, more and more Professional Associations were emerging, and the consequences of this for Comunn na Feinne, and its activities is addressed more fully later in the story.

At a meeting of Comunn na Feinne, on 5th December, 1879, it was acknowledged that a Cup had been donated by C.K. Pearson as one of the prizes for the 1880 Games.

At year's end David Hughes obliged with another of his rhymes welcoming the new year, 1880, and its traditional Comunn na Feinne Gathering. [The full poem can be found in Appendix 5 (c) Poems of David Hughes.]

COMUNN NA FEINNE, 1880

> Come Scotia's sons, prepare for the green,
> Christmas is gone now, and Ne'ar's (sic) Day is near;
> Come meet like brithers at Comunn na Feinne,
> Trying each ither's hearts there for to cheer.
>
> ....
> The year that's gone (may sorrow go wi' it)
> May eighteen eighty bring joy to each heart,
> May good times come once more to our Pivot,
> That those long here will not have to depart.
> ....

The *Geelong Advertiser*, as we have noted, often re-visited its theme regarding the harmony between the different national groups in Geelong, especially as displayed through the activities and goals of Comunn na Feinne. Its reason for again raising this matter had to do with its call to form a local movement to raise funds towards helping the poor in Ireland, where failing crops, disease and misery were daily afflicting the poorer classes. In addition to the natural disasters in that country, the *Advertiser* pointed to a further contributing factor to the misery, and that was the continuing political troubles daily afflicting the peoples, especially the peasantry. There was, said the *Advertiser*, a direct correlation between social disharmony and poor social conditions. Thus, on the day of the Comunn na Feinne New Year's Gathering, the newspaper, on 2nd January, 1880, took the opportunity of relating the national unanimity between the different peoples of Geelong, especially the Scottish, the English and the Irish, and how this harmony affected society, generally for the better: "here, thank God, the nationalities are welded together by social ties that recognize no distinction of race, and what affects one, for good or evil, affects all."

It was Comunn na Feinne's great achievement that it united, for a worthwhile purpose, "brither Scots and warm-hearted Irishmen and phlegmatic Englishmen …". The *Advertiser* suggested, on the basis of this unity, that a public meeting should be called to form a movement to raise funds to help alleviate the problem of hunger and disease in Ireland. On several occasions Comunn na Feinne was at the centre of such appeals helping to raise funds for the distress in Ireland as well as that in the Highlands and Islands of Scotland.

The 1880 Gathering witnessed only one slight incident, one which briefly disturbed the day's entertainments: this was the appearance, on the arena, of a latter-day prophet!

> The only occurrence which bordered on a scene was when an ill-advised individual appeared in the centre of the arena with a bible in his hand and commenced an extempore address on the mutability of human affairs and the follies of mankind in general. A dozen willing hands were ready to reject the offender, alike against religion and common sense, but two were equal to the task.

In the heavy games, new strong men continued to arise. The next legend-in-the-making was Mr Fred Worland, who first appeared at the 1878 Games, albeit without making much of a splash, but at the 1880 Games he was runner up to Peter Fleming in Tossing the Caber, and reversed those positions in Putting the Cannon Ball. Not all the ex-champions faded away quietly; long time competitors such as Denis Powell and John Clinnick found that their rivalry could continue in other events. They maintained their competitiveness, as we have seen, through other sports such as Tilting the Ring. For each it was a relatively new challenge but they soon showed a mastery over it. In the few years since they had entered this new event, they had managed to finish first and second in each of those years, the only change being the occasional reversal in the order in which they finished. At the 1880 Games, they were still 'learning the ropes', but doing much better than two of the crew from the *Cerberus*, who mounted steeds and rounded the course, tilting at the rings, though it is almost needless to add, without any other result than the breaking of the tilting rod.

Other crewmen from the *Cerberus*, however, acquitted themselves with more grace, skill and dignity, when competing at the Sailor's Hornpipe. Second place was awarded, after some difficulty due the closeness of the competitors, to J. Stone of the *Cerberus*, with two other crewmen finishing close behind. "[All] the men danced capitally and the judges experienced considerable difficulty in awarding the prizes." The *Cerberus* was to feature quite prominently at the 1880 Games. As well as the events already described in which some of its crewmen took part, the *Cerberus* Band also played at the Gathering, plus there was a special race for men from the ship's Band. At the race's conclusion, "one of the members of the band gave an exhibition of clog dancing, for which he received well-merited applause."

After a successful day, the Society's office-bearers, and others, including the Judges and some competitors, relaxed, "with a pleasant gathering at the Union Club Hotel, where a number of toasts were proposed, drunk with enthusiasm and responded to appropriately." It was also promised that next year's competitions would include "suitable prizes … for competitions for Poems, both in Gaelic and in English." This, combined with the previous year's announcement regarding an essay writing competition, indicated a partial return to a form of educational competitions as well as a continuing commitment to its Charter aim regarding Celtic culture. Gaelic

Orthography, Gaelic poetry and essay competitions had been part of the first few years of the Society's existence when Ossian Macpherson was a regular prize-winner.

At the Directors' Meeting held on the 17th December, 1880, and reported in the following day's *Geelong Advertiser*, it was agreed that at the 1881 Gathering the tickets for the Grand Stand were to be reduced from 2/6d to 2/-. This was an early sign that Comunn na Feinne was still having financial problems and that it hoped to increase the number of spectators by lowering some of the entrance prices. This is a subject which is taken up in more detail in the concluding chapter.

As the day itself neared, the *Geelong Advertiser*, on 31st December, 1880, supplied the customary publicity:

> An annual assemblage of the members of Comunn na Feinne will take place on the reserve at South Geelong. It promises to be very attractive, and as there are no other sports in the immediate vicinity of Geelong to clash with it, there is no doubt it will be well patronized. It has always proved a source of attraction to all nationalities, and there is no reason to believe that this year will be any exception. The members of several of the Societies, as well as the fire brigades and others, will march in procession to the grounds. A good programme has been arranged.

Comunn na Feinne was also keen to publicize its post-Games Scottish Concert which was for charitable purposes. It announced that its entertainment in the evening following the 1881 Games was to be devoted to raising funds on behalf of a destitute lady, the daughter of William Hone,* a philanthropist and writer of an earlier generation.

> FREE LIBRARY HALL.
> NEW YEAR'S NIGHT.
> GRAND SCOTTISH ENTERTAINMENT,
> Under the patronage of the Comunn Na Feinne.
> National music, vocal and instrumental, by Talented Amateurs.
> National patriotic address, entitled "Auld Lang Syne," by a Brither SCOT.
> And two inimitable Scottish Readings, kindly volunteered by Captain Gardiner.
> Commence at 8 o'clock.
> Chairs, two shillings,

Second seats, One Shilling.
Tickets to be had at Franks'.
Dinna' forget New Year's Nicht.

*[It is difficult to know if this refers to William Hone (1780-1842), the English bookseller and radical pamphleteer. Hone was certainly no "philanthropist" as he was constantly in a state of poverty and in and out of debtors' prison. It may refer to another William Hone altogether about whom we know nothing. Unfortunately, the *Advertiser* does not reveal the "distressed" lady's name.]

David Hughes struck again with his annual verse dedicated to Comunn na Feinne and its Highland Gathering and reminding all readers that although New year was a time of celebration and fun, death was just around the corner for everyone whether rich or poor! Just the message to cheer up the readers! [The full poem can be found in Appendix 5 (c) Poems of David Hughes.]

Christmas and Ne'ar (sic) Day's Here Again
And with it Vacant Chairs.

Another year is nearly gone,
And with it, friends to memory dear,
Have left behind a desolate home;
Who with us shared last Christmas cheer.
……………………………………..

Old Cameron* that has passed away,
Who helped Napoleon to subdue;
Like Wellington, he had his day,
And fought like him at Waterloo.
……………………………………..
Then after comes wild Scotia's day,
When brither Scots meet on the green;
To dance reels, jigs there, and strathspey,
While pipers play at Comunn na Feinne.

While I my stock I wish to sell,
And I the cost price won't refuse;
Those who want boots that will wear well,
Please give a call on David Hughes.

*[This is a reference to Donald Cameron who died at Geelong on 13th December, 1880. He had served in the 79th Foot – a Highland Regiment. He fought in many battles during the Napoleonic Wars and was so severely wounded at the Battle of

Waterloo that he had to be discharged from the army. He later came to Australia with his wife and family and settled at Batesford. He was aged ninety-four when he died.]

In its reporting of the traditional procession from Geelong to the grounds, the *Advertiser,* on 3rd January, 1881, took every opportunity of celebrating the diversity of the number of different groups taking part, and the coming together of the various organizations and societies of Geelong in a degree of harmony. However, as the *Advertiser* reported, this did not preclude the odd 'punch-up', though this was usually fuelled by drink rather than any ethnic bias:

> There were a few fights—just to vary the entertainment—towards the evening—in the immediate vicinity of the refreshment tent—but the police speedily stopped the combats; and the carelessness of a man who threw down a lighted match in the grass nearly caused the refreshment tent to catch fire. These little incidents, and a disposition shown by some of the Celts to object to the decisions of the judges upon the merits of some of the competitors who were successful in the Highland Dances, were the only occurrences to detract from an exceedingly harmonious and pleasant day's enjoyment.

For the 1881 Games, the Comunn na Feinne Games Committee had introduced a Handicap Flat Race, for members of the Geelong Rowing Club. This was the latest of its moves to involve specific sections of the wider community in its activities. The Society, as we have already seen, had established a Comunn na Feinne Iron Quoits Club, as well as a Cricket Club and a Football Club. Its involvement with voluntary bodies such as the Volunteer Fire Brigades, the Volunteer Brass Bands, the Volunteer Cavalry and the Volunteer Artillery units, has also been well demonstrated.* It now sought to draw in the Geelong Rowing Club and involve it in the annual Games.

*[See, for example, Appendix 14]

With such outreach came 'contacts' and it was able to enlist, as Patrons of the Society, the respective Mayors of Geelong, Newtown and West Geelong, as well as local members of parliament of all shades; this was no mean feat given the heat often generated by council rivalries and political factions!

The heavy games contestant, Mr Fred Worland, in 1881 truly came of age. He had already shown something of his talent by occasionally taking one of the major titles over the past few Games, but in 1881 he demonstrated his all-round brilliance by carrying off the Caber event (which he won amid great applause) as well as the Heavy Stone, the Heavy Hammer and the Cannon Ball, giving him a clean sweep for that year.

On the other hand, veterans, if not always bowing out gracefully, could sometimes do so with good humour. Captain Miller, of the Geelong Volunteer Fire Brigade, showed himself no 'stiff shirt', by letting his 'decorum' down a little, in the Firemans' race.

> This race was one of the most amusing of the day. Captain Miller, of the Geelong Fire Brigade, added *eclàt* to the struggle, just for the fun of the thing, by heading his men for a brief period, but the pace was too great for [him] and he had to retire from the task.

At the end of the Games there was the usual march back to Geelong and a shortened stay at the Union Club Hotel for drinks and speeches, as the Society was hosting a Charity Scottish Concert that evening.

> A number of amateur vocalists and musicians gave their services, Scottish songs and music only being rendered; and the singing and instrumentation being excellent, those present enjoyed the entertainment thoroughly. Captain Gardiner, of the Library, gave two Scotch readings in admirable style, and a "Brither Scot' lectured happily upon Scotland and its associations …the entertainment passed off very successfully.

The Society Directors' Meeting was held on 3rd January, 1881, and pronounced the New Year's Day Highland Games a great success. The *Advertiser* on 4th January, 1881, reporting that over 2,500 spectators had passed through the gates and, after paying all expenses, it was expected that the Society would make a profit of £50 on the day.

The passing of old members and office-bearers was becoming a common feature of the history of Comunn na Feinne as the years passed since its founding. The sudden death of the Chief, Robert de Bruce Johnstone MLA., on 19th November 1881, however, came as an unexpected shock which cast a pall over the Society, the town and its council (of which he was still a member), the State Parliament, and his many friends, as well as over the arrangements for the 1882, Highland Games. On hearing the news of Johnstone's death, the Geelong mayor, Cr Cunningham, "had the Corporation flag hoisted, half-mast, in Johnstone Park."

Robert de Bruce Johnstone had been one of the foundation members of Comunn na Feinne and was its Treasurer from 1858-68, and 1876-79; its President from 1867 until his elevation to the position of Society Chief in 1876, a position he held up until his death. He had served continuously on the Geelong town council from 1859-1881, and had served as Mayor for three terms. His funeral was held at Geelong on 23rd November, 1881, attended by many members of State parliament, the Geelong council, Comunn na Feinne office-bearers and members and a wide number of friends and other Geelong townsfolk and representatives from many Geelong organizations. The Hon. Francis Ormond* MLC accepted the offer to be the Society's Chief.

David Hughes, in one of his more reflective pieces (and without mentioning shoes!), contributed some verses dedicated to Johnstone and what he stood for, and the blow his death meant for liberalism in Geelong, and Victoria as a whole. [The full poem can be found in Appendix 5 (c) Poems of David Hughes.]

> Lines in Respect to the Memory of Robert de Bruce Johnstone
> ……………………………………..
>
> And death has made another call:
> De Bruce Johnstone is dead.
> Who now will fill the Liberal ranks.
> And in his footsteps tread?
> ……………………………………..
> And while he was chief magistrate,
> Justice then was his plan,
> His wish when seated on the bench,
> Do right to every man.
> ……………………………………..
>
> Who now will head auld Scotia's sons,
> When marching to the green;

> On New Year's Day take a leading part,
> Each year at Comunn na Feinne.
>
> Some Liberal now must fill his place,
> And in his footsteps tread;
> Like him, a man of sterling worth,
> Now numbered with the dead.

On the 5th December, 1881, the *Geelong Advertiser* carried an article reporting that, on account of their Chief Robert de Bruce Johnstone's death, "The annual gathering under the auspices of [Comunn na Feinne] on New Year's Day will not take place." Instead, the *Advertiser* reported, "a committee of management had been appointed for that purpose, arrangements having been made to lease the grounds." The *Advertiser* further announced that the Mayor, Cr. Cunningham, "has promised to give a prize of £5/5/0 to be competed for by boys working in factories."

The 1882 Games was thus under 'new management' which advertised the Gathering a "Caledonian Festival". The promoters' advertisement for the Gathering suggested business as usual, although the commercial impulse was evident. Tenderers were invited to run side-shows, confectionary and oyster stalls. The *Advertiser* gave its full support to the event, predicting that the upcoming Festival would be no different from what had always taken place. There were some differences, however, and commercialism seemed the main driving force behind the new promoters' idea of the Games. In pushing the side show franchise, they announced that they "anticipated that over five thousand persons will witness the sports."

The promoters' 'spruiking' went all out to raise the town's enthusiasm, and their advertisement of 30th December, 1881 was a combination of public relations-speak, commercial 'know how' and bold, unashamed *razzamatazz*. The order for the day was a long one.

> Captain Weber (of the Geelong Fire Brigade) the Grand Marshall.
> Master of Ceremonies,
> Troops of Yeoman Cavalry,
> The Augmented Military Band of the Geelong Volunteer Artillery,
> The Chief and Members of Comunn na Feinne, Visiting Scottish Societies,

The Order of the Society of St Andrew,
Pipers in their Highland Costume.

The Comunn na Feinne Caledonian Festival
100 Guineas in Prize Money,

The Pipers Playing the 'Gathering of the Clans'
Will wake the memories of a thousand years,
Till every Donald's name rings in each clansman's ears.
From the Land of brown heath and shaggy wood,
Land of mountain and the flood.

Geelong and Chilwell Fire Brigades,
God speed the firemen, gallant and brave,
The Geelong Salvage Corps,
Patrons, Judges and Committee,

The Rose, Shamrock and Thistle, this day shall entwine,
And all shall be toasted in bumpers of wine;
Success to old England, the land of the free,
And to Ireland, the loveliest gem of the sea,
With a toast nine times Bonnie Scotland to thee.

There was only a single event in the Heavy Games section, that of Putting the Stone. None of the main contenders entered and it was won by an outsider, E. McLellan. A bicycle race was, for the first time, introduced into the Games, but the *Advertiser*, beginning what was to be a long antagonism towards bicycles and bicyclists, dismissed it as "very uninteresting" and it drew only two competitors. Two other new events were introduced, a Two Hour 'Go as you please' distance trial, which attracted four contestants, and a Junior version (for those under 18 years), of one hour, which attracted sixteen competitors.

Despite this fanfare and the build-up to the January, 1882 Games, the crowd attending the Gathering did not quite reach the five thousand promised by the new promoters. The *Advertiser* estimated that there were about 3,500 but it did regard, "the enterprise, which was a private one, a decided success."

On 3rd October, 1882, the Comunn na Feinne appointed a Committee of

Management to take charge of the use of its Reserve at South Geelong. So much use was being made of the Society's grounds that it was decided to establish a committee to manage the Reserve on a more commercial basis. Apart from a basic donation, given by users of the reserve, Comunn na Feinnne appears not to have charged other organizations for the use of its ground up to this time. The potential loss of revenue probably explains the need to have a 'body' manage the grounds and the various requests during the year for the use of it. By October 1882, this body had been created, with James King, Robert Shirra and James M. Anderson appointed to handle bookings for the use of the arena.

The numbers being attracted to the Comunn na Feinne annual Gathering had dropped off since the heady days of its inauguration, with there now being a wider range of similar attractions on offer. There were Caledonian Societies in many of the country centres, as well as Melbourne, which would have attracted locals from those areas. Other New Year's Day entertainments had sprung up in the local district. The Society undoubtedly had stretched itself almost to financial breaking point. It relied greatly upon gate-takings and commission from booth holders as well as membership fees, and fees from competitors who did not wear tartan on the day, as its main sources of income. The total of its prize monies did, on occasions, exceed what was taken at the gate. While many of its prizes, by way of trophies, were gifted by benefactors such as Major Bell; the monetary prizes, which were small by comparison to what was offered by other, similar, societies, still had to be found from somewhere.

The Society's income from other sources, the holding of concerts etc., once expenses were paid, was used for charitable purposes. The Society had become a 'welfare agency' for sick and out of work members and it was, later, to endow a bed at the Geelong hospital. Its role in providing for local aborigines, although by the 1880s no longer a great expense, its night school project, its commitments to the two Geelong Orphanages and its relief for distressed workmen, constantly added demands on its purse. As we have seen, the Society's Gatherings embraced more and more activities and introduced more and more competitive events, all of which also added a strain on its funds and on its volunteer work force at the grounds. Conversely, the relatively low prize monies it offered were causing some star athletes to avoid the Geelong competitions. Comunn na Feinne continued to hold much to the principle of honour rather than sizeable money rewards for prize-winners, and this meant that Geelong offered a far lower scale of monetary prizes than did the other major Gatherings in the district and further afield. The truth regarding the fluctuations in the crowd numbers for the Geelong Highland Gathering probably lies in a combination of the foregoing.

Twice, in earlier years, Comunn na Feinne had been unable to stage its annual Gathering. The respect shown to the memory of its late Chief masked the fact that it was reaching the same point again, and some soul-searching was needed in order to regain the spirit which had motivated it in its earlier years. A meeting, held on 7th October, 1882, confirmed that the Committee was looking to revive the Society by taking the gamble of reducing membership fees. It had already reduced the price of tickets for its grandstand and the *Advertiser* reported, on the 8th October, that the Society now had resolved, as an inducement to former Members, to reduce the subscription to 5/- per annum, with new members being admitted on an entrance fee of 5/- and a 5/- yearly subscription." This was a gamble as the decision could result in reduced income if it did not significantly increase the membership list.

The death of Robert de Bruce Johnstone in 1881, was undoubtedly a serious blow to the Society. Robert Shirra, the new President, was the only founding member now remaining in an active role. It was he, along with Johnstone and, earlier, Archibald Douglas, now in New Zealand, who provided much of the moral heart of the Society. They were the champions of education, of the local aborigines, of the hospital, of the night school and of the working boys' school. There were few with the energy and the purposeful vision to take their place. The loss of those who set the 'philosophy' of Comunn na Feinne at its formation, represented a loss, in part, of the 'noble' purpose intimated in its foundation Charter and this left the Society, for a time, with only a weak grasp of what it stood for and where it should be going. The *Advertiser* wrote that:

> Perhaps it is symbolic of the lassitude now afflicting the Society that the grave of Robert de Bruce Johnstone was left unmarked, ironic for one who had striven to have the graves of the last of the local Aboriginals suitably memorialized.

There was no disrespect or lack of affection shown by Johnstone's fellow Society members which would explain this failure to attend to his grave stone. This oversight may initially have been due to the fact that Johnstone was unmarried and had no family in Australia to take responsibility for arranging such things as his burial and a suitable headstone. It took the lines of the local versifier, David Hughes, to bring this issue to the notice of the public and spur his friends, and Comunn na Feinne, to action. David Hughes reminded the people, and Comunn na Feinne in particular, of the centrality of 'service to others' a tenet which lay at the heart of its Charter. The *Advertiser*, on the 7th December, 1882, gave credit to Hughes:

> [Hughes] in his ordinary (versatile) effusion ... points out that the many friends of the Late Robert de Bruce Johnstone have neglected to place a headstone on his lonely grave at the Eastern Cemetery, Geelong, to mark the spot where the remains of the late Chief of Comunn na Feinne lie.
> [The full poem can be found in Appendix 5 (c) Poems of David Hughes.]

There's Not a Stone to Mark His Lonely Grave

In my ramble round the graveyard,
Where the rich and poor they lay,
I looked there for the grave of one,
Who lonely passed away:
Yes, one who was honoured while in life;
But, now that he is gone,
Around his grave I could not see
There, either fence or stone.
....
Great monuments I did see there,
Some mark of mammon's slave,
While he, the choice of Geelong West,
There's nothing marks his grave.

> ....
> Have all the leal hearts passed away,
> That met down on the green;
> If not, go look on Johnstone's grave,
> Once Chief of Comunn na Feinne.
> ....
>
> And when he died, our M.L.A.,
> Who bore an honoured name;
> Still, not a stone to mark his grave,
> Such is the burning shame.
>
> Oh, that it were but in my power
> Such, I would soon erect,
> And show there is one in Geelong
> Who honour does respect.
> ....

It is worthy of remark that, despite his long years of office, both in a Civic and in a Parliamentary capacity, Johnstone never sought to aggrandize himself in any way. He died without having amassed any personal or material wealth, having devoted himself to generously supporting many charitable organizations in Geelong over his lifetime.

An extra honour, done to the memory of Robert de Bruce Johnstone, took place in Council Chambers a few years later. The *Advertiser* reported on 1st October 1888 that a ceremony at the Geelong Town Hall took place when, "a large and well executed portrait of Robert de Bruce Johnstone" was donated to the council by "Major Hall of Clifton Hill and formerly of Geelong." The Mayor, in responding, "remarked that Robert de Bruce Johnstone, had been a man of extraordinary energy, and, it might almost be said he combined the character of a Philanthropist with that of a patriot." Members of Comunn na Feinne were present, and Robert Shirra made a brief speech. He concluded by moving a vote of thanks to Major Hall. "The portrait has been painted life size in oils and is three quarter length, its dimensions being 5 feet 6 inches by 3 feet 6 inches."*

*[This painting can still be seen hanging in the Geelong Town Hall.]

The *Advertiser* reported on the Society meeting held on 7th October, 1882, under the heading 'Scots to the Front':

> We learn that an extra effort is about to be made to give new life to the Society of the Comunn na Feinne which was established in December, 1856, and it is the oldest Highland Society in the Colony. In consequence of the death of Robert de Bruce Johnstone MLA., and other causes, it was deemed inadvisable to hold a Gathering on 1st January last but, in consequence of a strong desire on the part of the many friends, both town and country, [it was decided] that the Society's annual Gathering should be held as usual [for 1883].

Efforts were thus underway for Comunn na Feinne, once more, to take over the reins of the New Year's Day Gathering. Under Robert Shirra (now President), a Comunn na Feinne Directors' Meeting on 16th November, 1882, "unanimously decided to hold" a New Year's Day Gathering in 1883. The fact that the programme was to be deferred until their next meeting suggests that even at this late date it might have been uncertain whether or not a Gathering was to be held. The resolution at the 7th October meeting regarding the changes to fees to former members was ratified. The desire expressed to attract "former members" suggests that there had been some falling out over the Society's unwillingness to conduct the 1882 Gathering and that some members had left the Society. A further meeting on 23rd November heard from its President, "that a vigorous effort was being made to make the annual gathering on New Year's Day, a success". The *Advertiser*'s report of this meeting, on 24th November, asserted that new life was now showing in what had been almost a "defunct Society", and that there were optimistic signs that it was "back from the brink." A programme for the 1883 Gathering was drawn up and adopted, and the *Advertiser* wished the effort "every success."

A final meeting prior to the 1883 Games was held by the Committee on 21st December, 1882. It was announced that some donations towards Society funds had been received and that some new members had joined and arrangements had been made, "for the proper conduct of the Games on New Year's Day." The meeting also approved David Hughes' suggestion that he, under Comunn na Feinne Patronage, be allowed to sell his poems at the grounds with a half of all proceeds going to the fund to erect a proper memorial stone over the grave of Robert de Bruce Johnstone.

Further innovation, perhaps similarly aimed at swelling the Society's revenue stream, can be seen in the light-hearted events announced for the 1883 Games. The Society seems to have gone a little too far in its effort to introduce 'novelty' into its Gathering when it announced that the following events were to be tried out at the 1883 Games.

1. Prizes will be awarded to the prettiest Lady and the most handsome Gentleman present at the Gathering.

2. The tallest man on the ground will be presented with Longfellow's poems, printed in long primer, published by the eminent firm of Longman and Company, London. The gift of H. Franks esq., also prizes will be given for the shortest, the heaviest, and the lightest man on the grounds.

3. A handsome presentation will be given to the finest baby present under 12 months old.

Who would dare judge such events? It can probably be taken that no one (father or husband) would have had the temerity to judge the prettiest lady or the bonniest baby contests. Unsurprisingly, there is no record of these contests actually having taken place!

A novelty event carried over from the 1882 'private enterprise' Games was the 'Go as You Please' exercise which consisted of running for a prescribed time period. The winner was the competitor who had covered the most distance in the time allowed. Another event, which had been introduced in 1881, featured again at the 1883 Games; this was a bicycle race.

As we have seen, the *Advertiser*'s reporter found it hardly worth his time to report on the event when it first appeared at the 1881 Games. Indeed, the *Geelong Advertiser*'s editor was quite slow to warm to these 'newfangled contraptions' on, or off, the track. Bicycles, he wrote, were the cause of many accidents, were worse than wheelbarrows for frightening horses, and were, "an abomination" which should only be allowed out at night and, even then, only when it was foggy! Whatever the *Advertiser*'s reasons for adopting what seemed over-the-top antagonism towards bicycles and bicyclists, it missed no opportunity, as we will see below, of highlighting every crash, every broken crank, every bent wheel and every fateful meeting between that machine and the rest of the world!

In the early 1880s the *Geelong Advertiser* became less exuberant than previously in its coverage of Comunn na Feinne's New Year's Day Gatherings. For the 1883 Games, for example, the newspaper was able to fit into less than one column its report of the weather, the crowd, the procession from Geelong, the President's address of welcome, its description of the Games, and the results of all of the events! In addition to the foregoing there was also the reference, too, to the apology from the Chief, Hon. Francis Ormond MLC., for his absence due to his suffering from "an ulcerated throat." Peter Fleming continued to dominate the Heavy Games, once again winning the 'grand slam', but the reporter was obviously struggling to make interesting copy out of the day's events up to that point, finding no hard luck story and no humorous occurrence to colour his bare prose; other than the Chief's sore throat!

There were no misbehaving Cabers or near drownings in the water jump. There was no latter-day prophet, minor or major, calling down fire upon the Gathering, and there was a complete absence of carelessness involving dropped lighted matches or fractious horses or even 'feral' young boys invading the pitch! However, luck, or rather a case of someone's bad luck, was to throw the reporter a life line.

Despite its initial attitude towards bicycles and bicyclists, the *Advertiser* now found that these machines could, on occasions, provide good copy – usually involving pile-ups! So, when a reporter, covering the 1883 New Year's Day Games, was struggling to find anything fresh with which to ginger up his reports, this new and heaven-sent mechanical invention provided fresh ink for his nib. Machines, he became aware, provided a never-ending source of possibilities of things going wrong - crashes, breakdowns, protests and close finishes and, of course, bad luck.

Here was a new storehouse of 'plots' for the jaded reporter covering his umpteenth dancing and piping competitions! Thus, his introduction to his 1883 fateful bicycle crash story, while it is not up there with "It was a dark and stormy night," did, nevertheless, seek to 'grab' the attention of the reader.

> This was a most eventful event. On going the five rounds both riders fell, but mounted again. The next round W. Buckingham, in trying to pass his opponent, collided with him and they both came to grief. Buckingham's machine being much injured. He proceeded on another machine, but was unable to overhaul J.B. Riches, who had remounted and established a long lead and the latter eventually won easily.

The Society meeting held 9th January, 1883, confirmed the success of the New Year's Day Gathering. Most of all the expenses had been covered. "Nearly all of the prizes won at the sports had been paid, but there were still a few liabilities to be met." It was also the case, however, that "repairs to grounds and buildings" would amount to £50. Notwithstanding its financial situation, the Society did vote the secretary, William Field, a "bonus of £7/10/0. But financial worries continued to dog the Society and at the Annual Directors' Meeting on 24th September, 1883, it was reported that the financial sheet showed a balance of £6/18/8. It was also reported, according to the *Advertiser*'s account the next day, that further improvements to the fence and to the grandstand had to be carried out and this would require capital. It was decided, therefore, that there should be an effort to make the next Highland Gathering as profitable as possible, "as they desired funds to wipe off liabilities to be incurred in the improving of the Society's property."

At a well-attended Directors' meeting on 27th November, 1883, the programme for the upcoming 1884 New Year's Day Gathering was read and, with some small revisions, wholeheartedly accepted. Trophies had been promised as prizes from Messrs., Fisher, Pearson, and Hammerton, some of the jewellers of Geelong. It was also reported that a large number of donations had been received. Hon. Francis Ormond, the Society's Chief, had sent a letter to the Society together with a "substantial donation', and an intimation that he hoped to attend the 1884 Gathering. It was also agreed to reduce the admission charge for the grand stand from 2/6 to 2/-

The 1884 New Year's Day was greeted with "brilliant sunshine ... and the prevalence of dust was the only drawback to the general enjoyment." The Hon. Francis Ormond MLC., the man who replaced Robert de Bruce Johnstone as titular head of Comunn na Feinne, had not managed to be present at a Society Gathering until 1884, but Ormond, along with the Hon. James McBain MLC., attended these Games, although he did not remain to watch any of the events. The Chief opened the Games with remarks which epitomized the spirit of the Society. Here was a gathering at which people came together as one and where divisions were forgotten and where competition was based on athletic prowess rather than any narrow ethnic rivalry. At a luncheon with Comunn na Feinne officers, before leaving on the mid-day train back to Melbourne, Ormond elaborated on his earlier remarks. He said that he was pleased to see, "so many Englishmen, Irishmen as well as Scotchmen" present. In his own person, he continued, he stood before them as one with such a mixture of forebears that no one nationality could claim him, Scotland, Ireland and England could all lay claim at least to some part of him as well as, now, the State of Victoria. Judging his audience aright, and to great applause, he declared a preference to be known as a "Scotch Victorian."

J. Clinnick and J. Pywell, fought out the Tilting at the Ring event with Pywell taking the first prize and Clinnick runner up, among a strong field. The heavy events did not feature any of the well-known 'big' men and no one athlete stood out, the prizes being shared among various entrants. The Highland Dancing had an interstate winner, George Lapsley from Adelaide, and he took out first prize in the Strathspey and Reel and claimed second place in both the Sword Dance and the Reel of Tulloch.

However, it was the bicycle races which again gave the *Advertiser* reporter material enough to liven up his otherwise perfunctory coverage of the day's activities. The two-mile Bicycle Race had five starters. However, as the *Advertiser* reported on 3rd January, 1884, "Plant broke his crank just after he started, and Buckingham was thrown heavily after he had accomplished a mile and a quarter." This left E. Trengrove (off 200 yards) as first and E.A. Pearson (off 50 yards) coming second. It seemed that the secret of winning, or at least gaining a place, was to manage to stay on the machine!

The annual Directors' Meeting, held on 28th October, 1884, heard that a credit balance of £29/4/8 existed, which was, according to the *Advertiser*'s report the next morning, "considered satisfactory" by the meeting. However, it was also reported that the construction of the new fence and a ticket office for the grounds would amount to in excess of £50, "which would be reimbursed" from the takings of the next annual Gathering in January, 1885. The Society, it would seem, was playing the risky financial game of perpetual catch up! The popularity of bicycles was growing steadily and the *Advertiser*, on 29th December, 1884, reported that the Society's 1885 New Year's Day Gathering would again include a Bicycle Race over a distance of Two Miles, as well as the usual Foot Races for which a good number of entries had already been received.

At the 1885 Games, a familiar name, Peter Fleming, and another of the Worland dynasty, George Worland, contested the heavy events. Peter Fleming came a creditable second in Tossing the Caber and Throwing the heavy hammer and George Worland took the prize for putting the stone. Pywell and Clinnick repeated their previous year's performance in Tilting at the Ring by finishing in the same order, Pywell first and Clinnick second.

Comunn na Feinne returned to its tradition of holding a Concert in the evening following the Games, staging what was termed, "an international concert". This was held at the Mechanics' Institute Hall and, as well as Scottish, Irish and English entertainments, the "patriotic *La Marsellaise* was sung in a fine enspirited manner". It was, said the *Advertiser*, a very popular, successful and enjoyable evening. However, the term 'successful', when used to describe Comunn na Feinne activities, did not necessarily mean 'financial' success!

The Directors' annual meeting on 26th October, 1885, was reasonably 'upbeat' with the year having been regarded as a successful one, although this was hardly shown in the Society's balance sheet! The year had returned good income although the costs of the improvements to the grounds swallowed a quarter of this. With the cost of prizes and other expenses, the Society had a credit balance of £2/15/7. It was also reported that, as a result of a membership drive, two new members were admitted to the Society. The secretary also referred to a letter which had been received from Duncan C. Ross, "a Scottish Athlete in the colony." He was seeking to offer his services at the next Games (1886) and asking what terms the Society would make to have him appear. The meeting did not take any action on the matter and, with the Society's bank balance standing at less than £3/0/0, it is doubtful if the Society could have afforded Ross's services even if it had decided to hire him.

The 1886 procession to the grounds took place under skies threatening "unpropitious weather", but this failed to deter the marchers who, "undaunted and true", turned out in large numbers. The size of the parade was described as one of the largest and most varied and colourful for some time. As well as the Marshall, Fire Brigade Captain, Frederick Hodge, the pipers and Highlanders were in full costume, and members of Comunn na Feinne and the St Andrew's Society also were in Highland dress. Mr Ashmore's brass band, and that of the St Patrick's Society of Geelong, joined, in turn, with the music-making of the pipes. In addition, the Volunteer fire brigades of Geelong, Newtown and Chilwell, and Geelong West, along with the Ancient Order of Druids and the Salvage corps, also formed part of the Procession. The Marchers were swelled with the presence, "of about 300-400 members of Friendly Societies" thus making the Procession, "a well-organized and imposing one" as it snaked its way through town and down to the grounds at South Geelong, where, in the centre of the arena, "the emblematical flag with the Lion Rampant" was conspicuously waving. The crowd was estimated at over 2,500 people.

Peter Fleming, now at the veteran stage of his athletic career, demonstrated that he was not yet a spent force coming second to newcomer, Robert Horne, in

Tossing the Caber, and taking first prize in Throwing the Heavy Hammer and second prize in Putting the Stone. Excitement arose out of other events, too, where two contestants, J.T. Hickey and J. Mullen, vied for mastery in each of the three races in the Comunn na Feinne Handicap. In the first of these (150 yards), Hickey led Mullen to the finish line winning by a yard. In the second race (300 yards), Mullen led from the start and beat Hickey into second place. In the third of the races (440 yards), Hickey and Mullen, shot from the starting line together. Unfortunately, they were too much 'together' and they "soon collided," with Mullen coming to "mother earth" while Hickey, keeping his balance, went on to win the race. That rascal 'bad luck' had been busy - again!

The Handicap Bicycle Race (half mile) drew only two competitors, A.E Trengrove, starting off scratch and A.M. Dawson, who started off 350 yards. Dawson came in an easy winner. The reporter commented that the Course, "was a very bad one for bicycling" and, as this sport was a relatively new one, it was not yet subject to formal regulations as to the state of riding tracks, approved racing bicycles and official times, all necessary when working out accurate handicaps. The *Advertiser* commented that, "No times were taken of the different races, and we would suggest that in future, records should be made and the ground properly measured off."

Summing up the day, the *Advertiser* reported that the 1886 Gathering was a successful one and that this was, in part, due to its "excellent management." It added that Comunn na Feinne was associated with good work done in other areas, too, especially "in the direction of promoting education." Despite some faltering steps at times, the newspaper noted that, "the support accorded it [ie education] of late is sufficient proof of satisfactory resuscitation."*

*[Details of the extensive work carried out by the Society in the various areas of education including the 3Rs, the Eisteddfod, in volunteer organizations and in teaching practical skills, is covered in Appendix 14 which looks at Comunn na Feinne and its Wider Sphere of work.]

The Directors' annual meeting was held on 5th October, 1886, and reported with satisfaction the previous January's Highland Gathering. The credit balance was still low, £4/16/7, and more repairs were needed to the fence around the grounds, but the Society regarded itself as being back on an even keel and the Directors resolved that the 1887 New Year's Day Gathering should proceed. And proceed it did, with a substantial Procession to the grounds which had been given a great deal of attention, "with the view to making it attractive, and the happiest feature was a line of seventy flags, of various colours and shapes, suspended across the grounds and surmounted in the centre by the 'Scottish Lion'."

The opening ceremony of the 1887 Gathering, reported the *Advertiser* on 3rd January, was performed by the President, Mr Robert Shirra, who again apologized for the absence of their Chief, the Hon. F. Ormond, MLC. Shirra addressed an important point when he dwelt on the passing of the old guard of members, supporters, contestants and office-bearers and hoped, "that the young folks would not lose interest in the Society, but would continue to maintain it as their predecessors had." Not forgetting the slogan of the Society's Games, he hoped that the motto of 'fair play' would be observed by all." The crowd was estimated at about 3,000.

The *Advertiser* noted that the number of competitors for the athletic events was high, "albeit the prizes … were not large." It was, however, the dancing, with some competitors coming from afar, noted the *Advertiser*, which drew the best performances and the "warmest encomiums of the spectators for their artistic steppings …" The excitement of the athletics was heightened by the fact that finishes, "in the majority of the athletic events were unusually close …". But to the *Advertiser*, there was nothing like an untoward occurrence of some kind during an event to sharply focus the reporter's pencil. One such instance took place in the vaulting competition when one of the contestants, A. Scrivenger, at the top of his vault, in an attempt to clear the bar, had his vaulting pole snap beneath him. He had a heavy fall to the ground where he was knocked unconscious, badly injuring his shoulder.

It was the reporter's day, as in the Comunn na Feinne Handicap races the results came down to a tie in the number of points gained by the contestants, T. Scott and H. Hardcastle. The two runners decided to run over a distance of 300 yards to settle the first prize. The race was fairly even but, drawing close to the finish, Scott gained the lead and looked certain to win. However, he was "jostled and thrown down by Hardcastle, who endeavoured to pass him on the inside." The judges decided that the race should be run again.* The contestants, after having already run several races, plus the tie-breaker, decided not to trust to their flagging energies and divided the winnings between them rather than puff their way round the track again. P. Fleming was undergoing a resurgence of his career and took the Tossing the Caber and Throwing the Hammer events and came third in Putting the Stone. The Manx Race was re-introduced into these Games, and the Quoits Match, with the prizes of a Gold Medal (first) and Silver Medal (second), being donated by John Hammerton, a local jeweller, was decided in less time than at the 1886 Games!

* [This seems a lenient penalty given that a less physical challenge during the same event at the 1888 Games led to the offender being disqualified from that particular race and all other races for that day!]

The annual Directors' Meeting, held on 12th October, 1887, as reported in the *Advertiser* the next day, heard a preliminary report on the improvements which were being added to the South Geelong grounds. The arena was to be surrounded by a new picket fence and, "the running ground was to be lengthened and put in first class order." This work was estimated to cost between £35 and £40 and would be finished by 15th December ready for the 1888 Games. It was believed, "that the improvements would add greatly to the success of the sports." The financial report still showed a credit balance, albeit only of £10/15/0, but the cost of the repairs which were still to take place would more than swallow up this surplus.

In 1888, the number of spectators at the Games continued to increase into the afternoon when it was estimated about 2,000 were in attendance and, "the sons of Caledonia mustered in their customary strength, and the national bonnets and kilts were seen in many places around the arena." The *Advertiser* of the 2nd January, 1888, noted, with or without intentional sarcasm, that among the visitors was the Society's Chief, the Hon. Francis Ormond MLC.

Novelty events introduced at the 1888 Games included a Siamese Race and a Tug of War. Peter Fleming again won the Caber event, as well as Throwing the Hammer, and came second in Putting the Stone. Tilting of the Ring, that exciting sport involving man, horse, lance and suspended ring, was, without any explanation, still off the programme, and had not been staged since 1885. Inexplicably, too, there was no Bicycle Racing at these Games. The absence of each of these events robbed the day of the excitement which horse and rider, as well as bicycle contests can generate. Lack of money for prizes for these events may explain these omissions, although this was not mentioned at any of the Society's meetings either before or following the Games. Although no explanation was given for dropping the Bicycle races, a clue as to why they were not included in the 1888 programme might be related to the ground improvements which had been proposed a year before and which had not quite been completed. This seems to be borne out when, at a Directors' meeting on 11th October, 1888, it was mentioned that the grounds, "were in good order, the foreshadowed improvements of a year ago having now been effected, and a successful 1889 Gathering could thus be anticipated." But, despite the absence of these aforementioned events, the programme of contests was still a long one for the 1888 Games, and, wrote the *Advertiser* on 2nd January, 1888, it was "six o'clock in the evening before the last event was over."

The Directors, at their meeting on 11th October, 1888, had predicted a successful Gathering for New Year's Day, January, 1889. Unfortunately, according to the *Advertiser*'s report of 2nd January, 1889, the Directors of Comunn na Feinne had been overly optimistic. The usual Procession took place but the display, "was much inferior to those of former years." The day was exceedingly hot and the *Advertiser* expressed feelings of pity for the members of the Geelong Artillery Brass Band who were left without shade from a broiling sun. The paper took the Society to task for not providing some temporary shelter for the musicians. However, this did not detract from the high quality of the Band's music throughout the day which provided, "one of the best sources of pleasure to the spectators." This was just as well as, according to the *Advertiser*, everything went downhill from there. The absence of catering meant that the estimated crowd of 1,500 had to "shift for themselves" regarding food and refreshments.

The *Advertiser* also considered the standard of athletics, "scarcely up to that of last New Year's Day." Some of the racing was "rather poor" and the finish to "the Comunn na Feinne Handicap (prize of £20) – the principal event of the day – particularly tame."

It may have seemed "tame" in terms of an exciting race, but it was hardly dull. D. Fowler was disqualified, "for jostling and injuring H. Shea "when a short distance from home." Shea was carried off the ground and removed to the hospital in a cab! It also is something of a disappointment that the *Advertiser* saw nothing in the evergreen Peter Fleming's performance in what was the twilight of his career. He achieved a clean sweep of the heavy events winning the Caber, Putting the Stone and Throwing the Hammer events. For a few years, it had seemed that Fleming who, for a decade, had featured prominently in the winner's list in the Heavy Games events, was beginning to surrender to the realities of age. He was not so regularly in the winners' lists although he still managed to gain a place in his favourite events. However, he came storming back at the 1889 Gathering to lift all of the Heavy Games titles showing that he was not quite a spent force as a top Highland Games athlete.

The Society was dealt another blow when its Chief, the Hon. Francis Ormond MLC., died on 5th May 1889. He had held the office for less than eight years and, although generous with his donations, Ormond had attended only two Gatherings. Sir James Munro (1889-1894),* was elected in his place pending ratification at the next Annual meeting of the Society.

*[Munro seemed a strange choice to make as, at the time, he had been caught up in a financial scandal which brought about his ruin along with that of many others.]

At the opening of the 1890 Games, the President, Robert Shirra, paid tribute to the

Society's late Chief, Hon. Francis Ormond MLC., and announced that Sir James Munro who was, unfortunately, unable to be present as he was preparing to leave for Europe, had been elected in his place. Bicycling was again absent from the Games but Peter Fleming was still competing and he carried off first prize in Putting the Stone and in Throwing the Heavy Hammer.

There had been some disappointment with the 1890 Games and the Society set its goal to lift its performance for 1891. At the final meeting of the Comunn na Feinne committee on 30th December, 1890, details of which appeared in the *Advertiser* the following day, it was determined that a special effort would be made to ensure that the 1891 New Year's Day Gathering would be an improvement on that of the previous year. The meeting heard that there already had been a large number of entries for various events. These included the Comunn na Feinne Handicap Footrace (over 150 yards, 300 yards and 440 yards), the Hurdle Race and the one mile Handicap Race as well as the Handicap Quoit Match.

On the day of the thirty-fourth Games, the morning weather was kind, a good omen that the Gathering would be successful. The day, in fact, produced something of a novelty; an arena which was covered with green grass instead of the usual layer of dust!

> [M]ore favourable weather has not been experienced for the local celebration of Scotland's national holiday for many years past. … Yesterday … owing to the phenomenal character of the holiday season of 1890-1891, the novelty of a green grass-covered turf was experienced, and the arrangement good, the lengthy sports programme provided for the occasion passed off enjoyably for the spectators and the competitors alike.

Once the usual Procession reached the Grounds, Robert Shirra, the Society's President, opened the Games welcoming all who were in attendance and apologized for the Chief, Sir James Munro's absence. Shirra noted that Munro's letter of apology also contained, "a substantial donation to the funds." In addition to a new Chief, the Society had taken steps to welcome the new Governor of Victoria, the Earl of

Hopetoun, and to seek his official patronage for the Games. This was accorded but, as usual with Governors with better things to do, he pleaded his 'heavy duties' when tendering his apologies in advance for his absence from the 1891 Gathering!

Sir James Munro, who had been Premier of Victoria, had, as mentioned above, become embroiled in a scandal involving financial institutions and excessive speculations and he, along with many others, had been financially ruined. It is uncertain whether Munro was involved in anything actually illegal, but the taint of scandal followed him wherever he went and his association with the Presbyterian Church of Victoria, of which he was an active member, added to the disgrace. Robert Shirra, the Comunn na Feinne President (1876-1895), in his speech of welcome to the spectators, referred to their Chief, the Honourable Sir James Munro, who had recently returned from his overseas trip, as a man who had been a good friend of the Society in the past, and who had been re-elected Chief.

The Games having been declared open, the various competitions followed. Peter Fleming was back in the list of winners taking first prize for Tossing the Caber and for Throwing the Heavy Hammer, while also taking second place in Putting the Stone. Although other names were occasionally appearing as prize-winners in the heavy events, there was no new athlete regularly featuring in these competitions who was stamping his name on these events as some of the earlier champions had done – and, in the continued presence of Peter Fleming, were still doing. The music judges expressed their opinion that the piping was the best they had experienced, and this applied especially to the playing for the Pìobaireachd prize.

While reasonably pleased overall with the 1891 Games, a meeting of the Comunn na Feinne Committee, held late in December of that year, strove even more eagerly to further improve them. It was reported that, towards this end, the grounds had been, "considerably improved since last year". Care has been taken in several parts that formerly raised the dust, to have a thick coating of tar laid. Other improvements, included the painting of the grand stand, the planting of new bushes and the erection of a new room for the President. It was also reported that the Games Committee had worked hard to ensure that the traditional Procession to the ground would be, "a special feature" of the day. The report continued noting that, "The Militia Brass Band has been engaged to furnish the music of all nations, and the services of several Highland pipers from Melbourne have been procured for the delight of the sons and daughters of 'Auld Scotia' ... ". Also taking part, among other groups, were the members of the various town fire brigades, and members of the St Andrew's and the St Patrick's Societies. The Games were to open with a Highland Reel danced by all Highlanders in Highland Costume. A novelty, which was to be on exhibit at Comunn na Feinne's 1892 Gathering, was the presence of a block of ice, between 40lbs and 45lbs in weight, "within which have been frozen designs of flowers." This block was the product of the Geelong and Ice Refrigerating Company in Gheringhap Street and it was, "to sit at the head of the luncheon table at the Society's sports gathering at South Geelong tomorrow. The centre piece contained, in white floral letters, the words, "A guid New Year," which words were surrounded by prettily worked wreaths."

All of this effort appeared to pay off. Of the 1892 Gathering the *Advertiser* wrote on 2nd January, "in every respect, it was superior to meetings of the kind held for many years past."

Everything had favoured the day. The weather was "beautifully fine", the procession was, "more imposing than on previous occasions", and tartan costumed Highlanders seemed to be everywhere. The President, in his short address opening the Games, lamented the absence of so many of the usual faces, but he was pleased that these had been replaced by a host of young ones.

> Much enthusiasm among them had infused interest into the sports-gathering, resulting in a large attendance of spectators and competitors. The gathering was remarkable for the great number of men in kilts, and it would stimulate the young people, for they were shown that their motto 'Shoulder to Shoulder' was full of meaning.

The *Advertiser*, in remarking that there was an unusually large gathering of Highlanders in kilts, providing a fine spectacle, also commented on, "a novelty in the assemblage" which was "the presence of a young lady in Highland costume," which provided the sensation of the 1892 Games. However, it may just have been a sign of the times as, in 1892, young girls were now allowed, for the first time, to compete in the Highland dancing events. James Russell of Caulfield (age 13 years) won the Highland Fling competition with Miss Brown of Caulfield (age 13 years) and Master Norman Tait (age 9 years) tying for second place. "The competition was an excellent one, the public loudly applauding the dancers. The judges recommended that special prizes should be given to Miss Brown and Master Tait."

Apart from the excitement generated by the foregoing 'lady Highlander', there was more to be found in some of the other events taking place. In the Maiden Race (220 yards), closely won by A. Hopper, the contestants had to run the race again owing to the competitors having ran the wrong course! In the re-run the unfortunate Hopper, obviously puffed, did not feature in the first three places. In the seventh heat of the Maiden it was impossible to separate the first two runners, D. Young and A. McFarlane, at the finish. A re-run was ordered with Young (off 22 yards) narrowly beating McFarlane (off 18 yards) to the tape, both very much out of 'steam'. Peter Fleming was again champion of the Caber and Hammer events and a welcome return to the programme of events was Tilting at the Ring. The results showed another generational change with A.S. Pywell taking first prize over his father, J. Pywell, who tied for second place with H. McDonald. John Clinnick, who had been a long-time rival of John Pywell, seems to have hung up his spurs for good and did not compete.

Concern about the possible impact of the worsening economic recession in the State on the next New Year's Day Gathering, led to a special meeting of the Comunn na Feinne President and Office-bearers on 2nd November, 1892. This meeting acted as a morale booster for the Committee and encouraged the Society as a whole to rise above the social despondency of many in the community. The gathered office-bearers heard the report that the last New Year's Day Gathering had proved a great success. The financial report, however, was not so promising with a credit of only £1/15/0 in the bank. It was recognized that Victoria was in a state of economic depression and that this would obviously affect the wages of their supporters in Geelong. However, the treasurer (A.V. Rankin) remarked:

> [T]hat there was no reason why they should not make a success of the demonstrations next year if they worked together. Although the depression affected Geelong as well as other places, it would benefit Comunn na Feinne in one way for the people who usually went away for the holidays would remain in Geelong and patronize the local Gathering.

Francis Milliken, another of the directors, supported Rankin saying that:

> [I]t would ill become them as Scotsmen to show the white feather because of the depression, and he hoped they would make it [ie the Gathering] a great success. It was therefore moved and seconded and unanimously decided that the 1893 Gathering should go ahead [on] 3rd January, 1893.

The matter of the continuing Chieftainship was also raised. The Society discussed whether it should retain Sir James Munro as its Chief given his reverses and the scandal that was falling about his ears. Those attending this meeting were asked to live up to the truths behind Comunn na Feinne's name and to the 'spirit' behind its mottoes, and to give substance to the call, 'Shoulder to Shoulder'. The *Advertiser*, in its report on 3rd November, 1892, also regarded the decision as involving a matter of principle:

> Adversity is the test of true friendship and with his knowledge of this truism Sir James Munro, the present Agent-General for Victoria, will more deeply value the compliment bestowed on him last evening by Comunn na Feinne in re-electing him as its Chief. Delicate reference was made by several speakers to the reverses of fortune suffered by the Chief and the one sentiment to which voice was given was that Comunn na Feinne would be acting discreditably if it followed the usual example and had forsaken the allegiance paid to its Chief when the clouds of misfortune was still far below the horizon. It was remarked that there was little in the position, but Comunn na Feinne would show by its action that it still had confidence in Sir James Munro, and would continue to regard it as an honour that he was their Chief.

The general *bonhomie* towards the Society, exhibited by the *Advertiser*'s reports of the New Year's Day Gatherings, spilled over into another year.

> Notwithstanding the counter attractions that have regularly claimed a share of the patronage of holiday makers of latter years, the Comunn na Feinne

celebration continues to prove an unfailing attraction for 'guid Scots' and no small proportion of representatives of the other two kingdoms, not to speak of the assertive Australian who, despite the charge of irreverence, is not so entirely absorbed in football as to be unable to take an appreciative interest in the pastimes which have become venerable by their antiquity in the 'land o' cakes and thistles'. Yesterday was no exception to the rule, for the demonstration on the Comunn na Feinne Grounds … was as successful as any which preceded it.

Opening the Games, Robert Shirra, the President, "delivered his usual genial address of welcome" and mentioned that Sir James Munro had been re-elected Comunn na Feinne's Chief.

> The Society had felt honoured in the past having Mr Munro as their Chief, and would continue to do so in spite of the reverses that had been suffered by him during the general downfall of financial institutions.

Fleming took the winner's prize for the Caber event with a third both in Throwing the Heavy Hammer and Putting the Heavy Stone. In Throwing the Heavy Hammer Fleming's two prizewinning opponents each threw about ten feet longer than Fleming's best results, and in Putting the Stone they each threw two to three feet longer than Fleming, which may have indicated Fleming's waning powers or the greater physique of a newer and better trained second-generation offspring of the original settlers. Evidence, too, of the growing regulation of sports can be seen in the rise of Athletic Associations and Clubs, and the consequences of non-compliance with their rules. This was evident at the 1893 Gathering which was supposed to have included a friendly competition between the Richmond Military Club and the Geelong Athletic Club, but the latter fell foul of the Athletic Association and did not compete. There was some annoyance expressed at the non-appearance of the Geelong Club, "at a competition arranged for their benefit." The Richmond Military Athletic Club, under the command of Sergeant Cunningham, however, "gave an attractive exhibition" on its own.

The reporter's lyrical conclusion to his description of the Gathering at the close of the day ranged from his appreciation of the playing of Auld Lang Syne, which provided a bittersweet ending to the Games, to the scene of, "the Scottish flag, the broad ample folds which had fluttered gaily over the assemblage during the day, descending, as the sun, sinking behind the harvest-laden Barrabool Hills, flushed the evening sky with a parting smile."

The *Advertiser*'s warm and poetical mood at the close of the 1893 Gathering had, by the latter part of the year, become somewhat frostier. By late December the *Advertiser* was reporting, in fairly annoyed terms, that the Society's hierarchy had decided that there would not be any Highland Games for New Year's Day 1894, and that Comunn na Feinne was in financial trouble. But finances were not the only concern. The *Advertiser*'s report of 22nd December, 1893, indicated that even Members of the Society did not know what was going on and were dissatisfied with the decision not to stage the Games.* The *Advertiser* pointed out that the lack of notice and the failure to explain why the Gathering would not be held had caused disappointment, bewilderment and anger.

*[The Comunn na Feinne Minutes, together with most of its other records, have not been located so the inner machinations of the Society are not available to us. Some explanation of Comunn na Feinne decisions, therefore, have to be pieced together from hints which are garnered from newspaper reports as well as from the *Carmichael Notes*.]

Any hope of a last-minute change of heart, or the possibility of some other group taking over the Games for New Year's Day 1894, was not realized and the paper, on 2nd January, 1894, firmly declared that the Gathering was dead. "The absence of the usual sports gathering of Comunn na Feinne at the South Geelong arena caused some disappointment to the sons of Scotia resident in this town and district." The newspaper, on 3rd November, 1894, hinted at problems within the Society. A meeting of Directors had been called for on 26th October 1894, but had suddenly been cancelled. There had been something of a 'palace coup' within Comunn na Feinne's hierarchy, according to the *Advertiser*, which maintained that a "resuscitated" Society then met and approached Captain John Percy Chirnside MLA., of 'The Manor,' Werribee, to become its Chief, an offer which he accepted saying also that he would be attending the Games on 1st January, 1895.

A flurry of meetings was called and held at the offices of Hugh M. Sutherland, the new President (1895-96), to further discuss matters. With the Chief, Sir James Munro, replaced by Captain Percy Chirnside (1894-96) and the President, Hugh M. Sutherland replacing Robert Shirra, and George R. King taking over as Secretary from Robert J. MacDonald, events would seem to confirm the *Geelong Advertiser*'s suggestion of a palace revolution having occurred. Yet another meeting was held on 1st December, 1894, where arrangements for the January 1895 Gathering were discussed. Subsequently a Directors' meeting on 20th December, 1894 announced that the patronage of the St Patrick's Society, Geelong, and that of the Caledonian Society of Melbourne, were forthcoming and there was renewed optimism.

This meeting also indicated that the Society would be strengthening the promotion of Gaelic, which had formed part of its original charter in 1856, but which had waxed and waned over the years since. The new secretary, George R. King, who had been appointed 20th November, 1894, was responsible for restoring the Comunn na Feinne Literary Competitions which, for 1895, included some sections dealing with Gaelic. For example, a Gaelic Essay on Comunn na Feinne was set. There was also a competition to translate the famous 'Mercy' speech from Shakespeare's *Merchant of Venice* into Gaelic. A third category of competition was to write in Gaelic from Gaelic Dictation, "during the luncheon hour on the Society's Oval." The Gaelic poetry competitions also brought forth a number of entries which were judged by impartial Gaelic scholars in Scotland, with the winning entries being published in the *Oban Times*, a Highland newspaper. The following letter, which, along with a winning competition Poem, appeared in the *Oban Times* and indicates the outcome of one of these Gaelic poetry competitions.

An Australian Gaelic Competition

> We recently received from Mr Geo. R. King, secretary of the Comunn na Feinne society, Geelong, Victoria, Australia, an interesting communication inviting us to judge the contributions in a Gaelic translation competition held by the Society during their last annual gathering. In the course of his letter Mr King writes:-

At the last meeting of the directors of the above society it was decided to request you to act as judges in connection with the Translation Competition held by the society during their annual gathering.

I may state that the Comunn na Feinne, while originally a Fingalian Society, is at present a Scottish Association ... the oldest in Victoria, it having been established since 1856 and since then has continued to exist with varying success. ... To come to the matter of this letter ... I am enclosing the entries received, and I trust you will find time to judge them. The subject of the translation is Robert Burns "O', a' the airts the win' can blaw." You will, of course, judge the translations on your own standards. By way of recognition my Directors would be glad if you would publish in your journal the successful translation. ... By complying with the above requests, you will not only confer a favour on the society and on the Sons of Scotia, who are greatly interested in these Gaelic competitions, but you will help to form the chain - golden in its opportunities and advantages - which binds the mother country to colonies whose people link their tenderest associations with the brother (sic) country.

We need scarcely state that is has given us pleasure to examine and adjudicate the translations entered for competition, and help in this small way the Australian Highland Society which is so creditably fostering and maintaining in the far-off Colony the sentiments and traditions of Scotland and the Scottish Highlands. The competition itself is characteristic in an eminent degree, and is a striking evidence of how successfully the Gaelic language may flourish and be perpetuated in surroundings where it might most readily lapse. The contributions do credit to the translators, but we have awarded the first place to that signed "Dunvegan" (Mr A. MacDonald, Geelong) which in our opinion is the best.

The following represents just two verses of the winning entry for 1896. It is a translation into Gaelic of Robert Burns' poem, 'O' a' the airts'.*

*[The whole of this poem, including the disputed verses, along with other Gaelic contributions to Comunn na Feinne's Gaelic Poetry Competitions, can be found in Appendix 10 (a) Samples of Gaelic Poetry.
Results of the 1898 Competition can be found in Appendix 10 (b)]

>O' a' the airts the wind can blaw
>I dearly like the west,
>For there the bonnie lassie lives,
>The lassie I lo'e best,
>There wild woods grow, and rivers row,
>And monie a hill between,

But day and night my flancy's flight
Is ever wi' my Jean.

"Dhe 'n h-uile h-aird bho seid a ghaoth
'S ann thug mi gaol do 'n iar
Si sin an àird far bheil a tàmh
Mo ghràdh is àillidh fiamh
'M bheil coiltean-fas is sruthan làn
Is cnocan Ard cuir dìon
Ach tha momhiannsa ghnàth air sgiath
A là 'sa dh' oidhch le Sin.

I see her in the dewy flowers-
I see her sweet and fair.
I hear her in the tunefu' birds-
I hear her charm the air.
There's not a bonnie flower that springs
By fountain, shaw, or green,
There's not a bonnie bird that sings,
But minds me o' ma Jean."

Chì mi i's gach blàth fo dhriuchd
'S geal milis ùrar snuadh
Gu 'n cluinn mi ceòl aig eòin nam craobh
Dha bheil a ghaoth toirt luaidh
Chan fhaic mi flùr an doire dlùth
Ri bùrn, na leanag mhìn
Cha chluinn mi eunan binn a sinn
Nach d' thoir na 'm chuimhne Sin."

The *Advertiser* on 8th July, 1895 also reported that John Clark of Teesdale won the prize for his translation of Portia's Speech into Gaelic, Mr A. McDonald of Geelong won the best essay in Gaelic on the subject 'Comunn na Feinne', and Mr Samuel MacAulay, also of Geelong, was successful in the category of Dictation from Gaelic.*
*[Both Mr A. McDonald and Mr S. MacAulay were to be successful in these competitions over several years, and regularly had their poems published in the *Oban Times*.]

The *Advertiser*, with some half-hearted optimism, covered the 1895 Games and also offered some reflections on why Comunn na Feinne had waxed and waned over the years, especially over the previous decade. It also provided an analysis of why such societies often succumb to the effects of generational change. "Enthusiasm in regard to the observance of the National customs began to fail as the old identities made place for a generation without the traditions of the old land to fire their patriotism."

However, it is doubtful that this analysis could be applied to the Geelong Society, given the very rapid transformation of Comunn na Feinne into a general multi-national community organization. It is true that it had always retained a core of traditional Celtic games, music and dancing, and gave encouragement to the support of the Gaelic tongue, but its total athletics programme, as well as the majority of its other activities, reflected neither a Scottish bias nor an exclusivist agenda. Nor was Comunn na Feinne activity confined to an annual New Year's Day Gathering; it was spread throughout the whole year and over a large number of community concerns. Its influence is best seen through the activities of its individual members and supporters who were part of the many voluntary organizations and other community activities, and who carried the influence of Comunn na Feinne ideals into these many activities.

But, whether it was due to the new hierarchy or just the momentum arising from the desires of the Geelong folk to have their annual Gathering, the *Advertiser*, reported that the Games, "had been resurrected ... with encouraging results." It was also the case, as noted below, that this 'new breed' of office-bearers and members maintained the philanthropic momentum which had always driven the Society's various charitable endeavours.

Although the *Advertiser* was inclined to withhold its judgment as to the revived Games, it did praise the dancing which, it wrote, "was pronounced by the authorities to be of a superior character, and certainly it formed an attractive feature of the day's amusement." It also declared attractive, "the display by a team from the Athletic Club of the Geelong Battery, the members of which were heartily applauded at the conclusion of their performance." This Club obviously had all their 'papers in order', contrary to the Geelong Athletics' Club at the 1893 Games! Peter Fleming, still competing, won the Caber event in 1895. This 'Peter Pan' of the Heavy Games, continued to defy all-comers, as well as age, by also doing well in the 1896 Games where he won the Heavy Hammer event and came second in Tossing the Caber!

The new-found enthusiasm within the Society, demonstrated at the 1895 Games, continued throughout the year when, for example, the Annual Directors' Meeting of the Society, held 28th October, 1895, vigorously, and unanimously, agreed to hold a New Year's Day Gathering on 1st January, 1896. Some of the features to be introduced at these Games included a Sheffield Handicap foot race of 130 yards for £20, for which 40 entries had already been received. A grand handicap Bicycle Race was also to feature on the programme, and already 19 entries had been received for this event. There also was to be a Mile race in this category for which 14 bicyclists had already entered. As well as its activities relating to the New Year's Day Gathering, it was reported that the Society, "had also been active during the year in assisting in the way of providing employment and rendering assistance" to those in need. A successful Scottish concert had been held on 1st August, 1895 at which 300, "ladies and gentlemen sought for and obtained admission to the entertainment which was of a delightfully and pleasing description." Encouraged by this success, the October 28th Directors' Meeting appointed a sub-committee, "to make arrangements for a Scottish Concert similar to the one which had, so successfully, been held in August."

A series of meetings in November and December followed to prepare for the 1896 Gathering, and the *Advertiser* of 7th December, 1895, reported that:

> The committee of the Society has gone to some expense in getting the tracks in good order for the running and Bicycle events, and those who desire can obtain a permit from the secretary for the use of the grounds on payment of a small fee.

Trophies for the Bicycle races were put on display and prize money of £100 had already been subscribed. The *Advertiser*, which had been pessimistic, after the 1894 cancellation, regarding the survival of Comunn na Feinne, began to accept that the Society had indeed been saved while teetering on the brink of extinction. It believed in the possibility of a revived and a strong Comunn na Feinne, and welcomed, in its

2nd January, 1896 report, the new thinking going into the Games.

> The rejuvenated organization aimed at bringing the programme up to modern tastes and preserving, at the same time, the distinctive features of the Caledonian festival ... Their design has been well-realized, and the sports yesterday embraced all the new developments of outdoor amusements, as well as pastimes which appeal to national sentiment.

In fact, the Society was doing no more than it had always done which was to add new events to keep the Games always growing and always fresh and interesting, and dropping that which proved not to be popular. Examples of new items which had been added over the years included Bicycling, Sheffield Handicaps, Vaulting with the Rod and Iron Quoits. The Heavy events remained a popular and well attended section of the programme.

What had influenced the Society the most in bringing about changes to its programme and to its grounds, as we will see in detail later, was, in fact, the emergence of Professional Bodies which were laying down rules that affected the quality of running and athletic tracks, bicycling track surfaces, standardization of equipment and qualified judges. It was partly due to the emergence of those regulatory authorities that the Society ultimately decided to leave its old ground at South Geelong and to look for a more appropriate arena.

Another of the issues which had caused the Society to look to change was its inadequate income. This lack of financial resources brought pressure to bear on its ability to carry out its various charitable roles in the community. It was a financial supporter of the orphanages, of the Hospital, of the unemployed and of those in distress. It was also involved in the Industrial School and a Working Boys' night school, as well as other areas of community need. We have already identified the Society's use of public entertainments to raise funds. This work had lapsed for several years but the new committee restored such social evenings at which, as in the past, prizes were presented to the contestants successful at its New Year's Day Games. The concert which took place on 10th January, 1896 proved a great success, with Gaelic songs being sung by Samuel MacAulay and A. MacDonald who had been successful at the Gaelic dictation, composition and translation competitions.*

*[See Appendix 10 - Samples of Comunn na Feinne Gaelic Competition Poems]

By 1896, however, several things had happened to influence the thinking of the Society. There was a growing professionalism within athletic and music competitions, and a growing number of societies both within and beyond Victoria, which were drawing competitors and spectators away from the Geelong Gathering. Comunn na Feinne foresaw that a standardization of rules governing certain events offered for competition would have to be made in the interests of "fair play." There would also have to be a set standard of racing and bicycling tracks as well as suitable grounds for the other sports. As already noted, it had actually canvassed such uniform standards earlier in its history but had not received support from any other of the Caledonian Societies at the time. Lastly, the Geelong Society had realized that to attract people and competitors, prizes had to be made more attractive.

Athletics, and sports of all kinds, were entering into a new century in which contests were more 'tightly' regulated under the watchful eye of the relevant registration bodies such as the Victorian Amateur Athletics Association (V.A.A.A.) formed in 1891. Athletes had to be registered to compete and grounds had to conform to certain standards, and judges and handicapping all had to be approved by the relevant Associations. Bicycling, Dancing and Piping organizations all followed, some forming later than others. The Pipe Band Association, for example, although mooted in the late nineteenth century by Geelong's Comunn na Feinne, was not officially formed in Victoria until 1924.

Within the Society, too, changes were also taking place. The Constitution of Comunn na Feinne was being revised. As noted earlier, when the Society initially applied for title for its Grounds at South Geelong, the state government had merely granted the Society use of this land until such times as the government needed it for its own purposes. With its decision to seek another ground for its activities, title for its old ground at South Geelong was sought. Possessing title would allow the Society to sell the land, and a new and a more suitable and permanent site for its annual Gathering could then be found. In the event, no such purchase was ever made and the Society entered a nomadic life, as far as its Games' venue was concerned, until it settled at Kardinia Park in the 1920s.

At a meeting on 1st September, 1896, it was reported that Phillip Russell* of Osbourne House, had been elected Chief in place of Captain Chirnside. There was also yet another new President, Neil Campbell (1896-1902).** A change of venue for the annual Gatherings was also announced, when Comunn na Feinne, through its secretary, George R. King, had arranged with the Geelong Agricultural Society for the use of its Showgrounds for the next Highland Gathering. The *Advertiser*, on 11th October, 1896, reported that the Agricultural Society had agreed to lease its grounds for Comunn na Feinne events starting 1st January, 1897, on the basis that the Agricultural Society would receive half of the net proceeds. It would seem that the Agricultural Society must have been run by Scots! The 1896 Gathering was the last to be held on the old grounds at South Geelong.

[For * and ** See Appendix 3 (b) Short Biographies.]

The new President, Mr Neil Campbell, in his welcome to the spectators to the 1896 Games, as reported in the *Advertiser* of 2nd January, reiterated what had been a desire of the Society from the beginning, that of creating and maintaining social harmony. The aim of the Society was to create a community where all peoples would live together in peace. This laudable aim was in evidence throughout every Gathering, he continued, and, "Archibald Douglas, Robert Shirra, and all the other original members, would look favourably on the spirit which still existed in these games."

Bicycle races, re-introduced at the previous Gathering, proved, again, to be one of the reporter's favourite topics as they always promised a reasonable chance of 'disaster'; at the 1896 Games, the *Advertiser* was not to be disappointed. In one race, a contestant, "had to change his machine during the race through the breakage of the driving gear." In another of the races a contestant, "collided with one of the posts around the track, with results that were disastrous for the machine, though the rider escaped injury." Further disaster struck another two contestants, showing that the 'gremlins' were busy working overtime.

> Stoneham and Yeoman also started. One of the tires (sic) of the machine ridden by the latter burst while the fourth lap was being negotiated. Stoneham, who rode splendidly, secured the lead in the second last round, and was winning hands down when he was put out of the race through the fracture of the pedal crank. He got a nasty fall but was not hurt.

The *Advertiser* summed up the bicycling events with remarks which it soon came to regret. It reported that the failure of certain contestants was due to faults in the machines themselves. It reported that burst tyres, disconnected driving chains and fractured pedal cranks had led to crises during the race and, in one instance, to the defeat of a certain winner. The aggrieved manufacturer of the bicycle, ridden by H. Stonehaven, took umbrage at these remarks and made a visit to the *Advertiser* office, with 'slandered' piece of equipment in hand, to explain exactly what caused the pedal crank to fracture, and to show that it had nothing to do with faulty workmanship. There was a 'sort of apology' in the newspaper the following day.

> It was stated in our report yesterday of the Comunn na Feinne sports that, in the cycling contest, pedal cranks of bicycles were fractured and that H. Stoneham lost the two-mile race through the fracture of the pedal crank of his bicycle. This is not correct, as the damaged part of the machine, which was brought to this office yesterday, proves for itself. The fact was that H. Stoneham fell when racing round a corner in the course when the pedal of his machine struck the ground and the whole weight of the rider being thrown on one side, the 'spindle' of the machine, not the 'crank' was broken. The patent steel of the bicycle was only slightly bent showing that the material is of first class metal.

There you have it – don't blame the machine, blame the rider; and if you don't know the difference between a 'crank' and a 'spindle', best keep your opinions to yourself!

The following year, 1897, happenings outside the Ground competed for attention with those inside it. The *Advertiser* reported a spectacular accident involving one of the horse-drawn buses returning spectators after the games. Not since the day of the runaway Cobb and Co., coach in 1859 was there more excitement outside the ground than there was inside! And, to add to the reporter's luck, there was a similar accident conveying spectators to the grounds in the morning! However, there was no accusation on this occasion of poor manufacturing as the reason for the broken axles – the *Advertiser* had learned its lesson!

> One of the buses returning from Comunn na Feinne sports yesterday afternoon was brought to a sudden stand-still owing to the fracture of the axel (sic) of the front wheels. The heavy-laden vehicle dropped with a thud on the soft side of the road, and the outside passengers were landed upon terra firma with a suddenness that surprised them. Fortunately, the passengers [on] the disabled vehicle suffered nothing beyond a slight scare as the results of the accident. Whilst the procession was on its way to the grounds in the morning, the pole of the wagonette employed for the conveyance of the officers was broken in some way or another. The horses began to play up and the occupants of the vehicle, who did not wait for instructions in the matter, surprised themselves by the agility with which they [leapt] over the wheels.

Although the *Geelong Advertiser* was full of praise for the shift of venue to the Geelong Agricultural Grounds, it found the Society's claim that the new venue "enabled Comunn na Feinne to include events which could not have been brought off with success at South Geelong", was not substantiated, there being no augmentation of the 1896 offerings. The *Advertiser* continued, however, that the new venue was obviously appreciated by the public and the programme was still, "one of an extremely attractive character". The newspaper had even mellowed enough to include in its description, "a number of cycling events all of which produced excellent competition …" and, for the first time since their inception, there was no pile up or machine failure to be reported! Peter Fleming was still showing the younger breed of athletes that he was not yet a spent force. A first in Throwing the Hammer and a second, to George F. Worland (yet another of the clan!), in Tossing the Caber, were his rewards for an excellent performance.

As for the Gathering, overall, "the native-born successors to the founders of Comunn na Feinne must be credited with making the celebration of the birth of 1897 worthy of the occasion." Once again tartans and the green and gold of the St Patrick's Society mingled amicably in the Parade. At the grounds, the President, Mr Neil Campbell, addressed the spectators and, after apologizing for the absence of their Chief, Mr Philip Russell, welcomed all and alluded to the nature of the Society, "that had brought Scotch and Hibernians together in connection with the national celebration of the former."

But amid all of this *bonhomie* and praise for the new grounds, a voice of dissent arose, albeit directed only at the "inept" preparation of a small section of the total size of the new sports area.

> TO THE EDITOR.
> Sir, ... I, with other visitors, travelled to the Pivot on New Year's Day solely for the purpose of seeing a scientific exposition of the good old game of quoits, and seeing that not only the champions of your own district, but such doughty men as Cameron, Crowe, Redici, etc., turn up, one would not be disappointed, were it not that the authorities in charge of the sports, who advertise "clay ends," got some novice to prepare the ground, with the result that a bucketful of sand and mud, with a little water added, is the apology for same; I felt really sorry for those gentlemen who came all the way from Melbourne and other places on New Year's Day to enjoy and see a good game, for those men are genuine sports, and play purely for the honor of winning, and certainly not for the paltry prizes given, which are a disgrace to the town, considering the interest taken in the event. The whole of the management of the great "Highland gathering" needs remodelling, as it is carried out in a very unbusinesslike manner, and if things are not soon altered it will not only be quoit players who will strike (as on the last New Year's Day), but other competitors as well, and the ground, which should, if the sports were properly managed, be crowded to their utmost capacity, will be deserted by competitors and onlookers alike. Apologizing for taking up so much of your valuable space.
> *Pro Bono Publico.*

The correspondent's letter, as printed in the *Advertiser* of the 24th January, had made a passing reference to the derisory prizes awarded by Comunn na Feinne which were, it added, "a disgrace to the town". But the correspondent's claim that a "strike" had ensued among the contestants over the state of the Quoits' rink at the 1896 Games is not borne out in any contemporary account of this event. The *Advertiser*, for example, in its report of the Games, has no reference to such an action by Quoits' contestants, and the event took place without any apparent disruption or complaint regarding the state of the Quoits' rink. It is ironic, too, that barely two years after the Society had undergone a change in management, that this correspondent describes the running of the Games "unbusinesslike" and calls for a "remodelling" of Comunn na Feinne management. Obviously, not a happy customer! The *Advertiser*'s report on the 1897 Games does not mention any of the claims made in the correspondent's letter!

The newspaper's spirit of praise for the Gathering itself, as well as for Comunn na Feinne's management of the Games, spilled over into its 3rd January report on the 1898 Gathering where, it said, that although not innovative, the Society's balance between traditional games and newer sports was just about right.

> It must be conceded that on this occasion the directors of the annual Comunn na Feinne Gathering excelled all previous efforts ... The national characteristics of the holiday were preserved by the liberal provision made in the programme for Highland pastimes, but the directors were equally generous in regard to the sports which are sought after by cosmopolitan assemblages. ... The programme was so varied and extensive that several events were frequently to be seen in progress at one time. It was of a character to please everybody, for the tastes of both branches of the Celtic family were studied in the matter of dancing, and competitions in the athletic events, in which the Australian youth delighted to shine, was of a very excellent description.

Given the greater distance from the town to the new grounds, the usual procession was "abandoned" for 1898. However, a "kilted band" [ten pipers who played together on the day rather than an established pipe band] had made a reasonable attempt at it, "and with pipes full blast, marched up Moorabool Street and for some distance along Ryrie Street." But, as the *Advertiser* added, even the pipers had to resort to "cabs" to finish their journey! The day's proceedings opened with a parade of 'Hielan' men, "who assembled this year in greater strength than was ever experienced before in connection with the celebration." The display, "was warmly appreciated by those [in] whom national sentiment has survived transplantation amidst the more diverse conditions of Australian life."

The attendance at the 1898 Gathering was good but, noted the *Advertiser* longwindedly, "it did not realize expectations, [but] from the all-round expressions of appreciation elicited by the [crowd] it may safely be affirmed that the efforts of the Comunn na Feinne officials to enhance the attractiveness of their annual gathering will not go unrecognized." In other words, "well done". The *Advertiser*'s opinion that the Society had been revitalized, was borne out in its descriptions of the spectators' responses to performances. Everything, it wrote, seemed to have been better appreciated by the spectators than ever before. The dancing was excellent, the heavy games, and the strength displayed, "excited a great deal more enthusiasm than they would otherwise have evoked." The cycling events proved exciting enough even without the usual crashes! The Band of St Augustine's Orphanage in Geelong played to appreciative spectators and the boys from both Orphanages afterwards enjoyed the repast provided by Comunn na Feinne. If there was a surfeit of superlatives, this only reflected the spectators' own responses to the events.

Similarly, the *Advertiser* also saw something new in the Society's Scottish Concerts. Although these had regularly been staged by the Society, the *Advertiser* sought to present the latest one as an innovation and a new addition to Comunn na Feinne's offerings. Under the headline "Comunn na Feinne Revival", it reported the popularity of a "Scottish entertainment" held at the Mechanics' Institute. This concert was successfully repeated the following year on 20th September, 1899, again at the Mechanics' Institute Hall, to bring in some much-needed revenue. Scottish entertainers, locally and from Melbourne, amused a packed house. Repeated encores, demanded by the audience and, "generously responded to", kept the audience, and performers, to a late hour.

The annual Directors' Meeting for 1898 shared the general opinion that the Gathering was, "from a natural point of view a gratifying success." However, the attendance was not what was expected and, despite the excellence of the programme, a loss of £25 resulted. There was good news in that the Geelong Agricultural Society had refunded Comunn na Feinne £5 and had decided, rather than take fifty per cent of the net gate receipts for the Society's use of the ground, that, "only 12½ percent on receipts up to £100 and 10 percent on anything over that amount" would be charged. The Financial concerns of the Society were now a regular and more earnest topic of discussion at Comunn na Feinne business meetings. There was reference again to the Society's need for additional revenue to fund its activities and its charitable concerns. Appeals were made to the existing members to try and recruit more members. George R. King regretfully resigned from the secretary-ship of the Society due to the demands of his position at the Gordon Institute and Alexander McRae was elected to fill his place.

New Year's Day 1899 fell on a Sunday, delaying the Comunn na Feinne Games until the Monday by which time, after three consecutive days of above century temperatures, a drastic change, from scorching heat to wintry conditions, had occurred. This sudden drop in temperature had driven spectators from light summer wear and into, "woollen garments and great-coats". The conditions, "half gale, half rain squall," undoubtedly interfered with the box office, although the *Advertiser*, in its 3rd January report on the Gathering, remarked that:

> It came as an agreeable surprise to the directors that so many people could be induced to spend the day at an open-air demonstration under such unfavourable conditions. Nevertheless, the show ring was well fringed with spectators, and the grand stand was almost filled, and the gate receipts were better than those of the previous year, when more favourable conditions prevailed. It is pleasing to note this because the directors had made liberal provision in the way of prize-money to secure a really attractive holiday programme for the Geelong public.

With some of its masterly understatement, the newspaper's account of the attendance at the ensuing Games suggested, not so much a stoicism on the part of "auld Scotia's sons" in the face of discouraging weather, but more an example of a Scotsman's endeavour who, "having spent a saxpence," was determined to get his money's worth despite the uncomfortable circumstances!

The President (Neil Campbell) welcomed the assembly of spectators, competitors and officials and alluded to some of the prominent athletes and prize winners of the past, and other "old identities" from the early years of Comunn na Feinne, who were present at the current Games. These men were assembled in the ground's pavilion where spectators were invited to meet them. A number of these old-time competitors in the Heavy Games, such as John Clinnick and John McLennan were now passing on their experience as present-day judges of those events in which they had excelled. Reference was also made to the educational influence exercised by the Society in the early days when such men as Professor Kernot* and the Allen brothers* were proud, as school students, to gain its silver medal for educational excellence.

*[See Appendix 3 (b) Short Biographies.]

Group of Veteran Athletes.
L to R – J. McLennan, P. Fleming, J. Hennesy, F.L. Davidson, H.R. Frederico, C. Warner, H.D. Smith and J. Galbraith

The *Advertiser* had, in the last two Gatherings, decidedly warmed to the bicycling events, and the Games of 1899 found it still in this mood. "Cycling was a big feature of the programme and local riders cannot complain of want of encouragement so far as the Society is concerned." The newspaper recognized, however, that the weather conditions, especially the strong winds, were going to affect performances and, in the case of cycling, although all of the races took place as usual, the gales prevented, "any record performances" but, nevertheless, the contests were keenly fought out with some exciting finishes. The weather obviously had its own way of thinning out the numbers who started in some of the cycling races and it was truly a case of 'last man standing' in some instances. In the Three Mile Amateur Championship for cyclists, for example, the weather played a crucial part in determining the winner. There were eleven competitors who started in this race and by the last lap, this number had been reduced to five. However, only two out of the eleven starters actually finished the race, owing to an accident near the home turn. "Greenfield skidded and fell heavily and New, the Sydney amateur champion, rode over the embankment in endeavouring to avoid a collision. Shrimpton, who was riding splendidly, followed suit and the race was reduced to a tame go between the placed men." Courageously, Greenfield came out "immediately afterwards in two events, one of which he won." Shrimpton and New, unfortunately, were so affected by the crash that they were not able to participate in other races for which they had entered.

Cycling events at the annual Geelong Gathering continued to grow in popularity and increased in number, with some cyclists being drawn from interstate and with some of the races counting towards Victorian State titles. Comunn na Feinne also provided races for both amateur and professional riders. All of this meant, of course, that tracks had to be laid according to the standards of the cycling clubs which had now been established. Given the number of bicycling events being offered by Comunn na Feinne, the *Geelong Advertiser*, in its report of the 1899 Games, stated that, "local riders cannot complain of want of encouragement as far as the Society is concerned."

The annual general meeting of the Society for 1899 was held and the Report of the last games was prefaced with a self-congratulatory pat on the back. A credit balance of £16/14/11 was posted for the year, up from the £1/16/9 balance of the previous year, and the meeting was informed that the Society could anticipate a bright future for itself. Nevertheless, despite the less than overflowing bank account, the Society's support for other local bodies was not totally curtailed. Under the Society's auspices, for example, the Geelong Town Band gave a concert in November, 1899, in Johnstone Park, a venue named in honour of the late President, Robert de Bruce Johnstone who, when Mayor of Geelong, had been responsible for the Park's creation. The Band, ever-needy for funds, would have been pleased that the Benefit Concert cleared £27 for its coffers.

The Annual Directors' Meeting was held under the Chairmanship of the President, Neil Campbell, who, with wholehearted support from all present, moved to invite the Minister for Defence, "to accept office as a member of Comunn na Feinne." As we have seen, from its inception, it was not unusual for Comunn na Feinne to seek those whom it regarded as 'movers and shakers' in society to accept membership or position within the organization. The Society's strategy in extending such an invitation to the Minister for Defence had a definite purpose, and a request was soon made to the Ministry of Defence to allow the Victorian Scottish Regiment* to attend Comunn na Feinne's 1900 New Year's Day Highland Gathering. The Society had put some thought into how it would frame its request.

> Feeling certain ... that they would not be permitted to visit Geelong for show purposes alone, the Directors had drafted a programme of Military events ... It has been submitted to the Military Authorities for their sanction, and it was confidently anticipated by the Directors that, on New Year's Day, the Members of Comunn na Feinne, would have the pleasure of witnessing the Victorian Scottish Regiment, competing against a detachment from the various Regiments of the Colony.

*[The story of this Regiment is taken up more fully in Appendix 14 (b).]

A meeting of the Directors on 21st December, 1899, making final preparations for the upcoming New Year's Day Gathering, decided, as had been done on many other occasions, to invite the children of the two Orphanages and to entertain them with food and amusements. It was also announced that correspondence had been received from the secretary of the Victorian Scottish Regiment stating that approval had been given for the Regiment to appear at the next New Year's Day Gathering. The Regiment would take part in the pre-games Procession to the grounds along with other groups such as the Flinders School Detachment of the Gordon Highlanders, "headed with a miniature piper in full dress." During the day, the Regiment would give an exhibition of "Bayonet" and "manual firing" exercises, as well as competing against other Volunteer Defence groups involved in the Gathering.

The success in getting the Victorian Scottish Regiment to attend its Gathering proved to be a master stroke on the part of the Society. There was a growing sense of pride in the military forces and this was shown in the huge popularity of this Regiment. With the waning, in the later years of the nineteenth century, of possible military threats to Australia, the need for Voluntary defence forces fell away and most had been disbanded by the 1880s. The Volunteer Victorian Scottish Regiment, however, continued in a semi-permanent form and, after the outbreak of WW1 many of its volunteers took part in military action overseas as members of another fully professional Regiment. A new regiment was formed and many of the Volunteers joined this unit called the 5th Battalion Infantry Battalion (Victorian Scottish Regiment) and saw service at Gallipoli and Europe.

The Victorian Scottish Regiment.

New Year's Day, 1900, dawned hot with the promise of it growing even hotter! Despite the heat, the long march to the Showground was joined by 70 members of the Victorian Scottish Regiment, "in full dress, and [they] naturally formed the centre of attraction, their fine physiques being set off to advantage in their picturesque regimental garb." The Regiment provided an enormous attraction and, with its own Pipe Band, generated much excitement. Unfortunately, even in well regimented events, things do not always go as planned. The following year, for example, the Regiment, arriving at Geelong, assembled at the departure point with their Pipe Band and, due to a misunderstanding, immediately took off for the grounds setting a cracking pace orchestrated by its Band playing some "inspiring Scottish airs." However, the rest of the procession was still gathering at the departure point and was more or less left standing!

The local newspaper was full of praise for the first Games of the new decade giving its greatest pat on the back to the Victorian Scottish Regiment and praising the Society for the hospitality offered to the men. Also attending, and taking part in the Gathering, was a voluntary military group from Ballarat. Thus, the Games were very much enlivened by this Military presence especially as the soldiers went through their paces giving demonstrations of marching, bayonet exercises and volley firing. The Scottish Regiment wound up its performance with a mock battle, "storming the grandstand at the bayonet point." What the ladies (who normally sat in the grand stand) thought, or exclaimed, about their position being stormed by charging soldiers 'at bayonet point' is not recorded! Other activities continued the martial flavour. There were single stick events, fencing displays and a tug of war whose final, between the Regiment and a team from the Ballarat Voluntary Infantry, was a promoter's dream with the 'amateurs' being victorious over the 'professionals' - Ballarat carrying off the trophy!

A highlight of the Athletics was the appearance of the veteran John Clinnick, but this time in the Vaulting with Pole event! He secured second place. George Worland, of the Worland dynasty of Games athletes, several years a winner or place-getter in the heavy games, at last came into his own when, for the first time, he captured the triple crown of the heavy games winning the Caber, the Heavy Hammer and the Heavy Stone events. He was proving a worthy successor to the likes of Clinnick, Fleming and Powell, as well as to the long line of Worland family athletes.

A new championship event in Bag-piping had been introduced whereby the piper gaining most points over the three sections of piping – Pìobaireachd, Strathspeys and Reels, and Marches – was declared Champion Piper of Victoria, a title held for the year. J. Stewart was the inaugural winner at the 1900 Games and declared the first Champion Piper of Victoria.

The start of the new decade also became a time when the Society re-assessed its charitable role within the community. It formulated the idea of holding a series of country concerts, in aid of charity funds, which would also create a Comunn na Feinne presence in outlying areas including, initially, Winchelsea, Camperdown, Drysdale and Lara. The year 1900 also marked a change, somewhat, in the *Advertiser*'s reporting of Comunn na Feinne. Although still giving its report of the New Year's Day Gathering, the newspaper was now giving more coverage to the Society's events which were being held during the year than it did to the Highland Games. This was particularly so as it related to the amusements, balls, other social events and concerts either run by the Society or under its auspices. The central aim of these events during the year was, initially, to fund the variety of charities which the Society supported. Sadly, as it transpired, a great deal of the funds raised tended to gravitate towards paying the expenses of such concerts especially if the entertainers were professional or semi-professional ones from Melbourne, as was the case in the Society's first concert for 1900.

As the Society moved into the rest of the year with its activities, it held its annual 'Grand Scottish Concert,' on 1st August, 1900. The Mechanics' Hall was crowded from 'floor to rafters' so much so that another concert had to be promised for those who could not gain entry (a promise which was fulfilled by a concert on 26th September, 1900). The *Geelong Advertiser*, in its report of 2nd August, said that, "New life has been put into the Comunn na Feinne, one of Geelong's historic institutions, which was formed in 1856 … Convincing evidence of the revival was furnished at the Mechanics' Hall last evening, an immense audience being attracted to that place by the

Scottish entertainment given under the auspices of the Society." Well known Scottish entertainers from Melbourne, including Maggie McCann and Hector McLennan, were among the performers.

It is not clear whether these concerts were ever a major contributor to the Society's coffers. Sometimes attendances were large, sometimes not. The vagaries of the weather must have exerted some influence, as would the existence of a Hogmanay concert the previous evening. But, the main inhibitor to turning a good profit on these events was the aim to put on a good show. This meant using 'expensive' entertainers from Melbourne and, as a consequence, the net financial gain from such concerts could be considerably smaller after paying their fees.

This new-found energy of Comunn na Feinne, directed towards money-making, can be witnessed in the number of events, outside the sporting arena, in which it was engaging. The Grand Scottish Concert held on 1st August, 1900 had no sooner finished when yet another social engagement was announced for the next night! With barely enough time to draw their collective breath, Comunn na Feinne members, and Geelong and district folks, were out in force the following evening to attend a crowded dining chamber at the Prince of Wales Hotel for a Haggis Supper, "promoted by the Comunn na Feinne Society." Although Burns had written that, "the sure way to gain Scotland's grateful prayer is to 'Gie her a haggis' … there were many at the supper who undertook the investigation of the mysterious composition with no small amount of trepidation as to the after results."

Comunn na Feinne seemed to have concluded that its financial needs could only be met by turning its attention more towards activities which guaranteed a measure of profit rather than relying upon wealthy patrons or the flagship annual Gathering. By 1900 the Society was increasingly aware that it needed to be holding profit-making events more often, especially to meet its charitable commitments. As the *Advertiser*, rather unsubtly declared, the Society had to face the fact that the days when its supporters, such as Major John Bell, would provide Comunn na Feinne with a signed blank cheque to cover expenses, were mostly passed.

One attempt to increase income was to continue with its evening concert, after the New Year's Day Games, and devote the profits to its operating expenses. Such concerts operated from 1900 to 1929, usually outdoors, at Johnstone Park or Kardinia Park. The Society also provided a Hogmanay Scottish Entertainment at Johnstone Park on old year's night on 31st December, 1900, with between 3,000 and 4,000 people paying for admission. The evening was enthusiastically received by the crowds that attended. A large number of dances were performed by some of those who, the next day, would be competing for the medals on offer. Other items included songs and humorous recitations and the playing of the Town Brass Band which, after the concert, was driven around Geelong in a dray while playing Scottish airs. Midnight was brought in by the Band playing 'A Guid New Year,' and then, 'Auld lang syne.' It may have failed to register with many that they would be going to sleep as plain Victorians but waking up as Australian citizens in the new Commonwealth!

It is clear that Comunn na Feinne, despite its increasing financial woes, was not altogether neglecting its charitable role as can be witnessed in an open letter, published in the Geelong *News of the Week*, 24th August, 1900, by a recipient of such help.

> Sir, allow me to convey through your newspaper the deep gratitude of myself and children to the Comunn na Feinne Society, Dr John Small and all those who so generously assisted us in our time of trouble, and also to you for what you have done for us."
> I am etc
> John Cameron.

But Comunn na Feinne's own financial needs were by now extremely grave. The annual Directors' meeting on 8th October, 1900, revealed how precarious the finances of the Society had become due in part to the incompetence of the Treasurer. But it was not only the Treasurer who had been incompetent. The President, Neil Campbell, reported that it had been difficult for the Directors to gauge the financial position of the Society, "through the failure of their late secretary to supply them with a proper statement of the Society's position." Something like a disaster had only been averted when the Society's overdraft, held at the Commercial Bank, and all outstanding accounts owing by the Society were, generously, guaranteed by the Directors.

> [T]he Directors rose to the occasion, and by making themselves personally liable guaranteed that all claims against the Society would be met to the extent of twenty shillings in the pound.

George Raymond King, who had resigned his position as secretary of the Society a few years earlier, in the face of this latest financial crisis, was brought back and appointed Treasurer. Not for the first or last time, George R. King was to rescue the Society from financial chaos. With the removal of the secretary as well as the treasurer, James Galbraith was elected to the position. The President said that the Society, "had every reason to be thankful in having James Galbraith and George Raymond King to fill the offices as secretary and treasurer respectively."

Also present at this meeting was office-bearer Charles Shannon, who was to continue the vision of Douglas, Johnstone, Shirra and others, through his concern for street children and other problem youth of his day. Shannon, a Comunn na Feinne Vice-President, together with some other Society office-bearers and supporters, and some concerned townsfolk, later established, at Geelong, an organization called the 'Try Boys Movement'. Shannon had witnessed such an organization in Melbourne and had seen the good results that it was capable of achieving.

An unexpected attempt (and a perverse one given the desperate need for a general increase in members) to restrict membership of Comunn na Feinne to those of Scottish birth or descent was, by a large majority, defeated when put to the vote. The unpopularity of this motion was made clear when a counter motion that membership should continue to be 'open' was then put and overwhelmingly passed. A further resolution, having great bearing on the Society's need for increased finance, related to increasing membership fees. The discussion by members showed how unrealistic a majority of them were regarding fees. The existing fee included the privilege of the member inviting two guests to the Games without any extra charge. This effectively meant that three people were being admitted for the price of one! The motion, proposed by George R. King, and supported by the Directors, that subscriptions should be increased from 5/- to 10/6d in order for members to hold these same privileges was defeated. The long battle to improve the Society's finances in the face of unrealistic expectations of members, is taken up in more detail in a later chapter of this book.

After three decades of 'ups' and 'downs', Comunn na Feinne was now about to enter into a new century, and into the new Commonwealth, still plagued with the lack of a solid financial base and at a loss how to instill in all its members realistic fiscal common sense! Seeking maximum personal value from their membership fees, and insisting that fundraisers engage the best available entertainers were not ways to generate high profits with which to sustain the Society's philanthropic endeavours. However, over a good part of the next two decades the Society entered probably its 'golden' period. The key positions of Chief, President, Treasurer and Secretary were filled by men of leadership, ability and organizational skills, and they were to take the Society from the uncertainty of survival to a period of relative prosperity, stability and popularity. The outbreak of war in 1914 signalled the beginning of the end of this golden period and, as will be seen, marked the slow decline of the Society.

Chapter 5

1901 – 1920. "The Best of Times – The Worst of Times"

New Year's Day 1901 had an additional significance not only for the people of Geelong, but for the whole of Australia. Apart from the Society's usual Gathering, the first day of 1901 marked the beginning of the Commonwealth of Australia, "which was greeted with cheers and general good humour." The *Advertiser*, on 2nd January, 1901, warming to its subject, and with a measure of pride, reported that the colonies were now one people and, unlike the American states, there had neither been a war of independence with Britain, nor a civil war among her own states, in order to bring about this union. Australia, continued the paper, could offer a lesson to the world.

In fact, festivities had already begun, with Comunn na Feinne holding a large, crowded and boisterous Scottish concert on old year's night, Monday 31st December, 1900, at Johnstone Park.

> Between 3,000 and 4,000 people paid for admission, and the scene in the vicinity of the park Rotunda was one of remarkable animation. The crowd was in a most enthusiastic mood, and every number on the varied programme was well received. The entertainment started about nine o'clock, when the Society's hon. Piper, Mr D. McLennan, played 'Lochiel's Gathering,' …" Highland dancing and many Scottish songs were performed together with some pawky humour which was met with repeated calls for encores – which were met by the performers. The Geelong Town Band also provided "several numbers", both Scottish and English, which were "excellently interpreted." At midnight, the birth of the new century was welcomed by the bandsmen playing, 'A Guid New Year', and 'Auld Lang Syne,' and the audience spiritedly took up the refrain of the latter number. Subsequently hearty cheers were given for the

Commonwealth of Australia and Her Majesty the Queen, and with the singing of the National Anthem the crowd gradually dispersed.

Proving once more their stamina, the spectators seemed no worse for wear after their late-night experience in Johnstone Park, and it seemed to have done nothing to dampen their mood as, early morning, they wound their way to the Showgrounds for the Annual New Year's Day Highland Gathering. The *Advertiser* was kindness itself, maintaining its buoyant mood when, in its first editorial of the new year, it welcomed the new Commonwealth, the new Century and the New Year, all of which could be considered "auspicious" for Comunn na Feinne. This was evident in the record gate takings from the Gathering with the total amounting to £160. Of course, it added, harking back to points made in its editorial on the new Commonwealth, this did not happen without hard work and great effort on the part of individuals. The *Advertiser* reported that the new century had begun, as far as the Highland Gathering was concerned, with a pleasing display of tartan.

> Never before has the picturesque Highland garb been in such prominence here as it was yesterday. Apart from the [Victorian Scottish] Regiment one of the most gratifying features of the gathering, so far as the directors were concerned, was the large muster of adults and children of both sexes in the national costume.

While praise was given to the Scottish events on the programme, the newspaper said that these were not at the expense of the other items which were indispensable features of an outdoor meeting. The military exercises, and the variety of other games and competitions added to the enthusiasm already shown by the crowd of spectators. This was especially so when the Victorian Scottish Regiment gave its display:

> Besides treating the onlookers to well executed marching evolutions, the Regiment gave an exhibition of volley firing succeeded by a bayonet charge. Physical drill and bayonet exercise by squads also formed an interesting part of the performance.

Having learned from their previous appearance in the blistering heat of the previous New Year's Day, the Victorian Scottish Regiment, "did not parade in their new scarlet tunics, which are made of heavy material, but in the more serviceable war paint [informal uniform]; they were none the less effective, and the physique of the men excited the admiration of those who witnessed them on the march and at the grounds."

Although the games were a great success, the lack of attention to the actual sporting events given in the *Advertiser*'s report suggests that there was little exciting enough to comment upon. Dress and the display of the Victorian Scottish Regiment seem to dominate the description of the Games proper; the "marching revolutions of the kilted soldiers around the cycling track made one of the most picturesque features of the gathering that was in itself well worth a visit to the grounds." Cycling races were described with their routinely guaranteed smash-ups. However, with little more than skinned knees and abrasions resulting from the various collisions, these barely raised the paper's interest, or concern.

Similarly, the Tug of War competitions, with each side having eight men, did not generate much colour or excitement to put before the readers. The Scottish Regiment was victorious over Barwon, and Moodie's team defeated the Wharf Labourers, with Murphy's team being disqualified. All that brawn and no short fuses – unbelievable! Surely the *Advertiser* was looking the other way! The reason for the disqualification of Murphy's team is left unreported – and, probably, to the reader's imagination!

Although the 'giants' of the Heavy Games, such as Clinnick, Fleming, McLennan and Powell, did not make it into the new century as competitors in their favourite events, the Worland name continued past that milestone when yet another George Worland appeared among the contestants. But a new name also began frequently to appear in the results of these traditional Highland field events. Duncan Cameron (from Ballarat), at the 1901 Games, won the Heavy Hammer and Heavy Stone competitions and came a creditable second in Tossing the Caber, beating the favourite George Worland into third place. Cameron almost pulled off the 'treble' again in 1902 but missed out on the Caber event by mere inches to another newcomer, D. Creed. Comunn na Feinne had much to be proud of when its official Piper Donald ('Dosh') McLennan "secured the coveted honour" of Champion Piper of Victoria for 1901 with a first in the Pìobaireachd and with two second placings in the Marches and in the Strathspeys and Reels competitions respectively, beating the previous year's winner, J. Stewart, by a point. McLennan repeated his victory in 1902 with a larger margin but had to bow, in 1903, to the brilliant playing of Hugh Fraser, a piper, reported the *Advertiser* on 2nd January, 1903, with the Band of the Scottish Regiment, and a member of a family of champion pipers.

Donald 'Dosh' McLennan – Hon Piper to Comunn Na Feinne.

At a meeting of Comunn na Feinne on 13th July, 1901, the Society showed its gratitude to its Secretary, James Galbraith, for his untiring services at the 1901 Games and, "in recognition of the manner in which he has conducted the Society's business during the past 12 months," awarded him a bonus of £20. Reasons for this gesture emerged at the annual Directors' Meeting which took place in October of that year. Although the previous year's report was a discouraging one, the Society had been much uplifted by what had taken place over the year since then.

> The report on the previous year … whilst indicative of promise, was of a character, to say the least, disheartening. At the commencement of the year the finances showed a debit of £15/8/11, but with the work and the

unbounded enthusiasm of the hon. Secretary [James Galbraith], they were in a position to report a balance in the bank of £63/10/0.

The meeting further reported that the 1901 Highland Gathering had been, "the largest in the experience of the Society." The presence of the Victorian Scottish Regiment, the success of the Society's own Hon. Piper, Donald "Dosh" McLennan, and the support of the public, were all factors for which the Society was grateful. George Raymond King, the treasurer, was also singled out for praise in having "helped considerably to bring about the splendid financial position." Comunn na Feinne, its hierarchy believed, seemed poised to enjoy a period of success which might justifiably be called, "the best of times".

An addition to the Comunn na Feinne's social activities during the year, had been the setting up of a Fishing Club. This had its first outing on 30th October, 1901, and was duly reported in the *Advertiser* on 1st November. A large party, making up two teams, set out to see who could get the heaviest overall catch of fish for the day. Although a winning team was eventually declared, it was certainly not the one containing 'Dosh' McLennan, the Society's piper, whose individual contribution for the afternoon consisted of a single two-inch flathead drawn, after much struggle, "from the mighty deep."

Following lunch, and with bagpipes at full power, some of the party staged, on the dunes at Barwon, an impromptu re-enactment of the Gordon Highlanders storming the heights of Dargai. In the official account of the original charge, it is not recorded that the Highlanders had to stop half way up their ascent for a "wee drap o' mountain dew" with which to fortify their resolve, and to draw breath. Those acting out the mock ascent of the dunes at Barwon Heads found such a pause to be "expedient". So great was the effect on the party, and so much was extra "vigour" now inhabiting them, that "Highland reels and dances" instantly broke out on the sands of the beach, "to the accompaniment of the skirl of the pipes and the crashing ocean waves." With the national standard of Scotland, "unfurled by the proprietor of the Coffee Palace, floating proudly over the braes of Barwon Heads," and with the health of the Society's

President liberally toasted, the outing, regarded as a great success, came to a close.

A decision had been made in 1900 that the Society inaugurate visits by a concert party to outlying towns and that the profits be used for charitable purposes. This scheme was inaugurated on 12th November, 1901, with a concert party of about 50 people travelling to Drysdale where they entertained a crowded Free Library Hall to great acclaim. In a busy month of meetings in December, the Directors on 2nd December, heard the report of the successful Drysdale concert and agreed that such concerts be continued. Winchelsea was selected as the next target town, with details of the visit being confirmed at a further meeting on 16th December where it was also announced that a recruitment drive had proved reasonably successful with thirty-four new members being admitted to the Society.

The Directors met again on 23rd December, 1901 to finalize the New Year's Day Gathering for 1902 and to announce confirmation that 120 members of the Victorian Scottish Regiment, "accompanied by two bands," would again be taking part. The *Advertiser* of the 24th December, reporting the meeting, also noted that as the barque *Balmore* was visiting at the time, and that the officers and crew being, "all Scotsmen," the Society agreed that they be invited, "to attend the New Year's Gathering." Confirmation had also been received from the Geelong Council granting the Society permission to hold its New Year's Day Evening Concert at Johnstone Park.

The *Advertiser*, on the last day of December 1901, provided the upcoming New Year's Games with some last-minute promotion. It promised an attractive and varied programme with events such as would satisfy the range of tastes of the spectators, from Scottish Heavy Games to Bicycling and track events and from Dancing to Solo Piping. For the second year, the Geelong Agricultural Show Grounds was to be the venue. An announcement was also made regarding the presence of the Scottish Regiment at the upcoming 1902 Games and that it would stage a re-enactment of the Gordon Highlanders' "Famous Charge on the Dargai Heights," as it had done at the previous year's Gathering. The street procession would also take place and it promised colour and excitement as 120 members of the Scottish Regiment dressed in their new red doublets, along with their Pipe Band, would be part of the march to the grounds. In addition to this, there was to be a mass demonstration of Highland Dancing. Cobb & Co had also promised "to despatch a special coach from Portarlington, Drysdale and Bellerine, for the purpose of giving district residents an opportunity of attending the Comunn na Feinne Games."

This final Comunn na Feinne Committee meeting of the year further announced that a Scottish Hogmanay Concert was to be held at Johnstone Park with many Melbourne entertainers in attendance. Bands would provide music through the streets of Geelong leading up to the time of the concert and the admission price was set at sixpence. A large crowd gathered in the Park for this event and were well entertained by singers, dancers and musicians, until the New Year was announced.

The following morning the Procession from the town to the grounds took place amid great excitement with the Victorian Regiment's own pipe band and 120 men from the Regiment leading the march. "In their picturesque dress the Highlanders were an object of much attraction to the crowds that held possession of the streets." Unlike the previous year's misunderstanding, the Regiment waited until the whole procession had been assembled before taking off! St Augustine's Brass Band followed with Comunn na Feinne members and then a "creditable muster of boys and girls in Highland garb", falling in behind them. The Victorian Scottish Regiment proved, again, to be a big hit at the 1902 Games. Its marching, and manoeuvres, its bayonet displays, its mock battle scene and the playing of its Band were all very much appreciated and applauded. There was a very full programme of events and, concluded the *Advertiser*'s report, "it was late in the evening before the enjoyable proceedings were brought to a close."

And, at last, a return to some controversy! Who would have thought it that in the 'genteel' sport of 'tug-o'-war', some skullduggery would be alleged! But, indeed, it was the Tug-of-War contest which provided its own excitement with a controversial finish. The semi-final between Moolap Imperial and D. Moodie's team promised to be a close pull but, as it happened, Moolap won within one minute. Moodie's team was then accused of having used, not one but two, 'ring-ins,' Nixon and Purtle, who, it was claimed, were two members the World's Fair Team. Moodie's reduced squad, with the removal of these two men, had less pulling power and, "had no chance against Moolap's full team" which, later, went on to take the championship. But controversy was not confined to the 'grunt' events. In the Handicap Half-Mile Race, there were thirteen starters. The first to break the tape was W. Wilson but a protest was immediately lodged by Coles, the runner-up, who alleged that Wilson had run under another name at sports meetings in the Western District. Coles' allegation was supported by J. Beasland and, "as Wilson refused to make a declaration [the] officials upheld the protest and awarded the prize to Coles who had finished second in the race." Further controversy arose out of the same race when it was alleged that during the race:

> M. Heyward deliberately interfered with Allie and any chance the latter might have had was thereby destroyed. The official after very careful consideration decided to disqualify Heyward for life and other [officials] will be requested to endorse his action.

A Directors' Meeting was held on 30th January, 1902 and, as reported in the *Advertiser* the following day, the balance sheet for the Gathering showed a surplus of £60. "The result was considered highly satisfactory especially when it was taken into account that a good deal of expenditure was involved in bringing the Victorian Scottish Regiment to Geelong." It was agreed, after the success of Drysdale and Winchelsea, to continue the county concerts and that Portarlington and Lara would be the next target towns. It was further announced, in connection with these concerts, that "Hector McLennan, the well-known performer from Melbourne, had been engaged to assist [at these concerts.]" As previously noted, this use of 'professional', and 'semi-professional', entertainers from Melbourne, while greatly contributing to the success of these events, severely reduced any ensuing profit for the Society's charity fund.

Various social events were held by Comunn na Feinne during 1902 including, on 21st July, a musical night, with a limelight picture show of views of the Scottish Highlands, "and of the Black Watch Highlanders in full marching order", as well as views of other Scottish Regiments. Dr John Small, presided and many local vocalists performed, including a recital by George R. King. The Society's Annual Haggis Supper was held on the 12th August and this was rapidly followed by the Society's annual concert on 18th August, 1902, when the Mechanics' Institute Hall was filled with a large and enthusiastic crowd which was, "complimentary to the popularity of a Scottish entertainment and to the excellent … programme." Well known Scottish entertainers from Melbourne, such as comedian Hector McLennan and professional singers such as J. Gregor Wood and Miss Maggie McCann, gave good service with a variety of Scottish and Irish songs. Hector McLennan's performance, consisting of comic acting as well as singing, had "the crowd worked up to a state of enthusiastic applause." The audience, which encored nearly every act, kept the entertainment going to a very late hour.

At a Directors' Meeting of the Society on 11th September, 1902, the Treasurer, George R. King, brought to the notice of the Society that the Mayoral Chain of Geelong did not have a link, "to mark the terms of office of Robert de Bruce Johnstone, who was one of the earliest and hardest workers in Comunn na Feinne." The members immediately "subscribed the sum amongst themselves", and the present mayor was to be requested, "to have the link manufactured at the expense of the Society." The Society's Annual Meeting followed shortly on the heels of the Directors' one, and it was announced that, with the considerable number of new members enrolled for the year, the membership total now stood at ninety-eight and was rapidly increasing.

A significant change in the hierarchy of the Society took place when Dr John Small, the vice-President, was elected President in place of Neil Campbell who stood down from that position. Campbell remarked that, "if they were in a low position [financially and numerically] he would not ask another man to take charge, but he had been with them through troublesome times to prosperity, and he was now desirous of vacating the chair to give other members a chance of occupying the position. Neil Campbell was elected a life member for his services to the Society. Phillip Russell, last of the landed patrons of the Society, had been elected Chief of Comunn na Feinne in 1896 on the resignation of Captain Chirnside. In these two men, Dr Small and Phillip Russell, together with the secretary, James Galbraith, and the 'occasional' treasurer, George R. King, the Society had found an executive whose joint efforts in financial and practical affairs, stabilized Comunn na Feinne and took it to great heights. Their leadership and influence would carry the Society through the first two decades of the new century, including the war years 1914-18. Phillip Russell, the Chief, and a generous patron of the Society, left for Scotland on the 6th March 1903, on account of illness to try and recover a measure of good health.

The newly elected President, Dr John Small, reminding the meeting that Comunn na Feinne had long financially supported the Geelong Hospital, announced that the Society had decided to endow a bed at the Hospital. He was pleased, on behalf of the Society, to be able to hand over £100, "as the first instalment towards the endowment of the 'Comunn na Feinne Cot' at the hospital." In addition, Dr Small, in his role as office-bearer of the charity, the Ministering Children's League, thanked Comunn na Feinne "for their (sic) liberal donation raised by means of the sale of the Scotch Thistles at the Society's Haggis Supper …". It was clear, from the beginning of his Presidency of the Society, that Dr Small would lead Comunn na Feinne in the direction of fulfilling its charter aims as they related to "good works".

Dr John Small, President, 1902-1916.

The financial situation had improved and the move to the Geelong Agricultural Show Grounds had proved "an unqualified success". The visits of the Victorian Scottish Regiment continued to be a great crowd-puller and it was expected that these would continue. The meeting was charged with confidence as the success of its various events during the year was announced. It was said that, "perhaps the culminating point of the Society's success in recent days was reached on the occasion of the annual Haggis Supper, which was held on 12th August." Although it had returned a financial loss on the evening, it had resulted in the enrolment of 18 new members. Mention was made of the charitable purpose of the County concert visits and the good work in which the Society was engaged. The President moved that the report be accepted and added that, "not long ago they had been at a low ebb, and now they had a very substantial credit balance." The President added that he felt, "that the Society was stronger than ever it had been financially and numerically."

A voice from the floor (probably with a Scottish accent!) made the point that he, and some other members, thought the charge of £28 by the Agricultural Society for the use of their ground was excessive. It was explained that the charge was made on a percentage system thus the more the Society gained from the annual Gathering the greater would be the cost to the Society. The *Advertiser*, on 13th September, reporting this meeting, wrote that the Society's response to this question was to set up a committee, "to wait upon the Agricultural Society to obtain a reduction."

Dr John Small held the annual Fishing Party on 27th September 1903, where officers and members of the Society, "journeyed by Drag to Barwon Heads, where a pleasant outing was experienced followed by a fishing competition." The party, "scaled Mount Colite to the music of piper Donald McLennan", although there was to be no repetition of the charge up the dunes as had been attempted the previous year! A little more decorum, and less use of 'mountain dew' were observed this time and the guests settled for "an excellent luncheon in a marquee in the grounds attached to Neil Campbell's dwelling." It was found that "fish were very scarce" although some could boast of having been successful. Piper "Dosh" McLennan was again the recipient of the "booby prize." Modesty, or embarrassment, probably accounted for the lack of information regarding the number, or size, of fish caught altogether!

After such a busy time with meetings and charity fund-raising events, the Society looked to fine-tune its next New Year's Day Gathering. The search for novelty at the Games went on from year to year. As well as bringing back Tilting at the Ring, a novelty race in the Bicycling section in which, "competitors shall ride in Highland costume" was introduced. Anyone who has worn the kilts will understand how difficult this would make pedalling, let alone the maintenance of decorum! Another item was added, one designed to show off the skills involved in Highland Dancing, whereby 50 children, aged from 6 to 16, all in Highland Costume, and, "all at the one time", would perform Highland Dancing.

The annual concert by Comunn na Feinne on old year's night, 31st December, 1902, was held as usual and the *Advertiser* was effusive in its praise.

> Seldom has there been in Johnstone Park a more animated gathering than there was assembled in that place on New Year's Eve in connection with the 'Auld Nicht' given under the auspices of Comunn na Feinne. The park was crowded with a happy throng as each and all of those [attending] thoroughly appreciated the Scottish custom of giving the old year a jovial farewell and welcoming the new one in such a merry spirit. The music and song composed mostly of Scottish items were continued with, and though the evening did not terminate until after 11 o'clock, the enthusiasm was by no means waning at that hour, the people being apparently loth to leave the grounds.

This was, of course, just the 'warm up' to the New Year's Day Games!

Although regular transport to the coastal areas had made it possible for beach lovers to use the holiday as one for picnics and bathing parties, sufficient numbers were still drawn by the attraction of Comunn na Feinne's annual Gathering to stay home and attend the Games where "Celtic enthusiasm" abounded and where a popular sports programme was carried out.

Visiting dignitaries at the 1903 Gathering included the President, Vice-president and Secretary of the Terang Caledonian Society, the President and Vice-President of the Warrnambool Caledonian Society, representatives of Scottish Institutions in Footscray, Williamstown and Casterton and the President of the Thistle Club of Melbourne, as well the usual clutch of MPs. The pre-games procession again took place through the streets of Geelong and included 120 members of the Victorian Scottish Regiment and its Pipe Band, a large number of juveniles all dressed in Highland garb as well as the usual local organizations and their Brass Bands.

The Victorian Scottish Regiment, as well as providing competitors for many of the events, further entertained the spectators with drills and marches as well as mock battles and it was, as it had been since its first appearance, undoubtedly the main attraction of the day.

Comunn na Feinne had never failed to include among its guests at its Gatherings those who were supported by its welfare arm. Thus, the children of the Protestant Orphanage and the St Augustine's Orphanage, were again the guests of the Society, "and were generously entertained with refreshments by the committee."

The Piping and Dancing competitions were again dominated by, 'weel kent faces' and, in the Heavy Games events, yet another of the Worland dynasty, George H. Worland, was locked in a battle with the outstanding champion of the previous few years, Donald Cameron of Ballarat. In the Caber event Worland took first prize and Cameron came a close second. In Putting the Stone, the positions were reversed and in Throwing the Hammer Worland again bested Cameron. It was a close contest in all sections of the Heavy Games and keenly fought out and the audience was well entertained by the struggle for dominance by two crowd favourites.

The Directors gathered, on 6th January, 1903, for their usual assessment of the New Year's Day Games, and were reasonably pleased with the results, as the *Advertiser* reported next day.

> Receipts amounted to £224 and the expenditure £230. With the amount received from membership fees, a credit balance with which to start the year existed to the amount of about £100.

A further meeting at the Town Hall was held on 23rd January to honour the Society's official piper, Mr Donald 'Dosh McLennan. This took the form of the presentation of a new set of Bagpipes to the piper.

> The Pipes, which were specially imported from Scotland, regardless of cost, were mounted with Sterling Silver and Ivory, and are possibly the finest set now in the State, as the order was given to make the best that expert workmanship could turn out. The pipes are decked with a bannerette, on which is inscribed in art needlework, the Crest of Comunn na Feinne. On the reverse, it is intended to put the design of the Rampant Lion of Scotland.

It was decided at this meeting to commit a sum towards renovation of the grave of Robert de Bruce Johnstone. It was also agreed to hold a special Burns' night as close as possible to the national poet of Scotland's birthday, which fell on 25th January, which was a Sunday. Displaying a sensitivity which probably would have amused Burns himself, the Society, perhaps deferring to the "unco guid", held its concert, instead, on the eve of Burns' birthday! The large numbers attending meant that the concert had to be held at the Town Hall which accommodated a full attendance.

The evening was also used as an opportunity to present a gold medal in the form of a link for the Mayoral chain for which the Society had earlier subscribed.

> The Mayor, Alderman Frederick Hodges, acknowledged the link with thanks and complimented Comunn na Feinne on the important part it had played in the History of Geelong.

Later in the year, under the heading, "A Wee Scotch Nicht', the *Advertiser* of the 20th August, 1903, provided a report on yet another Society function, its annual Haggis Supper. Present were leading officials of many Scottish societies from Melbourne and the Western District. Dr Small presided over the large gathering;

> If there is one occasion more than another during the year on which local and visiting Scotchmen lay themselves out to spend the hours in jovial fun, that occasion is the annual Haggis Supper, which virtually takes the form of the annual 'gatherin' o' the clans' ... so successful did the affair turn out, that there were more present than was hoped for in the fondest anticipations of the Committee and officers of Comunn na Feinne, under whose auspices the affair was held. [They] assembled to partake of the mysterious mixture having the most prominent place on the menu, [and this] ... punctuated with copious draughts of the national beverage, made a feast sufficiently appetizing to gladden the hearts of all present, and help them in their desire to spend the night in mirth and glee.

It was rare for the Society to devote much time in verbally elaborating its charter aims, preferring to let actions speak louder than words, but at this gathering there was a re-statement made of its core 'philosophy' and an explanation of how its aims were being worked out in practical terms within the community. Dr Small made the most significant speech of the night when he posed and answered the question "What is the good of a Scotch Society?"

The scoffers, he pointed out, accused such Societies as their own, as being no more than self-centred organizations, inward looking and given to outbursts of sentimental nostalgia and nothing more. Dr Small threw back in the face of such critics what was the real answer to that particular question. The purpose of such societies in general, and of Comunn na Feinne in particular, was to look at the community and ask what could be done to help those in need. This, he continued, was at the heart of the Society's Charter and it was this that it had ever striven to do. Comunn na Feinne had always been at the forefront of those activities designed to advance the community educationally and to improve the conditions and opportunities of those who were needy, sick and unemployed. It had established a night school for working class boys and had been involved with others in the community in trying to save the disadvantaged from a lifetime of struggle and hardship.

Now, at the present time, said Dr Small, members of the Society had put forward "various proposals" to see what more could be done to continue its aims. One of these, endowing a bed at the Geelong Hospital, had already been put into practice. This was a practical action the result of which, he trusted: "would go on after they were all dead and buried [so that] what had been done in their lifetime might thus live and do good to other people ... He trusted that they would get more money, so that the movement would progress, and they would be able to have many beds kept up at the hospital."

He spoke, therefore, of the practical and solid work which could yet be done to improve their new homeland. But it would not have been a Scots' gathering without reference to the 'philosophical' nature of their people, to their poets and to the universal goals of which they wrote. In keeping alive the traditions, sports, music, literature and dance of their country, another of the speakers added, Scottish societies were also doing "a good work". But there was, he added, "a greater work in deepening the sense of brotherhood of Scotchmen throughout Australia, so that they might realize the grand ideal of their national poet, who speaks of the time coming when we shall brothers be for all that." This was no narrow, selfish national dream but, rather, a step towards realizing this as a universal goal encompassing all peoples.

At the Society's Monthly Meeting 1st September, 1903, it was reported that the annual concert had made a profit but the Haggis Supper had not. It has already been noted that hiring entertainment for such functions was costly. Quality entertainers did not come cheap, and providing them severely reduced any profits arising from such social occasions.

The Hospital Committee had worked on turning the Society's aim of endowing a bed at the Hospital into a practical reality and, "was resolved to submit its proposal to the annual meeting" which was to be held later that same night. This meeting attracted 60 members. It was announced that the Society currently had a membership approaching 200 and that finances now seemed to be on an even keel. The work of the charity committee was commended and the charity fund was growing, thus enabling more to be done in that direction. The charity Concerts, taken out to various country areas as far as Terang, had been well received and had attracted new members.

> Not only have the concerts been productive of financial benefit to the charity fund, but a greater interest has been aroused in the general work of the Society, with a consequent addition of new members.

A Comunn na Feinne Scottish Choir had been formed during the year and this, "had made a favourable impression at the annual concert on 19th August, 1903.

The motion that a member's subscription be fixed at 10/6 per annum was passed … [and] special praise was again given to James Galbraith the Society's secretary, "to whose credit is due the satisfactory position the Society now occupies." Appreciation was also given to the local press and others for, "the assistance rendered … in forwarding Comunn na Feinne interests, and we desire to tender them our sincere thanks."

The treasurer, George R. King, proposed that a history of Comunn na Feinne be published, and this was agreed to; further steps were to be taken by the Directors to turn this proposal into a practical reality. It was also agreed that the next country concert in aid of the Society's charity funds was to be held at Inverleigh on 9th November, 1903. George R. King had formed the nucleus of a Society Library* by donating, "three volumes of the poems of Ossian", and it was urged on other members to follow suit with donations of books.

*[This, later, became the Dr Small Memorial Library, after an extension was made to the Comunn na Feinne Hall. See below.]

A Directors' meeting was held 17th December to complete the arrangements for the 1904 New Year's Day Highland Gathering, and it reported that special trains had been chartered to bring Melbourne and Western District supporters to Geelong for the occasion. The *Advertiser* generally was supportive of the Society in its promotion of the New Year's Day Gathering and that planned for 1904 was no exception. It provided some highlights of various events which would be taking place and it announced that the best pipers and the best dancers in Australia would be present and competing for Australian championship awards. Additional cheering news was that the Step Dancing championships (attracting the best dancers from all over the State) were also to be held at these Games. The Victorian Scottish Regiment, which was again attending, was to be joined in "special displays" by the Williamstown Juvenile Naval Brigade. With such a line-up of attractions, the *Advertiser*, added that: "There is certainly no necessity for the Geelong public to go elsewhere for pleasure on New Year's Day, when Comunn na Feinne is catering so well for their enjoyment."

The Society further announced that it would be treating the children from both the 'Protestant' Orphanage and that of St Augustine's, in addition to children coming down from Birregurra, "by special train", to a special treat at the Games. An advance notice was given, too, to the celebration of the anniversary of Robert Burns' birthday on 25th January, 1904. These concerts always proved popular and were well attended by members of the public, as well as Society members, and all were advised to book early! But before this event, the Old Year's Night concert in Johnstone Park, to bid farewell to 1903, had to be so navigated as to leave the attendees fit for the New Year's Day Gathering!

The traditional Procession in 1904, reported the *Advertiser* on 4th January, was a lively one! The Victorian Scottish Regiment with its pipe band was joined by the Williamstown Naval Brigade and the St Augustine's Band, together with the usual assortment of pipers, as well as the Fire Brigade and the Town Brass Bands. According to the newspaper, "Inspiriting selections of music were played on the march to the grounds, and the procession was viewed by large number of sightseers …" The Gathering was opened by the Victorian State Commandant Brigadier-General Gordon, himself a Scot, who pronounced the Games, "the best of the kind he had ever seen" and he trusted, "they would admit him to membership of Comunn na

Feinne." After all of the foregoing, it seemed almost superfluous for the *Advertiser* to pronounce the Games, "a decided success."

Competition for the Victorian and the Australian crown in piping and dancing was keen, and the Society stated that the entries constituted a record for Comunn na Feinne Gatherings. The Society's own piper, Donald McLennan, came third overall in the Victorian Solo Piping Championships which was again won by that master-piper, Hugh Fraser, of the Victorian Scottish Regiment Pipe Band. J. Cameron was runner-up. The Heavy Events produced a new face, W. Nixon, who won the Caber competition.

Following the Gathering, the Society set the pace for its year ahead with its anniversary of Robert Burns' birthday celebration on 25th January, 1904, the guest speaker being Rev Arthur Davidson, Moderator of the Presbyterian Church of Victoria. The enthusiastic meeting was held in the brand new Masonic Hall (designed by Angus J. Laird, an office-bearer of Comunn na Feinne), and it was entertained with Scottish songs and music, as well as with illustrated scenes of Scotland referring to places mentioned by Burns in his works. Included were scenes of the unveiling of the Burns Monument in Melbourne which had taken place the previous Saturday.

The *Advertiser* of the 26th January reported that Dr Small also handed over to George Martin MLA., president of the hospital committee, another instalment of £100 towards the Comunn na Feinne hospital bed.

Comunn na Feinne's Grand Annual Concert, held at the Mechanics' Hall 6th July, 1904, provided a special treat for the audience. Miss Flora F. Donaldson, Scottish and Gaelic Prima Donna, and Gold Medalist, of Glasgow, and Gavin Spence, Tenor, of Edinburgh and Melbourne, were the guest performers. The Society's piper, Donald McLennan also gave a solo recital as well as playing for the Highland dancers. The 'stars' were recalled for several encores. So too were some of the other acts including violinist, Miss Maud Young, and tenor, A. Gibson, both responding generously to their respective recalls. The *Advertiser*, in its following day's report, said that, "Possibly the gem of the evening was '*Caismeachd Chloinn Chamrain*' ('March of the Cameron Men'), sung in Gaelic by Miss Flora Donaldson. Though the words were understood by few, reported the *Advertiser*, "the sentiment and spirit of the thing was apparent to all." Miss Donaldson also contributed another Gaelic song '*Ho ro mo Nigheann Donn Bhoidheach*' (My Brown-haired Maiden), along with many other popular Scottish songs.

But the Society was not quite finished with Burns for the year for, on 12th July, 1904, Captain James B. Leitch,* a Comunn na Feinne office-bearer, at a meeting of the Directors, presented the Society with a series of pictures to be hung in the rooms which it rented as its headquarters.** The pictures represented scenes from some of Burns' poems and had been "secured by Captain Leitch when on a visit to Scotland, and will form a pleasing addition to the gallery of the rooms." Leitch was a Geelong veterinarian who had served in the South African war in that capacity, gaining the rank of Captain. He was also a talented artist and sculptor and occasionally donated some of his work to the Society. It was also announced that the Society's President, Dr John Small, after a severe operation, was recuperating in Queensland. He was expected to return to Geelong by the end of the year.

*[See Appendix 3 (b) Short Biographies.]

** Although the Society had a variety of 'homes' where it held its meeting before obtaining its permanent home in Yarra Street in 1912, these particular rooms were probably in the Exchange Building, Little Malop Street, Geelong.

The *Advertiser* entered into the spirit of the moment in its coverage of the annual Haggis Supper on 8th September, 1904, beginning its report with some of Burns' memorable lines.

> Ye powers, wha' mak' mankind your care,
> An' dish them out their bill o' fare-
> Auld Scotland wants nae skinking ware*,
> That jaups in Luggies.**
> But, if ye wish her gratefu' prayer
> Gie her a haggis.
>
> *Skinking ware – a watery soup.
> ** jaups in luggies – splashes in wooden dishes.

What to many non-Celts might have seemed a strange and inexplicable ritual would not have been made any clearer by the *Advertiser*'s attempt to explain it:

> The principal item on the menu was the mysterious compound giving the supper its title. Nine large trays of this were carried aloft around the room by nine Highlanders, preceded by the Society's stalwart piper playing an inspirited air. ... The words of the national bard, 'Let Scotia's sons all agree to spend the nicht in mirth and glee', were enthusiastically observed. The advice on the menu card to have a wee drappie tae warm yi'r wame,* ma certie, we'll hae anither dram, and anither tastin' etc., was accepted with interest.
> *['wame' - a Scottish term for 'belly' or 'insides']

The significance of the evening was that Ladies were also in attendance, although their positioning in the hall may have made not a few of the husbands who were present, feel a little uncomfortable!

> In order to allow the wives and lady friends of the guests to become initiated into the mysteries of a haggis supper, the gallery of the Wool Exchange was set apart for their convenience. About 50 ladies watched the proceedings from this spot until a late hour in the evening.

But for all that, it is certain that some of the ladies would have come away with the view that here was no sacred or laudatory, hitherto secret and mysterious, ritual, 'endured' by their menfolk, but an excuse only for a lad's night out!

Along with the usual examples of self-deprecatory pawky humour, some of the speeches touched upon more serious topics including numerous allusions "to the good work Comunn na Feinne did in the cause of charity." And here, as if on cue, the collection plate was handed round, with the result that the Society's charity fund was swelled by £15!

The annual general meeting for 1904, held in September, was well attended and had a full roster of business to get through. The committee charged with revising the rules of the Society presented its report. The *Advertiser*, not entirely without a touch of sarcasm relating to a Scot's insistence on debating the fine points of any proposition to the nth degree, added that, "the national characteristics of members were evidenced here in the exhaustive discussion which took place on the various items. After two hours of dissection, the rules as submitted, with some few alterations, were adopted." These alterations were intended to put the Society on a sound footing, "consequent upon the increased scope of its operations." The annual report congratulated, "members on the continued prosperity that has followed the work of the Society." The total from entry fees of the competitors had risen dramatically and a satisfactory profit had been made on the annual Concert. The members were reminded of their commitment, "for the endowment of a bed at the Geelong Hospital at a total cost of £1,200 ...", and to honour this and, to 'live out', in their daily activities, their good works.

The illness of the President, Dr Small, (recuperating in Queensland), and that of the Chief, Mr Phillip Russell (seeking medical help in Europe), were reported, together with the wish for their complete recovery. James Galbraith, hon. Secretary, was again singled out for praise and appreciation for his "active energetic display" on behalf of the Society. The meeting also heard that "the reconstitution of the Society under the new rules" had led to the need, "to appoint a financial secretary" and George R. King was unanimously elected to that position.

It was agreed, too, that the Comunn na Feinne Ball, always very popular with members and public alike, would be held later in the year. A further effort by Comunn na Feinne to make its concerts entertaining and attractive to the whole community was its introduction of Scottish Country Dancing into its social events held during the year. The use of Scottish country dancing on the programme of these events allowed those uninitiated into the mysteries and intricacies of Highland Dancing, to join in general Scottish set dances which were quite sociable in nature and could quickly be learned with much pulling and prodding into place of the novices by those who already knew the steps. Highland Dancing usually was a solo performance with more discipline required in performance and demeanor on the part of the competitor who, more or less, danced staying in the one spot.

In addition to its rapidly filling 1904 calendar of activities in Geelong, Comunn na

Feinne also maintained its Country Concerts in 1904, dispatching its Concert Parties on, "a short tour in the Western District." The *Advertiser*, on 9th September, 1904, reported that the Society's assistance in fund-raising for worthwhile causes often took it beyond Geelong town limits. For example, it staged a Highland Concert at Camperdown in aid of the funds for a local library in that town, "with the result that £31 towards the fund" was raised. In these ways, as with its general charity work in Geelong itself, the Society was promoting and fulfilling its aim of 'doing good'.

It has already been noted that civilian Pipe Bands, as we understand them today, were rare in Victoria until the early twentieth century. There were many solo pipers, of course, who attended and competed in solo piping competitions held at the Geelong Gathering, and these pipers generally marched in the traditional procession to the grounds and also played for the various Highland dancing competitions. A feature of the usual Procession from the town for the 1905 Gathering was the presence of four champion Pipers each of whom was the Honorary Piper of his respective Society*. These were, Donald McLennan of Comunn na Feinne, Andrew Wattie of the Buninyong Highland Society, Allan Comrie of the Ballarat Caledonian Society and Charles McKinnon of the Caledonian Society of Melbourne. These men, along with Hugh Fraser of the Scottish Regiment Pipe Band, and other pipers from around Australia, all took part in the Society's Piping contests as well as contending for the award of Champion Piper of Victoria. Fraser, for the third successive year, won this award, while McLennan and McKinnon fought it out for second place, resulting in McLennan being pipped by McKinnon by one point.

Four pipers leading the Procession.

The rain which had driven the Hogmanay revellers from Johnstone Park to an indoor venue continued throughout New Year's Day itself. The Procession, in 1905, was shifted to the Geelong Eastern (football) Oval where, despite the rain, "which continued throughout the afternoon", the 3,000 spectators "thoroughly enjoyed the diversified programme" and warmly applauded the President (returned from his recuperation in Queensland), following his words of welcome.

The Heavy Games saw George Worland again among the prizes with a first in Tossing the Caber and a second in the Hammer event. The Victorian Scottish Regiment gave displays of drilling, bayonet exercises as well as the exciting 'charges' complete with 'war cries' fierce enough to alarm the faint-hearted! Bicycling continued to provide thrills, with many of the races being "determinedly fought out."

Although accidents were expected in the bicycling, the 1905 races seemed to be 'gremlin infested' judging by the number of falls and mistakes which occurred. There were some spills, and some miscounting of laps, to add to the excitement of the races. In the final of the Comunn na Feinne Wheel Race, for example, "the riders covered five laps instead of four" and the race had to be held again! Of the four finalists, one "withdrew in the third lap …" with two of the remainder falling when entering the last lap. Although they both remounted, the leader had an unassailable position by then and won easily. In the Caledonian Wheel Race (Two Miles), all four contestants fell in the first heat! That rascal 'bad luck' was obviously working overtime!

Comunn na Feinne's 1905 year continued through its cycle of concerts, special anniversaries, lectures and charity fund-raising. At a special meeting held 15th August, 1905, reported in the *Advertiser* the next day, George R. King was the recipient of a special award. Dr Small, in presenting it, said, "The sound [financial] basis on which Comunn na Feinne at present stands, is due largely to the efforts of G.R. King, who took up the treasure-ship of the Society when it was at a low ebb. …". King, because of the pressure of his other duties with the Gordon Institute, had, again, reluctantly resigned his position with the Society, but he left it, "strong numerically and sound financially." King's financial skills, and Galbraith's organizational genius, played a major part in the Society's revival in the previous few years.

At the Society's annual meeting, held on 12th September, 1905, it was announced that general agreement between all except one of the Scottish Societies in Victoria meant that a Scottish Union of Societies was to be formed. Reference was also made to the various cases of charity which had been supported during the year. One of the members present, John McLennan, "thought it inadvisable for donations [to the Society's charity fund] to be encouraged at the Haggis Supper. The affair was a social event and should be that alone." In responding, Dr Small, the President, in his puckish way, and no doubt with tongue firmly planted in his cheek, replied, "that he would not ask for anything, but if anybody, in consequence of the haggis, overflowed with the milk of human kindness and offered a donation, he would not refuse it!"

The *Geelong Advertiser*, in covering Comunn na Feinne activities, found, sometimes, more exciting or more humorous copy in incidents outside the arena than actually in it. Music may indeed have "charms to soothe the savage breast' but, so the *Advertiser* on 2nd January, 1906, noted, dancing, as some found, was loaded with violent potential!

> A Scottish piper who had arrived early to take part in the 1906 Highland gathering was proudly paying tribute to the new year with the skirl of his pipes when a band of youngsters, whose musical tastes did not soar above kerosene tins, challenged him. A duel ensued which resulted in the total discomfiture of Scotty, who was compelled to submit to overpowering numbers. Later on, the presence of another piper near the band stand in market square attracted a couple of persons who, to the music gratuitously supplied, took part in an impromptu dance contest. A collision between the two dancers was followed by a pugilistic encounter which, before much [physical] damage was done to either of the dancers, fell through on the whisper being passed around that the police were in the vicinity.

Good weather meant that attendance at the Corio Cricket and Football Oval for the 1906 Gathering was almost 40 percent higher than at the previous year's rain-soaked one, and it resulted also in a successful evening concert.

Among the notable members' deaths in 1906, that of Robert Shirra, following fast on the heels of John Clark of Teasdale, robbed the Society of two of its oldest links to the beginning of Comunn na Feinne. These deaths drew a letter, dated 1st February, 1906, from Western Australia, written by James Shillinglaw McKay who had been Comunn na Feinne secretary from 1873-1878, proof that ex-members still took an interest in the Society's affairs, and that journal of the Victorian Scottish Union, *The Scot at Hame an' Abroad*, was successfully spreading news of the affiliated Scottish societies quite widely. McKay first chided the *Advertiser* in its use of the definite article before Comunn na Feinne. As he pointed out, this is redundant as Comunn na Feinne in translation means 'The Society of Fingalians'. The real purpose of his letter, however, was not to correct the *Advertiser* regarding proper Gaelic grammar, but to mourn the loss of these early members and office-bearers of the Society. He reminisced regarding the founders and spoke feelingly of his time with the Society. When he departed for Western Australia in 1879, he had been presented with a medal and life membership on the motion of Robert Shirra, "the now deeply lamented Vice-President."

Comunn na Feinne, for long without an 'official' bard, now had a new voice, that of Allan Fullarton Wilson, a prolific maker of verse in Lowland Scots, which would have been familiar to those acquainted with Robert Burns' work. Wilson provided regular material, not only for Comunn na Feinne, but also for the Victorian Scottish Union (formed in 1904) and its magazine, *The Scot at Hame an' Abroad*, as well as for newspapers and other journals.

The Society's new poet contributed a verse, 'Scotland For Ever', which gives an example of his style and sentiment. [Wilson's full poem can be found in Appendix 5 (d) Poems of A.F. Wilson.]

> Scotland for Ever
> When Providence assorted men,
> In tae sae many lots,
> It kept a special breed ye ken
> An' ca'd them Picts and Scots.
> ....
> When He'ven had made this special race,
> An' intae it pit breith,
> It gied Auld Scotland topmost place,
> Wi' England underneath.
> ....
> An' there they are until this day,
> An' sae are like tae stop,
> For till the Earth shall melt away,
> Auld Scotland's aye, on top.

One of the gala occasions in Comunn na Feinne's calendar came to be its annual Highland Ball, the inaugural one being held on 4th July, 1906. This was held at the Corio Club Ball-room and on the night, "a steady stream of horse drawn vehicles" brought those attending to the entrance in LaTrobe Terrace. Scottish pipe music and highland dancing acts were provided by Comunn na Feinne entertainers. Following this, "the ordinary ball programme interspersed with several of the old country dances, were gone through [with] upwards of 120 persons dancing."

CNF Highland Ball, 4th July, 1906 at Corio Club Hall, Geelong.

Another popular charity-raising social function was the Haggis Supper and, as usual, this was well-attended and, given the presence of several politicians, the speeches were surprisingly short and to the point! George R. King, in proposing the toast to the Jubilee of Comunn na Feinne, said that he, "considered the early history of the Society was associated with the early history of Victoria. The Society was the first institution in the State to introduce any definite system of education, and amongst those associated with it in this respect was Professor Kernot*." There is probably little doubt that the Society did indeed have a part in raising teaching and curriculum standards, especially in Geelong and district, in the years before the Victorian Education Act of 1872, though to call that a 'definite system of education' surely was to exaggerate! The Society actually ran competitive examinations with a view to raising educational standards and influencing the curriculum. King, a noted educationist himself (as Principal of Gordon Institute), was correct in identifying Professor Kernott and his influence on education.

*[Professor Kernott was one of the early medal winners at the Society's annual Educational Competitions and went on to pioneer the inclusion of civil engineering courses at tertiary level. His brief biography is given in Appendices 3 (b) Short Biographies.]

At a Directors' Meeting on 7th August, 1906, news of the Society's piper, Donald 'Dosh' McLennan, who was recuperating after an operation, was given and the Society's best wishes for a full recovery were forwarded to the patient. It was also announced that the annual concert to be held at the Mechanics' Hall on 15th August was again proving popular and that tickets for this were "selling rapidly". The prices of tickets had been set at 2/6, 2/- and 1/- making them affordable to most working people in the community. The report continued that several well-known and popular entertainers from Melbourne had been hired for the Concert, as well as some local dancers and musicians.

The annual general meeting of the Society was held in the Exchange Building, Little Malop Street, on 12th September, 1906, where a full and encouraging report of the Society's activities and finances was given. The New Year's Day Gathering was, as were the various concerts held throughout the year by the Society, considered a great success. The Charity Fund was in demand again throughout the year and several cases of *ad hoc* need had been addressed. In addition to short term, and one-off cases, the Society also fulfilled its long-term, major, financial commitments to such institutions as the Hospital, the two Orphanages and the working boys' night school. A report on the Annual Ball was positive, and it was noted that old time Scottish Country dances were much appreciated by those who attended.

The meeting was also advised that the Society had managed to purchase the manuscript of the 'History of Comunn na Feinne', "so ably written by the late John Clarke, one of the Society's founders", and that, "the sub-committee appointed hope to have the matter [i.e. to have it published] in hand during the year."*

* [Although this subject was to be mentioned several times in subsequent years it appears that the book was never published. It was also later announced, in the *Advertiser* of 29th September, 1911, that the Society had, "After a lot of trouble … obtained the complete set of minute books from the date of its inception." However, the manuscript of the book, as with all the other Comunn na Feinne original papers, including the Society's minute books and financial records, disappeared when the Society eventually closed in 1946.]

This meeting further heard a report of the Games committee that the 1907 Games would represent the 50th anniversary of Comunn na Feinne's Highland Gathering. The *Advertiser* on 13th September, 1906, reported that the Society intended that special trains would be chartered, "to convey patrons to celebrate this historical event."

The Society also renewed its literary activity by giving prizes annually for essays on

Scottish subjects. The subject for the first of these was, 'The Influence of John Knox on the Evolution of the Scottish Nation', and a prize of £10 was to be awarded for the essay adjudged the best. This inaugural Essay Competition, in fact, led to joint winners as announced in the *Advertiser* on 29th December, 1906. It had been impossible to separate two essays as deserving of first prize, and it was decided to award equal first prize to the authors Mr W. Kennedy Smith and Mr T. Carruthers. Mr Fred P. Morris filled the third place. The equal winners, it was reported, "divided the first and second prize money …".

Members of Comunn na Feinne were now quite used to hearing, or reading, of the deaths of veteran members of the Society, but it came as a shock when it was announced that its popular and respected official piper, Donald 'Dosh' McLennan, had died suddenly. Although in the previous few months he had been ill and had undergone an operation in Melbourne, he had given every indication of having recovered his health and had entered into the life of Comunn na Feinne again. An announcement at the Annual Scottish Concert held 15th August, to the effect that he was well on the way to recovery had been, "received with applause". He had been present at the Haggis Supper in August, although it was his brother who had carried out the piping duties that night. He had been well enough, as one of the two delegates from Comunn na Feinne, to attend the Victorian Scottish Union Conference held at Rushworth early in September, 1906. However, while out driving in a buggy with his brother, reported the *Advertiser*, he died suddenly from a heart attack on 26th September, 1906. Not since Robert de Bruce Johnstone's death had the Society been hit so hard with shock and this extended beyond his fellow Comunn na Feinne members. He was also well known for his charity work in the area of Barwon Downs where he had his farm.

> It is, however, in his own district that the deceased will be most missed, for there he occupied a unique position in the respect with which he was regarded by everyone. In times of trouble it was to "Dosh", by which title he was more familiarly known, the old and the young would go for comfort and advice. Like Goldsmith's village preacher, he was "a man to all the country dear".

The Society's bard, Allan Fullarton Wilson, summed up Donald McLennan's life and his memory in a brief but moving poetic testimony:

> Loved and esteemed by all who knew him here;
> The future he has little cause to fear.
> His was the heart to feel for others' woe
> He never wronged a friend, nor feared a foe,
> His aim it ever was to do the right,
> His life was blameless, and his honour white,
> 'Tis passing strange that death should ever choose
> Those men the world can least afford to lose,
> Many have lost in him a generous friend,
> And with sad hearts lament his early end.
> Not simulated is that grief they feel,
> But heart-felt sorrow, deep, sincere and real.
> He won and earned his fellow man's good will
> And leaves a gap it will be hard to fill.
> Untimely closed, alas his too brief span
> Here lies at rest an honest gentleman.

At the monthly meeting of Comunn na Feinne on 1st October, 1906, it was unanimously decided to ask Murdoch McLennan, the brother of Donald, "to accept the position of Hon. Piper to the Society." A letter had been received from Rev. William Naismith, of the Presbyterian Church, Birregurra, asking Comunn na Feinne to assist in erecting "a memorial to their late piper." The minister's letter continued:

> Donald McLennan for years … carried out the duties of Secretary of the Presbyterian Church at Birregurra, and as he manifested a special interest in its welfare, his most intimate friends suggested that as the present building is old and too small for requirements, the erection of a new church would be a fitting memorial to the departed Highlander.

The cost of the Church [£825] was beyond the resources of Comunn na Feinne, but it was determined to work with others towards achieving the required amount. The Society, and other groups, did go on to raise £825, and the new Church was eventually opened in 1908, but with a cost overrun of £300! The *Advertiser* reported, on 1st December, 1906, that the Society would be busy in the next few months appointing collectors and holding various fund-raising activities in response to Mr Naithsmith's request. It was also announced that a bust of the late Donald McLennan:

[Was] executed by James B. Leitch, an office-bearer in Comunn na Feinne and a fervent admirer of his late comrade. The work reflects great credit on James B. Leitch's ability as a sculptor, and will doubtless be long treasured by the Society, to which James B. Leitch presented it, as a memento of a good and true man.

Bust of Donald 'Dosh' McLennan by J.B. Leitch.

In the meantime, arrangements for Comunn na Feinne's next New Year's Highland Gathering were proceeding, and the Society announced, on 2nd December, 1906, that confirmation had been received that a contingent of the Victorian Scottish Regiment, together with its Pipe Band, would be taking part in the New Year's Day Gathering for 1907. At a further meeting of the Society, held 11th December, "It was decided to include a State School Championship race over three distances, "for boys 15 years and under." It was also decided to invite, "by special invitation", as many of the "old pioneers" from the early days of Comunn na Feinne, who still lived locally, to be present at the 1907 Gathering. If such a group could be gathered it was intended to have a special photograph of them taken to hang in the Society rooms. Efforts were to be made, too, to have medal winners from previous years in attendance and to display their medals at the Gathering. One who responded to this request was W. H. Sinnott from the General Post Office, Melbourne, who won educational prizes from 1857 to 1861.

The *Geelong Advertiser* gave generous space to Comunn na Feinne and the celebration of its approaching jubilee, entering into the spirit of the occasion and devoting many column inches to it throughout December. The Society, it reported on 31st December, was anticipating that there would be a record number at its New Year's Day, 1907 Gathering. It had its first Gathering 50 years ago and, "has extended its usefulness in many ways …".

Under the heading 'Jubilee Celebrations – 50th Annual Highland Gathering,' for example, the *Geelong Advertiser* wrote that Comunn na Feinne had done "splendid work" over the half century of its existence. It had "inculcated" in its members a "true spirit of charity." The poor and distressed had been aided and, in every direction, the Society had spread its charity. Its services to education before the 1872 Act had been significant. Its influence had pervaded the community creating a 'spirit' of brotherhood and harmony. The Society, it reported on 31st December, was anticipating that there would be a record number at its New Year's Day, 1907 Gathering.

The *Advertiser* also highlighted the lengths to which the Society had gone in order to convenience Melbourne and country Victorians.

> The Society has gone to the expense of commissioning two special trains, one from Melbourne and the other from Camperdown to encourage participation by the public. The Scottish Regiment, headed by the Pipe Band, will arrive from Melbourne by special train which is timed to leave at 8.25 a.m. They will give a display of physical exercises during the day.
> [The train] from Camperdown … will bring a large number of members of the Camperdown and Colac Caledonian Societies. It will also pick up excursionists at Birregurra, Winchelsea and Moriac. The train leaves Camperdown at 6.40 a.m., and returns at 7.40 p.m.
> The boys of the Protestant, and St. Augustine's Orphanage will not be forgotten, and the committee has arranged that they shall be entertained at their respective institutions. They will also be invited to attend the sports.

The jubilee will be further celebrated in the opening by a concert in Johnstone Park. The Scottish Regiment Pipe Band and the Artillery Band will give selections, and appropriate biograph views will be shown by Messrs. Alex. Gunn and Sons, of Melbourne.

On 2nd January, 1907, the *Advertiser* once again highlighted the Society's contribution to education. Before the introduction, in 1872, of a compulsory state educational system, that was also free and secular, Comunn na Feinne, through its setting up of educational competitions between pupils at schools in Geelong and district, had raised the level of teaching and influenced the widening of the school curriculum. Many are the examples, said the *Advertiser*, of those who were prize winners in the early Comunn na Feinne education competitions who had gone on to important and influential careers.*

*[Some of these have been shown in Short Biographies Appendix 3(b).]

As much as the *Advertiser*'s analysis gave praise to the Society for its wide charitable and educational activities, it was only after a half a century that Comunn na Feinne, belatedly decided to give women honorary membership status. At its meeting on 26th March, 1907, a proposal was put forward by James B. Leitch, "that ladies be admitted to membership of the Society. After some discussion, a resolution was carried that ladies of Scottish descent be admitted as *honorary members* at an annual subscription of 5/-." Cultural norms have changed, of course, but it still seems incredible, looking back from today, that the Society could have so under-appreciated the role women played in its activities through the years. Lady pipers (and lady Highland dancers, over 16 years of age), were not allowed to take part in those two areas of competition until the twentieth century! It had, of course, allowed ladies to compete in the Archery contests, albeit at some distance from the actual Games arena, and from the spectators, at South Geelong!

Comunn na Feinne relinquished its usual Hogmanay Concert to the Volunteer Geelong Town Band which staged the old year's night concert on 31st December 1906 at Johnstone Park. It kept very much to the usual formula and its programme, "was thoroughly in keeping with the occasion (New Year's Eve)." Appropriate music, dance and biograph views made up the night which carried on until late for those who wished "to see the old year out."

In opening the 1907 Gathering, Dr Small, president of Comunn na Feinne, welcomed those who had come and those who were representing Scottish Societies in Colac, Camperdown, the Metropolitan areas and the Western District generally. He also made a touching and sincere reference to the loss of their official piper, Donald McLennan. In honour of his memory, he continued, they had been told that the people he worshipped among were badly in need of a new Church building and that Comunn na Feinne had opened a Fund towards this purpose. To this fund, he hoped all would give their support. The list would soon be closed, "and those who wish to honour a good man … should do so at once, according to their means."

The *Geelong Advertiser*'s coverage of the Society's Jubilee gave a picture of a movement which was committed to the community – the whole community. Thus, its activities stretched far beyond the periphery of its sports' ground and even further beyond its social activities altogether. Its charter aims took it into every aspect of community well-being and its multicultural openness, with regard to its activities, contributed to the harmonious relationship between the various national groups which had settled in Geelong. Here was a Society whose deeds were its loudest testimony – one whose jubilee deserved to be celebrated, said the *Advertiser*'s editorial for 2nd January, 1907.

> COMUNN NA FEINNE
> The society has inculcated in its members the true spirit of charity. Its charitableness has extended in many directions, and many a deserving case has been relieved out of its funds. A Society that seeks to hold out a helping hand to the poor and distressed as the Comunn Na Feinne does, and has done for many years, is worthy of the best support of the public, and it is gratifying to note that the Comunn Na Feinne is continually gaining in membership. Its influence is for good and it is a decidedly useful body in the community. In the days when scholarships were not known in Victoria, the society keenly interested itself in the spread of education by giving medals for educational work.

Once the speeches and the welcoming remarks were over, the Games began in earnest. G. Worland again starred in the heavy events, taking first prize in the Caber event and in Putting the Stone. Only long-time rival, Donald Cameron, from Ballarat, who had returned to the Geelong competitions after a period of absence, denied Worland the grand slam when he won the Hammer event. Hugh Fraser again crowned as Champion Piper of Victoria for the fourth time in the five years since the award's inception, and had only missed the previous year's contest because he was in Sydney where he won the Piping championship of that State!

The jubilee theme continued into the evening when the usual Scottish concert took place in Johnstone Park and, "was attended by a very large crowd." The *Advertiser* reported that this also proved to be a great success with the Victorian Scottish Regiment parading through the Park, "and the usual programme of dances, pipe selections, band music and biograph views was presented. It was a fitting windup to the successful Gathering held on the Oval in the afternoon."

Following the appeal made at the New Year's Day Gathering, the President of Comunn na Feinne, Dr John Small, and the secretary, Mr James Galbraith, on 8th February, 1907, "launched the Donald ('Dosh') McLennan, Memorial Fund." Through donations and sales of work stalls, the Society was to raise a good sum towards the total required for the building fund. Contributions also came from the Colac Caledonian Society, the Camperdown Caledonian Society and the Birregurra Presbyterian Church congregation, with help also coming from other sources. In fact, the amount raised did not cover the eventual cost of building the Church which ended up running several hundred pounds over the original costs supplied by the builder. The Church was opened with a memorial service on 3rd December, 1908.

The half-yearly meeting of Comunn na Feinne took place on 26th March, 1907, and, reported the *Advertiser* the next day, the members heard that: "good progress had already been made regarding the formation of a Pipe Band." Evidence of this was provided in a pipe selection played by Master Duncan McIntyre, a lad of about eight years of age. He rendered 'Cock o' the North' in the style of an old veteran, and his effort was received with much applause." The President remarked that he was "proud to see such youthful talent" and quipped, "If he could make that much noise now what would he do when he grew up?"

It has already been noted that Pipe Bands, apart from those associated with Scottish Military Regiments, did not exist at this time. The South and Port Melbourne Thistle Society's Pipe Band has staked a claim to being the first non-military Pipe Band in Victoria, although there is no documentation to indicate that it was actually formed in 1897 as claimed. The first recorded Pipe Band contest appears to be that held at the Ballarat South Street Eisteddfod in 1907. The winner at this competition gained the title of Champion Pipe Band of Australia. Comunn na Feinne formed its Band in 1906-07, and the first Pipe Band Competition held by the Society at its annual Gathering was in 1910 when the Collingwood, Comunn na Feinne and Camperdown Pipe Bands took part.

Dr Small, in his President's report, briefly re-told the story of Comunn na Feinne since its inception in 1856. He outlined its charter with emphasis on its service to the community and he trusted, "that the Society would not forget [this] original purpose for which it was formed." He recounted, also, the dark days [in the period of the 1870s leading up to the end of the century], when the Society appeared to be languishing and gave credit to some of the leadership for striving to revive it. The "chief credit, however, was due to the secretary, James Galbraith, who, he maintained, was one in a thousand. The Society now numbered 200 members and was, consequently, a power in the land."

On 1st May, a social evening was held in the Society's rooms, "to celebrate the bicentenary of the Union of Scotland and England. Representatives of the St George's Society were present and a lecture on 'The Union of the National Flags' was appreciatively received. Scotland and England may well have left old hostilities behind but, as shown below, the campaigns waged by the Victorian Scottish Union against what were seen as present-day slights to Scotland, demonstrated that Scots would not be passive in the face of what they regarded to be attempts at 'airbrushing' Scotland out of public news, out of history!

The Burns' Night on 26th January, 1907, the Annual Scottish Concert, held 13th August, the Haggis Supper and the Highland Ball, were among other social activities which the Society held throughout the year, all of which continued to prove very popular with the audiences. Of a more formal character was the hosting, from 9th – 11th September 1907, of the Victorian Scottish Union Conference by Comunn na Feinne, at Geelong. In his opening address, Mr John Burt Stewart, President of the Victorian Scottish Union (VSU), referred to the success the Union had in establishing a uniform set of regulations for Scottish National Games and pastimes in Victoria. Stewart also referred to the campaign the VSU had waged to get the press and other bodies to use the term 'Britain' or 'British' or 'Great Britain' when it was dealing with the whole of the UK, instead of using the term 'English'.

Stewart went on to affirm that the VSU was determined to foster the Scottish principle of educational opportunities for all, of being an influence for 'good' in society, and of caring for the destitute and those in distress. He continued that their aim should be the realization of 'the universal brotherhood of man', idealized by Burns, and, "they were determined to foster this to such a degree by the inculcation of national principles that it would be reflected in the Commonwealth by the wider development of true citizenship." Here, then, was Comunn na Feinne's 'vision' of a caring and harmonious community writ large!

Amid all the celebratory and complimentary comments at the Society's 50th Annual Meeting, in 1907, Dr John Small said that the Society, "had always fostered Scottish tradition in every way" but, more importantly, it also fostered some greater 'vision' within its own members, and in the community generally. He said that he was confident that, "In works of charity it [the Society] had always been prominent, and this charitable spirit is inculcated in every member." The fiftieth anniversary of Comunn na Feinne Gatherings was an occasion whereby both members and the general public could reflect on the Society's purpose in the community and whether the Society still held to its 'creed', as it had been laid down half a century before. Amid all the celebratory and complimentary comments, Dr Small said that he hoped the Comunn na Feinne 'spirit' would never grow weak and fade.

In practical terms, he continued, the Society had gone to great expense in making the Jubilee Gathering a success. Trains were chartered from Melbourne and Camperdown, and special invitations had been sent to the pioneers and other special guests, all of whom had to be accommodated and catered for. But, for all that, the report went on, "the accompanying balance sheet will show the Society to be in a sound financial position." The crowd at the Jubilee Gathering was one of the largest for some years and the events were watched with great interest. The New Year's evening concert at Johnstone Park had drawn "an immense crowd" and other activities, including the Burns' Night and the annual Haggis Supper, also had drawn large numbers. In terms of the Society's presence in the community, it was reported that the year saw many cases of need tended to by the Charity committee whose funds had been heavily drawn on but a credit balance of almost £20 still remained. The annual Highland Ball at the Corio Club rooms was also a success "from a social point of view", and the presence of the Scottish Country Dancers was, "a feature of the function" which added to its attractiveness.

It was reported, too, that a Comunn na Feinne Pipe Band had been established in the past year and that 13 pupils, "were making great progress under the tuition of Hugh Fraser* of Melbourne, and hope to make their first public appearance at an early date." Dr Small also announced that a momentous change had taken place during the year when the Rules of the Society were altered, "so as to provide for the admission of ladies to the Society" and, he continued, "we extend a hearty invitation to ladies to become members and interest themselves in the Society's affairs." Society Membership stood at 200, and the overall balance sheet showed that the Society had a credit balance of £9/0/11.

*[See short biographies Appendix 3(b).]

The passing of time had affected Comunn na Feinne in other ways too, but some of these changes, as already foreshadowed above, were dictated by people and organizations outside of Comunn na Feinne itself. There had been changes in sports, standards and equipment in the past half century with which Comunn na Feinne had come to grips. The growing professionalism of athletics and other competitive sports, the need for more realistic prize purses and the better racing track surfaces and the introduction of new events involving machines, such as bicycles, had brought better athletes and better outcomes in some competitions. Although many of the hazards and accidents of former years had been reduced, they had not entirely been eliminated. That silent competitor 'bad luck' still made its appearance on occasions. Arena improvements, such as the foregoing, had not altogether rendered sporting events accident free and there was still the chance of a wayward Caber or of an out of control Single Stick competitor or even that of a stray arrow! Bicycling, too, still provided the best chance of an unplanned catastrophe. The *Advertiser*, on 2nd January, 1908, wrote, for example, "In one of the finals four riders came to grief. One of them turned a somersault as he fell over two prostrate riders, but happily he escaped with a few cuts and abrasions about the face."

To some extent, the spirit of the Jubilee Year still inhabited the spectators and the competitors at the 1908 Highland Gathering, or so it seemed to the *Geelong Advertiser*. The procession to the grounds was all that could be wished. The colour of the tartans and the various uniforms on display, the music of the Prahran Pipe Band, the Society's own pipers and the St Augustine's Brass Band, among others, ensured that the colour was matched by the sounds of celebration. The absence of the Victorian Scottish Regiment did, somewhat, diminish the spectacle of the day. Unfortunately, the 'B' Grade Brass Band Contest and a quickstep contest, which had been arranged, meant that the Society did not invite the Regiment to take part at the 1908 Games due to the overfull programme. As it was, the Brass Band competition fell through but it was too late to then bring down the Regiment. Duncan McIntyre, who had so impressed Dr

Small some time before when, as an eight-year old he had played 'Cock of the North', won the piping competition for boys under 16 years, with James Galbraith's son, Alford Galbraith, taking second place.

There were no surprises in the Heavy Events with George Worland and Donald Cameron again dominating the field. Worland took first prize in the Caber and the Heavy Hammer events and Cameron was runner up in each of these contests.

The evening Concert held in Johnstone Park was, as usual, counted a great success by the *Advertiser*. The music, song and dance were much appreciated by the large crowd as were the biograph pictures which, in place of the overseas scenes which usually had dominated this part of the programme, featured "amongst the amusing subjects … 'A Wife's Hat' and, 'The Runaway Van.' Moving pictures were here!

A special Comunn na Feinne meeting was held 30th January 1908 to welcome back the Society's Chief, Mr Phillip Russell, after a long absence in Scotland where he had sought some recovery from his ill-health. In fact, earlier in the day, the Geelong Agricultural Society had also welcomed back Phillip Russell and had wined and dined him. Hardly having time to wash his hands, Russell was whisked off to a similar function by Comunn na Feinne. Dr Small, in his speech of welcome to the Chief, restated a now familiar theme. He said the Society was motivated by the clear 'vision' it had of its role. It existed for the good of others and for the community as a whole. Dr Small set right those who, even after so many demonstrations of its falsehood, perversely still described Comunn na Feinne as being a 'Scots only' club whose main occupation was patting each other on the back and exclaiming, 'Here' tae us! Wha's like us!' Precious few – an' they're a' deid!' Evidence would give lie to this charge.

> People often asked what was the good of having a Comunn na Feinne in Geelong which existed for the purpose of 'blowing' about Scotland. This showed their ignorance.
> In the early days, Comunn na Feinne had done a lot in the way of fostering education, but education had now become so common that every boy and girl in the land was now [no longer] forced to educate himself.
> He had always tried to uphold the traditions of this Society, and he had to congratulate the members on the good work they had carried out.

Comunn na Feinne's half yearly meeting was held on 23rd March, 1908 when Dr Small presided over, "a large attendance" of members. George R. King, who had been of great assistance to the Society on many occasions, was honoured by being made a life member. The half-yearly treasurer's report showed that the Society was in credit and that £175 had been placed on fixed deposit and the Charity fund, which was much used, had a balance of £17/16/5.

By 23rd July 1908, the Society was able to announce that the newly formed Comunn na Feinne Pipe Band numbered twelve pipers and the band was making "splendid progress" under Hugh Fraser's tuition. "They are enthusiastic and eager to make themselves proficient, and will be of great service to Comunn na Feinne on the occasion of the annual gathering and entertainment." When it was known that the band still required six sets of pipes to fully equip it, the Society's Chief, Mr Phillip Russell, donated a sum of £20 to buy two sets." The *Advertiser* on 29th July added that a further gift, from a 'patriotic Scot', covered the cost of the other four sets.

Comunn na Feinne Pipe Band

The Society's bard, Allan Fullarton Wilson, dedicated a poem, 'The Bagpipes of Scotland' to Comunn na Feinne's Pipe Band on the eve of its first public outing. [The whole of this poem can be found in the Appendix 5 (d), A. F. Wilson's Poems.

'How shall a doggerel bard portray
The secret o' the bagpipes' sway,
That mak' the Scotsman hot tae slay
An' maim an' wound,
Whilst his opponents curse the day
They heard the soun?
....
In fac' nane save the foremost place
Exac'ly suits our Scottish race;
Tae win it aft they've had tae face
The jaws o' hell.
Gie them the pipes, man they wid chase
The deil himself!
....
An' oh! When rises in the air
Their note o' sorrow, deep an' sair,
What grief unspeakable is there
In that refrain!
Thae wailing accents o' despair
Wid melt a stane.

During the rest of the year the Society followed a full calendar of events. On 20th August 1908, the annual Scottish Concert was held at the Mechanics' Institute Hall and an overflowing audience was well entertained. This was made special by the first public appearance of the Comunn na Feinne Pipe Band, headed by Pipe-Major D. McDonald (in the absence of Hugh Fraser). The Band marched, playing, through the streets of Geelong to the Hall and, during the interval, it mounted the stage and played 'The Barren Rocks of Aden', "the dozen or more pipes, together with the drums, producing a great volume of sound. For this they were encored, and gave "The 92nd Gordon Highlanders." The Concert consisted of singing and dancing. James Galbraith's talented children, Ettie, Walter and Alford Galbraith, together with Miss A. Mitchell, danced the 'Hopetoun Reel' and, later, the 'Clansmen's Sword Dance'. Many of the artists who performed were from Melbourne.

The Annual General Meeting on 29th September, 1908, at the Society's rooms in the Exchange Building, had a large attendance, and the President, delivered his annual report. He referred to the number of successful social events held by the Society, including the Burns' Night and the St Andrew's Night. The annual Haggis Supper which had been held at the Town Hall was also well received, as was the Highland Ball at the Corio Club, though it did not make a profit. Reference was also made to the charitable work done throughout the year as well as to the large task of hosting the Scottish Union conference. The lecture series had been held as usual and the Society, it was reported, had purchased a Picture Lantern, "with a view to assisting the lectures". It was also decided that Ladies be admitted to these lectures. The various balance sheets of the different parts of the Society were presented - all showing a credit balance. It was proposed that an early attempt be made to secure the Victorian Scottish Regiment for the 1909 New Year's Day Gathering. The evening was rounded off with entertainments in the forms of Scottish slides with J.B. Leitch manning the Lantern, with accompanying song.

Comunn na Feinne did manage to secure the Victorian Scottish Regiment for its next Gathering in January, 1909, along with the Regiment's Pipe Band. The usual Procession took place with plenty of noise and colour in its midst and, by the time it reached the grounds, it was found that it had drawn "a large number of persons, who had followed the march." The Society's own Pipe Band, along with St Augustine's Brass Band and Camperdown Pipe Band, "enlivened the proceedings with music."

The scheme, which had now been operating over a few Games, whereby there were two categories of contestant, amateur and professional, in many of the sports, seemed to have been a success. To encourage local athletes to participate, and to protect them against the professionals now dominating the Geelong, and similar, Gatherings, Comunn na Feinne had, over the past two or three years, run some duplicate events with one set open only to those living within a radius of 25 miles from Geelong and restricted to non-professionals. The Open events still attracted the big 'stars', while those now held only for locals, gave the 'week-end athlete' a chance to shine. The Society had also introduced a similar division in its solo piping competitions where there were separate contests for those living within twenty-five miles of Geelong and for those who had never won a piping competition, in addition to the usual Open event.

The *Advertiser* found it difficult, on occasions, after so many years of covering the Games, not to become somewhat repetitious in its reporting of events, or to rise above simply providing the bald results. Colourful imagination seemed to have deserted it altogether, however, when, at the 1909 Games, it could mention that there was a wrestling contest among, "the members of the Scottish Regiment", without mentioning a single eye gouge or below the belt tackle! However, it did comment upon the large numbers attending and how well the Games were carried out, giving James Galbraith great credit for his usual efficiency in organizing the Gathering and seemingly being everywhere at the same time.

The evening concert, following the day's Games, was held at Kardinia Park with the Comunn na Feinne Pipe Band and the Caledonian Brass Band providing the musical entertainment. There was also "an excellent show of moving pictures" presented for the people's enjoyment.

The Galbraith name was again to the fore as the Society held its annual Burns' concert in the new Masonic Hall on 28th January, 1909. Comunn na Feinne talent made up the entertainment together with the Society's own pipe band and its own Reel Dance Party (containing three of Galbraith's children), providing some of the entertainment. There was also singing and piping; the night was considered a great success, and there were no Melbourne artistes to pay!

Among the other events during the rest of the year, the annual Haggis Supper was held on 9th September, 1909, again at the Masonic Hall. It was a large gathering, and guests included Sir Thomas Gibson Carmichael*, Governor of Victoria, with John Cameron, "acting minister for Public Works ... accompanying His Excellency." Other politicians who were present included Donald McKinnon MLA., William Plain MLA., and C.L. Forrest MLA.

*[Sir Thomas Gibson Carmichael was Governor of Victoria, 1908-1911]

The *Advertiser* was quite descriptive, if not a little irreverent, in its summing up of the night. It allowed the pipes to loom large in its account:

> The proceedings were even more enthusiastic than usual. The pipers skirled before and during the supper; they hailed the great chieftain of the puddin' race; blew the Governor a wail on his way to the station, and marched thrice around the hall before the second part of the speeches could be resumed.

The presence of representatives from St Patrick's Society, the Cambrian Society and the St George Society, together with so many politicians of different stripes, presented a good example of the inclusiveness which Comunn na Feinne Society had always sought to promote, and the Society bard was on hand to deliver some verses* honouring the Governor's visit.

*[This poem can be found in Appendix 5(d), Poems of A. F. Wilson.]

The annual general meeting was held in the Society's rooms at the Exchange Building with Dr Small presiding. The usual reports were heard with the treasurer declaring that the Society to be in a state of credit to the amount £6/6/6. A special vote of thanks was delivered to "the Burns of the Society", Allan Fullerton Wilson, for his poem 'Welcome to the Governor, Sir Thomas Gibson Carmichael', which was recited at the meeting. This poem also appeared in the *Geelong Advertiser* on 9th September, 1909.

The Society's Pipe Band had been making good progress in its playing and a set of new uniforms was provided through the generosity of the Chief, Mr Phillip Russell, as well as from other donations. Russell also promised to "equip the band with plaids and brooches."

The Society also announced, as reported by the *Advertiser* on the 10th December 1909, that the Victorian Scottish Regiment would be at the 1910 Gathering and the Society would again be chartering a train from Melbourne to carry them and others who would be attending the Gathering. It made the point that, for the 1909 Games, 650 persons had used the specially chartered train from Melbourne to attend the Gathering. It was further announced that at the Gathering there was to be a Pipe Band

Competition between the Camperdown, Comunn na Feinne and Collingwood Pipe Bands, and it was also noted that Collingwood Pipe Band, "had given great support in the forming of, and in raising funds towards, … the Comunn na Feinne Pipe Band, [helping also] with kilts and pipes."

The 1910 New Year's Day Gathering started propitiously with the weather being, "warm but favourable." The Melbourne train, among its hundreds of visitors to the Geelong Gathering, also carried 70 members of the Victorian Scottish Regiment. Unfortunately, the Warrnambool Pipe Band and members of that town's Caledonian Society, who were supposed to have travelled by train to Geelong, were not able to do so due to a coal strike at Newcastle which had meant that their train was cancelled. The Society's chartered trains from Melbourne and Camperdown were not affected by this strike.

At the 1910 New Year's Day Gathering, Comunn na Feinne's own Pipe Band paraded for the first time in complete Highland Dress. Several Bands, including St Augustine's Brass Band and the Bands playing in the Pipe Band competition, took part in the traditional procession to the Geelong Football Oval. As usual there were many guests from different Caledonian Societies in Victoria and, significantly, H.D. Smith, secretary of the Victorian Amateur Athletics' Association (V.A.A.A.), was also in attendance, as well as "other representatives from kindred societies." Runners from Melbourne and Ballarat, as well as from two Geelong Harriers' Clubs, competed at the Games.

The heavy events saw George Worland back in winning form taking the Caber event and scoring a second in Throwing the Hammer and a third in Putting the Stone. The Pipe Band competition resulted in Collingwood coming first with Comunn na Feinne's Pipe Band a very close second, only two points separating first and second placings.

The usual evening concert following the Games was held, for the second time, at Kardinia Park. There was a large attendance and the Society, according to the *Advertiser* of 4th January, 1910, used an innovation in the form of night lamps and 'night lighting' was introduced for the first time!

> Eight large LUX LAMPS had been erected on the oval, and the different pipe bands were enabled to go through marching exercises. Scottish dancing and other items were included in the programme.

Thus, as noted earlier, over a century before Geelong Football Club played 'under lights' at Kardinia Park, Comunn na Feinne had introduced the idea at its night Concerts as early as 1910.

A Directors' Meeting was held on 11th January, 1910 and the Society was delighted to share a letter which they had received from the Victorian Amateur Athletics Association, "congratulating the Society on the success of the carnival [and] acknowledging the kindness extended to its representative." The V.A.A.A. representative expressed himself satisfied that the Association's standards had been met at the Society New Year's Day sports and, as a consequence, he added that the Association's presence next year would be double that of its 1910 showing. The champion heavy games winner, George Worland, himself 43 years old at the time, "promised to give a veteran's trophy for the Stone, Hammer and Caber events at the next Gathering …" There was a stipulation that the competitors for the trophy had to be over 55 years of age!!! No one seems to have taken up the offer.

A balance sheet was delivered showing that the recent New Year's Day Gathering had made a profit of £40, "which the directors considered very satisfactory." There was also a letter from Alexander Robertson, Chief of the Warrnambool Caledonian Society, "expressing regret that the coal strike had caused the cancellation of the special train from Warrnambool on New Year's Day, and promising that the Society would be strongly represented at the next Gathering in Geelong." That is, presumably, if the coal strike was over by then! It was also decided that the Comunn na Feinne Pipe Band would compete at the South Street, Ballarat Competitions later in the year. It was reported that the pipe band was practising hard and the pipers were showing satisfactory improvement.

The 54th Annual General Meeting of Comunn na Feinne was held on 7th September, 1910 with the treasurer's report showing the Society to be, "in a sound financial position". James Galbraith, the secretary, commented "that it was the best balance sheet submitted during his ten years of office as secretary." The "best of times" was continuing for the Society.

Many of the usual events took place during the year and were well patronised by members and public alike. At the annual Haggis Supper, Rev R.M. Fergus,* the minister of St Andrew's Presbyterian Church, Geelong, who was also a poet and songwriter, proposed the toast, in verse, to 'The Land o' Cakes'. [Two verses are given here, with the full poem in Appendix 5 (e) Poems of R.M. Fergus.]

> Dear Brither Scots, sae far frae hame,
> I hope I may escape your blame,
> If what I say prove a' too lame,
> For theme sae grand;
> We've met to glorify the name-
> 'Oor Native Land'.
>
> Here's tae the Land – The Land o' Cakes-
> Whose mystic charm our love awakes;
> An' to the dear ones, for whose sakes
> We fain wid be,
> Where heather blooms an' Thistle Shakes,
> Far ower the sea.

*[Rev. R.M. Fergus also published poetry and songs, as well as prose works. See Appendix 3 (b) Short Biographies.]

At this Haggis Supper, reference was again made to the fraternal feelings which existed between the various national groups in Geelong. Dr Small, in toasting Kindred Societies, specifically mentioned Clove Myers, the representative of the St George Society, and Mr J.T. Kerley of the Hibernian Society. Each of these men responded in turn with J.T. Kerley referring, "to the fraternal feelings existing between the national societies in Geelong." This had been, as already noted, a feature of Comunn na Feinne from its formation. The Society's philosophy was again re-stated by the President when he referred to the harmony and to the spirit of good works which characterised the Society's aim for the local community, and beyond. This formed the *ethos* of the Society and, he emphasized, if that ideal did not influence members' roles as individuals in the community, quite apart from any specific Comunn na Feinne activity, then they were not fulfilling the essence of the original charter.

Great stability and purpose had been added to the Society over the previous decade mainly under the leadership of the President, Dr John Small, the sometime treasurer, Mr George R. King, and the superlative organizational abilities of the secretary, Mr James Galbraith. The executive was well backed up by the united, able and hard-working committees and sub-committees. Comunn na Feinne's presence within the community, and beyond, had greatly increased, it was financially stable and its ability to undertake charitable work had expanded. Looking at the history of the Society as a whole, and at the previous decade in particular, it might accurately be said that this was, indeed, for Comunn na Feinne, "the best of times"

Such a view of the Society and its work, as the foregoing, was echoed by the *Geelong Advertiser* when, on the eve of the 1911 New Year's Day Gathering, it provided a short and affectionate history of Comunn na Feinne. It commented that the Society, "has never been stronger than at present, and the members anticipate a record gathering." A Pipe Band Contest, involving the Comunn na Feinne, the Camperdown, the Warrnambool and the Collingwood Pipe Bands, was to be one of the highlights of the day.

On New Year's Day, all of the ingredients were present for the "record gathering" hoped for by the Society. The *Advertiser* in its report on 3rd January, 1911, said that the weather was "perfect", the Procession through the town, was delayed because of the "late arrival of the train from Warrnambool", but the crowd at the starting point "waited patiently" and the march went ahead when the Warrnambool folk arrived. And it was a Procession, wrote the *Advertiser*, which made the wait worthwhile.

> The Collingwood Pipe Band and the Victorian Scottish Regiment … held pride of place, and made a fine display. The Warrnambool Pipe Band, Geelong Artillery Squad, Comunn na Feinne Pipe Band, [the Society] banner and

members, and the St Augustine's Brass Band were other features of the parade.

Despite the *Advertiser*'s ambivalent attitude over the years to the large number of Highland Dancing competitors taking the platform every year, its 'hardened' heart could be softened at times especially by the 'cuteness' of some of the very young dancers. It reported in 1911, for example: "There was hardly a lull in the dancing contests, and a little mite named Ruby Brown, celebrated her third birthday by dancing reel, hornpipe and strathspey, to the enjoyment of all present."

Ruby Brown (3 years old) with Major W.K. McKirdy.

The Victorian Scottish Regiment, with its marching, drilling and bayonet exercises, was again the star attraction at the Games. But it was its participation in other activities, too, especially its wrestling contests between individual members of the Regiment, that also drew so many spectators. "The wrestling contest by the Scottish Regiment was highly popular with the crowd who became so absorbed that cycling and pedestrian events were overlooked in its favour." This wasn't completely the case, of course and the *Advertiser* noted, "that the Worland dynasty was still producing heavy games champions, with George Worland, at 44 years of age, again winning the Caber event and being placed in the other heavy events."

Cycling was not altogether overlooked, however, and the *Advertiser* commented, "The cycle fields were large, and the finishes good and a good contingent of Melbourne harriers put life into the track events." But not all of the excitement involving bicycles and the rest of the world occurred on the racing tracks. There were incidents *en route* to the arena, outside the grounds, which also were newsworthy, especially as they involved bicycles and animals!

> One of the horses bringing St Augustine's Band to the Scottish Procession yesterday morning, stumbled opposite Dr Marwood's residence in Latrobe-terrace, and came down heavily. It was cut about the legs and flank, but not so seriously as to prevent the resumption of the journey.

Then there was animal and machine! Not only was travelling to Comunn na Feinne's Gathering fraught with risk, reported the *Advertiser* on 3rd January, 1911, returning from the Games presented its own dangers.

> Whilst returning from the Comunn na Feinne sports yesterday afternoon, a youthful cyclist collided with Mr J. Farrell's cab in the Botanical Gardens Drive. Mr Farrell pulled up, and finding the lad had not been badly hurt, reported the matter to the police, claiming that he was driving on his right side of the road at the time.

Like the horse, the boy went on his way. Nothing, however, is said of the fate of the bicycle - presumably it was humanely put down!

Then it was the machines by themselves! It appeared, sometimes, that there was nothing that could keep the mention of bicycles and Comunn na Feinne out of the news!

> A Melbourne cyclist named Matthews reported the theft of his cycle from Williams' restaurant, Moorabool Street, yesterday morning. He had been training in Geelong for a week for the Comunn na Feinne Sports, and was deprived of his ride by the thief. The machine was Melbourne built, was enamelled red, and had Major Taylor racing handles.

The evening Scottish Concert in Johnstone's Park took place where, "there was an enormous attendance" and the evening was greatly appreciated by the crowd. Comunn na Feinne's own Pipe Band presented two tunes, "and the drummer, Mr G. Bell, attracted much attention by his dashing manipulation of the sticks."

There were occasions when, away from the arena, and away from the social functions and entertainments, Comunn na Feinne's Charter was more visibly displayed in the activities of its members in daily life. Members, as individuals, were committed to work to realize the caring community. As individuals, they were enjoined to carry the Comunn na Feinne vision wherever they found themselves in society. In work and at play, in the family and in every other situation, they were to fulfil this calling. This was especially so in the years before such things as government-funded social services, pensions, child allowances and sickness benefits existed. Thus, it was expected that members would be involved with charitable groups, in local and wider politics, with Orphanages, with working Boys' Schools, with Industrial schools, with the Try Boys' Association, and in every area where there was a need. In this way, Comunn na Feinne was able to accomplish far more good through its influence on individuals who, in turn, had an influence on the community, than it could ever have achieved simply through the events which, as a Society, it staged or promoted.

A roll call of Comunn na Feinne members would find them involved in local, State and Federal Politics, in education, science, business and industry. It would find them in volunteer organizations, charitable institutions and in every movement pertaining to good works. They took the injunction to be 'leaven' in society very seriously.* This is not to say, of course, that many others, not belonging to Comunn na Feinne, did not have the same aims. Other societies in Geelong have been referred to throughout this book, and their members shared similar concerns for those with needs and they worked as volunteers in different community services.

*[Details of such activities, too numerous to include here, can be found in Appendix 14 (b).]

A very large crowd attended a fund-raising concert, on 1st April, 1911, for the Society's Pipe Band, and the principal guest act was the Melbourne Caledonian Kilties'

Brass Band. Before the evening Concert, the Band paraded the streets of Geelong marching and playing. They followed this up, according to the *Advertiser*'s account on 3rd April, 1911, "by giving a brilliant concert in the evening." Without outside assistance, they kept a bright and smart programme going for nearly three hours, the frequency of encores helping to extend the programme." One of the reasons for its popularity lay in the Bandmaster's willingness to feature items which were "out of the ordinary" in his programme. These included, "their descriptive fantasia, 'A Trip to Blackpool' which was capitally done", as well as the "popular cornet polka duet, with plenty of triple tongueing."

The fact that Comunn na Feinne, now over fifty years since its founding, still did not have its own offices or hall, or even a permanent headquarters, led, according to an *Advertiser* report on 21st September, 1911, to the following suggestion being raised.

> Captain J.B. Leitch, one of the directors of Comunn na Feinne, spoke strongly at the annual meeting on Thursday night in favour of securing a hall. At the present Comunn na Feinne has a sum of £200 on fixed deposit at the Commercial Bank, whilst general funds show a credit of £62/4/4.

The *Advertiser* also made mention of the ongoing efforts being made by Comunn na Feinne to "retain, in Geelong, Piper John Kidd, the 'Hero of Dargai* … He has made many friends in Geelong, and is taken with the district. A scheme is afoot to enable him to comfortably settle here."

*[The Gordon Highlanders' successful charge at the Heights of Dargai, took place 20th October, 1897, after a typical bit of British nineteenth century military blunders. The Dargai Heights are in Pakistan near the Afganistan border.]

Piper John Kidd had emigrated from Scotland with his wife and family, in 1911, to settle in Victoria. When Comunn na Feinne found out that he was in Melbourne it brought him down to Geelong as its guest and sought to induce him to stay. The Society was able to achieve success in that regard when it announced, at a meeting held 26th October 1911, that Piper John Kidd had settled on a small holding at Belmont which the Society had been able to obtain for him. He quickly became an active member and was thoroughly involved with the Society, tutoring its pipe band and being part of the annual New Year's Day Gathering, as well as its other activities. [Piper Kidd's story is told more fully in Appendix 3 (b).]

Piper Kidd

LHS Piper Milne -RHS Allan George Findlater - Centre John Kidd, Three pipers with the Gordon Highlanders when they stormed the Heights of Dargai. All three were wounded.

Comunn na Feinne's welcome to New Year's Day 1912 took the form of a verse from a popular song from the nineteenth century which has become something of a traditional start to the New Year even down to this day.

> A Guid New Year tae one an' all,
> And monie may ye see
> An' during a' the years tae come,
> O happy may ye be.
> An' may ye ne'er hae cause to mourn
> To sigh or shed a tear,
> Tae ane an' a' baith great an' sma'
> A hearty guid New Year.

New Year's Day 1912 saw the Highland Gathering competing for spectators with a Test Match in Melbourne and district horse racing. The *Advertiser* of 2nd January, 1912, reported that the Society's Gathering still attracted a reasonable crowd, although smaller than the previous year. The pre-games march again went by a route that passed the Geelong Hospital and the Benevolent Asylum, for the benefit of patients in those institutions. Leading the Procession was the Geelong Artillery Band. This was followed by a good turn-out of about one hundred men of the Victorian Scottish Regiment. The *Advertiser* commented that their appearance, as usual, was a big attraction adding, however, that this may have been the Regiment's last appearance "as a branch of the State Defence Service." With the formation of the Commonwealth of Australia in 1901, the various State defence systems were gradually being replaced with Commonwealth forces, although this changeover was somewhat progressive and did take time. The participation of the Victorian Scottish Regiment in various events, apart from their military routines, was appreciated, as always, by the spectators. This was especially so in the wrestling and tug of war events and, for those who appreciated the finer points of 'sweat and toil,' there was Wrestling and Physical Drill with Arms, to keep them satisfied.

The Pipe Band contest, held in 1912, saw the Comunn na Feinne's Band a popular winner, with Warrnambool Scottish coming second and Melbourne Pipe Band taking third position. An enormous response from the spectators arose when the three aforementioned Pipe Bands, in a display of massed pipes and drums, led the Victorian Scottish Regiment and the Melbourne Kilties around the ground. The marching skills of the Victorian Scottish Regiment and the Melbourne Kilties' Band later thrilled the crowd with a display of some intricate *manoeuvres*.

The *Advertiser* tartly reported that the Highland Dancing was, "watched with interest, despite the quantity of it." But once again the reporter was won over by a little girl dancer, Ruby Brown who, for the second year running, won the hearts of all the spectators. This diminutive performer was the daughter of George Brown of Melbourne (himself a champion Highland dancer).

> [She] gained the heartiest applause for her pretty hornpipe. She was the smallest Highland lassie on the ground, and even when off the dancing board, could not resist the temptation to jig to the tune of the pipes.

The evening Concert included pipe music as well as some lively music by the Geelong Municipal Brass Band. Other entertainments included "bioscope films" and Scottish dancing.

It was reported, 11th January, 1912, that the Comunn na Feinne Pipe Band, under John Kidd, had, "lately made rapid progress." Some good news was also delivered by the financial report for 1912 which, again, was an encouraging one. Financially the Society was in good health with assets standing at £707/16/3 and with no liabilities. The Charity Account also showed a credit balance.

At the monthly meeting of the Society on 3rd June, 1912, "It was agreed to revive the annual Highland Ball which had lapsed since 1908.

There were three issues which tended to dominate the second half of 1912 as far as Comunn na Feinne was concerned and these will briefly be looked at in turn. The first lay in the proposal to buy property on which to establish a 'home and hall' for itself. This involved an effort to 'sell' its old ground at South Geelong. The second issue related to the need for title for its old ground before it could be sold. The third of the issues to occupy the Society was that involving a proposal by the government to ban the wearing of kilts in its Scottish Regiments.

Not having used the grounds at South Geelong for some years, and having flitted around from ground to ground holding its annual Highland Games, the Society was anxious not only to find a permanent ground for its Gatherings, but also a settled home for itself to use as a Hall and offices. There appears to have been some unofficial contact between St Andrew's Presbyterian Church in Yarra Street and Comunn na Feinne with the possibility of the Society buying the Church building and grounds. Various sums between £3,000 and £3,500 had been bandied about but there had been no official meeting and the matter had not yet been put to the members of the Society. The St Andrew's Church managers were seeking to relocate and to sell their Yarra Street premises and grounds. Further gossip around the town had stated that Comunn na Feinne had made an offer of £3,500 for the property. Attached to this piece of 'unofficial' information was the further rumour that that the Society was seeking to sell the old grounds at South Geelong and that an offer of £700 had been made for this property. It was also reported, on 24th September, 1912, that the Society, "had asked the Government to take over the grounds vested in it for recreation purposes at South Geelong, for a consideration, on the understanding that the amount is to be expended in a hall [for the Society]."

[Note: The following newspaper coverage of the meeting, which decided upon the purchase of St Andrew's property, is quoted in full in Appendix 4 (b) CNF Grounds. It is given at length in the Appendix as it shows how the proposal was received by the members generally and how it relates to the Society's on-going debt problem, and it demonstrates how the seeds of the Debenture holders' debt, which was to trouble the Society to its last days, were sown at this time.]

> At a special meeting called of Comunn na Feinne members, under the chairmanship of its President, Dr John Small, the matter of the sale of St Andrew's Church and grounds was fully laid before the membership. The secretary read a minute from the directors that the following sub-committee had waited on the St Andrew's Church managers, who had offered to sell 171 feet of land in Yarra Street, with a depth of 131 feet 6 inches along McKillop Street, with the church buildings and appointments thereon for £1,500.

The Chairman proposed that the scheme be carried through, and the *Advertiser* reported:

> Mr J.B. Leitch seconded [the motion]. It was a wonder to him that C.N.F. had existed for 56 years without its own home. This might not be in the centre of the city, but it would soon be the way things were progressing, and if they waited for a block in the city they would wait till doomsday.
> Mr Aikman said as the land was under offer it was the wisest thing C.N.F. could do to buy it. He thought the members would finance it.
> Mr Sinclair said his experience was that members were not quick to put their hands in their pockets.
> [The Chairman said [that] such loans from members would be repaid with interest.]

The *Advertiser* of 31st October, 1912, reported that after some discussion, the proposal to buy was carried unanimously, "with applause", and the directors were empowered to act for the Society in the purchase.

> It was decided to issue a circular to district and country members appealing for assistance to carry the project through. Sums from £1 to £100 advanced will be allowed the current rate of interest.*

[*Those giving money under these terms constituted the 'debenture holders' much mentioned in the latter stages of the Society's life.]

The second concern for the Society was the need for title to the South Geelong grounds before it could sell such land. [See also Appendix 4 (c)]

Comunn na Feinne actually had no title to the land at South Geelong which originally had been granted to it, for temporary use only, as a Highland Games arena. The Society had not used these grounds for several years and it now sought to 'sell' this land. It first had to obtain 'title' by applying to the government for it, knowing full well that it had no right to it. Surely a colossal nerve on the part of the Society!

William Plain, a Victorian State MLA., and long-time Comunn na Feinne member and office-bearer, had been busy with efforts to 'oil the wheels' of the decision-making machinery in the state parliament. This pertained to the application by the Society for

Title to the grounds at South Geelong and, also, to have the government purchase back its own land!

It has already been pointed out that Comunn na Feinne avoided party politics and denominational religious matters, and practiced a non-discriminatory attitude when it came its membership and to participation in its activities. However, as we also have seen in the land issue involving its grounds at South Geelong, it was not averse to using political 'contacts' to further and 'speed up' its cause. The issue of Title was dealt with by a Government Bill introduced into parliament on 29th November, 1912, and was passed less than two weeks later, on 11th December, 1912. In a report regarding the land bill issue, the Society stated that it had received a letter from Hon. Hugh McKenzie MLA., (Minister for Lands) acknowledging the Society's gratitude, "for his assistance in pushing the Bill through Parliament for the disposal of Comunn na Feinne land at South Geelong, [and] intimating that he would be pleased to accept the invitation to attend the opening of the new Hall."

On Tuesday 3rd December, 1912, a preliminary deposit was paid to the Church's Trustees with possession of the property available almost immediately. It was intended that an early start was to be made on the necessary renovations and extensions.

The *Government Gazette* of 15th February, 1913, gave notice of the intended sale of the Society's old ground at South Geelong. Following this notice, a letter appeared in the *Geelong Advertiser* on 18th February, 1913, critical of any scheme that would allow a single buyer to gain the whole block of land and critical, too, that this would mean that the land would not be used to build affordable housing for the working classes.

> Sir - In your issue of *Geelong Advertiser*, Saturday 15th February, 1913, Government notices, I see the Comunn na Feinne site is to be sold in one lot the whole of the purchase money to be paid within a month (A splendid chance for a working man). Now, sir, considering that the land agents are asking £3 per foot for blocks in that vicinity, I consider it is not right to allow any person, or syndicate, to acquire one whole block fronting four streets where allotments are so valuable. Hoping the member for the district will endeavour to stop the sale of the same in the interest of the advancement of Geelong. Why does not Trade Council act for its members in such cases? Signed 'Working Man'.

Predictably, 'Working Man's' plea went unheeded and at the sale it would seem that there was at least 'a nod and a wink' between all of the parties involved that would see the whole enterprise 'sewn up' between 'brithers a'.

> There was a big attendance of speculators half a dozen of whom bid spiritedly for the land. The upset price was £700, and bids rose rapidly to £900. Two fought out the purchase to the end, and the site was knocked down at £990 to Neil Campbell and Company for William Volum. The good price realized gave satisfaction to the Society, which will secure a percentage of the takings towards the purchase of St Andrew's old Church, for their hall.

It seemed almost superfluous for the *Advertiser* to note that W. Volum, "is a member of Comunn na Feinne." It could have added that so too was Neil Campbell who was, in fact, a past-president of the Society, and now operated as an auctioneer and real estate agent. A subsequent advertisement in the *Advertiser* on 28th March, 1913, offered for sale, "18 Magnificent Residential Sites [with] Frontages to Bellerine, Balliang and Fyans streets (all made roads)." W. Volume lost no time in highlighting the other advantages.

> Special attention is directed to this sale, as each block commands a High and Healthy Situation, with Perfect Drainage, and is indeed an Ideal Spot for Building Purposes. The land has frontages to Wide Made Streets by Extensive Depths to a right-of-way.

The new South Geelong Electric Tram in course of erection will run within a few minutes' walk of the Site.

The third issue which captured the concerns of Comunn na Feinne, and which caused it to set itself on a collision course with authority, was the Government's proposed abolition of the kilt for Scottish Regiments in Australia. The Society held its annual meeting on 11th September, 1912, when the reports of the various activities over the past year were delivered. Among other matters of discussion was that involving the Government's attempt to abolish military use of the kilt. Objections had been lodged by Comunn na Feinne at government level. The President said, "that they were now hopeful that, largely as the result of efforts put forward by Comunn na Feinne, the Minister would find it possible to allow the Scottish Regiment to retain its national dress." This went beyond being an 'ethnic' campaign, carried on by an 'ethnically inclusive organization,' attempting to impose its narrow view on the rest of society. It related only to the Victorian Scottish Regiment, initially a volunteer force. James Scullin* pointed out that banning the kilt from this Regiment would be detrimental to the building of an Australian nation, bearing in mind that even its native-born children had parents most of whom had come from one of the three main divisions of peoples in Great Britain. Antagonizing one or more of these divisions of peoples was hardly the way towards a united sense of nationhood. The building up of Australian sentiment would not be accomplished, "by casting aside all the best traditions of the old world."

*[James H. Scullin served as Labor Prime Minister of Australia, 1929-1931]

James B. Leitch, a member of the Comunn na Feinne executive, and President of the Victorian Scottish Union at the time, "mentioned the arguments that had been used by the deputation to the Minister. The matter, he thought, would be debated in Parliament on the 5th October. It was to be a non-party question." At yet another meeting of the Society, held 12th December 1912, it was reported with great delight that word had been received that the attempt to abolish the kilt, "as the official dress of the Victorian Scottish Regiment" had been defeated by a large majority. The Society took further satisfaction in the fact that it had initiated the resistance to the Federal Government's original plan and it was appreciative, too, of the help of other organizations and of those members of parliament who had spear-headed the opposition to the Government's intention. So effective was the lobbying and the challenge within parliament itself that, "the official decree was smothered.

Notices of the passing of old members and supporters regularly appeared in the local press and cast gloom over the Society at the removal from the scene of the veterans. One of these, Alexander McRae*, one-time secretary of Comunn na Feinne, and a long-serving member of the executive, died in November, 1912. He had been a member for 50 years. He was a Gaelic scholar and had regularly helped the non-Gaelic speaking members through his explanations of Gaelic words and phrases.

*[See for some details in Appendix 3 (b) Short Biographies.]

A gift to the Comunn na Feinne also reminded it of another stalwart of the Society, Major John Bell, who had been its President (1862-67) and, later, its Chief (1873-76). He had been an enthusiastic member of the Society's executive, and a generous financial supporter of the Society and he had died, after a long illness, in 1876. The Society had, on the 18th December, 1912, received news regarding a portrait of Major John Bell, "which was to be hung in the Society's Hall. Major John Bell "was a noted Stone, Hammer and Caber thrower (sic), and was never beaten at the Society's gatherings". His biography – an extract from the *Geelong Advertiser*, occupying two columns – accompanied the picture. John Bell won the Gold Medal at the Paris Exhibition at the age of 18 years as the most powerful athlete in Europe." Tales of his strength, and demonstrations of this, passed into Geelong folk-lore.

Despite the fact that Comunn na Feinne was, with great regularity, losing, through death or removal from the district, members of the Society, both young and old, its activities continued and its energies, both emotional and physical, were needed in preparing the annual Gathering as well as staging it. It was, therefore, business as usual as the New Year, 1913, approached. The *Advertiser* carried several notices in its last issue for the year, advising of the upcoming Scottish events in January 1913; the promotion of military and naval demonstrations unwittingly, perhaps, foreshadowing the coming of war.

Part of the notice appearing in the *Advertiser* for 31st December, 1912, read:

Comunn na Feinne
56th Grand highland Gathering
Military Tournament and Pipe Band Contest
On the Football Oval
New Year's Day
Splendid Entries for All Event
Grand Military and Naval Events.

The *Advertiser* opened its report on the New Year's Day Gathering, on 2nd January, 1913, with praise for the size and the attractiveness of the traditional procession to the

Geelong Oval. With the Victorian Scottish Regiment and the pipe bands of Port and South Melbourne, Richmond, Warrnambool, and the Society's own band, all taking part, there was no shortage of stirring music to encourage the marchers. The Geelong Harbour Trust Brass Band also took its turn, "giving odd spells from the skirl." On arrival, the President, Dr John Small, welcomed the crowds and the bands and competitors. He also greeted the "representatives of the Linton, Warrnambool, Colac and Numurkah societies", and conveyed the greetings which had been received from kindred societies including, "Brunswick, South and Port Melbourne, Prahran, Numurkah, Collingwood, Camperdown. Colac and Warrnambool, and the Hibernian Club."

While welcoming all present to the 1913 Games, Dr Small particularly drew attention to the presence of Alexander Robertson (President of the Launceston Caledonian Society, Tasmania), some veterans who had competed in the games in the early years of the Society, and visitors from Warrambeen. His short address drew its biggest cheers when he mentioned that, "through the action of Comunn na Feinne and Mr J.B. Leitch, the Scottish Regiment had retained the kilts, and he hoped they would maintain the traditions of their ancestors." He also mentioned the fact that the Society had taken steps to provide a home for itself.

Although the *Advertiser* could momentarily be charmed with the sight of a tot like Ruby Brown competing in the Highland dancing, it could, on other occasions, also display an impatience with the amount of this dancing at the annual Gatherings. At times, it must have seemed to the reporter that there was a veritable multitude of kilted 'ankle biters' who year after year, in increasing numbers, waited their chance to perform the same dances, to the same pieces of pipe music. However, there was praise from the reporter at these Games, especially for the "juveniles" who "were an extremely clever lot."

Group of dancers (under 12) waiting their turn to compete.

The cycling races, too, could sometimes stir even the most jaded spectator, even a bored reporter, to a bout of enthusiasm. There was excitement and some close finishes in the cycling, and these contests were, "lifted from mediocrity" by some excellent riding by the Camperdown cyclist, E. Perrett, and the Melbourne contestant, T. Moloughney, also gave some entertaining racing.

The Pipe Band contest results, saw Comunn na Feinne's Pipe Band running second to the Port and South Melbourne Pipe Band, with Richmond and Warrnambool coming third and fourth respectively. Apart from the excitement and thrills of the day, the event closing the Games added a special 'tingle' to the air. This was, "the march past of 60 Pipers and Drummers and 100 Kilted Warriors of the Regiment" in a 'massed bands' display.

The traditional evening Concert in Johnstone Park was as popular as ever with singing, dancing, and music. A demonstration of physical exercises by, "the Naval Cadets and members of the Artillery" was enthusiastically applauded and, for the less strenuous, biograph views were also shown.

Although the building to be used as its new Hall and headquarters had not yet been fully renovated, the Society's directors met on 16th January, 1913, for official business, for the first time at their new Yarra Street 'home', with Dr Small in the chair. He took the opportunity of impressing on those gathered the need for the building to be re-modelled as soon as possible and for them, "to rally round and complete the building proposal [which would], make their property something to be proud of." Committees were set up to, "supervise various works connected with the scheme." James Galbraith reported that several cash donations had already been received towards the building fund. The meeting was recorded the next day in the *Advertiser*, which reported that Allan Fullerton Wilson's poem "Oor ain ha'." written especially for the occasion, was read and received with "considerable enthusiasm".

Tenders for the Yarra Street building and renovations were advertised 1st March, 1913 with Laird and Buchan, Architects, having already had been awarded the contract for planning and design. Angus J. Laird and Thomas Buchan were closely associated with Comunn na Feinne, as members and office-bearers! On opening the first lot of tenders, for renovating the church building, on 12th March, 1913, the Society felt that, "the prices were very high, and action was deferred" until amended offers were received. New Tenders were subsequently received and it was the firm of Drew Bros and Ebbels of Geelong, whose tender of £1,350 was accepted.

As might have been expected, the various meetings of the Society during the year were dominated by discussions and reports on the progress of the Hall and, of course, appeals for donations. The monthly meeting held 31st March, 1913, reported next day in the *Advertiser*, heard a progress report on the building and fund-raising activities. A circular had been sent out seeking donations and loans from members, "and the response had been most liberal, the sum subscribed now totalled £1,550/10/0, with the Chief, Phillip Russell, "showing his practical approval by subscribing £500, and other donations ranged from £100 down to 10/-."

On 3rd April 1913 William Plain, again using his position as a Parliamentarian, arranged for a meeting between a Comunn na Feinne delegation and Mr John Thomson, acting Minister for Lands. The delegation, consisting of Dr John Small, Captain James B. Leach and Mr James Galbraith, met with Mr Thomson to enquire the best procedure as to the transfer of title to the St Andrew's church land. John Thomson advised that the best course would be to transfer the land to the crown and then elect trustees. Hot on the heels of this meeting, the election of Trustees for the Comunn na Feinne Hall site took place. Elected were, "Dr John Small, Captain James B. Leitch and James Galbraith and, along with Phillip Russell and George R. King", they were to form the general trustees of the Society's property. This was announced in the *Geelong Advertiser* 7th April, 1913.

The Hall and its progress continued to dominate Society meetings, with regular progress reports being delivered. The monthly meeting on 1st July, 1913, for example, heard that the building work on the hall was progressing well and that it was expected that the first meeting in the new premises would take place, "with Highland honours … about the end of August." The Minister for Lands, Hon. Hugh McKenzie, "had consented to perform the opening ceremony." There was also a report from the concert committee to the effect that the annual concert to be held in July would feature Madame Stirling and "her clever daughter Miss Mary Stirling …". It was also agreed to erect a "tablet" in the Hall to indicate to visitors that the building was originally St Andrew's church whose first minister was the Rev Andrew Love. The announcement that a prize, the Society's Gold Crest, to be awarded to the member who introduced the largest number of new members by the end of the year, had been a stimulus to bringing in new recruits. The Society's membership had increased by 100 to total 400 over the course of that year.

Despite the changing nature of the Highland Games and the removal of so many of those actually born in Scotland, sentimental song and verse still proved patently effective. At the annual concert a new Scottish song, 'Where the Heather grows', was sung for the first time. It was written by Rev R.M. Fergus, the minister of St Andrew's Presbyterian Church, who also set it to music. [The full song can be found in Appendix 5(e) Poems of Rev. R.M. Fergus.]

> Oh, the hills and the valleys where aince I did stray.
> An' the burns an' the birdies, that gladdened the way.
> An' the Lang days that lingered in summer sae fair,
> Shall I see them, or hear them, or tread them nae mair?
>
> *Refrain*
> Where the heather is blooming on Scotia's far hills,
> Where the lav'rock is thrilling the life wi' his trills,
> Where the leal herts are bounding sae joyous an' free,
> Oh its there that ma hert is an' fain I wid be.
>
> Oh I see them, I see them around my hearthstane,
> But the circle is small noo', sae many are gane;
> An' tho' sair be the sicht, yet I ken they're all weel,
> An' we'll all meet again i' the land o' the leal.

The concert was, as usual, crowded out and many were the encores which called all of the artistes back again and again. Twenty nurses from the Geelong Hospital were present as guests, as well as visitors from the Western District. Representatives from the Geelong Football Club also attended, "at the invitation of James Galbraith, an ex-Geelong champion footballer, who was the vice-president of the Football Club and president of the Junior Football Association." Before the Concert began, the Comunn na Feinne Pipe Band had "marched, playing, through the city" and it was this Band which opened the Concert with "a Highland selection." The singer, Miss Maggie Stirling,* born in Geelong and, a popular singer at Scottish Concerts, was encored over and over again. The Rev. R.M. Fergus's song, 'Where the heather grows', was sung by her at this concert and, according to the *Advertiser* of 22nd July, 1913, this was its first public performance. Her daughter, Miss Mary Stirling, made her public debut at this event. She was so well received that she ended up having to sing five songs instead of her scheduled two! In addition, she also sang duets with her mother. Other entertainers included the baritone Pat Coleman and the humourist, Arthur Douglas, "the Australian Harry Lauder."

* [Maggie Stirling's details can be found in Appendix 3 (b) Short biographies.]

The Annual Meeting, on 15th September, 1913, was held at the Fire Brigade Hall with Dr Small presiding. The purchase and the renovation of the new Hall continued to be high on the agenda of Society affairs. It was anticipated that, after its own new Hall was completed, the Society would be able to run regular monthly socials. The Society's charity work had not been neglected with many deserving cases having been helped through the Charity Fund. It was also reported that £100, "had been placed to the credit of the Geelong Hospital endowment fund." Various donations were acknowledged and a glowing report of the annual concert, especially the singing of Miss Maggie Stirling, was given.

The President in summing up the evening said that:

> [A]fter 50 years of existence in Geelong, Comunn na Feinne was holding its last annual meeting as a homeless body. From its inception, it had been obliged to meet where it could. At last a home was in sight. At an early date, it was expected that a haggis supper would be the means of entertainment by which the new Hall was to be opened. Fears had been expressed at the large cost of patching an old building, but he was of the opinion that what was worth doing was worth doing well, and they now had a hall which was a credit to those who had designed the alterations.

The treasurer's report was equally 'up beat'. The Society had a credit balance of £965.3.6 and the Pipe Band also returned a credit balance of £11/12/3. Twenty new members of the Society were also admitted into membership.

The Hall was officially opened with great fanfare on 1st October, 1913, and the ceremony was performed by Sir Alexander Peacock, the Minister for Education. It was related that the building and land cost the Society £1,500 and the restoration and alterations amounted to a further £1,700. After the official opening, the meeting then held a Haggis Supper. The opening was celebrated with a little pomp and much noise. The Society's Pipe Band marched, playing, up Yarra Street at the head of a procession which included Sir Alexander Peacock, Senator McColl, Senator William Plain, Donald McKinnon MLA., Phillip Russell, Dr John Small, and the Rev. J.A. Forrest. A large crowd had assembled outside the Hall to welcome the official party. Electric lights, in red, white and blue, shone above the building. Sir Alexander Peacock gave a short opening speech, apologizing for the absence of the Minister for Lands (Hugh McKenzie who was ill), who had asked Peacock to deputize for him. Following the preliminaries, "over 150 sat down to the Haggis Supper which proved to be one of the most enthusiastic and successful gatherings of its kind held by the Society …". Verse and song, by Rev. R.M. Fergus and the Society's bard, Allan Fullarton Wilson, also featured during the celebrations.

The Comunn na Feinne Hall, Yarra Street, Geelong.

As noted, local politicians as well as State and Federal politicians were in attendance as were representatives from many other Scottish Societies. Senator McColl spoke briefly commending the Society for its vision in acquiring such a home from which, "they would be able to extend operations as soon as they were able. They were going to radiate from this place an enormous influence on Geelong and the State generally …" The various toasts were proposed and responded to and James Galbraith, the secretary, Dr John Small, the president, and Mr Phillip Russell, the Chief, were singled out for special praise. Under the leadership of these three, the membership had gone from 100 to 400.

It seemed that, for Comunn na Feinne, it continued to be, 'the best of times'.

The Comunn na Feinne Pipe Band was active during the year, competing, for example, at the New Year's Day Gathering at Geelong and playing at Beaufort Caledonian Society Sports on 24th March, 1913. The Society's Chief, Mr Phillip Russell, paid for its trip to Beaufort. As we have also seen, the Band had an active part in the opening ceremonies of the new Hall on 1st October 1913. Later, in the same month, the Society's Pipe Band once again entered South Street, Ballarat, competitions. Although the South and Port Melbourne Pipe Band took first prize, Comunn na Feinne Pipe Band was by no means disgraced and it came a close second with only five points separating the two Bands.

On 31st December, 1913, the Society's secretary, James Galbraith, announced that Dugald Rankin, "now living in Melbourne, [one] of the originators of this historic institution, would endeavour to be present" at the 1914 New Year's Day Gathering at which there would be, "a grand march past by the Scottish Regiment heralded by 50 pipers" at 3pm during the Games. Members of the Society honoured their president, Dr John Small, with their first Hogmanay in the Society's new home in Yarra Street.

The Procession to the grounds for the 1914 Highland Gathering was led, again, by the Victorian Scottish Regiment with senior officials of the Society and visiting bands and Society members following. While welcoming all present to the 1914 Games, Dr Small particularly drew attention to the presence, among other visitors, of Alexander Robertson (President of the Launceston Caledonian Society, Tasmania), and Dougal Rankin, one of the original members and a promoter of Gaelic, who had helped form the Victorian Gaelic Society. Also present were some veterans who had competed in the games in the early years of the Society. The *Advertiser*'s report on 2nd January, 1914, records that further welcome announcements were made by Dr Small to the effect that the Society had, at last, obtained a 'home' for itself and that "the final payment* of £800 had been made on the last day of the year."

*[This announcement seems to sit at odds with the later reference to the continuing debt which the Society owed and it probably refers only to the final payment to St

Andrew's Church. The Society continued to have many debts such as interest payments due to the debenture holders, for example, as well as the £1,700 debt owing for the renovations to the building which had to take place before it could be used by the Society. The ongoing debt thus would have referred to the large costs involved in renovating the building plus interest on loans, such as was owed to debenture holders and to the bank overdraft.]

While the *Advertiser* was generally supportive of Comunn na Feinne's annual New Year's Day Gathering, as well as its other activities, it occasionally let fly with both barrels when it thought the Gathering was so terrible that it should be put out of its misery. The newspaper's opinion of the 1914 Games fell into that latter category. It was critical of cancellations of certain events and, summing up the January 1914 Gathering as a whole, it said that, "a good wood chop" would have been better than "half a dozen tame and monotonous events." Although not identifying the "tame and monotonous events," the *Advertiser* had never been secret about its ambivalent attitude towards the large number of Highland Dancing and Piping events. Its coverage of the Piping and Dancing competitions, therefore, did not always find the reporter in a charitable frame of mind, and his reports of these two events showed, sometimes, his lack of patience.

The Pipe Band contests at the 1914 Games saw Comunn na Feinne's Pipe Band take first place, with Colac and Warrnambool taking second and third places respectively. There was the now familiar march past consisting of the massed bands and the Victorian Scottish Regiment and this, reported the *Advertiser*, was also received well. Similarly, the *Advertiser* did not stint in giving credit to the less 'dull' activities such as cycling events (always good for the inevitable spill of cyclists and their machines), and the wrestling bouts (always the chance of a bit of 'biff and eye gouging') although the latter, it said, was "delayed till many people left the ground wearied." But, wearied or not, sufficient of them attended the traditional concert at Johnstone Park that evening where they were entertained by the Society's Pipe Band, the Geelong Harbour Trust Brass Band, and singers and dancers, as well as with moving pictures."

The first monthly meeting of Directors for the new year was held on 6th January,

1914, and it was decided that the Society would hold a Burns' Night on 24th January, the nearest suitable day to Burns' actual birth date of 25th January. There was also a report on the illness of Francis Milliken who had been a member of the Society for forty-four years. A letter of sympathy was sent to his family wishing him a good recovery. This was part of Comunn na Feinne's general welfare policy where those with a sickness or some other form of physical or mental problem were contacted and, if necessary, medical fees, expenses and other costs might, if needed, be shouldered by the Society. At the monthly meeting of 3rd February, 1914, it was reported that James Galbraith (secretary) and James Patterson had visited Francis Milliken and had found him recovering from, "a serious operation and making satisfactory progress towards good health."

A Special Director's Meeting was called on 20th January, 1914, when the accounts for the Prizes awarded at the Highland Games, an amount of £247, "were passed for payment." Perhaps an announcement which held a more solemn foreboding, given the impending WW1, related to Captain James B. Leitch. Captain Leitch, a senior member of the Society, had held the rank of Captain when serving in the forces as a Veterinarian in the African War, and it was announced that he was promoted, "to the position of Captain in the Commonwealth Forces."

It was also announced that the collection of photographs of all past presidents, since the Society's formation in 1856, had now been completed and framed. This was unveiled at the half-yearly meeting held on 24th March, 1914, before a reasonable turnout of members. Pleasing news was delivered, too, by the treasurer who reported that the finances were in "a very substantial state." It was also announced that the Comunn na Feinne Pipe Band, together with the Ballarat Caledonian Society's Pipe Band, had travelled to appear at the Beaufort Highland Society and were guests of Phillip Russell, chief of Comunn na Feinne.

Collection of photos of Office-bearers over the years.

Perhaps the most popular overseas name to perform in Geelong, to that time, was that of Sir Harry Lauder, the internationally known Scottish comedian and singer, whose visit was hosted by Comunn na Feinne. On the 20th May, 1914, it achieved the biggest boost to its activities to date when it welcomed Sir Harry Lauder, "The £1,000-a week Comedian", to Geelong. The Society was actively involved in promoting his visit and organized the time he spent in Geelong.

In a dense throng at the railway station, Thursday, when the midday train brought Sir Harry Lauder and his company from Melbourne, the Scottish Humourist and his wife were parted. "Where's Mistress Lauder?" he called, and repeated it until the reassurance came that the little lady was safe in James Galbraith's keeping. They had experienced a rough passage [getting] to the Motor cars decorated with the Highlanders' flags and many tartans. As for Harry Lauder, everybody wanted to get near him, and he wanted to get near the Comunn na Feinne Pipe Band. He complimented them, there was cheering, and a motor whisked him to the Victoria Hotel, where the Comunn na Feinne leaders spent a few happy minutes with him in the sitting room [where] Dr John Small briefly told the story of Geelong.

The *Geelong Advertiser*, seemingly fixated by Lauder's presumed weekly wage packet, gave an effusive review of his show, concluding that whatever the size of Lauder's wage envelope, it was no more than he deserved.

> The four figures-a-week Scot made a record; every seat was booked, and the pack of disappointed cash patrons outside was dense. They had some solace in seeing the comedian walk up to the front of the theatre behind the Comunn na Feinne Pipe Band. Many of them were glad to pay for standing room on the stage behind the side scenery. Harry Lauder soon showed the audience some of the main characteristics that command a £1,000 a-week salary. He enunciates perfectly, even in a whisper, and is careful to put abundant burr on his r's. His tongue is not particularly broad, and no effort is required of the auditor to understand him. Here was the world's record maker in his line showing the bottom rung of the ladder to budding artists. Then his facial expression is wonderful, and goes a long way to that £1,000.

Sir Harry Lauder at CNF Hall 20th May, 1914.

With the excitement of the Harry Lauder visit quickly fading, the Society turned its attention to the immediate problems to hand, including the matter of the Hall debt. It has already been noted that Comunn na Feinne had belatedly recognized that women should be allowed to join the Society and had opened up membership (with some restrictions) to the ladies. They, of course, had always played an important (though rarely acknowledged) part in the Society's life and this was never more pronounced than when it came to fund-raising. The female portion of the Society was to the fore when the Comunn na Feinne Hall Committee announced on 21st May 1914, the formation of a Ladies' Committee to assist with the Building Fund. A group of fifty ladies met and elected Mrs N. Wilson to head the group. And so, not for the first, or the last time, ladies stepped in to support worthwhile causes and this Committee very quickly arranged several functions, "to be supervised solely by ladies", to take place during the year, and which were expected to raise "a good sum" towards paying off the debt on their Hall. This Committee was soon in action and on 29th June a Comunn na Feinne Concert, organized by it, was held. The numbers attending were more than the Hall could accommodate and this successful experience led the Comunn na Feinne executive to recommend increasing the size of the Hall, though they were still not debt-free regarding the costs of the initial renovations.

CNF Ladies' Fete Committee

The Society after some discussion considered reviving competitive examinations for schools, which had occupied such a large part of its activities in the early years up to the introduction of the State Education Act in 1872. Comunn na Feinne was proud of the fact that many of the individual pupils who had been medal winners had gone on to have important careers in medicine, education, law and administration. (See Appendix 3 (b).

> A sub-committee was appointed to consider the advisability of renewing the competitive examination, as [conducted by] Comunn na Feinne [in its] early history, for scholars of the schools.

Coincidentally, at this time, a reminder of one aspect of Comunn na Feinne's earlier activities regarding its educational competitions was provided through the discovery of the die for the medals which the Society had issued as prizes.

> Some excitement was occasioned by the discovery amongst some litter in the room at Strachan Wool Store, the original screw-press die with which these medals were struck. It was imported for the Society in 1860, through Strachan, Murray and Shannon, and was mislaid for a long time. About 12 months ago it was, evidently, surreptitiously placed by a modest donor inside the door of the meeting room, and not until last night was its value devined (sic). The directors were delighted with the restoration of the old relic.

After having discussed the issue of reviving its role in educational competitions, and re-instituting Essay-writing competitions as a first instalment towards realizing this aim, the Society, in March 1912, began a series of competitive Music, Dance and Elocution events for school-age children of Society members. Comunn na Feinne, however, did not revive the educational competitions after the pattern of those of the early decades of its life. It quickly came to realize that in its recently introduced Music, Dance and Elocution competitions, it was also engaging in education, but more widely defined. Just as it had gained plaudits from educationists in the nineteenth century for its influence both in improving the teaching and the educational curriculum in schools, so too was it to gain similar praise regarding its musical competitions in the twentieth century.

These competitions were variously called the Eisteddfod or the Musical, Elocutionary and Dance Competitions, and the Society regarded this venture as a continuation of its education policy which it had begun in 1858. The subject areas, initially, were confined to music, dance and elocution and were only open to the children of Comunn na Feinne members. In June 1914, however, these competitions were extended to school-age children generally. The *Geelong Advertiser* on 15th June, 1914, announced the Comunn na Feinne Musical, Elocutionary and Dance competitions with an explanatory piece identifying these as being in the spirit of the Society's original role in improving education.

> In the early meeting of Comunn na Feinne, Educational examinations were held annually, and many leading citizens were amongst the prize winners. It is the intention of the Society to re-new these, and a start will be made tonight, when elocutionary and singing competitions will be held. A very encouraging entry has been received, 32 for the elocution section alone.

These contests, which were now, "not confined to [children of] members", drew "a large audience" and were considered successful. A concert and dance followed the end of the contests.

The venture began quite slowly, with just a handful of children competing mainly in music and elocution, but it very quickly blossomed, and, by 1928, over two thousand men, women and children were taking part in the ninety-two sections on offer. These ranged from classical singing, musical instrumental performances and dramatic acting to choral work, duets and comedy performances.

The Society's newly-opened hall was used as the venue for the Eisteddfod in 1914 but, as the competition expanded, additional venues had to be used. As time went on members earnestly, but no doubt with partisan motives, began to press the civic dignitaries who opened each annual Eisteddfod to make good on their pledges of support by erecting a concert hall for Geelong. Needless to say, they asked in vain! More hurtful was the failure of the Town Council to provide any monetary support for the growing Competitions. Despite the numbers the event brought to the district each year, Council hid behind the Local Government Act, which it claimed tied its hands. (Ballarat felt no similar constraint when it came to supporting the South Street Competitions, nor did Bendigo council when similar competitions were begun in that town.) As the Eisteddfod grew so did the expenses associated with it, especially hall hire, judges's fees and prize monies. For the latter, local businesses were regularly canvassed for financial donations and trophies, but success in this regard was not spectacular, although the Melbourne *Sun* newspaper, commencing in 1925, contributed thirty pounds annually for an operatic aria competition.

Some effects which flowed from the Eisteddfod were immediate and local. The Society encouraged the formation of choirs in local schools and workplaces to enrich its choral competitions (The International Harvester Choir is one surviving example of the tradition of workplace choirs). Geelong teachers of dance, music, singing and elocution were able to use the Eisteddfodau to develop and hone the skills of their charges; and, when advertising for new students, they did not fail to draw attention to the successes of their pupils. Unsurprisingly, given the competitive nature of the whole enterprise, one of its proudest outcomes was the discovery of highly talented young performers. Thomas Goodall, Rita Miller and Elena Danelli were winners at the Comunn na Feinne competitions and some went on to enjoy domestic and international success.

Singers such as John Brownlee, Marjorie Lawrence and Norman Menzies were enabled to study in Europe with Brownlee and Lawrence becoming international 'stars'. Initiated by Nellie Melba a mutual support network of sorts emerged among the successful Comunn ne Feinne singers, backed by the wider Geelong community, which could see prize-winners showcased at an annual concert. John Brownlee won success at the 1918 competitions, and was encouraged by Melba to undertake training in Europe. He did so and eventually sang, to great acclaim, at the Paris Opera, La Scala in Milan and the Metropolitan Opera in New York. While abroad he gave encouragement and support to other Australia singers seeking to further their careers. These included Marjorie Lawrence, winner of the aria contest in 1928, who had a stellar career on the international stage. With sad irony, the letter Marjorie Lawrence wrote to the (then) Secretary of Comunn na Feinne, James Galbraith, detailing her struggles to succeed overseas and acknowledging the support received from the Society, arrived after he had resigned his post because the Society had withdrawn from the staging the

Eisteddfod!

Nellie Melba sang at a local fund-raising concert for Elena Danelli (her protégé), and a series of similar concerts in February and March 1932 raised a staggering seven hundred and sixty-five pounds to support Norman Menzies' overseas studies. Menzies career, due to an early death, was a short one, but he and his wife sang at the coronation of George VI and in Oratorio in England.*

*[A more detailed account of Comunn na Feinne and its Eisteddfodau can be found in Appendix 14.]

It is clear that the ever-expanding financial and human costs of running the Geelong Eisteddfod between 1912 and 1928 became a huge burden to Comunn na Feinne, and were a major factor in the decision to withdraw from the event. This decision, announced on 31st January 1928, revealed just how deep was the commitment of certain members to the furtherance of education in the performing arts. James Galbraith, himself father of three Highland dancers and pipers, had served the Society for thirty years as secretary; an ex-Geelong footballer and club vice-president, a moving force in organising the Pipe Band Association and other public regulatory bodies, he had taken responsibility for arranging the Eisteddfodau for many years. When the axe fell, he resigned as Secretary (though not from the Society itself) and immediately joined a new committee, with fellow-Society member Senator Plain to re-stage the Eisteddfod under the name, the Geelong Competitions. Comunn na Feinne did not hesitate to charge this new body for the use of its hall!

Although this may seem a departure from Comunn na Feinne's Scottish activities, it was, in fact, an extension of its role in education* in the same way as were its earlier arena competitions to improve volunteer fire-fighting and military skills such as rifle marksmanship and sword play.

*[A detailed consideration of Comunn na Feinne's understanding of the term 'education', and how it implemented this in many ways, is too extensive to include here but a detailed account of this subject can be found in Appendix 14 (a)]

The Society, as we have seen, had successfully arranged for 'Piper' John Kidd to settle in Geelong and had also provided a piece of land at Belmont where the piper and his family could settle. However, its concern for the wounded piper did not end there. A fund-raising social evening, for his benefit, "the Hero of Dargai", was organised by members of the Comunn na Feinne Pipe Band of which, John Kidd was tutor.

> The stage had a novel setting representing the officers of the Gordon Highlanders in camp and holding a social evening before going into active service.

The event was well attended and an amount of £20 was donated to Piper Kidd. In addition, Mr R. Howe donated one of his own oil paintings, "an Australian river scene", to be used as a fund raiser for Piper Kidd's benefit. James Galbraith, the Society's secretary, was to arrange, "to dispose of it by art union." [a 'posh' raffle!]

For almost fourteen years, Comunn na Feinne had gone through the best period of its life. It had a stable, hardworking and successful team of leaders, it had acquired a property as its permanent home, it had established and trained a successfully competitive Pipe Band, and it had revived its flagging annual Highland Games. The Society had also initiated a new series of competitions largely based on the 'arts' – music, dance and elocution – which were to bring added gloss to its already praised contributions in the area of school education. It had, in this period, maintained its commitment to the core aims of its charter including its work with the hospital, with the town orphanages, with troubled and unemployed youths and with other charities. In terms of the foregoing and in many other ways, these years continued to be, for Comunn na Feinne, "the best of times."

If the years 1901 to the outbreak of the first World War in 1914, could be regarded as the 'best of times' for Comunn na Feinne, the period from the outbreak of the World War in August 1914, to the end of the decade, undoubtedly deserves the description, 'the worst of times.' It had endured periods of financial hardship, and periods of almost being moribund, in its early history, but the effects of the Great War were widespread and longlasting; it could be said that Comunn na Feinne's final decline could be traced back to these effects.

The declaration of war, which involved Great Britain, almost immediately drew in Australia, and it soon impacted on Comunn na Feinne, as it did upon society generally. Once war had been declared, practically the whole of the eligible members of Comunn na Feinne's Pipe Band enlisted,* and of the twenty-three pipers who volunteered for military service only three remained in Geelong as they had been rejected on health, age or other grounds. The Society had then to start from the beginning in creating a new Band, and it was not long before a set of youths was learning the pipes and being taught by Piper John Kidd. As well as its Pipe Band, the Society's President, its Chief, and many of its office-bearers and ordinary members, all volunteered for service even though some, such as Dr Small and Phillip Russell, were in poor health and were older men.

*[The members who volunteered are listed in Appendix 9 (c).]

At the Society's annual meeting in their new Hall, held on 22nd September, 1914, Dr John Small delivered the annual report and, alluding to expanding the Hall, he said that finances did not allow for any extension of the premises for the time being but, "we are only temporarily standing fast and in a little while hope to proceed to enlarge our premises so as to give more comfort and convenience to our members, and also to those who rent the Hall from time to time." The president also gave support to a suggestion of members doubling, for one year, their annual subscription. If this were done, he said, "ample money would be forthcoming to wipe out the deficit existing on the Hall." Already, he added, "many members have complied with this request." Although the income for the year had been large (£2,443/15/4), so too had been the expenses (£2,440/9/11), leaving a credit balance of £3/5/5. The heaviest expenses were the Building Fund (£859/10/1) and an extra piece of St Andrew's land (£800) which the Society purchased. At this meeting, the Society also appealed to the members for donations for the Geelong Patriotic Fund and £27/6/0 was immediately raised.

The issue of the War, although not discussed directly at this meeting, obviously had an affect upon the Society. Dr Small's annual report was coloured with some sombre words*. Like most organizations in the community, Comunn na Feinne was affected by the numbers of its members volunteering and was faced with having to adjust its activities accordingly. It was to the Society's own members, and to the community in general, that the President concluded his report with the hope that those members who had enlisted, and all volunteers in general, would be spared to return. Those giving their lives, he said, they would highly esteem. It was a just cause in which they were engaged. The sentiment expressed by Dr Small was then put in the form of a proposal which was, "carried with acclaim. The National Anthem was then sung."
*[See Appendix 9 (a) For Dr Small's full and robust opinion of the War.]

Initially, however, Comunn na Feinne activities continued without too much disruption. A concert and dance was held on 6th October, 1914, with the proceeds going to help the expenses of sending Comunn na Feinne's Pipe Band, whose enlisted members had not yet been posted, to compete at the South Street, Ballarat competitions on 17th October, 1914. It had been announced that nine bands would be competing in the Pipe Band section. The Society Band had been practising hard, especially its marching, "and it was expected that they will give a good account of themselves." The results of these competitions showed that the Band had indeed given a "good account" of itself. However, it was 'pipped at the post', again, by the South and Port Melbourne Pipe Band, losing by only four points.

The Society decided that, despite the war, the Highland Gathering for 1915 would be staged as usual. The *Geelong Advertiser* carried notices for the upcoming games to be held over two days, Friday 1st January and Saturday 2nd January, 1915. Comunn na Feinne had gone all out to present a huge Gathering for the New Year and the notices appearing in the *Geelong Advertiser* reflected that enthusiasm. It was noticeable, however, that Brass Bands had replaced Pipe Bands in the listed competitions:

> Comunn na Feinne
> 58th Highland Gathering
> Inaugural 'C' Grade Brass Band Contest
> On the Geelong Oval
> Friday January 1st and Saturday January 2nd.
> 25 Entries for Novelty Motor Cycling Events
> Don't Miss
> 175 Bandsmen Playing as One Band
> (Under the Baton of Mr J.W. Beswick, of England).
> Considered the greatest of all treats.
> To Conclude With A Grand Concert in Johnstone Park.

The continuing effect of the war on pipe bands around the state can be seen, for example, in the request, in 1916, from the Colac Empire Demonstration committee for the services of the Comunn na Feinne's Pipe Band to take part in a general patriotic demonstration. At the Directors' monthly meeting held on 3rd May, 1916, the request was received and the Society's reply told a common story as far as many of the state's Pipe Bands were concerned. "The secretary, J. Gibb, was instructed to reply that, owing to 20 members out of the total of 23 members of the Pipe Band being at the front, the request could not be met." Brass Bands were competing in place of Pipe Bands at the 1915 Highland Gathering for this same reason.

The traditional procession to the grounds was watched by a large crowd and the Brass Bands, which had entered the competitions, together with St Augustine's Band, played as they marched to the grounds. Although there were no Pipe Bands present, individual pipers from Comunn na Feinne's Band, joined with similar members of the Collingwood, the St Kilda and the Ballarat Pipe Bands, to play together as one united massed Band for the spectators at the ground. The Society, the *Advertiser* reported on 4th January, 1915, had engaged in a greatly enlarged programme for these Games. With this goal, it continued, there was, "greater financial responsibility." In other words, the Society was taking a financial gamble having the Games over two days and especially with the inclusion of the 'C' Grade Brass Band Competition, as it had no idea how such a competition involving Brass Bands would be received. Costs involved in transport and the awarding of prizes were also likely to have involved the Society in a large commitment of its resources. Even the *Advertiser* had reservations which, it was happy to admit, turned out to be groundless.

> It is many years since Geelong has had a brass band contest, and the inclusion of the "C" Grade event in the Comunn Na Feinne annual festival on Friday and Saturday was a new attraction. So successful did it prove that the directors are already agreed that it should be on the programme next year.

Another new inclusion at the 1915 Gathering was that of motor-cycle 'dare-devil' racing. If the Society had been looking for some activity which offered skill, danger and excitement with which to thrill and bring spectators to their Games, the introduction of motor cycle shenanigans certainly filled the bill. Mr Vic Balfour 'revved' the excitement level to fever pitch with, "a clever exhibition of motor-cycle fancy riding." Motor-cycles, with and without sidecars, and their daring riders, became a regular event from 1915. Bun-biting competitions, "for side-carists" (sic), were an exciting feature of the second day's activities whereby the passenger on a side-car platform attempted to 'bite a bun' attached to the ground while speeding past it at a heart-stopping rate. Whether the 'bun-biting' side-car daredevils earned their share of buns or not, their exciting antics, according to the *Advertiser*, drew involuntary gasps and, probably, not a little stomach-churning from the spectators!

To add to the fun and the excitement, the motor-cycles also took part in an obstacle race as well as in a variation of musical-chairs, called musical flags. Each time the music stopped playing, the sidecar passenger had to grab a flag. As there was always one flag less than the number of motor-cyclists, one competitor had to drop out each time. The *Advertiser*'s report enthusiastically concluded that these new events "were a distinct success."

The more regular bicycle events continued to provide their own brand of excitement, albeit at a slower speed! There were the usual spills with cyclists flying through the air at regular intervals! A spectacular crash involving three riders, Grundell, Bond and Bell, left Grundell, the anticipated winner, with a bad injury. That 'rascal' bad luck again intervened in a race when, W. Ramsdale, just within reach of the finishing line, had the wheel of his bicycle touched, sending him to the ground. But a thought must also be spared for those riders in the final of the Comunn na Feinne Cycle Race (Two Miles) when, after the finish, the Judges, not satisfied with the race, ordered it to be run again! Unfortunately, the winner and place-getters were different from those when the race was first run!

To calm the shattered nerves of the more delicate section of the audience after experiencing the 'thrills and spills' of cyclists, whether pedal or motor driven, the Games introduced a novelty event to provide some amusement. This included exhibitions involving a bicyclist, six feet two inches in height, riding a bicycle standing only seven inches tall. Travelling at speed, and travelling carrying someone on his back, whether riding on the Society's bicycle tracks or riding on the dance platform, made no difference to the cyclist's balancing skills. These were just some of the stunts performed by the performer, Mr H.A. Tipper. He had, he said, travelled the world with his act and had covered 40,000 miles in doing so – presumably the whole of this distance was not on his 7" bicycle!

In the solo piping contests Hugh Fraser, as usual, dominated all sections and emerged, yet again, as Champion Piper of Victoria. There was, of course, Highland Dancing. Ruby Brown, now six years old, who had first competed when she was only 3 years old, danced in the Highland Fling contest, "and in appreciation of her effort the judge … presented her with a special prize." Another familiar name from the Worland dynasty (yet another George), took out first prize for Caber tossing. Five competing Brass Bands, Ararat, Beaufort, Brighton District, Brunswick City and Geelong West took part, with the Ararat Band being the ultimate victor.

Following the close of the Games, an evening concert was held at Johnstone Park and a large gathering was present to see and hear the Bands and the other performers, including Mr Tipper who gave another exhibition of riding his miniature bicycle. Biograph pictures were also shown.

With Sunday intervening, it was not until Monday 4th January, 1915 that a social function was held at Comunn na Feinne's Hall where the awards to the Brass Bands and to the sporting champions were presented by the Mayor Cr. W. Brownbill. He congratulated the Society for taking the initiative regarding staging the 'C' Grade Brass Band championships. Aware of the financial risks to the Society, he added:

> If Comunn na Feinne was willing to conduct the contests, then the municipal councils should help financially. It would pay the City Council to give £100, and Geelong West and Newtown and Chilwell each to give £50. That would provide a handsome prize of £200. The councils would be well repaid, for the ratepayers would get all of the money back, if not directly at least indirectly, because the Bandsmen must spend money here. He thought the Councils should seriously consider this matter, and he hoped that in the near future they would be able to run 'B' Grade contests. This was the home of good bands. They had three 'A' Grade bands, each of which had won the big contest at South Street, Competitions, Ballarat.

James Galbraith, Comunn na Feinne secretary, commenting on the Mayor's remarks and without much conviction as to their genuineness, said facetiously that the Society would accept the money from the Council, "if it was forced on them." After all, it would not be the first time that Council promises turned out to be empty ones, without any follow-up. After the presentation of the awards, and the speeches were over, there was much mutual admiration expressed between the members of the competing Bands, and congratulations were voiced for the Ararat Band which achieved "the fine double". James Wighton, a solicitor in Geelong, and a member of the Comunn na Feinne executive, who made the presentations, remarked that it was excellent to note the spirit in which defeat had been accepted by the other bands. They had, "certainly played the game." Everyone expressed their satisfaction with the judges and the Brighton Citizens' Band said, they were perfectly satisfied that they had been [fairly] beaten by Ararat."

Encouraging news was also received in a letter from the Licensed Victuallers' Association which said that the members of the Association wanted to subscribe individually to the next Brass Band contest. The *Advertiser*, on 2nd June, 1915, reported that the letter was received with thanks and that, "a sub-committee was formed to draw up the programme for the contest." However, there was no escaping the influence of the war upon the Society. By 1st June, 1915, at the Directors' monthly meeting, a sub-committee was formed to prepare a suitable Board of Honour,* "in memory of those members of the Society who had gone to the front."

*[See Appendix 9 (c) for more details.]

The Society's Elocutionary and Singing competitions, due to their success, had been added to the regular activities on the Society's calendar. For the 1915 competitions, the Society had arranged for some of the contests to be 'open' events rather than to confine them to members and members' children, and there had been, in terms of numbers, "a very encouraging entry." In addition to the original Elocution and Singing events, competitions now included Tenor solo, Baritone solo, Soprano solo and Contralto solo contests, as well as Humorous Recitations for Ladies, and for Gentlemen; these were open to all those over 16. It was also a condition of entry that the competitors had to be *bone fide* Amateurs. Amateurs in this sense, said the Society, "will mean all who have never received payments other than out of pocket expenses for services rendered at a concert performance or other entertainment." The *Advertiser* of 8th June, 1915, reported that the Comunn na Feinne directors had intimated that the 1915 competitions would extend over three nights and they foreshadowed the possibility of "extending the programme" for 1916.

Apart from its catering role for organizations hiring the Hall, the Ladies Committee, for the past two years, had been beavering away with socials aimed at raising money for the building fund. Their aim was, "to lessen the liability on the Hall" and, to this end, they held another function on 27th June, 1915. The Hall was crowded and the *Advertiser* reported that the entertainment was well received.

The Society's annual general meeting was held on 19th September, 1915, and though away at camp on military duties, Surgeon-Major Dr John Small, the President of Comunn na Feinne, was present in spirit with the members at their annual meeting through the medium of a suitably fiery, pugnacious and accusative presidential address which was read on his behalf*. This was recorded in full in the *Geelong Advertiser*'s report of the meeting on 20th September, 1915.

*[See Appendix 9 (b) – Dr Small's report for 1915 includes his references to the war and to Germany, "the most ruthless, barbarous and treacherous military despotism that has ever disgraced the annals of warfare. All the attributes of civilization and Christianity are mocked by the German war-lords."]

With a measure of understatement, given that the Society's Pipe Band had enlisted almost to the last piper, the report continued that, "The Band has not been to the fore as usual, but, thanks to the assistance of Pipe Major Donald J. McDonald, a fine combination of young players is coming along. Presentations were made to each bandsman leaving for the front."

A surplus balance for the year of £30/14/7 was announced and £47/17/0 was the amount of interest paid on the debentures. Revenue from the Hall came to £94/19/6, but the amount of £67/7/0 had been paid out to members (this was in addition to the interest paid to the legal debenture holders) who had loaned the Society money towards the purchase of the Hall and other expenses related to this.

Although the war did mean that some interruption of normal Comunn na Feinne activities was necessary, it directed its energies to increasing its charitable fund-raising, especially in support of the war effort. This meant that social activities, as the main means of raising funds for charity, continued throughout the year. George R. King also brought the distress in the Scottish Highlands to the attention of the meeting. This had largely been brought about, "through so many men having gone to the War. Something might be done by the Society," King said. It was agreed to vote £10 from the funds, and subscriptions in the room raised another £10/15/0. The secretary was requested to make an appeal for public contributions. The Society thus added to its list of causes including, for example, Red Cross support as well as the War Highlands Distress Appeal and the Disabled Soldiers' appeal. In addition to its own efforts in raising funds for the Red Cross, the Society was also involved with promoting similar appeals by others. For example, Dame Nellie Melba, in one of her several associations with Comunn na Feinne at Geelong (her father David Mitchell had been a member of the Society in its early years), gave notice that she would stage a Concert at Geelong in aid of Red Cross on 24th and 25th February, 1915. This concert raised the large sum of £1,500 for that charity.

Sadly, news relating to the first of the war deaths of Comunn na Feinne members or associates, was reported, a message which was to become all too common at Society meetings. The *Advertiser* reported on 20th September, 1916, that fatalities included the death of Brigadier-General Linton, "while leading the 22nd Battalion of the 6th Brigade, in a charge at Gallipoli. The late officer had taken part in many of the Society's functions. Reference was also made to the loss sustained by Thomas McKenzie Kirkwood in the death of his son at Gallipoli.* The father had officiated at the Society's annual gatherings for 14 years. Another casualty of the war was the son of a favourite singer of Comunn na Feinne, Maggie Stirling, whose only son, Robert Riddell, was killed while fighting in France in 1918.

*[See Appendix 3 (b) Thomas McKenzie Kirkwood's son, Corporal Athol Macgregor Kirkwood, DCM, 323, 6th Btn. Australian Infantry, AIF, was killed in action 27th July 1915, aged only 20, at Gallipoli.]

At a meeting on 5th October, 1915, with Dr Small presiding, Comunn na Feinne's Honour Board was unveiled by Donald McKinnon, Attorney-General for Victoria. As well as praising the Scots and the Australians at the battlefront, McKinnon was at least politic enough to refer also to the fighting capabilities of the Irish!*

*[See Appendix 9 (d) for McKinnon's speech at the unveiling ceremony.]

> Out of the 38 names on the Honour Roll**, of Comunn na Feinne men who had so far enlisted, sixteen had been associated with the Pipe Band, which seemed to indicate that there was something in the association with the Scottish Pipes that brought out the best that was in a man. He congratulated the Pipe Band on its splendid contribution towards the manhood of Australia in the war. In conclusion, the Minister asked James Galbraith, secretary of Comunn na Feinne, to remove the veil from the Honour Roll.
> "James Galbraith [then] gave a brief sketch of the members who had gone on service, and in memory of the late William Tosh, who fell in action, the audience stood while Donald McDonald piped 'Flowers of the Forest,' the Scottish National Lament."

**[See Appendix 9 (c) for list of names on the Honour Board.]

The sad news of the war deaths of members (and the sons of members), was duly announced. It was also the case that those wounded and those who had been invalided back to Australia were given a warm welcome by Comunn na Feinne. For example, Sergeant C.R. Buchanan, a former piper with the Pipe Band, who was wounded at the Dardanelles Landing, and invalided home, was welcomed and looked after by the Society.

Every year since the war commenced the Society had discussed whether it should suspend the New Year's Day Gathering and its other activities for the duration of the conflict. The Society made its decision at the end of each year and, so far, it had agreed that even if it meant sustaining a financial loss on the day, the Gatherings would be continued for the sake of morale. This decision was also made for the 1916 Games at which it became apparent that the war was seriously affecting such public gatherings as those at Geelong. The *Advertiser*'s mood was a sombre one and it was a muted notice that it carried regarding Comunn na Feinne's New Year's Day Gathering for 1916. The Society's advertisement noted only that the 59th Highland Gathering and Brass Band Contest would be held on Saturday 1st January, 1916 and the *Advertiser*'s 3rd January report on the gathering was not much longer than Comunn na Feinne's advertisement for the Games. Its account could not avoid referring to the war even if it was only to explain the deficiencies in the offerings of the day. The customary Procession took place together with the Bands which, later in the day, would be competing, together with the Brass Bands of St Augustine's Orphanage and Winchelsea, all contributing music on the way to the grounds.

Although the war brought extra concerns for the Society, it did not forget its charitable role in the community. Under the heading 'For Distressed Scots' the *Advertiser* gave space to an appeal that was made at the start of the 1916 Comunn na Feinne Gathering, thus honouring a pledge made in February, 1915.

> Scottish Societies in Victoria have joined in collecting for the Home Fund for the relief of Scottish folk who have lost their breadwinners at the war. At the C.N.F. gathering on Saturday Mr A. McKenzie (president) and Mr J. Keith (secretary) of the Ballarat Caledonian Society, brought down the balance of the tartan souvenirs with which £50 was raised in Ballarat in one day a fortnight ago for the fund, and by permission of the C.N.F., offered them for sale

amongst the crowd. All were speedily sold and £57/3/0 secured for the distressed Scots.

The *Advertiser* led off its 2nd January report of the 1916 Games identifying the war as continuing to have an impact on public gatherings like that of Comunn na Feinne, although it was pleasantly surprised at the public support.

> GOOD CROWD AT THE OVAL.
> Comunn Na Feinne's annual Highland gathering and 'C' grade band contest was commenced on the oval on Saturday in perfect, weather. The curtailment of band entries through the war was regarded as a foretaste of public patronage, but the directors were agreeably surprised. The Society was loth (sic) to register a break in its gatherings at the 59th year, and was determined to hold the carnival even at a loss.

The procession from Geelong to the grounds was maintained and the competing bands, along with the local St Augustine Brass Band and that of Winchelsea, 'provided abundant music." At the opening of the 1916 Highland Games, in the absence of Dr Small through illness, the vice-president, Mr Alex Lowe, provided the welcome which, inevitably, referred to the war that was still raging. Pipe Band competitions were still off the programme due to the large number of pipers from all centres who had enlisted and who were fighting abroad. Brass Band competitions, as already noted, largely replaced pipe bands at the various competitions around the State. The huge number of Brass Bands which existed, together with the fact that older men and youths made up a good percentage of the players, meant that there was sufficient of these Bands to enter for competitions such as those which Comunn na Feinne conducted at its Games.

The report on the physical events was brief and to the point, with the 'obligatory' crash in the bicycle races. "The cycling and athletic events were disposed of in the early part of the afternoon, and the former were particularly well contested." Hugh Fraser again showed that he was practically unbeatable, and a true Master Piper, with his clean sweep in the solo piping competitions. The familiar name of Worland, which had continually cropped up over a period of fifty years in the prize lists of the Heavy Games competitions, was again present in the shape of yet another of the 'clan'. Colin

Frederick Worland, son of an old competitor, George Henry Worland,* took part in the Caber event.

*[See reference to the Worland dynasty in Appendix 3 (b) Short Biographies]

Despite the continued excellence of Hugh Fraser in the piping solos, and the excitement of the cycling, and the performances at the heavy games and the track and field competitions, it was, according to the *Geelong Advertiser*, the Brass Bands contests which were the centre of attention at the 1916 Gathering. The Royal Park Military Band under Bandmaster R. Davis, "was the most popular, and enjoyed the distinction of being the only band applauded on the march." As much as the spectators appreciated the Royal Park Military Band, however, it was the St Kilda Brass Band which carried off the winner's award." But, though "music be the food of love," little respect was shown to the judges by losing bandsmen, sore about adjudications and the merits of other bands. Unlike the previous year's Contests, there was a high degree of criticism both for the judges' placings and for the merits of the other bands, giving rise to angry words. In former days, we might have guessed some quarrel over the Caber, or jostling in the races or faulty mechanics in the bicycle events would have lain behind such a discordant cry. However, the causes lay in a different direction. Amidst the soothing and, at times, stirring music of the Brass Bands, there was decidedly sounded a 'sour note' in the form of protests.

Immediately after the results were announced, which had St Kilda first (with 357 points) and Caulfield the runner up (with 351 points), two protests were made and submitted to Mr Albert Echo, member of the Victorian Brass Band Association (VBBA). The protest against St Kilda was based upon an infringement of the VBBA rules by playing an unregistered player. The other protest was against the appearance in the competitions of the Royal Park Military Band as, it was charged, that Band was not registered with the VBBA. The protests had to be lodged with the VBBA for a decision. But that was not the end of the protests. The F.W. Walker Trophy, valued at £5.5.0, was awarded, "for the band securing the greatest number of points for discipline during the contest", and this was awarded to the Royal Park Military Band. But controversy yet again showed its head. Geelong West Brass Band was disqualified for not turning out for the Street March and St Kilda suffered the same fate for including within its Ranks a player from outside the Band. Despite this furore, and the disqualification of the two Geelong Bands, a judge of the Brass Band competitions said that, overall, "he had never heard such playing by 'C' Grade bands. The standard of music especially from the leading bands surprised him." So, for at least one person, music did soothe "the savage breast."

The evening concert was held at Johnstone Park as usual, "where a large assemblage" enjoyed the entertainments which included "some of the visiting Bands." No protests were evident!

The second day of the Gathering, according to the *Advertiser*, proved to be a dismal affair both weather-wise and in the low attendance of spectators. The day was mostly given over to musical contests where the Brass Bands were judged on their "Test Pieces" and their "Own Choice" selection and where solo Brass instrumentalists also competed for individual awards. The numbers entered under this latter category "were satisfactory", and the solo contests were held, in the forenoon, at the Comunn na Feinne Hall, "in the presence of a fair attendance of members." In the afternoon, and before the Brass Band competitions got under way, there was the completion of the, "local Highland Fling Competitions for boys and girls under 14 years of age", which were continued from the previous day. The *Advertiser* praised the Comunn na Feinne organizational skills, "and not a moment of unnecessary delay occurred in the bands taking their places in the stand." During the Brass Band 'own choice' selection, and then the 'test piece', it unfortunately started to rain. The *Advertiser*, rather cryptically, reported that although the rain was "discomforting" it made "little apparent difference to the playing." However, the spectators who had gathered showed spontaneous appreciation of the Bands as they each played their respective choices. The poor crowd at the ground for these second day contests, with gate takings yielding only £17, led the *Advertiser* to doubt that the Society would cover its costs.

Despite troubling financial times, Comunn na Feinne managed to continue some of its charity work. A notice appeared in the *Advertiser* on 31st January, 1916, regarding the Society's efforts on behalf of those in the Scottish Highlands who had been badly hit by the losses of men in the war. It reported that, "The Comunn na Feinne has collected £32/10/6 as a donation towards the fund for the relief of distress in the Highlands caused by heads of families having fallen in the war."

Less than a week from the closing of the 1916 Gathering, the Society suffered its severest blow of the war years when, on 9th January, 1916, the death of its President, Dr John Small was announced. Dr Small, like Comunn na Feinne's Chief, Phillip Russell, had enlisted at the outbreak of the war, and was serving in a medical capacity as Surgeon-Major. His death was received with great sorrow. The *Advertiser* reported on 10th January, 1916:

> With great regret, we record the death of Surgeon-Major Dr John Small, who passed away in the early hours of yesterday morning. His end was hastened by a chill he contracted about six weeks ago through a motor breakdown after a visit to Queenscliff with military officers. ... He is to be accorded a military funeral this afternoon.

This was, for Comunn na Feinne, the worst of news indeed, in what was, "The worst of times."

Dr Small's service - to the community, to Comunn na Feinne and, latterly, to the nation - provided him with a public epitaph - publicity he would not have sought.

> The Comunn na Feinne had no more enthusiastic member, and he had been president since September, 1902, succeeding Neil Campbell. Towards the establishment of the Comunn na Feinne Hall and Pipe Band he gave liberally. For many years it had been the custom of Dr Small to entertain members of the Committee of the Comunn na Feinne on New Year's Eve night, but it fell through this year owing to his failing health. In the Scottish Gathering on New Year's Day the well-known figure of Dr John Small was greatly missed.
> As surgeon-major of the A.G.A., he never missed the Easter Camps, and was the life and soul of the officers' mess. While acting as senior medical officer at the Geelong military camp, he gained the esteem of the officers and men, by whom his death is greatly regretted.

Dr John Small, was a member of the community of Geelong, he was essentially Scotch, and combined the characteristics of the Scottish temperament in a marked degree; loyalty, determination, dislike of humbug and a keen sense to detect the shallow and superficial. Like a true Scot he possessed a deeply religious nature. Dr John Small also played a leading part in the public life of Geelong … Whether we agreed with him or not, we had to admit his business acumen and sagacity. Matters involving heavy expenditure had to prove themselves up to the hilt. In public affairs, he was a personality to be reckoned with. Like all Scots he was a tough fighter and when he was beaten he went down fighting. Of his charity he gave freely, but unostentatiously and brightened the lot of many old people.

On 21st March, 1916, a Directors' Meeting was held in order to discuss the election of a new President and the directors had resolved to invite J. Angus Laird to accept the office. The new President officially took over the Chair at the Society meeting on 6th June, 1916. He gave some encouraging words to the Society and he was proud that, in the face of the various troubles at present, when other societies and organizations were suspending or scaling down their activities, Comunn na Feinne had sought to keep its various outreaches alive. It was reported that during the period that Dr Small was President, "the Society had contributed nearly £200 to the Geelong Hospital fund," in addition to its support for the many individual cases of distress and also for the Red Cross military aid appeal.

The Society held another function on 22nd August, 1916, and it was clear that raising funds for the Hall was, more and more, coming to dominate Comunn na Feinne activities. This event was called, 'a Caledonian Tea,' and it was organized for the afternoon and evening by the Ladies' committee. The proceeds were for the reduction of the Hall Fund Debt but, as it transpired, they were used to help balance the Society's books that financial year. Financial pressures were building! Nevertheless, at the annual meeting, held on 17th September, 1916, it was decided that a 'Dr Small Memorial Library for Scottish Literature' be built, attached to the existing Society Hall. The appeal for funds was to be a continuous one but already, it was announced, the project was well in hand. It was also stated, even before a public appeal had been announced, that £100 had already been donated towards the costs. It had been necessary for the Society to buy some adjoining land behind the present Hall upon which to erect the proposed Library and this had been finalized, "at a cost of £170." Much of Dr Small's personal library was to be bequeathed to the Society and many other gifts of books were to come, over time, from a variety of sources.

> The gift of a much-prized copy of Robert Burns' poems was received from Mrs Morris of East Geelong. The Book, which had been in the possession of the Lady's family for 65 years, was considered to be one of the original copies and it was described by Senator William Plain, as invaluable. The secretary, James Galbraith, was directed to write to the donor, thanking her for the gift, and assuring her that the book would find an honoured place in the Society's Library.

Despite the lower than usual gate takings at the 1916 New Year's Day Gathering, it was reported that the total of expenditure over revenue was only £26/7/3. However, James Galbraith, the secretary, was able to announce that the recent 'Caledonian Tea,' together with, "outstanding subscriptions" having been paid, "wiped out the deficit." It is evident that the Ladies were proving invaluable in their fund-raising activities but were having no control over how these funds might be spent. The financial situation as outlined by Galbraith demonstrates, however, just how close to the edge the Society continued to teeter.*

* [The subject of the Society's financial history is more fully taken up in a later chapter.]

There had been little, if any, controversy involving the Society and the War issue, especially with regards to the potentially divisive Conscription debates of 1916 and 1917. There had been no doubt that the War, as defined by its President Dr Small, was a just one. However, the issue of conscripting young men to fight that war may not have been so clearly seen as being 'just'. One of the few references to Comunn na Feinne and the first WW1 conscription issue was made on 25th October, 1916, when it was reported in the *Advertiser* that a Comunn na Feinne committee meeting had, "affirmed the principle of conscription" and had urged a 'Yes' vote in the upcoming referendum.

At a well-attended meeting of the directorate and ladies' committee of the

Comunn na Feinne, held last evening in the Society's Hall … [t]he following resolution was unanimously agreed to: "That this society affirm the principle of conscription as being necessary to retain our forces at their full strength, and pledge ourselves to do everything in our power to obtain a 'Yes' vote at the poll on Saturday next and would further place on record our cordial approval of the action taken by our vice-president, the Hon. William Plain*, in furthering this end."

*[William Plain, later Chief of the Society, was a Labor Party member of the Victorian State Parliament Legislative Assembly, but had split from his party's position over the conscription issue which he supported. Plain was expelled from the party for his stand on the issue.]

There was a monthly meeting held on 28th November, 1916, at which the Society again agreed to continue its activities throughout the duration of the war, including its New Year's Day Highland Gathering. The Society was still without a Pipe Band, but it optimistically reported that the young lads who had already begun learning were progressing well.

Support for the war effort also continued through fund-raising activities. On the 28th December 1916, for instance, Comunn na Feinne held a concert for war funds at which the Kilties Concert Brass Band from Melbourne was a welcome and entertaining guest act.

The *Advertiser*'s report of the Society's New Year's Day Gathering for 1917, was highly coloured by the fact that it was the Comunn na Feinne's New Year's Day Highland Gathering Diamond Jubilee, thus celebrating its 60th Annual Gathering. J. Angus Laird, the new President, officiated and mentioned, with feeling, the loss through death of their, "trusty friend and leader," Dr Small. Laird said he was glad, "of the opportunity of welcoming home again Lieut. David Ross, who left here nearly two years ago and, for bravery on the field, had received his commission," In one of the few direct encouragements to the enlistment campaign by the Society, the President said he hoped that, "every Scot and every son of a Scot," whether born in Scotland or Australia" would consider enlisting.

The war continued to take its toll in different ways and, for the second year in a row, there was a reduction in the number of events and competitors at the Games. The *Advertiser* reported that the Programme for the day, "was principally notable for the great number of dancing items" and that, "A bugle band competition was introduced for the first time and proved most successful." Brass Band and Bugle Band competitions had replaced the Pipe Bands as the main musical contributors at the Games. The *Advertiser*'s comment regarding the number of dancers would seem not to have been an exaggeration. The number of juvenile dancers was 226, "which is said to be a record for the Commonwealth." As we have seen, with the curtailment of other events, especially some of the Athletic and the Pipe Band Competitions, because of the War, Highland dancing emerged more prominently, as did Brass Bands competitions.

The post-games concert, held at Johnstone Park in the evening, took place as usual. Much of the entertainment, before a large and enthusiastic audience, was provided by the Kilties' Concert Brass Band which was described, "as the most popular band in the State." A surprise announcement at the beginning of the Games, made by William Plain MLA., was that the Prime Minister, Billy Hughes, was present at the gathering and had consented to say a few words.

> William M. Hughes, who was greeted with three cheers, said that he had been brought there to hear the music not to speak. He was not a Scotsman, but had done his best to remedy that defect by marrying a Scots woman, so that his children in some measure could claim kinship with them. At such gatherings as these they were bringing back to their minds memories of the land from which they or their parents come. As a brother Celt, he was glad to be with them and to revere those memories which were interwoven with the most glorious episodes of the world history. They were stirred by the knowledge that on every battle-front the men from Scotland were bearing aloft the banner of their race. Scotsmen had won glorious traditions which they were right to treasure.

The Prime Minister's presence was certainly a surprise, but the bigger surprise was that Hughes made no reference to Conscription, the Referendum or the Irish 'Troubles", all of which were highly contentious issues at the time and about all of which Hughes, normally, had much to say! He praised William Plain MLA., for having the courage of his convictions which had led, as in Hughes' own case, to expulsion from his political party in 1916 by supporting a cause (i.e. the Referendum on conscription) to which their own party (i.e. Labour) was opposed. It was on such a principle as believing in one's position as 'right', said Hughes, that both he and Plain had been expelled, and it was on such a principle of 'right' that the war was being fought and, "we must be resolved to do our duty to the end, whatever it may cost.

The Society held its half yearly meeting on 28th March, 1917, with war-related information darkening the mood a little. News from the military authorities was received and published in the *Geelong Advertiser*, and it was noted that Private Ralph Fraser, wounded in the war, had been, "invalided back to Australia." The *Advertiser* announced on 29th March, 1917, that Private Fraser would officially be welcomed back by Comunn na Feinne.

At its annual meeting on 17th September, 1917, Comunn na Feinne passed a vote of thanks to the ladies' committee, "for the good work, particularly in Red Cross and patriotic affairs," which they had carried out. They had raised £70 for the Red Cross and £174 for the Kitchener Memorial Fund. This meeting also heard that 65 members of Comunn na Feinne, including Rev. R.M. Fergus, the well-known minister of St Andrew's Presbyterian Church, Geelong, and Comunn na Feinne member, had now enlisted. Out of a total of 325 members, one fifth had enlisted and, to date, three had been killed in action and others wounded. This figure is all the more telling when it is understood that the 65 members who had enlisted constituted nearly the totality of the membership eligible and able to enlist.

On the 17th November, 1917, the Society received a visit from a representative of the Victorian Brass Band Association (V.B.B.A.), which had its headquarters at Ballarat, "to ask Comunn na Feinne to include a brass band marching contest in the New Year's Day programme." The Society, discussing this request, "proposed that the event should be open to all grades of Band." Comunn na Feinne was also assured by the V.B.B.A., if it agreed to stage this contest, that, "two judges from Ballarat [would journey] to Geelong, and only charge their bare expenses." Comunn na Feinne, always wary of costs, was satisfied with the proposal and agreed to this request. It was also announced that at the next Gathering, on 1st January, 1918, a Drum and Bugle contest would again be held and that already there had been twelve entries received.

It was reported at the monthly meeting of Comunn na Feinne, held on 29th December, 1917, that the Society's membership, despite the many veteran members who had died or shifted away from Geelong, and counting those who were serving at the front, was still a credible 300. It was announced, too, that the Pipe Band, after being depleted by 20 of its members going to the front, was rebuilding its ranks and, "was now in full swing with young pipers."

The balance sheet showed a debit balance of £103/7/1. Against this, the Society had an asset in the land purchased at the rear of the Hall for £170, of which £129/19/0 was already paid." However, as this land was acquired for the purpose of building the Dr Small Memorial Library, it could hardly be regarded as a saleable asset.

At the opening of the 1918 Games, it was obvious from the vice-president's remarks that the Society had, for the fourth time, pondered whether or not the 1918 New Year's Day Games should be held and, for the fourth time, it had decided that the Gathering should go ahead as usual. The Vice-president, and now Senator, William Plain, deputizing for the President, J. Angus Laird, rationalized the affirmative decision, albeit somewhat unconvincingly, in his speech opening the Games on 1st January, 1918. He said: "While this gathering was [being] celebrated, the minds of all would travel across the sea to those fighting for our freedom." The war, and the growing casualty lists, continued to cast a shadow over the competitions. Although the *Advertiser* reported, on 2nd January, 1918, that the New Year's Day Gathering, "was the most successful since the outbreak of the war," it was obvious, from the lack of competitors in some of the athletic events and in the continuing absence of pipe bands, as well as in the lower numbers entering the solo piping events, that the war was continuing to have an impact on the Gathering and on its usual festive air. Even the dress of those attending reflected a sombreness.

> The piping events did not attract many entries, as most of the adult kilties are at the front; and many veteran Scots who were formerly in attendance fully

rigged in the garb of the Gael, wore English clothes, many of them with a black arm band.

The *Advertiser* reported that there was little to whet the appetite of the veteran spectator. There was some momentary excitement at the cycling when a competitor came off his bike during a race and, "striking a knot of spectators, was thrown to the ground. No one was hurt." The cadets from the Ascot Vale physical training club, gave an interesting display of gymnastics, "including Swedish drill, marching exercises and Pyramids." In addition, the Bugle Bands provided an entertaining substitute for the former pipe band marching and playing contests. Although twelve of these Bands had entered, only nine bugle bands actually competed. Quite obviously, the Society took a more up-beat view of the Gathering than was expressed by the newspaper. James Galbraith, secretary to the Society, announced great satisfaction at the numbers and the financial results of the Gathering and felt that the "display had surprised the committee in view of the present conditions."

The usual New Year's Eve concert, following the Gathering, had generally been held in Johnstone Park, but for 1918 the venue chosen was Kardinia Park, although no reason was given for the change. This was the second time that Kardinia Park had been used and, as on the previous occasion, outdoor lighting had been used to illuminate the ground only this time it was with generated electricity and not Lux Light.

> The pipe band and bugle bands and many of the winning competitors fell in at 7.45pm., at Bright and Hitchcock's corner and marched to Kardinia Park where a large gathering of people had assembled. Dancing and pictures, chiefly of an amusing nature, formed the programme.

Comunn na Feinne members, and others, joined together in celebrating Burns' birthday with a Burns' Night. It had been scheduled for Burns' actual birth date, 25th January, but that night had been unsuitable for many and the entertainment had been postponed. Senator William Plain, the Society's vice-president, provided an outline of Burns' life and there were songs, music and recitations making up the night's entertainment. The Society also staged a successful 'Comfort Fund Concert' in August,

1918 raising £69. There was also held that month the Highland Ball, which took place on 6th August, 1918, and, according to the *Advertiser* report, this proved to be as popular as ever and, "250 dancers were present."

The annual meeting of the Society was held on 16th September, 1918. The Chief, Phillip Russell, on a very rare visit to Comunn na Feinne, was in the Chair. James Galbraith noted Russell's very generous donation of £500 towards the Hall Fund. Financially the Society showed a credit balance of £88/13/9, but the Pipe Band account was a staggering £245 in debt. Without the original financial records, there is no way of knowing how this debt was incurred. The death of Captain H.H. Storrer as a result of the war was regretfully announced and it was pointed out that the Honour Roll now totalled 68.

Although the armistice was signed on the 11th day of November, 1918, the Society staged no special events in recognition of this fact. There were no special meetings, concerts or any other recognition given by Comunn na Feinne that the war had ended. There were, of course, various rallies and so on in Geelong itself and members of Comunn na Feinne would have been part of these as individuals. The Society carried on with its usual round of meetings, and the *Geelong Advertiser* reported, 31st December, 1918, on the final one for the year, giving some detail of what would be happening at the January 1919 Gathering, including the evening concert which was again to be held at Kardinia Park.

> The final meeting of directors of the Comunn na Feinne [for the year] was held in the hall last evening. Mr D. Rankin* (who was at the first gathering 62 years ago), and many other old patrons, have signified their intention of being present. A special invitation is extended to Anzacs and returned soldiers who are visiting the city, to be the guests of the Society. The Khaki Girls' Band was also announced as being a feature at the upcoming 1919 Games. They were to have the honour of leading the march past of all the competing Bands at the close of the ceremonies. Following the end of the Games all of the Bands were to reform and march to Kardinia Park for the evening concert.

Group of CNF Veterans including (from Left to Right) Dugald Rankin, William Sinnott, William Armour, and J. Young with Angus Laird (CNF President).

*[Dougal Rankin died on 21st February, 1919, aged 82. See Appendix 3 (b) – Short Biographies - for more details of his life.]

The *Advertiser* carried two notices relating to upcoming Comunn na Feinne activities and the Society was again at the Geelong Oval for its annual New Year's Day Games.

> Comunn na Feinne
> 62nd Highland Gathering on
> The Geelong Football Oval and in
> The evening in Kardinia Park.
>
> Dancing Tonight
> In Comunn na Feinne Hall
> Come and Dance the Old Year Out and
> The New Year in.
> Ladies 1/-; Gents 1/6
>
> Special Visit of the Khaki Girls' Bugle Band.
> At 3.30pm a March Past of Bugle Bands and Pipers.
> Admission to Geelong Oval 1/- (plus tax)
> Admission to Kardinia Park 6d.

The Society's New Year's Day Gathering, the first without the war overshadowing it, was held at the Geelong Oval on 2nd January, 1919. The Procession marched, "to the strains of bagpipe and bugle" from the town to the grounds and, for the first time for several years, there was a return to the old colourful mixture of tartans, regalia and uniforms worn by the different groups and individuals taking part. The Khaki Girls' Bugle Band led the procession and was followed by the Comunn na Feinne's own pipers and various other Bugle Bands from, "North Melbourne, Elsternwick and Malvern and the Caulfield Scouts." Members of Comunn na Feinne had returned to wearing their kilts and "other regalia" as they marched. The attendance was well up to the best of past years and the *Advertiser*, which had given a low-key coverage of events during the war years, adopted, for these Games, a more buoyant reporting mood. The Americans had their fourth of July and the Irish their St Patrick's Day but the Scots, it reported, had their New Year's Day and, "yesterday he (sic) celebrated well and truly", and the day and evening events were a "success" for the Society. Although the war had ended the previous November, there were still no Pipe Bands to join the marchers, nor were there any pipe band competitions (although there was solo piping events), as many of the pipers who had enlisted, and who had survived the war, had still not rejoined or reformed their old Pipe Bands. Special applause was given to the Khaki Girls' Bugle Band.

> Among the most interesting items was the display by the Khaki Girls whose marching and bugle playing evoked applause. At the conclusion of their final manoeuvre they were met in front of the stand by the Pipers' Band playing Cock o' the North, and at the call of the Kilties' leader, Drum-Major Reid, three cheers were given for the girls.

Highland dancing dominated the programme of events, although some traditional heavy events also took place as did some Bicycle races and a Bugle band competition. The New Year's evening concert, following the Games, saw a large crowd congregating to enjoy the open-air entertainments. The Society had been progressive in its use of 'modern' technology such as its introduction of flood lighting via Lux-Lights at the 1910 Gathering at Kardinia Park and, later, with generated electricity. This innovative spirit was also in evidence at the 1918 evening concert at Kardinia

Park. The Khaki Girls' Bugle Band, which had drawn applause for its marching and playing skills at the afternoon Games, drew an even greater response at the evening open-air Concert, with their innovative use of electric bulbs on their caps producing a colourful display when they were marching and manoeuvring on and around the grounds.

> The programme consisted of a moving picture display, Scottish airs by the Pipers' Band, and illuminated evolutions (sic) by the Khaki Girls. With electric globes on their caps, the girls paraded to the enclosure, and produced a pretty effect. The night was ideal for a concert, and promenading round the oval was made a popular item by many.

It has been noted several times that the Society had many official bards over the years (and some unofficial rhymsters, too!). Allan Fullarton Wilson, who had served as Comunn na Feinne's official bard for some years, and who was a prolific versifier, had died on 16th August of 1917. Such was the appreciation of his verses that Comunn na Feinne arranged to have some choice pieces published as a small volume, "and members were asked to give their hearty support so that their own poet's work may be remembered." His verse, mostly in Scots, the language of the poetry of Ferguson, and, later, of Burns, appeared in *The Scot at Hame an' Abroad*, the official journal of the Victorian Scottish Union, and newspapers including the *Geelong Advertiser*. A list of some of Wilson's poems, which would form the contents of the proposed book, was presented to the Society for approval and Comunn na Feinne subsequently announced on 1st February, 1919, that a collection of Wilson's poems had been published by John Purdie newsagent and stationers, Geelong.

> [Wilson's*] wit and satire so often brightened the pages of the *Advertiser*. To those who knew the man, and appreciated the charm of his style, no praise and no introduction are necessary; for others, a foreword is provided. Geelong will be the better for reading them. Wilson's style showed "a remarkable affinity with Burns due, perhaps, to a striking similarity in temperament and the buffeting experiences of life. … The poetry gives proof of fine powers of versification, joined to humour and imagination. There is here, too, something of the Robert Burns' touch in the protest against the social order, and no less in his spirit of independence.

*[Further details of A.F. Wilson can be found in Appendix 3 (b) – Short Biographies]

Like Burns, some of Wilson's satire is every bit as relevant today as it was in his own time. His barb on parliament, for instance, could have been written for contemporary readers. "Some of his election pieces tingle with irony …"

> "Parliament was aince for statesmen,
> That has passed away;
> Now the needy politicians
> Fecht for place and pay.
>
> Patriotism! Love o' country!
> De'il ha'e they a bit;
> They only love the country for
> What they get oot o' it!"

"Of Wilson one could truly say, "He was a fellow of infinite jest," most of his writings for the Press had a touch of canny (and often, very uncanny) humour; but he was as versatile as he was profound, and in his day ranged as wide as any man, from grave to gay, from lively to severe." … This is a volume to be read and reread by all who loved the man, admire talent, or desire to see the mirror held up to Nature, for the betterment of their souls."

A list of the contents shows the Title of the poems included under a variety of sections. There is quite a large number under the division headed 'The War.' A contemporary and touching example of this was that of his 'prayer', "God End the War!" [The full poem can be found in Appendix 5 (e) Poems of A. F. Wilson.]

> God End the War!
>
> Lord God we thee entreat
> Our enemies to defeat,
> God end the war.
>
> Let thy wrath on them fall,
> With fear their hearts appall,
> Destroy them one and all,
> God end the war.
> ....
> Sorrow and heaviness
> The hearts of men oppress,
> God end the war.
> On thee do we rely

To grant us victory;
Hear us, oh Lord, who cry
God end the war.
....

To us who trust in Thee
Give thou the victory,
God end the war.
Thou art our shield and guide,
On Whom we do confide;
God end the war.

Allan Fullarton Wilson died at Geelong on 16th August 1917, in his sixtieth year leaving a widow, and eight children, the youngest being only six years old. The following lines, written by the deceased, a week prior to his death, were read by the Rev John Sinclair, of the old Gaelic Church, Geelong, who officiated at the grave-side on the 18th ultimo, in the presence of a large gathering of the public and members of Comunn na Feinne.

My Plea: Excuse of Extenuation none; none being possible to me.
My Certainty: That great as is my sin, His mercy is great enough to cover and hide it as the snow covers the earth.
My Hope: That He will extend that mercy to me.
My Prayer: The only one befitting me, that of the publican –'God be merciful to me, a sinner.'
Wherefore I am conscious of no fear, but only of a cheerful hope.
Signed Allan Fullarton Wilson.

A new era involving the location of the Comunn na Feinne Games was foreshadowed at a general meeting of social and sporting clubs in Geelong with the Geelong council on 19th May, 1919. It was announced that a new Oval at Kardinia Park, costing £6,000, was to be established and the likely total rent which could be raised from the different groups in the community using the facility were estimated as following.

Geelong Fire Brigade	£60
Junior Football Association	£60
Comunn na Feinne	£25
Cycle Club	£25
Harriers	£10

Gordon College	£10
Pictures entertainment	£50
Demonstration	£60
Eight Hours Committee	£20
Total	£320

Comunn na Feinne heartily supported this scheme.

At a Monthly meeting of the Society on 6th September, 1919, it was remembered with pride that practically the whole of the Society's Pipe Band had enlisted and served overseas. There was now an attempt to re-assemble the Band and it was intended that it would enter the Pipe Band Contests at South Street, Ballarat on 18th October, 1919. At its annual meeting on 15th September, 1919, reference was again made to the Society's war effort. Various deaths were recorded and it was announced that its Honour Board was to be enlarged. It was reported that, "Out of a membership of 300, over 70 enlisted … [which was] … practically the whole of the eligible members." The Society's financial position was also commented upon and it was reported that it would close the financial year with a deficit of £165/6/7, although it was noted that collections since the books were closed had effectively reduced this debit to £34.

The immediate post-war period showed how much the legacy of the war continued to affect Comunn na Feinne, and society in general. One of the post WW1 initiatives taken by the Society was to set up a Soldiers' Club Committee. It had also decided to postpone the holding of the 1919 Haggis Supper until later in the year. The Pipe Band was in rehearsal for the South Street, Ballarat competitions in October and, "had been strengthened by the return of some soldier members from overseas". It had been doing well at these practice sessions, in playing and in marching, so much so in fact that the Band's supporters were confident of the Band's chances at the October competitions. When it had last competed at South Street, in 1914, it had missed achieving first place by only two points, and it was considered that it would do better at the Ballarat competition on 18th October, 1919. The extra practice and the drilling obviously paid off and the Pipe Band returned home victorious. It was also the fact that, according to the *Advertiser*'s report on 21st October, 1919, "there were returned men" from the war making up the pipe bands and this included the Comunn na Feinne Band. What was also pleasing, reported the *Advertiser*, was the wide mutual respect which existed between pipers who had served during the war. This was demonstrated in the public's response to all of the Pipe Bands and, "amongst those who were most hearty in their congratulations were members of the defeated Bands."

The Society staged a concert on 21st October, 1919, which included a full range of Scottish songs, recitations and dancing. The *Advertiser*'s report the following day of the function, noted that the Comunn na Feinne Reel Party danced the Reel of Tulloch, and it was also pointed out that all of the dancers making up this troupe had been taught by Miss Ethel Hughes. The president, J. Angus Laird welcomed visitors and congratulated the Pipe Band on its recent success and wished them well for the competitions which the Society hoped to re-start at the next New Year's Day Gathering on 1st January, 1920. He added that there was to be an emphasis, in the coming year, on Comunn na Feinne Socials as such activities broke down "stiffness" and encouraged a greater openness between members. He omitted to refer to the hope, too, that such social events would help raise revenue for the Society's various funds – especially the Hall debt!

In the run-up to the New Year's Day Games for 1920, the *Geelong Advertiser* on the 29th December, 1919, declared that the Society stood alone in its field with the forthcoming Games celebrating 63 consecutive years of Gatherings. It announced that these Games would form around the two themes of a Peace Gathering, and a Reunion of Old Associates.

> Portraits of the whole of the presidents from the inception of the Society in 1856, to the present, adorn the walls of the [Society's] Hall ... Old patrons of the Society will have an opportunity on inspecting the Hall on 1st January.

Given the difficulties re-forming Pipe Bands after the war, the Society continued to look to Brass Bands (and sometimes Bugle Bands) to provide the main musical entertainment during the day, and the only New Year's Day Band Competitions it held, were between such Bands. As a consequence of this, it was the ambition of the Society to make Geelong the centre of competition on New Year's Day for 'C' grade bands. With inducements, said Harry Shugg, an official V.B.B.A. adjudicator, it would be possible to broaden such competitions so that bands of different Grades might also join the competitions.

The event most looked forward to at the forthcoming 1920 New Year's Day Gathering, therefore, was the Brass Band "C" Grade Competitions which the Brass Band Association had persuaded the Society to stage. The *Advertiser* report of 31st December, 1919, described the arrival of the South Yarra Brass Band with a degree of excitement. The newspaper anticipated, "much music in the streets, as the various bands arrived and marched [playing] to their respective hotels."

The South Yarra Band, which had success at a previous Comunn na Feinne contest, was under Mr J.W. Holmes as Bandmaster. Holmes had previously played with the Geelong Harbour Trust Brass Band. There were also Bands coming from Brunswick and Coburg, but the Geelong West Band was the only one of the local Bands actually taking part in the Competition. The judging of the playing was to be carried out by Mr Harry Shugg who had been Bandmaster of the Geelong Harbour Trust Brass Band and who now held the similar post with the Malvern Tramways Band. The V.B.B.A. provided separate judges for the marching, presentation and dress.

The *Advertiser* also reported that the New Year's Day programme for 1920 was going to be a lengthy one and it would be conducted at more than one venue. The Brass Solo events and some Highland Dancing competitions were to take place from 9am on New Year's Day in the Society's Hall. At 10am the Bands were to assemble for the Procession to the Eastern Oval. The sports were to begin at 12.30pm and at 2pm the Bands were to gather for inspection following which, at 3pm, the Quickstep competitions would be carried out. Mr Harry Shugg, the overall Band Competition adjudicator, was then to conduct the massed bands in a Peace Reveille and this would be followed by some further displays.

Sandwiched between the Band contests, there were to be other competitive events involving Highland dancing and solo piping as well as bicycle and harriers' races. If this programme was not crowded enough, there was also to be some entertainment provided by Mr H.A. Tipper, "The world's wonder cyclist", who had appeared as a novelty attraction at the Society's 1915 Highland Gathering. He intended bringing several diminutive machines for boys to ride and with which to compete in races. The day was to conclude with the final of the two-mile cycle race at 5.30pm, the last track contest on the Geelong Oval that day. The Bands and competitors were then to assemble and march to Kardinia Park where the contests were to continue in the evening from 7pm. The grounds were to be lit up with "powerful electric lights" to enable the spectators to see the Brass Bands performing their 'Test' Piece and their 'Own Choice' Piece. Probably, as it had done on a previous occasion, and to set at rest the fears of any 'nervous nellies' who intended being at the electrically illumined arena, the *Advertiser* reported that Inspectors from the Electric Supply company had checked the illuminations and attested to their safety!

The increasing role played by various professional sporting and music bodies was apparent at the Society's 1920 Games and this subject is dealt with more fully in another section. However, it is important to see the effort, at these 1920 Games, on the part of the various athletic and cycling organisations, to promote their respective sports and to encourage the formation of local Associations. The Victorian Amateur Athletic Association (V.A.A.A.), for example, announced that it was sending some of its officials to Comunn na Feinne's New Year's Day Gathering on 1st January, 1920, "to assist in carrying out the events which included some of the Melbourne Club's best performers," and to oversee the formation of the "Geelong Amateur Runners". A short time later, on 7th February, 1920, the Chief Officer of the Victorian Bicycling Association (V.B.C.A.) came to Geelong to inspect the "wheel track at Kardinia Park to ensure that it conformed to Association Regulations. A trial was to be carried out at a later date.

The *Advertiser*, frequently critical of the pre-Games procession to the Grounds, did its best to generate interest in this part of the proceedings. It reported that Comunn na Feinne's own pipe band would lead the various local and visiting Brass Bands from the assembly point in Little Malop Street to the Eastern Oval where, from 12.30pm, "every moment will be occupied with harrier races, cycle races and Highland Games."

With the foregoing build-up of the 1920 annual Gathering, and with the Oval in perfect condition due to summer rains, everything seemed set for a successful Gathering. The *Geelong Advertiser*, reporting on the day, as it had since the staging of the first Games in 1857, said that the attendance numbered "several thousand" and the weather, although not the best for spectators (being cool), was suited to athletic sports. The newspaper, on 2nd January, 1920, while full of general *bonhomie* towards the Gathering, could not, however, overcome its occasional antipathy towards Highland Dancing and to bagpipes. It was praiseworthy of the Brass Band Competition but critical of the arrangements whereby, during the Quickstep event for Brass Bands, Highland dancing, to the accompaniment of bagpipes, was also taking place.

> It was impossible for spectators to enjoy either event, and how the judge was able to carry out his duties amidst the noise of skirling bagpipes was a mystery.

It is interesting, however, that on the judge's score-sheets, which are fairly detailed, as given in the newspaper account, there were remarks about the effect strong winds and physical distance from the Bands had on audibility, but not a word about the sound of bagpipes causing any distraction whatsoever. The *Advertiser*, despite its own criticisms of some aspects of the 1920 New Year's Day Gathering, was prepared to provide the opinions of other attendees even when they differed from their own. For instance, visitors from other Scottish Societies throughout Victoria and, "officials who have been connected with the Society for many years [said] that this [was] the most successful gathering held for five years."

Comunn na Feinne played a significant role in the post-war revival of Pipe Band contests. The Society's own Pipe Band performed at the 1920 New Year's Day Games, and, "had created a favourable impression". So much so, in fact, that two "well-known members" of the Campbell Clan, supported by another enthusiast, promised to subscribe £5 each towards the next year's Pipe Band Contest where the prize money was to be £40. This, it was thought, would be an inducement to bring Pipe Bands to Geelong. This led to a challenge being laid down to those of other 'Clans' similarly to increase the Prize Pool in order to draw Bands from all over Victoria. On the 4th February, 1920, the secretary, James Galbraith, was pleased to announce that there had been a good response to the challenge, and the latest donation was from the McIntosh clan. The McDonalds, too, had responded with Alexander McDonald forwarding, "a cheque for £25 towards the President's scheme."

There was a mild flutter of excitement when the Geelong mayor, Alderman Hitchcock, announced that he had received from Mr W.M. Hughes, prime minister of Australia, advice that His Royal Highness the Prince of Wales would be visiting Geelong during his forthcoming tour of Australia. The *Advertiser* added, on 5th February, 1920, that it was due to the mayor's "representations" that Geelong was being included in the royal tour. The newspaper recounted the several previous visits of royalty to Geelong, tactfully leaving out the Duke of Edinburgh's visit in December, 1867, with its disastrous "free picnic" riot at the botanical gardens. The Duke of Cornwall and York (later King George V) had passed through Geelong in the 1880s, and again in 1901 when he visited the country to open the First Federal Parliament. These were both, literally, 'whistle stop' visits, confined to the Geelong train station for a few minutes on each occasion. On this present visit, however, the *Advertiser* wrote that this Duke of Cornwall and York, Prince of Wales, "our future King – should spend a longer time here on this occasion."

At its general meeting on 20th May, 1920, Comunn na Feinne discussed the intended visit of the Prince of Wales on 1st June, 1920, and it was agreed that two veterans of the India Campaigns, Councillor Robert Williams and Piper John Kidd, be invited to meet the royal visitor. The *Advertiser* slightly mixed up the account of Piper Kidd's experience at Dargai Heights, writing:

> Cr Robert Williams took part in the great march made by Lord Roberts from Kabul to Kandahar, while Piper John Kidd was in the Gordon Highlanders when they made their famous charge at the Dargai Heights, and though wounded in both legs, continued sounding the pibroch.

However, the world, and the attitude of some Geelong folk, had changed over the past 50 years. The great enthusiasm which broke out with the news of the very first royal visit to Australia; the Duke of Edinburgh's visit in 1867, was not quite repeated when the news of the intended royal visit was made known. The *Geelong Advertiser* revealed that not everyone, apparently, was looking forward to welcoming the Royal Visitor.

"Labour not interested in the Prince of Wales," was its heading over the relevant news item.

> In many parts of the State motions have been carried by members of the Trades (sic) Unions urging Labourites not to allow their children to take part in any demonstration in connection with the visit of the Prince of Wales.

A letter to the *Advertiser* on 24th May, 1920 from a Union official, expressed this mood more pointedly and with a local application.

> Dear Sir, I have to inform you that the Geelong members of the ASE., do not want any time off for the Prince's visit unless paid for the same. Trusting you will notify the employers to that effect.
> Yours truly, Secretary, Geelong Branch.

However, despite the less than welcoming spirit expressed in the foregoing pieces, the Duke's visit to Geelong on 1st June, 1920 was enthusiastically received, especially by the children. The Duke spent a mere 1½ hours at Geelong, and said and did everything without mishap. Crowds there were aplenty, children of course, and the ubiquitous Comunn na Feinne Pipe Band, naturally! There were visits to an Exhibition* and to various industrial sites, within easy reach, with the Prince charming everyone he met. Then it was over, hand-shakes all around and a collective sigh of relief that, despite some rain at times, there were no 'damp squibs', whether unionist or republican, to spoil the occasion; and there certainly was no free picnic in the park!

*[This was an Exhibition, staged at Dennys Lascelles' Store, to show off and promote, "the potentialities of our (i.e. Geelong's) primary and secondary resources."]

In another attempt to get back to a state of post-war normalcy, Comunn na Feinne announced on 5th September 1920, that the regular Comunn na Feinne Concerts, which had been discontinued during WW1, were to be re-instituted, with the first one to be held 13th September 1920. In further keeping with the aim of providing regular entertainments, the Society announced that there also was to be a reunion concert, in September, 1920, featuring Miss Ethel Hughes and her dancers who had raised such a large sum of money during the war years for charity.

'Haggis with Honours,' was how Comunn na Feinne announced the reinstatement of another of its most popular annual entertainments; and what better day could they have chosen than the 30th November, 1920, St Andrew's Day, to re-launch this event? It attracted the largest attendance in its history and representatives from "every Scottish Society in Victoria" attended, along with the usual clutch of politicians and members of the St Patrick's Society and the Society of St George.

The Society, at its last meeting for the year, reported the *Advertiser*, promised that the 1921 Gathering would be "the biggest yet staged." Special reference was made to the work of the ladies over the past year and to the magnificent performance of the Pipe Band, which had won the Championship prize at the 1920 South Street, Ballarat Competitions, 1920, subsequently gaining the title, 'Champions of the Commonwealth'.

CNF Pipe Band-winner at South Street, Ballarat, 1920.

At this meeting the secretary, James Galbraith, read the annual report and the balance sheet remarking, with a degree of understatement, that there had been difficulties, but despite these, "the Society had kept the flag flying." A directors' meeting on 8th December, 1920 discussed the forthcoming January 1921 Games. Reference was made to the £100 Sheffield Handicap purse (the winner of which would also receive the Society's blue ribbon), and to the Sprint and Cycle races, all of which were receiving large numbers of entries. This enthusiasm was re-iterated at the following weekly meeting where it was reported that the number of entries so far received was pleasing, bringing in revenue from the entry fees, and that the closing date was 16th December, 1920. Already, it reported, "Upwards of £50 in Sheffield Handicap foot-running entries have been received." This was case, too, for the number of cycling entries.

The meeting further reported that the President, Mr J. A. Laird, "has in hand the designing of an up-to-date board which will record the number of competitors, time for the race and colours of the winner. Competitors will race in different coloured jackets so there will be no difficulty in the public picking out the winners." The Society was also conducting yet another campaign to enrol new members and, as an inducement, it was announced, according to the *Advertiser* of 15th December, 1920, that new members would be able, without further cost to them, "to participate in the whole of the privileges for the year."

The Society, itself, adopted an 'upbeat' attitude announcing that, "entries in the other events constitute a record," and the secretary, James Galbraith, was further reported as saying that he had received from the Chief, Mr Phillip Russell, "a letter of appreciation of the efforts being made for the success of the gathering, and enclosing a substantial donation towards the funds." There was to be a Highland night at the Society's Hall on Hogmanay (old year's night), where singing and piping and dancing would 'see in' the new year. Following the Games on New Year's Day, the *Advertiser* promoted the concert to be held at the Society's Hall where, "a splendid evening's entertainment [would be presented] by Melbourne artists. (sic)"

On the eve of the Games, the *Geelong Advertiser* on 31st December, 1920, presented an exciting picture of what spectators might expect to find at the grounds the following day.

> Comunn na Feinne's 64th Highland Gathering is causing keen interest in pedestrian and cycle circles. The entries received for the cycle events constitute a record for Geelong. Local riders have had the opportunity of training on the track. … and their opinion is that it is on a par with other sprinting grounds. The winner [of the foot race] the Sheffield Handicap, will be decorated with the Society's blue ribbon … as a token of the first £100 competed for in Geelong." The newspaper also reported that a new "Quoit rink" had been prepared "under the shade of the trees for the quoit match for which a good entry has been received.

It was, thus, from a period of 'highs' and 'lows', that Comunn na Feinne came to the end of another decade of activities, prepared to face its 64th New Year's Day Gathering on 1st January, 1921. As we have seen, the period from the birth of the new century up to 1914 had constituted, for Comunn na Feinne, "The best of times". However, the war, with its lists of the fallen and the death of Dr John Small; its impact on the Pipe Band and the falling membership rolls, caused a grim mood to settle upon the Society constituting, for the years, 1914-1920, "The worst of times."

The new decade was to bring its own challenges as the Society sought, once again, to build up 'a head of steam'. There is little doubt that, in one activity at least, its annual Eisteddfod, which had been running since 1912, Comunn na Feinne was to reach great heights. To the *Advertiser*, however, it seemed that Comunn na Feinne, as a whole, was slowly 'running down'.

Chapter 6

Running Out of Puff – 1921-1929

The first Gathering of the new decade gave evidence that the community, and society in general, had not yet returned to a state of normalcy following the first World War. The New Year's Day Comunn na Feinne Gathering for 1921 took place at its new grounds, Kardinia Park. The *Advertiser* reported, on 4th January, 1921, that the day was, "Successful, but marred by heat and withdrawals." Weather, and events involving people, always test a reporter's store of adjectives and the *Geelong Advertiser*'s scribe was no exception. The day, of course, was "sweltering", the crowd "large" and visiting dignitaries were "numerous" and were "royally treated" and their Highland dress was "resplendent." Many officers of other Scottish Societies including, from interstate, Mr A. McLeish, president of the Kalgoorlie Society of West Australia, were present resplendent in their Highland dress.

As well, there was the usual clutch of local MPs and dignitaries who, as a species, had managed, it seemed, to surpass even the Scot at spotting 'an eye to the main chance.' Being seen and, better still, being heard at such events never did one's election or re-election chances any harm! The tartans added "colour" and the kilted men, with 'tammies' to match, "made a pleasing combination." The day, like the *Advertiser*'s report, provided a mixture of good and bad. Few attended the morning session and even those, "sought the shade" provided by the Stand or, with more frequency, the refreshment tents! The Refreshment Rooms were "capably managed by the Comunn na Feinne ladies [and] were well patronised."

The projected Brass Band contests for the 1921 New Year's Day Gathering was dealt a series of blows and sank without a trace, "due to misunderstandings between the Victorian Band Association and the Metropolitan Band Association." The *Advertiser* reported that, because of this "misunderstanding", none of the nine 'C' Grade bands which had entered from Melbourne would now be taking part in the competitions. The newspaper continued saying that the contest, had it gone ahead, "would have meant some 200 bandsmen and supporters coming to the city." The second of the 'blows' fell when it was learned that the two bands from Wonthaggi, which had entered, "will also be prevented from coming owing to the coal strike." Finally, it was announced that the two bands which had tied in the quickstep event the previous year, the South Yarra and the Toorak bands, which were to play out the tie at the 1921 Games, "did not put in an appearance." The *Advertiser* hastened to point out that the cancellation of the Brass Band contest, "was in no way the fault of the promoters."

The bicycle races offered the usual excitement and, for those Quoit enthusiasts, an iron pitch had newly been laid out although it only "attracted desultory attention." In fact, the Society was to establish its own Iron Quoits Club (see below), which held matches at different times throughout the year and, despite Quoits being a very popular pastime, with many clubs existing throughout Victoria, the lack of interest at the 1921 Games seems puzzling. It may have been, as the *Advertiser* suggested, that the distance of the rinks from the main arena brought about the lack of an audience for the Quoits competition.

Commenting on the Games programme in general, the *Advertiser* noted that when compared with previous years, "there was a marked falling off in the arena events." It did, however, have some praise for the dancing events at which a "large number of lassies competed" in what was "an unpleasant day for the dancers, who displayed remarkable endurance." The chief Highland Dancing Judge, Mr T. Paterson, said, despite the fierce heat of the day, that the dancing was superior to that of the previous year. In fact, he commented that each year improvement was seen in the dancing over the year before, and this was to be applauded. Bouquets, too, were awarded to all of the dancers as, "the heat of the day had been most trying, but the Geelong girls have wonderful spirit. They have made no trouble and have not disputed a decision. Even adverse judgments have been received with smiles." Equal praise was given to the two pipers, Ralph Fraser and John Kidd, who laboured away in the heat, accompanying the multitude of dancers. But the judges did not stop at the dance competitors or the accompanists; they directed praise, too, towards the whole organization.

> The officials of Comunn na Feinne are to be congratulated on the events of the day. They offered liberal prizes, and it is a pity there were not more competitors. Despite handicaps, which must be heart-breaking to the organisers of a sports' gathering, the function must be termed a successful one.

As for the heavy events, the *Advertiser* concluded that given the distance such sports were from the spectators, "all the crowd saw were several middle-aged gentlemen straining on the wooden Caber or bending under the stone." A little below the belt, perhaps, and, probably, not a remark to be repeated within earshot of the "middle-aged" gents referred to!

Overall, the *Advertiser* summed up by stating that, compared with other years, the arena events were poor as far as, "quantity and variety were concerned." There was further disappointment when it was announced that the Harriers' Races, "Owing to the small number which entered for them … had to be abandoned." This meant, continued the *Advertiser*, that bicycling tended to dominate the time, "which provided an interesting day." But, it was more than just "interesting" and the newspaper did highlight some excitement on the bicycle track when it reported, in one of the heats of a cycle race, "the front tyre of one of the machines blew out" with the rider being flung to the ground. "The crowd held its breath as three cyclists fell over the first, but fortunately no injuries were sustained except a few scratches." The cyclist was quick not to lay any blame on the cycle track itself and said that it, "was the natural result of a single tube bursting."

The Society's Blue Ribbon (as well as the £100 first prize purse) for coming top in the Sheffield Handicap foot racing event was awarded by Senator Plain to W.H. Thompson. This purse was, "the largest stake which has yet been competed for, in its class, in Geelong." No doubt, because of the size of the purse, the event proved to be very popular and attracted a large number of entries.

Overall, the *Advertiser*, despite the various pieces of bad luck which had prevented the attendance of many of the Bands, managed to play the 'glad game' by praising the Society and, generally, concluding that after all, the Gathering was a success. It was true, the reporter wrote, that the Brass Band contest did not take place and that this was a "serious disappointment". However, the absence of the Brass Bands, the report continued, meant that, "the provision of music [was left] to the Pipe Band which stepped into the breech manfully." There was a moment of *Advertiser* light-heartedness, too, when the reporter, under the by-line "Fire Causes Amusement" wrote that, "Not the least entertaining incident at the Highland sports on Saturday was an unprogrammed event – to wit, a grass fire …" This fire broke out at the area where the Caber tossing event was taking place, however the attempt to extinguish the fire by rolling a Caber over the flames, though ingenious, had no effect. With the flames rapidly spreading, it took several men, with bags and underbrush, a period of vigorous beating of the flames before the danger had past. Though treated humorously by the *Advertiser*, the paper did don its serious face when recognizing that, "with all the grass on the arena [being] in a dry condition … had the fire got beyond the control of the few officials, the outbreak would have been more disconcerting than amusing." So, there were at least some saving graces which could be picked out of the day's entertainments!

After the Games had ended, but still with some 'spleen to vent', the *Advertiser*'s reporter turned the 'blowtorch' on the traditional New Year's evening concert, and it was obvious that the writer, after enduring a long hot day's sports, and looking forward to a relaxing evening of entertainment, was in no mood to be charitable in the face of what was regarded as second-rate talent. The report was as terse as it was uncharitable!

The "attendance was poor, as was the Concert itself ..." There were, however, mitigating circumstances beyond Comunn na Feinne's control which the reporter might well have taken into consideration when composing his review. The private electricity supplier pulled the plug, literally, by announcing that they would not allow the Society the necessary power required for the evening's lighting. Only after the intervention of Senator Plain was it decided that a limited amount of power would be allowed and the concert could proceed up to 10pm. This reprieve came too late to inform the Melbourne performers that the Concert was going to proceed after all, and they had already returned to Melbourne. The other major drawcard, the biograph programme, also had to be cancelled because of power shortage, and the Concert ended abruptly at 10pm when it was, quite literally, lights out!

The *Advertiser* had held over its report on the visit to the Games of some 'old-time' members and past competitors until its issue of the 5th January, 1921. It referred to the presence at the New Year's Day Games of several veterans from the earliest days of the Society. Mr William H. Sinnott, "was the only survivor present of those who attended the first Comunn na Feinne Gathering." Mr William H. Armour was another of the aged veterans of the early Gatherings who was in attendance at the 1921 Gathering. "Despite his advancing years, William Sinnott* makes it a point to attend each Geelong Comunn na Feinne Gathering", and since its inauguration in 1857, the paper added, "he has missed very few". William Sinnott had been successful in the Education competitions which the Society had inaugurated at the 1858 Gathering, and he had with him a clutch of medals, including a gold one, which he had won at these competitions.

*[See short biographies in Appendix 3 (b)]

William Sinnott "little Billy Sinnott" to his friends, said that he had been present at the very first Gathering in 1857 on the grounds at South Geelong. He had also attended the first Gathering on the Geelong Oval and, latterly, the first Gathering at Kardinia Park. "There were more men at the old-time gathering", he remarked with a quiet smile, "who were born on the soil of Scotland, but many of the games they took part in, such as tilting the ring, have since been discontinued." Despite this, there appears to be greater interest in the function than ever. William Sinnott was extremely shy when a camera man appeared on the scene. However, a good snap was secured.

As the year 1921 got underway, all seemed to be business as usual. The first of the regular monthly meetings of the Society for the year was held on 2nd February, 1921. It was foreshadowed that a Robert Burns night was being planned as well as a concert for Society members. At a Monthly meeting of Directors on 2nd March, 1921, "It was decided to entertain the Comunn na Feinne Ladies' Committee and the Pipe Band at a picnic at Queenscliff." Later in the year, at the monthly meeting, held 3rd August, 1921, it was agreed that the Society take steps to woo the Victorian Brass Bands Association to allow the staging of Brass Band contests at the 1922 New Year's Day Gathering. The emphasis on Brass Band music and contests would indicate that there still was difficulty in attracting enough Pipe Bands with which to stage a competition.

At the Society's 66th annual meeting, held 20th September, 1921, the treasurer's report was discussed, "and approved of." It was further agreed that the Society would, as it had done at the 1921 Games, include on the programme, "a Sheffield Handicap … [with prize money] … of £100." The meeting also learned that a positive response had been received from the Victorian Brass Bands' Association and, as far as the next (1922) Highland Gathering was concerned, the Association had granted the Society permission to stage the 'B' Grade and the 'C' Grade quickstep contests, with the Society itself offering a prize of £75 for the winner of the latter.

Although the Society was still finding it difficult to get enough pipe bands to stage a competition at its New Year's Day Gatherings, its own Band was competing at South Street, Ballarat each year. It was announced that at the October, 1921 South Street competitions the Comunn na Feinne Band had come a creditable second.

Continuing its pattern of offering as many social events during the year as it could fit in, the Society held another concert on 27th September, 1921. This was followed up later in the year with a Haggis supper, on 30th November, for which event the

Advertiser was full of praise. In contrast to its earlier savaging of the post-Games Society Concert, mentioned above, the *Geelong Advertiser*'s report the day after the Haggis Supper, adopted a very complimentary tone in its description of this social event. The catering was "the most efficient", the attendance was "representative", the speeches were "above average" and the music was "the best". What more could be said! After that the *Advertiser* seems to have run out of superlatives!

The *Advertiser*'s last issue for the year, on the last day of the year, offered a tantalising glimpse of some of the attractions which were to appear on the programme for the New Year's Day Games for 1922. An event capable of conjuring up all sorts of imaginative pictures was, "the wrestling match on horseback between naval men from the *Platypus*. This event, the *Advertiser* drily noted, "promises to be very amusing" and was keenly looked forward to by the naval men themselves. The Gathering was to begin on Saturday 31st December, 1921 and, missing Sunday, to conclude on Monday evening the 2nd January, 1922, as the number of heats in various events meant that extra time was required to stage them all. The Geelong West Cycle Club would be taking part and entrants from that Club would, "run their first heat, to be followed by ten heats in the 75 yards' sprint," on the first day of the Gathering and three heats "in the half mile handicap" would also be run the same day. In addition, opportunity was also to be taken to stage the 'C' Grade brass band Quickstep contest, and the various Bands' 'Own Choice' selection, on the Saturday. The evening programme of events was to include a "concert" for which several leading artistes from Melbourne had been engaged.

Although the Games were never held on a Sunday, the Society did hold a fund-raising concert towards its financial commitment to the Geelong Hospital on that day. The programme consisted of the Essendon Citizens' Band, together with the Geelong Returned Soldiers' Band, providing a "sacred concert" of suitable music.

The Games continued on Monday 2nd January, 1922 with one of the highlights again being the £100 Sheffield Handicap foot race. Mr J. Burke, who had already won the £200 Melbourne Cup Stakes, was an entrant for the Geelong race and would be starting "off the 5½ yards' mark." The *Advertiser* concluded its promotion of the 1922 Games by referring to the Monday evening concert, following the closure of the Games, which was to be held in the Society's Hall, "when a full jazz band will be engaged." Truly, a new age was dawning!

As noted, some of the heats for various events were conducted on Saturday, 31st December, 1921, and there was a good crowd for the Games and this was reflected in the 3rd January's *Advertiser* headlines, "C.N.F. Celebrations Again Successful", and, "65th Annual Gathering Attracts Big Crowds." However, it did qualify these headlines when it pronounced the Gathering as "almost" a success. Its conditional "almost" was again due to the events involving Brass Bands. The Victorian Brass Band Association was anxious to add Geelong to its roster of Band competitions each year and had arranged to stage a contest at the New Year's Day Gathering at Geelong in 1922. Indeed, Comunn na Feinne had donated a prize of £75 for the winning Band, but the event turned out to be a disaster!

Over the years, the *Advertiser* had regularly reported various 'dust ups' between athletes, bicyclists and even runners, all of which had brought the inevitable 'protests.' However, in its report on 3rd January of the 1922 Games, it was clear that no disputes in the past came near to the number of challenges raised by the Brass Bands (and their Association). In fact, all but three of the Bands had withdrawn before a single note ('good' or 'bung') was sounded. This left only three Bands in the Contest. But worse was to follow. Two of the remaining three Bands (Colac Citizens' Band and the Geelong Returned Soldiers' Band), were disqualified due to playing unregistered players. These Bands were allowed to take part but were disqualified from being awarded any of the prize monies or being officially 'placed'. This left only one Band (Essendon City Band) legitimately qualified to compete, so there was no real contest at all, concluded the report.

This failure of the Brass Band contest overall was very disappointing to the Society, although it was not responsible for what happened. The Victorian Brass Band Association (V.B.B.A.) had specifically requested that the contest take place and it is difficult to understand why some of the Bands pulled out, especially given that Comunn na Feinne had provided a reasonable sized prize purse (£75) for the winning Band. It was disappointing, too, for another reason. It had been hoped that Comunn na Feinne would subsequently provide the venue for the Australian Brass Band Championships; but, although no fault of the Society, the poor turn out at the 1922 Games did not help their case. The Society had also offered a Pipe Band Contest at the 1922 Games, but this also had to be cancelled altogether due to the number of bands withdrawing their entries.

The Society had utilized the Saturday before the games to conduct the preliminary heats of the Sprint Handicap and the Mawallock* Handicap, "for which the Society had offered £10 and £100 respectively. There were ten heats in each of these events, which provide great interest for the followers of foot races." The heats of the Cycling competitions were also held on the Saturday with the finals, like that of the foot racing, being contested the following Monday.
*[Mawallock was the name of Phillip Russell's property at Beaufort.]

The *Advertiser* remarked that, at the 1922 Games, "although there were a number of Scotsmen" in Highland Dress, and a number of representatives from other Scottish organizations across Victoria and from other States, and although traditional Scottish sports did feature on the programme, "the principal attraction was provided by the pedestrian and cycling events. For these, the Society was fortunate in securing a very large number of entries." A new professional body, the Victorian Athletics Association, had recently been formed and it was also noted by the *Advertiser* that the Geelong sports, "were run under the auspices of the V.A.A." The Society was aware that the focus of the Gatherings over the years had shifted towards being a more general sporting event, and it saw this as evidence of its success in creating a wide appeal to the whole community.

The Society's Evening Scottish Concert on Monday 2nd January, 1922, was held at Kardinia Park and, with no threat of electric power restrictions being evident, it attracted a large attendance which was "most appreciative" and which "demanded many encores" of the performers. The singing and the humour were much applauded and the Comunn na Feinne Pipe Band, "rendered enjoyable selections and Highland dances were contributed by a band of lassies. Solo dances were performed by prize winners from the Games' dancing events."

Two other important events in the life of Comunn na Feinne occurred during this year. The first of these, on 22nd August 1922, was the official opening of the Comunn na Feinne Hall extensions which included the addition of the Dr John Small Memorial Library building. This was to house the Society's collection of books and, later, the extensive library of books which made up Dr Small's personal collection which had been bequeathed to the Society. The Executors of the late Dr John Small's estate advised Comunn na Feinne, on 25th April, 1924 of the gift to it of Dr Small's own library.*

*[This seems completely to have disappeared when Comunn na Feinne folded.

> The executors of the estate of the late Dr John Small who was a president of Comunn na Feinne some years ago has donated "the whole of his valuable library to the Society. The library includes works by such authors as Ruskin, Dickens, Scott, Burns etc., while there is also a handsome History of the Great War. The Society will also receive from the Estate a Steel Engraving of Scotland Forever, and a group Photograph of the Directors of Comunn na Feinne that was presented to Dr John Small during his fourteen years as President. The Photographs will be given a prominent place in the Hall in Yarra Street. The collection of the works was made by Miss Hall, a niece of Mrs Small. They will be greatly treasured by the Society, amongst whose members the late Dr John Small was a general favourite.

The second important event was the holding of the Victorian Scottish Union Conference at Geelong. Alan MacNeilage, the Society's bard since Alan F. Wilson's death, provided an appropriate poem welcoming the delegates to Geelong. The verse reflected that duality which is said to characterize the Scottish soul. At once 'pawky' and 'philosophical', the verse illustrated the continuing aims of Comunn na Feinne which were to be put into effect through the lives of members in the community. This might involve influencing politics and developing their new home-land and welcoming and caring for new immigrants, all of which demonstrated the continuing relevance of the Society's charter.

[The full poem can be found in Appendix 5 (f) Poems by Alan McNeilage.]

> Welcome to Delegates at Geelong Conference – 20th September, 1922.
> A' the Scots folk are geth'rin the gither again,
> For the slogan has peal'd o'er hill, valley an' plain;
> They are leavin' the ledger, the forge, an' the pleugh;
> A' their vows o' true frien'ship ance mair tae renew,
> An' a leal kindly welcome awaits them, I ween,
> Frae the lassies an' lads o' Comunn na Feinne.
> ....
>
> Here Highland an' Lowland, the-gither will blend,
> Here Liberal, an' Laborite winna' contend,
> But, provin' their hairts tae auld Scotland beat true,
> Still this fair land "Australia," they loyally love.
> God! Prosper the union! Undimmed be its sheen
> An' may kind fortune favour Comunn na Feinne.

The South Street, Ballarat, Pipe Band Competitions were held October, 1922 with Comunn na Feinne's own Band again entering. For the second year running, it came a close second with only 3½ points separating first-placed Melbourne Highland, from the third-placed Band. Although its own Pipe Band contest failed in 1922 because of the non-appearance of several Pipe Bands, Comunn na Feinne was doing its best, in the form of inducements, to attract Pipe Bands to its upcoming Gathering on 1st January, 1923.

The Society met towards the end of December providing the latest news on its forthcoming New Year's Day Gathering. It had been desperately seeking new members and this meeting, as well as providing information about the Gathering, also provided a reminder to all the members of what the Society had done in its history, and what more it could achieve with an enlarged membership. When it came to the programme for the 1923 Games, one ploy used to draw spectators was to ensure that there were big names signed to compete. These included two well-known athletes of the time, C. Milburn "the champion sprinter" and R.J. Corbett, "the speedy Ballarat footballer who played for Melbourne last year." C. Milburn had performed well in the Ballarat Gift on Boxing Day and both men had entered for the Sheffield Sprint of 75 yards at the upcoming Comunn na Feinne Games. Some well-known cyclists of the day, "J.L. Fitzgerald, Fox Edwards and Beasley" were also expected to be competing and some exciting contests were anticipated.

In addition to the athletic drawcards, the Society announced the appearance of the South and Port Melbourne Ladies' Pipe Band which would, "render items during the afternoon." This Band had been formed during WW1 and was very popular with the public. It was further announced in the *Advertiser* of 29th December, that, "on the Sunday, the Ladies' Pipe Band and the Pakington Street Choir will render several sacred items of Choral work, in aid of hospital funds." It should be noted that Ladies' Pipe Bands and Ladies as solo pipers were not, at this time, allowed to compete at Highland Games in Victoria, although some Societies, such as Comunn na Feinne, did allow them to participate in their Games as a non-competitive Band. Neither could lady pipers play in a pipe band alongside male pipers. Ladies' Pipe Bands were not officially recognized and, indeed, were treated with hostility by many officials and by the newly formed (1924) Victorian Pipe Band Association (V.P.B.A.), and thus could not compete or do anything which would have fallen under the Association's area of control. In fact, it was not until the 1940's that Ladies' Pipe Bands were officially recognized by the Pipe Band Association in Victoria! Wilfully, and bravely, however, an Australian Scottish Ladies' Pipe Band (despite its title it mostly was made up of lady pipers from Victoria), defied the Pipe Band Association, and despite obstacles put in its way, travelled overseas on a world tour in 1925. The Band was a great success wherever it played and achieved awards in Piping and Dancing at Competitions in Scotland.*

*[A brief history of this Band and its tour can be found in Julia Church's article 'Ladies and Bagpipes: the 'world's greatest novelty', in *Memento* Issue 38, 2010, pp 10-12, National Archives of Australia. Some details can be found in Appendix 4 (b).]

Australian Ladies' Pipe Band at Robert Burns' Cottage, Ayr, Scotland, 9th October, 1926.

It is noticeable, even with the few Society social functions, cited as taking place during the year, that, by 1922, the increasing success and expansion of the Society's annual Eisteddfod* was curtailing the Society's fund-raising socials and concerts. The presence of large gatherings, either competing or as the audience, during the many weeks of artistic competitions meant that income-generating lettings, at least for the duration of the Eisteddfod, were denied to Comunn na Feinne. Comunn na Feinne's secretary, James Galbraith, made an important announcement regarding extensions to the Society's new Hall because of the success of the Eisteddfodau, and the increasing number of entrants which, for 1922, had reached 900 (compared with five in 1912). The period over which they were now held had stretched out to almost three weeks and that period was to eventually extend over three months.

*[An extensive history of the Eisteddfod is more fully dealt with in Appendix 14 (a).]

The annual Games were occasionally spilling over two days, as it was found increasingly necessary to hold preliminary heats in some events, such as bicycling and foot racing, before the actual Gathering day. This meant, of course, further expense for the Society and an even greater reliance on 'professional' judges. One element of this growing professionalism in athletics was the expectation of good, audible and reliable starting signals. Another was a rising need to so schedule events that athletes could move between meets, competing in a circuit of Games.

One of the demands from athletes at the 1923 Gathering, therefore, concerned a better method of sounding the start of a race. Before the day was out, however, it was a case of being careful for what you ask! The *Advertiser*'s description, in its report on the 1st January, 1923 Games, gives many of the reasons why athletes were unhappy with 'Starting Methods' and why, perhaps, they regretted opening their mouths!

> Varied were the methods adopted by the starters at the Comunn na Feinne sports at Kardinia Park on Saturday … and particularly was this so in the Sheffield Handicap. Whistle and handclap were employed with more or less success. The gun, however, was not an effective weapon in the hands of the starter of the Sheffield. On several occasions when the runners were crouched on the mark ready for the signal the pistol refused to perform its functions, but clicked audibly. A repetition of this performance resulted in many of those behind the pickets advising the starter to "get another gun." Starters are only human after all, and when the gun clicked again, he threw it on the turf in disgust. A burly constable then came on the scene and handed over his revolver which was loaded with live shells. As soon as this fact was known, there was a general scatter in the direction of the fence, and even the runners, now bent over their marks, cast apprehensive glances behind them, for the starter was indeed handling the gun in a rather dangerous manner. But even the policeman's gun wouldn't act, and as a last resource, the starter despatched the runners per medium of a hand clap.

The cyclists having seen or heard about the loaded gun being used as the starter's signal, decided on caution rather than valour, and opted for the starter for their races using an ordinary whistle! Experience had taught them that even in the most perfectly run race, the unseen contestant, 'bad luck' could strike in numerous ways. They preferred not to add to that list by having a loaded pistol anywhere near their unprotected heads!

The large increase in Bicycle racing, and the number of heats having to be contested, meant that extra time was required to complete these contests. Although the greatest excitement generally was found in the final races, on occasions the heats could also raise the spectators' blood pressure by providing colour and excitement, both on and off the track. In the preliminaries of an important race, for example, the *Advertiser*'s report of the 3rd January, 1923, spoke of no gunshot injuries on the racetrack, although at times, it was nearly the case of last man standing, literally!

> In the first heat of the Caledonian Wheel Race, Watts of Mildara (sic) fell opposite the grandstand, owing to his striking the back wheel of the cycle in front of him. He fell heavily and had to be carried off. In the next heat of the same event, J.A. Abbs (Werribee) fell when negotiating the south-western turn of the track. T.G. Hughes who had been close behind him, collided with him, but escaped injury. Abbs was severely shaken and had to receive attention in the dressing room. There was another spill in the Kardinia Scratch Wheel Two Mile Race, when J.J. Beasley was thrown to the ground. Two other cyclists were also brought down. These had the presence of mind to get up and continue the race by running with their cycles until provided with new mounts. As there were then only three [left] in the race, they came second and third.

No marks to the bicyclists but full marks surely to the stretcher-bearers who were working non-stop ferrying the 'victims' from track to first-aid post, and full marks, too, to the bicycle mechanics working overtime to repair the damaged machines or, humanely putting them out of their misery!

The weather forecast had given favourable hopes of a successful Gathering. Even a short, sharp shower late in the games, along with stiff wind blowing across the arena, did little to dampen expectations. The presence of a Ladies' Pipe Band, playing Scottish airs, provided something of a novelty at these latest Games, and again at the 1924 Geelong Gathering.

The Worland dynasty continued to shine in the Heavy Events (Open) at the annual Gathering with Mr George Worland winning in the 'grunt' sections. At the 1923 Games he took the Caber, and the Throwing of the Heavy Hammer prizes and ran second in Putting the Stone. Yet another Worland, James Worland, won the Caber event reserved for local competitors.

It was pleasing to Comunn na Feinne that, with electricity rationing firmly behind them, the Society's post-games evening Concert at Kardinia Park was again, "brilliantly illuminated". After a performance by children, the concert was given over to song and dance with all of the artistes enthusiastically received by the audience.

The report that the field sports had been completed early to allow some contestants, who were to compete at Maryborough the following day, to catch the evening train for that town, was not accepted too well by at least one spectator. His letter, included in the *Advertiser* the next day, and signed, 'Disappointed,' aired his grievance that the Games, as a whole, "were not worth the admission money." Among things upsetting this correspondent included the decline of the pre-games procession, the timing of the start of the sports and, a hardy annual, the presence of too many people on the competition arena itself.

Sensing a good story, the *Geelong Advertiser* invited a reply from Comunn na Feinne, and James Galbraith, its secretary, obliged his explanation appearing a day later. Timetabling was being looked at, but, he explained, good competitors followed the circuit of Highland Games, and other Sporting events, competing in as many Gatherings as they could for the prize money. However, in order to attract such 'draw cards' it was necessary to stage these events at a time convenient for these travelling athletes. The timetable for the late Games, therefore, "was the result of a pre-arrangement between the Competitors, Maryborough [Caledonian Society] and Comunn na Feinne. Maryborough considered it a good idea as it allowed the runners to compete in Geelong and to be finished in time to, "catch the 5.25pm train that evening thus permitting of their appearance … at Maryborough [Games] on the Monday." However, Galbraith added that, "the result of the experiment was unfortunately not satisfactory to the promoters, but they have benefited by the experience so gained."

Galbraith went on to deal with the other matter, that of "empty" spaces during the second day of the Games. In doing so he provided an insight into the problems which some contestants found in financing their appearance at the Games and the "difficulties" which last minute withdrawals by athletes posed for the Games' organizers. He said that had all the Brass bands who had entered actually turned up to compete, there would have been a full programme, "as originally drawn up" and, "there would have been ample competition to take up the two days ..." But, continued Galbraith, with Brass bands especially, the matter of finance becomes a crucial factor in their appearance or non-appearance on the day. When the Games' day draws closer, many Brass bands, which originally had entered for the various competitions, find that they now could not do so as, "they cannot raise the wherewithal to travel." Thus, with last minute non-appearance of contestants, difficulties arise that, "only the promoters ... running a big gathering could fully realize."

Galbraith added that, for the next Games, several innovations might be tried which will enable a full two days programme to be delivered but if this could not be done, then the Gathering would drop back to "a one-day meeting."

In the course of dealing with the foregoing complaint, Galbraith affirmed, "that it was not the policy of the Society to enter into any controversy." Rather, Comunn na Feinne had long promoted community harmony and regarded its 'flagship', the annual Gathering, as a place where this 'harmony' might best be displayed.

The Society therefore continually strove to perfect this day and to eliminate anything which might tend towards acting against, or not promoting, a sense of enjoyment, fair play and harmony. Timetabling of events was an area which had caused some dissatisfaction and therefore it was being looked at.

Another innovation planned for the 1924 Gathering was to divide the ground into signposted sections, each one representing a different part of Scotland. This would make it easier for people from the different regions of Scotland to meet others from the same town or district.*

[*This 'innovation' is still carried out at the present-day Geelong Highland Games]

The annual Directors' Meeting, held 9th January, 1923, heard, among other matters, that the Programme for its Eisteddfod for April, 1923, had been prepared and was being printed. The meeting drew notice to a new event which, it believed, would attract attention towards these competitions.

> It will include what is claimed to be an entirely unique feature so far as competitions of this kind are concerned, viz., Old Testament Character. Competitors are allowed to select their own Old Testament character, and write their reasons for the selection in a short paper which will take not more than five minutes to deliver as an oration.

The Society was, of course, desirous to reach that same level of community participation in all of its other activities as it sought for its annual Eisteddfod. Throughout 1923 the Society continued its policy of providing entertainments to raise funds for charities and to meet its own expenses Public dances held in its Hall were performed to contemporary popular music, and also attracted revenue from the promoters of these events. But the Society did not merely hang out a 'Hall for Hire' sign. It also conducted its own popular dance nights to music provided by its own contemporary band. It advertised such a Dance for Monday 9th April, 1923, where the Comunn na Feinne Jazz Band would be playing the latest numbers, "just received from Melbourne and Sydney."

On occasions Comunn na Feinne organized events which were of a more solemn character, both for the Society and for the community in general – Anzac Day was one of those occasions. The 1923 Geelong Anzac Day Memorial Service was held at the Comunn na Feinne Hall at 8pm. The *Advertiser*'s account on 26th April, reported that a lone Piper played a suitable Lament and the 'Last Post' was sounded by a Bugler and Keith Hall* recited, 'This is Anzac Day.' The Society, in particular, had reason to commemorate this day, "as out of membership roll of 300, 78 enlisted. A number took part in the landing at Gallipoli and many paid the supreme sacrifice." Comunn na Feinne maintained a general association with Anzac Day commemorations and usually provided the piper (even wounded ones!) for the services.

> It would take more than an injured knee to prevent Pipe Major A. Linton of the Comunn na Feinne Pipe Band from taking a part in the annual Anzac Day March. On Saturday afternoon, he took his place with the Band and with a decided limp marched and played in the procession from the Returned Soldiers' Club at Kardinia Park.

*[Keith Hall was a regular competitor in the elocutionary and acting categories at Comunn na Feinne's annual Eisteddfod. He later joined the Allan Wilkie Shakespearean Company and toured with them in Australia as well as throughout New Zealand]

Comunn na Feinne's year passed with its usual programme of events, starting with the Gathering in January and then a scattered series of concerts and other social functions in the following months. The Society's annual Eisteddfod for 1922 had attracted 900 entries, and had been staged over three weeks. As well as having to find substantial prize monies and volunteer labour to sustain it, the indebted Society also lost opportunities of renting out its Hall for the duration of this event. Obvious strains were continuing to show, but the Eisteddfod, yearly, continued to grow in terms of the categories of competitions offered and in the numbers of contestants taking part. This 'success' also had the consequence of straining the voluntary manpower on offer!

In reporting the 'Members' Night' at these competitions the *Geelong Advertiser* put its full support and encouragement behind the Society and its financial needs. There was a variety of reasons why such a venture should be supported, and not the least of these, wrote the newspaper on 30th April, 1923, lay in the Society's 'ideals' which flowed out of its founding charter.

> There are high ideals behind the holding of these annual competitions but high ideals in themselves will not foot the prize list bill of £350 to which the Society is committed. It therefore behoves the public, by attending the sessions in adequate numbers to do its share in making the festival the success it ought to be. By so doing, Comunn na Feinne will be encouraged, not only in its effort to place Geelong in line with South Street, but in its higher ideal of bringing out our developing latent talent.

The *Advertiser* was also pleased to report, therefore, that Members' Night at Comunn na Feinne's annual Eisteddfod, which took place on 28th April, 1923, drew large numbers.

> The hall was packed and, the ordinary accommodation proving inadequate, forms had to be brought in. The attendance was the most gratifying since the actual competitive work opened nearly a fortnight ago, and a continuance of support on a similar scale would do much to relieve the anxiety of the

committee as to the financial side of the contests.

During this evening the secretary, James Galbraith, expressed the Directors' appreciation of the magnificent attendance, but asked for increased support from the public. He stressed that the Society was taking a big risk in staging its annual Eisteddfo and said on-going support was needed. So far, the attendances had been fairly good but not as good as he believed they should have been. These competitions were meant to fulfil part of the Society's educational aims, insofar as these related to such things as music, in its instrumental and vocal forms, the spoken word and a wide range of occupational skills, as well as promoting community harmony.

The Annual Meeting was held on the 12th September, 1923, and among its business was the election of a new Chief of Comunn na Feinne. The long-serving Chief, and generous benefactor, Mr Phillip Russell, had tendered his resignation citing his continuing ill-health. This was received with regret by the executive and members generally, and it was noted the many times he had financially supported the Society. Senator William Plain was unanimously elected as Comunn na Feinne's new Chief. A review of the Society's activities over the past year was given by the President, Mr Charles A. Smith,* who, "traced the work of the Society … and what it was doing for the benefit of the youth as well as the adult."

When the business side of the meeting had concluded, a Scottish concert of songs, music and anecdote were enjoyed.

*[Charles A. Smith succeeded J. Angus Laird as President. Laird had stood down from that position at the 1923 general meeting and Smith, a vice-president, was elected to the post.]

With the Society's Eisteddfod over for 1923, Comunn na Feinne turned its attention to its Pipe Band which had entered for the South Street, Ballarat competitions to be held on 20th October, 1923. Unfortunately, the Band was not able to compete as it had disbanded, due to lack of finance and of experienced players. This was just one more example of the instability which had existed in the Society's Pipe Band since WW1 when it had enlisted almost to the man. This problem, judging by the poor attendance of other Pipe Bands at Comunn na Feinne's annual Gatherings, was general among the Victorian Pipe Bands. However, the President's remarks at the annual general meeting would seem to suggest that the Pipe Band had been left very much to fend for itself. The President had alluded to this in his remarks that, "when certain work which the Society had in hand had been completed, more attention would be devoted to the musical side of the Comunn na Feinne's activities." It was the case that the Society Pipe Band seemed not to be high on Smith's concerns.

If not already stretching itself to its limits of finance and manpower, the Society initiated, on the 23rd September, 1923, yet another new series of entertainments which it called, "One Hour Concerts." The *Geelong Advertiser*, in its review the next day, said, "doubtless as they become more well known, the patronage will increase." Sadly, such concerts of this type, originally for the purpose of raising charitable funds, were now also being used to raise money in aid of the Hall debt and to keep the Society afloat*. One was held on 21st November, 1923, and was considered, by the *Advertiser*, a great success.

*[The issue of the Society's financial problems is dealt with in detail in Chapter 7]

Following close on the heels of this Concert was the Society's annual Haggis Supper on 2nd December, 1923. In line with the Society's habit of courting those in important positions, the *Advertiser* reported, "that there was a strong Parliamentary, Educational, Municipal and kindred Society representation, including the Premier of Victoria, the Hon H.W. Lawson; the Hon Minister for Education (Commonwealth), John Gordon, the Director of Education (Victoria), Frank Tate and the Mayor of Geelong, Councillor Robert Purnell." Music accompanied the evening with, of course, an endless list of Toasts. The Hibernian and St George Societies were also represented and were duly toasted.

As the final function for the year, Comunn na Feinne celebrated Hogmanay night. This was the night on which the Scot, said the *Advertiser*'s 31st December 1923 issue, "submits himself to revelry, conviviality and a true bond of friendship according to the traditions of his race," and where all disagreements throughout the year are forgiven and forgotten in the spirit of Burns' 'Brotherhood of Man.' The *Advertiser* promised that a treat was in store at the New Year's Day Gathering at Kardinia Park. The mood of the day would be set with the procession to the grounds of the popular and innovative Kilties' Brass Band leading those competing bands arriving by special train, in a march to Kardinia Grounds, arriving there at 11.30am. "Every moment, except during the luncheon hour, will be occupied until 6pm." Indeed, as he had promised earlier, James Galbraith had delivered a programme with no 'empty spaces' for the 1924 Gathering. The Games offered a crowded programme with "two hundred entries having been received for the cycling events alone." There was to be, at 3pm, a Pipe Band contest, "something not seen for a while at the Society's Gatherings." At the close, a massed band demonstration was to be given, followed by Community Singing, led by the Kilties' Brass Band, from 5.30pm.

After a tea-break the programme was to re-commence with, "a big concert in the Park by the Kilties' Brass Band, Melbourne artistes and pipe bands."

The newspaper emphasized that it was the Society's 67th Annual Gathering and, as well as drawing attention to the "antiquity" of the Society, it also focused on one of its noteworthy activities. Its early work of holding competitive school examinations had produced many current prominent citizens and educationists. The *Advertiser* also reported that another recruitment drive by the Society was underway and that, "intending members can enrol and participate in the whole of the privileges for the year for self and lady for New Year's Day, and for self at all functions, such as Burns' Night, St Andrew's Night, and several concerts during the year." It added that several new members had already signed up, and that the Society had now 300 members on its roll.

A record attendance was recorded at the Gathering, and in describing the day's activities, mention was again made, by the *Advertiser*, of the presence of the South and Port Melbourne Ladies Pipe Band which took part in the Procession from Geelong to the Games arena and, later, in the Pipe Band competitions, although as previously noted, the Pipe Band, being female, was actually barred by the newly-formed Pipe Band Association from 'officially' taking part in competitions. Reference was also made to the provision of a renewed bicycle track. Whether or not this was the result of the previous year's race mayhem and crashes is not made clear! However, the existence of a Bicycle Racing Association more than probably had something to do with the changes.

The Worlands, George Henry and Colin Frederick, were among the prize-winners at the heavy Games in 1924 with G. Worland again winning the open Caber and other heavy events. His brother Colin, also competed in the heavy events with some success, being runner up to brother George in the Caber tossing. Colin Worland won the local Putting the Stone event (reserved for local competitors), and came third in the open Putting the Stone event and took third place in Throwing the Hammer. The display cabinet must have been groaning under the collective weight of the Worland family trophies over the years! The traditional concert following the Games in the evening was held at the Kardinia grounds, and the usual entertainments made the evening pass pleasantly.

Comunn na Feinne, which had struggled to consistently maintain a Pipe Band since the outbreak of the first World War, announced on 25th February, 1924, that a new Boy's Pipe Band had been inaugurated after the New Year's Day Games. It had held its first practice, with fourteen boys receiving tuition from Piper John Kidd. It was hoped, as these learners progressed, that they would help fill the ranks of the depleted senior Band, and there was a degree of optimism about the Band's future. Comunn na Feinne's Pipe Band demonstrated its improvement when it entered the competition at the Ararat annual Boxing Day gathering on 26th December, 1924. The Band was ably supported by the presence of Comunn na Feinne's Chief, Senator Plain, its President, Charles A. Smith and its Secretary, Mr James Galbraith, along with other members. The "recently re-organized Band was successful in winning a double, the Quickstep and the Selection." The fact that this was supposed to be a 'new' band, and had won at a competition less than ten months later, suggests that there must have been many experienced players along with the 'novices'!

To build interest in the 1925 Games, the *Advertiser* announced on 24th December, 1924, that the Society, "in conjunction with the Geelong Motor Cycle Club," had included in the programme for the New Year's Day 1925 Gathering, "a solo flag race, flag race with side-car, solo bending race, side-car bending race, a flat race of five laps to the mile, a Ford 'aquaplane' event and a match race of one hundred yards." As well, many years before the current annual Puffing Billy event in the Dandenongs, Comunn na Feinne offered such a test in the form of a race between, "a pedestrian [running] and a motor cyclist." None of this was deterring the usual wheelmen and the Society announced that the programme would also contain the more orthodox bicycling races and that entries for these had been received, "not only from riders in Melbourne and the Western District but also from several in Bendigo".

On the social side of the Gathering, Mr W.H. Armour, now aged 70, was making his 68th annual visit to the Games. He was born in 1855, the year before the 'birth' of the Society itself and, counting the visits from when he was carried as an infant, he had been present at every Gathering. Mr Armour said that he had seen many alterations over the years not the least being the disappearance of so many of the "old familiar faces" but he retained, he said, "a deep and abiding interest in the doings of the Society", and intimated that he would again be in his place at the forthcoming Games.

In addition to drawing attention to Mr Armour's record for attendances, the newspaper promoted the 1925 Gathering with further news of what visitors to the Games could expect. The Gathering, it said, had always provided an opportunity for the re-union of Scots, "from all parts of Victoria" and, following on from a suggestion made after the 1924 Games, placards bearing the name of Scottish counties would be placed at different parts of the grounds. At each of these spots spectators who had originally come from one or other of these different parts of Scotland could write their name in a book supplied at each of these points around the ground, and, "In this manner those who scrutinize the books will be enabled to find their friends and perhaps renew acquaintances that were broken for years." One of the *Advertiser*'s most frequent remarks was about the warmth of feeling expressed as old friends renewed acquaintance. The Gathering, it said:

> [A]ffords a pleasant opportunity of once more greeting old friends and of making new acquaintances among the hundreds of fellow countrymen or descendants of those from the Land of Heather. ... Reunions were quite numerous yesterday, and it was with a feeling of pleasure that friends were seen to greet one another with real Scottish warmth and to talk over old times.

The *Advertiser* also announced that a Pipe Band contest, under the rules of the recently formed Pipe Band Association, would take place at its 1925 New Year's Day Gathering and that the Northcote and Preston Pipe Band as well as the Collingwood, St Kilda, Footscray, Comunn na Feinne and the Melbourne Caledonian Boys' Pipe Bands would all be competing. There was also to be some demonstrations from the hugely popular Melbourne Kilties' Brass Band throughout the day. A further innovation at the 1925 Games was a competition based on the marching of the Bands in the procession from the town to Kardinia Park. For this competition, "the C.N.F. Society's gold crest will be awarded to the band gaining the highest number of points for street marching, discipline and punctuality."

The 1925 annual New Year's Day Gathering took place at Kardinia Oval on 1st January, 1925, and the *Advertiser*'s report of the day was, to say the least, an effusive one! Comunn na Feinne was a "progressive society," the Gathering was, "one of the most successful" ever held, and the attendance "was enormous." The day was one, said the *Advertiser*, which transcended all boundaries of age or birth or nationality.

> To athletes, lovers of sport, but more particularly to Scots, all roads led to Kardinia Park yesterday, where the 68th Grand Highland Gathering of the Comunn na Feinne Society took place in delightful weather.

The *Advertiser* regarded the Pipe Band contest, probably because of the long absence of such a feature, as, "the most important event of the day." Each of the Bands, on their appearance on the oval, "was enthusiastically greeted by the spectators...", and a keen interest was taken in the different parts of the contest, the playing, the marching, the drilling, and the inspection of dress. All of the entered Bands, except Footscray, attended the Games and competed. Despite its recent victory at Ararat, a double tone, "from start to finish on one set of pipes," sank Comunn na Feinne's Pipe Band's hopes in the Selection, though it did come second to the Northcote and Preston Pipe Band in the Quickstep. While the marks for the various parts of the performances were being tallied, there was an impressive display provided by the massed bands, "under Drum-Major Feegent of the Northcote and Preston Band."

Although the Comunn na Feinne Games for 1925 had managed to attract six Pipe Bands (including Comunn na Feinne's own Band), attracting Pipe Bands to the Geelong New Year's Day Gatherings on a year by year basis continued to prove difficult. For example, at the 1926 Gathering only two Bands were present – Northcote and Preston Pipe Band and the Footscray Pipe Band, competing the Quickstep, Selection and Drill contests. The viability of the Society's own Band tended to fluctuate throughout the year from fully operational to a state of near collapse from a shortage of players or from financial problems or from neglect by Comunn na Feinne itself, and support from the new President, Charles A. Smith, seemed half-hearted, at best!

As well as the Pipe Band contests, all of the usual competitions were held with the Heavy athletic events and Highland dancing attracting keen interest. Not one but two Worlands again appeared in the prize lists for the heavy events. Colin F. Worland won the Caber event and Throwing the Hammer and came second in Putting the Stone. Yet another brother, John Henry Worland, was placed second in Tossing the Caber in the 'local' section of these competitions.

The events using motor cycles added a few twists to previous performances and also drew the attention of large numbers of onlookers. The feature, "Motor Cycle Races, under the auspices of the Geelong Motor Cycle Club was also conducted," and provided its fair share of 'thrills and spills'. The "aquaplaning" races whereby contestants, mounted on "flat wooden planks' and drawn by motor-cycles racing, "at a very fast rate of speed," provided many "hair-raising incidents" and near crashes which were "fortunately averted, although W. Pilgrim, when near the southern end of the oval, skidded and was thrown from his machine. Another competitor diverged from the track, and rode between the goal posts at a rapid rate, but he retained control of the motor cycle and his effort was given 'two flags', at least by the spectators!

Ironically, it was the more 'sedate' bicycling events which provided the injuries to contestants. In the third heat of the principal race, "the Comunn na Feinne Cycle Race of two miles", the most spectacular crash of the day occurred when one of the cyclists, in the most dramatic fashion, "fell from his machine … Fortunately his injuries were not serious".

The 1925 Gathering, on all accounts, was considered a successful one and it was attended by large numbers of spectators with both the Society's Chief, Senator W. Plain and its President, Mr Charles A. Smith, announcing themselves pleased with the turnout and declaring the Gathering equal to anything that had gone before. With these Games now over, the Society, buoyed by the return of Pipe Band contests to its programme, got on with the business of attending to its yearly activities which included organizing programmes for the number of bodies bearing the Comunn na Feinne's impress.

As noted, the Society had formed new and various clubs during its history. Along the way, for instance, it had established a Comunn na Feinne Fishing Club, a Comunn na Feinne Football Club, a Comunn na Feinne Cricket Club, among others and, now, in 1925, it established an addition to its list, a Comunn na Feinne Iron Quoits Club. The Society, in one of its many outreaches to the community, had now decided that a Club would benefit Geelong if open for players all year round. The *Age* newspaper, on 23rd January, 1925, announced the formation of the Club giving its Highland pedigree.

> As an ancient highland game, 'iron quoits' has always had a place in the programme for the Comunn na Feinne sports. That body has now decided to give further encouragement to the pastime by establishing a rink alongside its hall, and this will be at the service of the recently formed Comunn na Feinne Iron Quoits Club.

The newspaper was not quite accurate when it claimed that Quoits had "always" been a part of the events at the Society's Gatherings, but the sport had certainly been part of its New Year's Day Games for many years. Despite occasional reports in the *Advertiser* of limited spectator support, the first Club Tournament was held towards the end of January and the *Age* provided the results of the event which had ended on 30th January 1925.

The Society, as we have seen on several occasions, had never been reluctant to court political influence in furtherance of its causes, but it had never openly favoured any political candidate when it came to elections. This position was to change 1925 when it openly campaigned on behalf of its Chief, William Plain. In pronouncing its support for Senator Plain, the Society came as close as it ever got to promoting a partisan political position, albeit in a non-party way! Plain was seen as "our Senator", in the sense that he represented not a party but the general public. It saw itself as standing in the tradition of historic liberalism and thus committed to the practical realisation of what this 'philosophy' considered was the 'good' society. It was a purpose most frequently identified in the words, and in the humanism, of Scotland's national poet, Robert Burns. Senator Plain was presented as the personification of the 'spirit' of the Society, standing for the 'Brotherhood of Man'; not a 'party' man but an 'everyman'. He possessed "steadfast ideals and fixity of purpose" and his "unselfish deliberations" of the matters which came before him would provide, "a steadying and leavening" influence within the Senate and, through its work, within society in general.

Comunn na Feinne's annual concert was held 21st September, 1925, and played to a large audience which enthusiastically enjoyed the night. A long programme of vocals, humorous turns and instrumentals, as well as dancing, followed the concert proper. The remainder of the year followed a normal course of meetings as well as carrying out its social programme of events. Unfortunately, the Haggis Supper, due to be held on St Andrew's Day 30th November, 1925, was postponed in respect to the memory of Queen Alexandra who had died that month. The planning meetings for the next Highland Gathering were held in December as usual and the programme was confirmed for New Year's Day.

The *Advertiser*, under the heading "Your Ain Folk", led off its report on the 1926 annual Comunn na Feinne Gathering remarking that it had become such an institution that without its New Year's Day "skirl o' the pipes," Geelong, "would lack a distinguishing feature …" The traditional march from town to the Society's grounds at Kardinia Park was enlivened by the playing of the Northcote and Preston Pipe Band and the Footscray Pipe Band. This preamble to the actual reporting of the Games included the *Advertiser*'s praise, again, for the innovation of erecting placards at different spots around the grounds to indicate a meeting place for Scots, or their descendants, from one or other of the named areas. In an extension of this idea, there was to be a special invitation, "extended to Gaelic-speaking people from Inverness and other parts, and, if possible, a Gaelic scholar will be in attendance to converse with visitors." Many of those attending the Games could well have been third generation Australia-born descendants of Scottish settlers returning to an identification with the ancestral homeland, as well, of course, as post WW1 immigrants.

Any hope that the inclusion of Pipe Band contests at the Society's annual Games would give "new life" to it, and that there would be a revival in its circumstances, proved futile. The Society never seemed to concern itself with, or to examine why its Pipe Band lacked stability. Only two Pipe Bands had entered to compete for Comunn na Feinne's 1926 New Year's Day Highland Gathering, and the Society had to deliberate on whether to go ahead with a contest of sorts involving quickstep, selection and drill. As the V.P.B.A. rules stipulated that at least three Bands had to be entered for a contest to take place, it was decided to forego the competition. The two Pipe Bands which had entered did, however, perform their competition programme for the benefit of the spectators, and the judges, Lieutenant F. Bernard and Ralf Fraser, awarded first place to the Northcote and Preston Pipe Band with a total of 606 points over the Footscray Band's total of 588 points – all unofficial, of course.

There was, however, no uncertainty regarding the appearance of the Games' other categories which drew sufficient entries for each of its contests. Bicycle races and the Heavy Games, along with Athletics, Highland Dancing, Solo Piping and Quoits, filled up the day's programme of events and these were enjoyed by the crowd of 2,000. Colin Worland, following the Worland family tradition, came first in the Caber and in the Heavy Hammer events, and came third in Putting the Stone. A surprise contestant in the Heavy Events was Tom Fitzmaurice, captain of the Geelong Football Club. He demonstrated that his entry was a serious one by winning the Putting the Stone event and coming second in Throwing the Light Hammer, with Colin Worland relegated to third place. The positions were reversed, however, in the Throwing the Heavy Hammer event.

The Society, which had always been unafraid to introduce new elements into its presentations, including that of the early use of floodlighting, continued its innovations with special lighting being employed at Kardinia Park for its evening open-air Concert. It announced (and not for the first time), both for publicity and also to reassure spectators and performers alike, that it was safe and that, "a special lighting scheme over the stage has been inspected by a sub-committee and found to be such that there will be no defects, either from the point of view of the performers or visitors." It is to be hoped that the "sub-committee" included at least some who had a knowledge of electricity! As well as the special effects, there was to be a full line up of much admired singers and humourists from Melbourne. In addition to Pipe Band music, the Geelong City Brass Band, if available, would also be taking part.

If the Society had any worries about the success of the now, "customary open-air concert," these would quickly have disappeared when they saw the size of the audience which was greater than that of recent years. The crowd was an appreciative one and the presence of local winners of Highland dance and solo Piping competitions at the Highland Games held earlier in the day, proved a great hit with the audience. Appreciation was also shown of the strong group of singers and other entertainers from Melbourne. The dancers and singers were accommodated on a platform which had been erected in front of a section of the grandstand, both of which were illuminated by coloured electric lights The Bands performed their playing and marching around the grounds under other flood lighting, and proved a colourful spectacle.

Comunn na Feinne activities in January continued with the holding of a Haggis Supper, held over from the previous November. When the postponed Haggis Supper was announced as taking place on Burns' birth date, the enthusiasm was palpable and the attendance filled the Society's Hall. The *Advertiser*'s headline the next day, "Large Gathering of Scots," introduced its report of the event and its headline was no exaggeration. As might have been expected, in attendance was the usual bevy of local, state and federal politicians, as well as office-bearers from other Scottish organizations.

This was another opportunity for the Society to educate its audience, if that was still necessary, into what it was that energized it to act as 'leaven' in the community. The regular activities took place with toasts and entertainments and with tributes to Burns the poet and also to the humanism which spilled out from his verses. Hearing Burns' lines, said Senator Crawford, one of the political guests, "had been in the nature of a liberal education" and a call to every hearer to put into action in his or her life and work what was being taught. The Society's Chief, Senator William Plain, was able to say with feeling, given his own experiences, that reverses were common and battle should be expected in a Scotsman's life as, "he would always express his thoughts where necessary." But the call to do one's best for others was not addressed to Scotsmen only, Plain continued, for even among those gathered at this celebration there were representatives from England, Ireland and Wales all sitting under the poet's 'teaching'. Burns' call was to everyman.

However, the Society's responsibilities in putting Burns' words (and its own charter) into practice in the community, was steadily increasing its financial burden. Much more of its energies and time were being taken up with fund-raising activities, such as the "Scottish Fair", conducted by the Society over two days, 23rd and 24th September, 1926.

Senator William Plain was the last Chief of CNF.

For the life of Comunn na Feinne, since its beginning in 1856, it had no other Scottish Society in Geelong to challenge its position. A St Andrew's Society and a Scottish Lodge had both existed for many years but the office-bearers of these organizations basically were the same as those of the Society, as were the memberships, and thus there was no rivalry between them. Over time, the Irish, the English and the Welsh Settlers each formed their own national associations but these organizations, much due to Comunn na Feinne's policy of inclusiveness and its desire to maintain harmony within the community, were never the source of antagonism between the respective memberships. However, on 3rd September, 1926, the Geelong Caledonian Society was formed and this was to test this spirit of brotherhood. Initially it seemed that good relations would exist. For example, among those who were present for the occasion were Charles A. Smith, president of Comunn na Feinne, who wished the new organization all success. By the 27th September, 1926, it was announced that the new Caledonian Society already had a membership of 180 and that it was thriving. At a further meeting of this Society on 7th October, 1926, when an election for office-bearers took place, it was announced that its two honorary pipers were John Kidd and Donald McDonald, both of whom also happened to be Comunn na Feinne's pipers! It would seem, therefore, that Comunn na Feinne wanted to establish a friendly relationship with this new organization. Achieving, and sustaining this relationship, as we will see, proved to be elusive.

Comunn na Feinne's 70th annual general meeting was held on 28th October, 1926. "The revenue during the year was £2,042 and, notwithstanding enforced alterations to the Hall to comply with the Board of Health regulations, the year finished with a balance above its liabilities." The ever-popular Highland Ball was also (yet again!) to be revived. Reference was made by [the president] to the 70th Annual Highland Gathering to be held on New Year's Day 1927, and the special attractions organised for this included Brass and Pipe Band contests, despite the previous difficulties experienced with both!

In an attempt to make the Society more family oriented and better known to children and their parents, it was decided that a children's members' roll should be started and that special events, once a quarter, would be staged for them. The first of these nights was on 9th November, 1926, "when Mary Gumleaf of 3LO fame would give a talk to members' children and their friends." This entailed considerable extra work for the secretary, James Galbraith, who was accorded a vote of thanks by the Society. In reply, Galbraith declared that his motivation was the fact that Comunn na Feinne was dedicated to a wider purpose than mere entertainment; the Society, "was doing a noble work, and should be encouraged." At this same meeting, it was also reported that 18 new members were received into the Society.

Comunn na Feinne's St Andrew's Night concert was held at the Society's Hall on the 30th November, 1926, and a huge and enthusiastic crowd enjoyed the evening. The death of Mrs Galbraith (wife of the Society's secretary), on 26th November, 1926, a lady who had been held in high regard for her church and charitable work, had cast a pall over the evening and the entertainment was moderated accordingly, but the night went well. "Reverently with bowed heads, the audience stood while the Lament was played by Pipe Major Kenneth McAulay. It was a touching tribute to Mrs Galbraith's memory."

The Society again met on 6th December, 1926, to fine tune the programme for the 1927 Gathering. Comunn na Feinne in announcing the next New Year's Day Games, its 70th anniversary, referred to the appearance of veterans of the first games. It was announced that Alexander McDonald, now of Melbourne, who was approaching his century had determined to be in attendance. He looked forward to renewing acquaintance with the 'youngster' Donald McPherson, now only 96 years of age! Also in attendance would be William H. Armour who still lived in Geelong and who had been at the first Gathering in 1857 as, 'a babe in arms'.

A fitting tribute was paid to Comunn na Feinne on its 70th annual New Year's Day Gathering by the official magazine of the Victorian Scottish Union, *The Scot at Hame an' Abroad*. The Society, it said, was now regarded as, "one of the institutions of the State." Geelong, it continued, had progressed much recently and Comunn na Feinne has matched this progress. It could even be said that the Society, in fact, had progressed further and had pulled Geelong with it." Excessive praise, perhaps, but the sinews of Comunn na Feinne did run through the whole of the community, touching and influencing, through the work carried out by its committees and individual members, the major institutions of the town. Its early pioneering work in the area of education, the backbone it provided to various volunteer bodies, the support it provided in hospital and orphanage work, its contribution to the arts, its influence and financial support for working boys' night school tuition and its contribution to the founding and running of the Try Boys' organization, all provide examples of the extent of Comunn na Feinne's work and influence. The presence, too, of many of its members serving in local councils, in a variety of positions, was an extension, too, of its goal of every member 'being useful' and acting as a leaven in the community.

The Games in January 1927, the magazine continued, were to be, "bigger and brighter than ever." The call, to local readers, and to those throughout the whole of the State, was, "to be at Geelong on New Year's Day and see this Comunn na Feinne celebrate its seventieth birthday with the biggest gathering ever." The *Advertiser* provided a complimentary report on the New Year's Day activities; its report bore the headline that the Gathering on 1st January, 1927 was, "the 70th Annual Comunn na Feinne Gathering."

> Several old Highlanders came to Geelong for the New Year's Day celebrations of Comunn na Feinne on the Kardinia Park Oval. Scotsmen and their families showed their loyalty to the cause by attending in large numbers … and about 3,000 attended. The programme was warranted to delight the heart of any true Scot, and it was worthy of the oldest Scottish Society in the Commonwealth.

There was music, of course, and those attending were treated to a feast of it, and there also was a "lavish" display of tartan. The *Advertiser* pointed out that many of those attending the 1927 event, were "veterans" whose attendance showed their continuing belief in the 'cause'. And 'cause' it was. These veterans, and many others besides, were showing support not just for an entertainment but were, as well, affirming that they still believed in, and supported, the aims, philosophy and spirit of Comunn na Feinne. John Cameron, for example, dated his first attendance at the Games back to 1862. He had joined the Society in 1882 and had been a director and had officiated at the heavy games for over forty-five years.

Other loyal supporters such as John McGillivray had partly been instrumental in forming Scottish societies elsewhere and he had been Chief of the Camperdown Caledonian Society and also President of the Colac Caledonian Society, formed in March 1906, of which he was a foundation member. Many who were involved with other Caledonian Societies, like John McGillvray, had been inspired to be part of the founding of these groups by the example of Comunn na Feinne, and perhaps came to the Geelong Gatherings not only as to the shrine of Scottish Games in Victoria, but because of what the Society stood for. Other examples of the presence of many past performers and long-time spectators was evident in the person of Alexander McDonald, of the Yarraville Pipe Band. He had been attending the Geelong Gathering for forty years and was accompanied by eight other band members. He was born at Inverness and met up with Norman McDonald, the recently arrived champion piper from Skye, who had immediately become a member of Comunn na Feinne. Another local resident in attendance, John McPherson, had danced at the Games more than thirty years ago when they were still being held at the South Geelong grounds. Yet another veteran of the dancing was Angus Lawson, who once held the championship for the Irish Jig and Sailors' Hornpipe in Australia. He had attended the Games for thirty years and held to the spirit of the Society by still dancing for charitable causes.

A member of almost thirty years was Captain James B. Leitch who, over a long period, had served on the committee of Comunn na Feinne and also had been President of the Victorian Scottish Union. And, the count went on, "there were dozens of others who had twenty years' attendance, and more, to their credit, and are yearly qualifying to go higher up the veteran ladder." Attempts to gather and publicise veterans continued at the 1928 and 1929 Gatherings; whether the strategy inspired a younger generation to attend or to compete at the Games, or to become socially active is, however, a moot point.

Unhappily, three of the assembled veterans at the 1927 Gathering would not live to see another New Year's Day. During 1927 Alexander McDonald, Alexander Aikman and Archibald McDonald, late of the Education Department, Melbourne, all died; their deaths being reported in the *Advertiser* on 9th October, 1927. Their ages "aggregated 252 years, with an average of 84 years each" and each's birth year pre-dated the founding of Geelong and even the settlement of Melbourne! Truly, "The flooers o' the forest are a' weid awa'," would be an appropriate description to give to the passing away of these links to a past era.

> Their association with Comunn na Feinne dated back to its first annual gathering over 70 years before. Archibald McDonald was the only one of the three to attend the first gathering, while Alexander Aikman was a successful competitor in the Highland Dancing Competitions held at a later date. Though he lived in Colac, Alexander McDonald had closely allied himself with the Society since 1872. All three were fine members and always generous in their association with Comunn na Feinne.

The deaths of this earlier generation continued in 1928 with the passing of Alexander McDonald of Warrion, Colac (who left £100 to the Society), Mrs Phillip Russell (wife of the long-serving Chief, Mr Phillip Russell) and Mr James Wighton, the Geelong solicitor and veteran charity worker with Comunn na Feinne. Wighton, a

Vice-President of the Society, had been active with many others in Comunn na Feinne in forming and supporting a Night School to teach vocational skills to young people who had missed out on these earlier in life. He was also associated, from its beginning, with the Try Boys' Association in Geelong, along with another Vice-President and long-time member of Comunn na Feinne, Mr Charles Shannon, as well as others both from within and without Comunn na Feinne ranks. All of the foregoing tells its own story of a Society which had been around for a long time and which, through age and death, was losing contact with its past and, maybe, to some extent, in the community's eyes, its relevancy.

The Society had also invited 360 youths who were part of the Young Australia League to attend this 70th anniversary Gathering. This organization had been formed by a businessman, J.J. Simons, in Western Australia in 1905. It promoted service, sport, music, travel and self-reliance. The organization also promoted youth migration and, during the 1920's, it sponsored 192 young men from the UK to Western Australia. A group of these, visiting Geelong, was welcomed by the Mayor, Cr J. Solomon, and Senator William Plain, who congratulated them on their appearance and behaviour, "and also reminded the boys of their good fortune in being able to see for themselves what was being done in other parts of the country.

The *Advertiser*, in reporting the various contests which took place at the 1927 Gathering, was generous with its praise for the cycling events and the fact that twelve Victorian Cycling clubs took part. For the second year, Tom Fitzmaurice, captain of Geelong football team, participated in the Heavy Games with some success. He won the Stone Putting event although tossing the Caber and throwing the Heavy Hammer events he found beyond his athletic skills this time, and he was unplaced in these. Colin Worland, however, added more lustre to the family record coming second in Tossing the Caber and third in Throwing the Hammer.

The Society's usual Concert, in the evening following the Games, presented a fine cast of performers in the musical and dancing numbers and, as in previous years, it enjoyed great success with many encores being called from the artistes.

An indication of the pressures on Comunn na Feinne officers and members was the task, following directly after the annual Gathering, of immediately beginning preparations for their Eisteddfod in March, 1927, which the *Advertiser* announced in its 7th January issue.

> Now that the 70th annual Gathering of Comunn na Feinne has been successfully negotiated, the directors have turned their attention to the preliminary arrangements for the 15th Annual Musical and Elocutionary Competitions [which have] of late years grown to such importance the directors have taken into consideration the extension of the various events to be competed for and have from year to year included extra items in the schedule.

The last of the functions for the year associated with Comunn na Feinne's Eisteddfod was the Pleasant Sunday Afternoon function on 1st October, 1927. These social events, founded by James Galbraith, were occasions for raising money in support of Comunn na Feinne's extensive work with charities in Geelong. A large attendance gathered at the Palais Royal to be entertained by many of those who had competed at the Society's 1927 Eisteddfod. James Galbraith, the Society's secretary, supervised the occasion.

> He said the Pleasant Sunday Afternoons had been held since April and the Society would hold them again next year. He expressed the thanks of Comunn na Feinne to all the artists who made [the] success of [these] functions possible … the Society had been able to raise approximately £200 and the money had been divided up among local charities and to alleviate cases of necessity.

The Society's St Andrew's Day concert, on 30th November, 1927, marked the last of its social events for the year and, "there was a large and distinguished gathering of members, friends and visitors, to enjoy the excellent programme." On Christmas Eve, the Society officially welcomed, Piper Norman McDonald from Skye, who had, "arrived earlier in the year" and, as noted above, immediately had joined Comunn na Feinne.

Comunn na Feinne's New Year's Day Gathering for 1928 was met with good weather and a bright *Advertiser* report, noting a "large attendance" albeit slightly less than that of the previous year. This it blamed on the large number of "counter-attractions" which were taking people away from the annual Geelong Gathering that year. The *Advertiser* wrote:

> New Year's Day at Geelong always seems to be Comunn na Feinne Day, and the progressive bayside city would hardly start the New Year right without its famous Highland Gathering. This year the Society celebrated its 71st function of the kind, and attracted a large and enthusiastic attendance, though perhaps in figures the attendance did not outstrip that of previous years; but that is scarcely to be wondered at, considering the great number of counter attractions.

The usual procession to the grounds at Kardinia Park took place, with the *Advertiser* reporting that spectator interest was returning to the Heavy events.

> Events of this character produced competition of a very spirited nature, and there were some splendid feats of skill and strength. Amongst the competitors were several Scots well up in years, who have earned a wide reputation in this branch of athletic [sports].

The post-games evening Concert in 1928 was held at the Society's Hall and the *Advertiser* reported that the building was filled to bursting. Some top artistes from Melbourne, as well as local dancers and singers, made the evening a stand-out success. The *Advertiser* could find nothing but praise for the evening. "A splendid night's entertainment concluded with a feelingly rendered 'Auld Lang Syne' by everybody - the end of a full day."

As in previous years, the Society also held its Pleasant Sunday Afternoons for the duration of the Eisteddfod. First conceived of by James Galbraith, these events, as already noted, had proved popular and the funds raised were devoted to the various charities which Comunn na Feinne supported. The Society was able to present some important speakers at these functions and 1928 was no exception. For example, at the last of these Pleasant Sunday afternoons, held on 18th June, 1928, the guest speaker was, said the *Advertiser*, "one of Melbourne's leading young barristers", Mr Robert G. Menzies." This was, of course, the future Prime Minister of Australia!

Sandwiched in between all of this activity, a function, on 2nd June, 1928, was held at the premises of the Victorian Pipe Band Association (V.P.B.A.), Melbourne, to honour the service of James Galbraith, "The pivot of every Comunn na Feinne function … [and to] whose organizing ability the success of yet another Gathering must be mainly attributed …". Galbraith was also lauded for his work with other associations. He was the secretary of the Victorian Pipe Band Association (V.P.B.A.) and, along with Senator Plain (who was its President), had much to do with its formation. Senator William Plain, in his presentation speech, said Galbraith, whose energetic and organizing efforts on behalf of the formation of the V.P.B.A., including his term as secretary of it, was well known to some, but this current honour would be to all, "a constant reminder of the fact that the Association realized and appreciated his efforts."

Comunn na Feinne ended its year of socials with a well-attended Hogmanay Night on 31st December, 1928, which featured the Comunn na Feinne Pipe Band (reformed again!), playing inside the Hall as well as marching through the streets. In addition to Highland dancing and singing, there was old time dancing for the patrons.

At the time of the 1929 Games, the *Advertiser* commented that the older members of the Society, "felt that the young Scots, men and women, should come to the fore and show a greater interest in the movement, reflecting perhaps the strategy of courting veterans in recent years." A veteran of the nineteenth century Games was John McPherson of Belmont who had been attending Highland Games at Geelong, and at other centres, for 60 years and had first entered the Highland Dancing events in 1878. He regretted that the dancing was now open only to children and he reminisced about the time when only men were allowed to compete. But the lure of the 'good old days' does not always appeal to the young! Like many of the older members, veteran competitors and spectators from past days, McPherson expressed his disappointment at the poor attendance at the Games as compared to those of past years, and he appealed to the old spirit which had inhabited the movement and the people in earlier days.

The Society thus continued with this 'passing of time' theme for its 1929 Gathering. There was an effort, again, to promote the long history of Comunn na Feinne and, following the practice of recent years, many veterans of the Games were introduced to the spectators with the hope of encouraging the next generation of potential members and contestants. However, this may have tended to present the annual New Year's Gatherings as associated with the past and thus not relevant to the rising generation.

> Although the Comunn na Feinne Pipe Band played its way to the grounds on New Year's Day, the usual general procession from Geelong to the arena was absent. The attendance numbered about 500. Members of the Society, however, were present in large numbers, and included in the gathering were several of the old Scots who have been regular participants at the annual C.N.F. meetings. Older members of the Society expressed disappointment at the small attendance, and while realising that many had journeyed to the holiday resorts and to other places on pleasure bent, they said it was a pity the young Scots people did not show a greater interest in their national gathering.

The *Advertiser* provided its usual coverage of events and duly described names and results and the occasional "exciting finish" to many of the Bicycling races. It added that, "There was a good entry for tossing the Caber, in which spectators showed special interest." There was no animus towards the Games or towards the Society itself in the newspaper report. Perhaps, if anything, its coverage was tinged with sympathy. The cooler evening drew the people out, and the "Scottish concert held at Kardinia park was attended by a large gathering" and was, "of a high standard."

The low turn-out at the 1929 Gathering was not part of a longer trend of diminishing audiences for the Games. In fact, the years leading up to 1929 had witnessed some very large gates. Unfortunately, those within the Society who may have had the desire to see the end of these labour intensive and, at times, expensive Gatherings, were to seize on the historically low number to justify their aim.

Comunn na Feinne, which had, in 1928, instituted regular social evenings just for children, held another 'Children's Night' on the 23rd January, 1929, at the Society's Hall, and the *Advertiser*, the following day, pronounced it a great success. Miss Hazel

Maude, "the little Kookaburra" of 3LO, entertained the 150 children in attendance with songs, dances and stories until 9pm. This move to woo the parents through the children may itself have been an indication of the waning interest in the Society by the general public, but there was no 'spike' in membership as a result of these children's socials.

Since the end of WW1, Comunn na Feinne's Highland Gatherings, as well as its social calendar throughout the year, gave every indication of the Society being alive and well. Certain collapses at the New Year's Day competitions involving Brass and Pipe Bands, cannot be laid at the feet of the Society. Apart from the foregoing Band Competitions, the usual Game events were flourishing. It is true that the Society's Pipe Band was finding it difficult to maintain a consistent standard, although it was still able, on occasions, to perform well at the South Street, Ballarat and other Pipe Band Competitions. However, Pipe Bands in general, throughout the state, were also experiencing problems of re-forming, and problems of stability, since the end of WW1. Part of the problems affecting Comunn na Feinne's Pipe Band can be attributed to the lack of attention being given to it by the Society's hierarchy. It was, perhaps, unfortunate, too, that the Society in this last phase of its life had a President, while able, did not seem to understand, or perhaps even believe in, the 'vision' of Comunn na Feinne.

The exponential growth in participation in its annual Eisteddfod, and the added costs, financial and in manpower, which accompanied this, and the persistent Hall debt, all commanded almost the total attention of the Society's hierarchy. Comunn na Feinne itself was facing seemingly insuperable problems. The foregoing issues eventually led to two momentous announcements being made by the President. The first was to the Directors on 31st January, 1929, and the second was delivered at the end of the same year.

Both decisions seem to have been taken without much, if any, discussion or general member involvement. The first decision was that Comunn na Feinne would divest itself of the responsibility for organizing its annual Eisteddfod and all costs associated therewith. At a general monthly meeting of Comunn na Feinne 30th January 1929, "a resolution was passed that it be a recommendation to the incoming board of directors to discontinue conducting the Music, Dance and Elocutionary Competitions (the Eisteddfod), as it was felt that the Society could no longer accept the financial responsibility with respect to these Competitions. The meeting of the Board of Directors, following at the close of the general meeting, decided to adopt this resolution. This meant that Comunn na Feinne ceased immediately from conducting these Competitions, and this included the 1930 Eisteddfod. Presumably this was not just a bolt from the blue, for the meeting also heard that, "A committee of prominent townsmen quite apart from Comunn na Feinne, with James Galbraith as secretary, has been formed to conduct the Competitions." Senator Plain also joined this new committee. Galbraith had immediately resigned as secretary of Comunn na Feinne, and the Board of Directors, "passed a resolution placing on record their appreciation of his long service to the Society." James R. McDonald was appointed interim secretary.

Matters moved fairly quickly following this decision regarding the Eisteddfodau. At a Comunn na Feinne social evening, catered by the Ladies' Committee, held on 15th March, 1929, it was announced that the Comunn na Feinne Competitions Committee, "had leased the Hall for the forthcoming competitions" to the new body which had taken them over. The Eisteddfodau were to continue, but now the Society was to make a profit from them!

The Board of Directors of Comunn na Feinne met on 7th May, 1929, when the financial situation of the Society was discussed, "and it was reported that in this respect it was in a good position." The Society's Hall was "letting well" with some bookings being for 12 months. There was also discussion relating to the holding of a Highland Ball. Letting the Hall for profit at every opportunity carried with it, as the Society embarrassingly discovered, some hidden hazards. The general meeting of the Society, for example, scheduled for 10th September, 1929, had to be altered to the 11th September, 1929, when an embarrassed executive realized that, in its haste to commercially let its Hall at every opportunity, it had actually let it for the same date as its meeting! Even the Society's own Pipe Band, which had not been treated well under Smith's administration, suffered 'eviction' from its space in the Hall and had to find premises to rent elsewhere!

The general meeting on 11th September, 1929, was dominated by business relating to Hall bookings, and it was announced that four nights of the week had been permanently booked, and that income from the letting of the Hall was now more than double that of the previous year. It was, perhaps, no surprise that the enthusiasm of the directors and other officials of the Society for the hiring of the Hall was at a high level. The annual balance sheet showed that the Society's financial position, "was much improved" and this "impressed the members present." This response to the annual report would have been pleasing to Smith because the inclination, over the past year, of the President, and some of his supporters on the executive, had been to concentrate efforts on maximizing income; thus anything, any activity, which did not deliver a profit was to be subject to cancellation. In pursuit of profit, monthly social evenings were to continue, and a Highland Ball was mooted for later in the year.

On the last day of 1929, Smith dropped his second bombshell that there would be no New Year's Day Highland Gathering for 1930. The timing of this latter announcement may suggest that the argument for scrapping the Gathering had only just been won; if, indeed, Smith bothered about such a debate. The *Advertiser*, on 2nd January, 1930, noted Smith's decision, "The Highland Gathering, the Comunn na Feinne's annual gathering, had been dispensed with for the coming year." No explanation was publicly given and, in fact, the news caught many intending competitors, and the public generally, not to say also many members, completely unawares. Only ostensibly for that year, the cancellation of the Games was, in fact, to be a permanent one.

An article in the *Geelong Advertiser* on 13th April, 1929, had referred to the removal, in that same year, of the old Comunn na Feinne grandstand* at the South Geelong grounds. This, now, must have seemed somewhat symbolic, foreshadowing for some, the collapse, too, of the New Year's Day traditional Gathering and, perhaps, presaging the approaching end of the Society itself.

Comunn na Feinne's attempts to stir up interest in the New Year's Games by featuring 'veteran' members as well as 'veteran' ex-competitors with their references to the 'old days', failed to bring any significant increase in membership figures. The presence of the 'veterans', with their memories of the 'golden age' of the Society's annual Highland Gatherings, may have given a picture of a sense of the curtain coming down on a long running play that had reached the end of its run – and its relevance. Arthritic actors, moth-eaten costumes and scenery and deflated pipe bags – all bespoke closure of a once popular and long running entertainment.

In contrast, the social events throughout the year such as concerts, haggis suppers, Burns' nights, and the like, generally were crowded out and usually made a profit. This obviously had an influence upon the Comunn na Feinne executive's decision to not proceed with a Highland Gathering in January, 1930 and to concentrate its energies elsewhere; especially on profit-making activities! The January Gathering, with its regular failure to generate large, if any, profits, had probably determined its likely fate.

The 'worst of times' obviously had not ended with the conclusion of the war in 1918. The removal by death of the Society's president, Dr John Small and by ill-health of the chief, Mr Phillip Russell, and the resignation of its treasurer, Mr George R. King, and of the secretary, James Galbraith, over the Eisteddfod issue, left Comunn na Feinne without the quartet which had raised it to its highest point of popularity and solvency. The more grievous loss was, seemingly, that of the original 'vision splendid'.

The end of Comunn na Feinne was to be a laboured and, at times, a painful exercise, stretching over the next decade. This came about, as we will see, rather ingloriously and, "without a shout."

Chapter 7

The Death of a Vision 1930-1946.

A Drama in Three Acts

Act 1 "Change and Decay' - The Beginning of the End 1930-1933

The announcement, in the *Geelong Advertiser*, on 31st December 1929, that there would not be a New Year's Day Highland Gathering for 1930, was received with great disappointment, and not a little shock. It was certainly true that there had been a loss of £64 on the 1929 Gathering and attendance had been an all-time low. The Press offered, as explanations, competition from horse-races and international cricket matches at Melbourne, rival sporting events in the Geelong locality an alleged decline in interest in Highland sports, and exceptionally hot weather and the consequent lure of the seaside, as reasons for this situation. The impact of the news was exceptionally severe especially as it was not made public until the very last moment. Nor was it only the local paper which was caught by surprise at Comunn na Feinne's decision. It was, strangely, a Melbourne paper which expressed this disappointment more strongly and which tried to offer an explanation. The Society, wrote the *Australasian*, on 4th January, 1930, had, "decided to abandon the New Year gathering because since motoring to the coast became popular, interest in the sports has declined."

The President's explanation for the cancellation of the 1930 Gathering seems rather weak. It was true that the number attending the 1929 Games was an historically low figure but this was not just the latest sign of a downward trend in attendance numbers. At the 1928 Gathering the *Advertiser* had reported that "a large and enthusiastic" crowd of spectators had gathered to enjoy the Games. Over the years, in fact, there had been occasional fluctuations in the numbers attending from one year to the next, but the numbers evened themselves out when taking a longer period for analysis. It may be that a better explanation for this decision could lie in the possible attitude of the President, and some of his supporters, whose desire it was to concentrate on activities which required minimal manpower and which were low cost and which raised maximum profit. None of these criteria is to be found in the Society's Charter as a reason for its existence!

In the broader context, the terrible flu epidemic and the world economic downturn, both of which followed the ending of the Great War, severely impacted ordinary working people. The slow recovery of society in general was further challenged by the immediate post-war depression, and then the further, worldwide, 'great depression' following the 1928 'Wall Street Crash'. This meant, in general, that unemployment was again rife and spending money scarce for large numbers in the community. Later still the outbreak of the second world war in 1939 provided further disruption to the day-to-day lives of the people. These foregoing factors could be said to have had the most impact, and, conveniently, be pointed to as the hurdles which a great many institutions, including Comunn na Feinne, were unable, over the long-term, to clear. However, it is rare that history offers such neat 'cause and effect' explanations for significant occurrences and, in the case of the demise of Comunn na Feinne, other factors, too, including the attitude of some of the Society's executive, have to be considered. It could, realistically, equally be argued that it was the President and his executive who, at the time, were making the decisions about the Society's directions; decisions which contributed to its ultimate demise and which may not have had any role for the ordinary members.

The following sections, therefore, do not, by themselves, offer a single, clear and definitive explanation for Comunn na Feinne's closure. Given its quite valuable assets, Comunn na Feinne was not irrevocably heading for economic disaster as a result of the great depression nor from the outbreak of the second world war. Lacking the original minute books and original correspondence and 'official' financial records, has meant that certain deductions have had to be made from what evidence, mostly newspaper accounts, has been available to the authors. Whilst this is examined under several discrete headings, there is no doubt that many of the factors explored below were both interconnected and interlocking.

1. Financial

Comunn na Feinne was a 'not for profit' organization. It was, initially, primarily funded from such sources as the ticket revenue from its annual New Year's Day Highland Gatherings, by membership fees, by the generosity of members of its committee and by donations from supporters. While the Society aimed at providing entertainment for members, and others, who would gather at its sports ground and at other venues, more importantly it initially attached greater importance to its charitable and its community work and sought to promote this.

There were various points during its history when Comunn na Feinne faced serious financial problems and, as a consequence, had to curtail some of its activities, reduce its subscription fees and lower the cost of public entrance tickets to its annual Highland Games. As early as 1867 the financial and physical drain of the Duke of Edinburgh's visit to Victoria (and to Geelong in particular), resulted in Comunn na Feinne not staging the 1868 Highland Games, but, instead, handing them over to the Geelong Volunteer Fire Brigade. This was the case, too, when a decision late in 1881 had been made to cancel the January 1882 Gathering out of respect for Robert de Bruce Johnstone, the President of the Society, who had died suddenly in November 1881. However, the decision also could relate to the financial straits of the Society.*

[*The Society's financial records, like its other official papers, have not survived. Given the absence of such records, the financial story has been pieced together from other sources such as newspaper accounts of general meetings as well as from personal notes maintained by a long-time member of Comunn na Feinne. Where it has been possible, these financial details are included in tabular form along with the various Appendices referred to throughout this book.]

The lowering of the membership fees in order to attract back ex-members, as well as to recruit new ones, was part of an arrangement to allow the 1883 Games to go ahead. The *Advertiser* on 7th October, 1882, reported that this involved the dropping of the 5/- nomination fee leaving only a 5/- per annum membership fee which also got the card holder into the grounds.

We have also noted how the Competitive Education Examinations, which Comunn na Feinne conducted from 1858, had become an economic albatross around its neck. In 1862, scurrilous, and anonymous, accusations of cheating on the part of one of the competing schools led Comunn na Feinne to institute a system which rendered cheating well-nigh impossible.* The elaborate means taken to ensure a fool-proof system came, however, at a great financial cost to the Society. The crippling costs involved in providing a secure system, in addition to issuing expensive medals, led Comunn na Feinne to abandon these examinations for a less expensive system based upon teachers' assessments of their classes. While it continued its involvement with the schools, Comunn na Feinne replaced expensive inscribed medals with book prizes and external examiners with the advice of classroom teachers, in order to rein in costs.
*[This accusation of cheating, and its vigorous refutation, is elaborated in Appendix 14 (a)]

In the early years, the Society sought as its Chiefs those who were prominent in the State. Thus, for several years, the succeeding Governors of Victoria served as Chiefs to Comunn na Feinne. Such requests were always accepted, along with the generous donation the new Chief bestowed on the Society. Later, prominent politicians, philanthropists and wealthy squatters filled the role as Chief, or as patrons of the Society and, again, most were generous financial supporters as were, to some extent, office-bearers, members and general supporters of the Society. This financial backing helped the Society not only in its promotion of the annual Highland Games but, more importantly, in their ever-growing list of charitable causes. Two men, especially, were to be financial mainstays of the Society and its activities. These were John Bell of Bell Park and Phillip Russell of Mawallock. Bell was the President from 1862-67, and Chief 1873 to 1876. Phillip Russell was Chief from 1896-1923. Both men were generous financial providers towards the Society and its activities and, especially in the case of Bell, an eager 'hands on' President, and later, Chief. Whether it was through direct donations of large sums of money or through the provision of material aid in the form of cups and medals for prizes, or by kitting out the Society's pipe band or the Voluntary military units, or through support for the many social and charitable causes taken up by the Society, the contributions of these donors to the life of the Society, and their support of its aims, were genuine and generous.

It was, perhaps, because Comunn na Feinne was an organization run by volunteers and one which was committed to promoting charitable and selfless behaviour towards the community in general, and to needy cases in particular, that it did not seek to accumulate wealth for its own sake. Even its eventual acquiring of a 'home' for itself should be seen in terms of this providing the Society with greater means of fulfilling its charter, rather than in it accumulating assets. While it engaged in providing many events during the year, apart from its centre-piece Highland Gathering on each New Year's Day, profits, if any, were ear-marked for one good cause or another. Comunn na Feinne's balance sheets presented at each annual meeting of the Society generally demonstrated how close to the edge it sailed in terms of being financially solvent. On several occasions when its balance sheet found it 'in the red' its own office-bearers and members, as we have seen, stepped up and cleared the deficit.

Part of the Society's financial problem lay with the impractical expectations of its members. For example, a member, having paid his 5/- annual membership fee was entitled to take two friends to the New Year's Day Highland Gathering, and that included even the friend's entry into the grandstand, without further charge. Why, it was asked, would anyone join up as a member and pay 5/- when, for paying 4/- at the gate, two non-members could gain admittance! However, instead of seeing the obvious way of overcoming this (i.e. by increasing membership fees or by disallowing members the privilege of bringing along two companions without any charge), the ensuing members' discussion, in fact, favoured *increasing* the privileges of a member! This totally unrealistic motion by members of bringing along not *two*, but *three* non-paying friends, would simply have increased the loss to the Society and, after some discussion, a compromise was reached whereby each member would be allowed to have two ladies given free entry to the grandstand.

It is interesting that when the Caledonian Society of Melbourne was being revived in 1884, the main cause for its demise after 1861, as can be seen in the following passage, was laid upon its failure to match membership fees with expenditures. A lesson Comunn na Feinne did not learn! See, for example, Alec H. Chisolm *Scots Wha Hae-The History of the Royal Caledonian Society of Melbourne*, Angus and Robertson, 1950, Chapter 3.

> Eventually, on 12th June 1884, a meeting was held in the Equitable Co-operative Society's Hall, Melbourne, for the purpose of reconstructing "the present Melbourne Caledonian Society" on "a more workable basis". ... Mr Munro said that various causes had united to bring the Caledonian Society to the verge of extinction; ... One of the chief causes of the Society's decline, Mr Munro added, was the smallness of the entrance-fee and subscription-a statement which seems to suggest that the Scots of the day imperilled the existence of their Society by under-charging themselves!

Increasing memberships was, of course, another way to increase income. At a Comunn na Feinne meeting, held 14th October, 1892, A. V. Rankin, an office-bearer of the Society, moved that the nomination fee of 5/- should be abolished and that the 5/- subscription fee should be considered enough for membership and privileges. This was passed by the Society and led to an immediate increase in new members. However, the loss of the 5/- nomination fee would have cancelled out any immediate financial benefit. To increase profitability such membership growth would have to be both substantial and sustained.

Even before the Society's Hall purchase, the cost of improvements to the Society's original South Geelong grounds had added to the strain on the Society's purse. For the 1892 Gathering, for example, in an attempt to beat the dust problem at the South Geelong ground, the Society arranged to have a sound coating of tar laid down. The *Advertiser*, reporting on this December, 1891, meeting, added that, "a new room for the President [had] been erected [and] the grandstand painted, and steps [had been] taken to complete the decoration of the pavilion with green bushes, and to adorn the place with flags."

Such necessary expenditure did not always sit easily with the fact that Comunn na Feinne was, in financial terms, an organization which existed, literally, to give all of its income away. With such a philosophy, therefore, it should come as no surprise to find regular references to its precarious financial position. A sample of some 'bald' annual financial statements relate the story clearly enough. For example, in 1885 income totalled £255/0/2 with expenditure being £252/4/9. This left a balance of £2/15/7. In 1887, the balance of expenditure over receipts left a credit of £0/15/0. While this may have satisfied Charles Dickens' Mr Micawber, it was a parlous way to run an organization! The annual reports quite often, therefore, refer to the Society starting the financial year with an overdraft which needed attention and it was obvious that sufficient reserves were not being kept in order to meet contingent expenses! At a Directors' Meeting 25th September, 1883, for example, it was stated that the Directors intended making every effort to ensure the next Gathering was profitable, "for they desired funds to wipe off liabilities … incurred in the improving [of] the Society's property." This was a regular state of affairs and, almost a decade later, as the *Advertiser* reported, on 15th October, 1891, a similar financial situation still existed with the Society beginning the year with a bank overdraft of £31/13/9.

Given this pattern it was hardly surprising that in the twentieth century, on three separate occasions, Comunn na Feinne had to be saved from financial collapse by the efforts of 'sometime treasurer', George R. King, who was principal of the Gordon Institute. His abilities, together with his standing in the community and his political contacts, made him a trusted and competent worker on behalf of Comunn na Feinne. In the darkest days of the Society during the 1930s, he was entrusted with the delicate and sensitive matter of re-arranging Trusteeship of Comunn na Feinne's property so that no liability would fall upon specific members of the Society.

Occasionally, factors outside the Society's control did arise to create immediate problems. The Depression of the 1890s affected the whole of the Colony, reducing employment and wages among the working people of Geelong and district. This, in turn, was affecting the gate-takings, donations, and the growth of membership, but the Society, it was urged, should show its most determined face at such times. Hence, at the meeting held on 14th October, 1891, it was suggested, because of the Society's poor economic standing, and the economic crisis that existed in Victoria at the time, that the 1892 Games be cancelled. This proposal was rejected. It was argued that with new measures in place to reduce costs to members, and the public, and with all pulling their weight as far as the annual Gathering was concerned, a successful New Year's Day Contest could be delivered. From the various comments made at this meeting there was obviously a fair degree of 'fist-pumping' taking place! Hardship for Scots, it was inferred, was a test of spirit and brought out a renewed determination to face problems, not with hopeless resignation, but with a belief that they could overcome them. Comunn na Feinne members were urged to show this spirit and to wrestle the present conditions to advantage. The *Advertiser*, in a supportive piece, duly praised this determination to continue in the face of the general depression and the "grit" which would carry the Society forward, "against any odds."

The precarious state of the balance sheet demonstrated how much the Society still had to rely upon the good-will of sponsors and donations from the succession of Chiefs and other office-bearers and patrons over the years. The Treasurer's report of the year's income and expenditure was not exactly encouraging and showed that "grit" was only just prevailing! The receipts from all sources had amounted to £238/0/9, including £92/0/6 as gate money, and the expenditure was £251/5/0, leaving a [deficit]." Despite these shaky figures, the Treasurer tried to sound an optimistic voice regarding the future of the Society and its activities. The spirit of the Society's slogans was again appealed to as ensuring a way through the hard times. The Depression, it was pointed out, might even benefit Comunn na Feinne, as those who normally left Geelong for the holidays would, through budget constraints, remain at home and "patronize the local Gathering," There was, therefore, every reason to be optimistic! But these were 'Pollyanna' economics; the Society finished the year some £13 in debt and subsequently had to cancel the 1894 Games. Rumours that internal disruption followed this decision led to speculation that dissidents would form a new Society, and this is explored later in the Chapter. Such financial brinkmanship explains why the goodwill of the Chiefs, office-bearers and patrons was sometimes necessary to keep the Society afloat!

By 1895 the *Advertiser* announced that Comunn na Feinne was a "rejuvenated organization" whose aim was to bring the Society up to date while not entirely leaving behind "the distinctive features of a Caledonian festival." With a parlous financial situation – the balance sheet showed a balance of less than two pounds – the Directors nevertheless opted to press ahead with a New Year's Day Gathering for 1896. It was to be business as usual!

The switch to the Geelong Agricultural Show Grounds for the staging of the Highland Gatherings, starting with 1897, proved to be popular with the public. The Gathering that year was the largest in 15 years. However, despite increased numbers, the takings left Comunn na Feinne coffers with a £25 loss and with the President appealing to all members, "to put their shoulders to the wheel." It was obvious from this that the 'success' of a New Year's Day Gathering, in terms of numbers attending, or even in the amount of appreciation expressed for the Programme of events, was no guarantee of financial 'success' or stability. There was an understandable tendency to deem ventures successful if they drew, and pleased, good crowds, even if they incurred financial losses.

Throughout the 1890s, a trend emerged which saw other Comunn na Feinne activities during each year subsidizing the losses incurred by the Highland Games. This was a decided change, and the Society began to look more and more to activities beyond its annual Highland Gathering to generate funds for its charitable and other ventures. The costs of staging the Games, more often than not, exceeded the gate takings, and the need for such cross-subsidizing was clearly illustrated each year. But at every opportunity, there were those who also sought to 'talk up' the Society on the basis of the attraction it had to the public. It was only the most supreme optimist who could regularly praise it on its success when the financial statements were showing no evidence of the Society's economic improvement. For example, at the Annual Meeting of the Society, held 16th September, 1899, the Report on the previous games was prefaced with a self-congratulatory pat on the back. Activities during the year had delivered them a slight profit and this resulted in an overall credit balance of £16/14/11. That the President could congratulate Society members on "the flourishing state of the Society" may, indeed, have been the clear result of looking at life through the wrong end of the telescope! But his report then assumed a rather pessimistic tone lamenting the days now gone when wealthy patrons financially supported the Society with great liberality. The obvious conclusion was that members would have to step up to fill this loss of revenue. This meant, at the very least, an increase in membership dues and in 1901 this was again brought before the Society, at the annual Directors' meeting of October, 1901.

The meeting took place amid a very confident and buoyant mood. A debit balance of £15/8/11 at the beginning of the year had been turned around with a Bank Balance now showing £63/10/0. Mr G.R. King, now temporary treasurer again, was singled out for praise in contributing to the success which had met the Society's year. The matter of membership fees was again raised and dampened the euphoria a little! It was proposed that the fee should be increased to 10/-. Another proposal suggested that membership should be 5/- with a further fee of 5/- to gain entry to the games. Such a move, to the *status quo ante*, would hardly attract new members as the ordinary spectator could gain entry to the Games without having to pay the 5/- membership fee. Once again members wanted value for money from their dues, and the yardstick for this was their 'privileges' on New Year's Day. It was obvious that there was no real agreement and the Society, in true Scottish Presbyterian fashion, set up a sub-committee to look at solutions, including any changes to the Society's Constitution which might be necessary to bring the Society into the new century and, more importantly, to render it financial – with members wanting this without paying for it!!!

As well as membership fees, the related issue of membership numbers arose regularly at Society meetings as the question of finances came to be addressed. Among the schemes used to encourage membership, which the *Geelong Advertiser* reported on 12th September, 1912, was the use of prizes for those who signed up the most members in a year.

With such a struggle from year to year to fulfil its financial commitments, it may seem to have been reckless for the Society to venture out on a scheme, the acquisition of a permanent home for itself which, for some years at least, would have greatly increased the Society's indebtedness. From the time of its inception in 1856, Comunn na Feinne had never had a home to call its own. It had met in a series of Hotels, the Mechanics' Institute rooms, the Exchange Building and anywhere else it could, 'lay its head.' However, as we have seen, in 1912, the President, Dr John Small, announced the proposal to buy the Society its own building which would be its permanent home. The old St Andrew's Presbyterian Church in Yarra Street was subsequently purchased. Certain changes had to be made to the building – over time it was renovated and extended, and adjoining land was acquired – all of this adding substantially to the debt into which the Society had entered. It now became clear that there was an even greater focus on money-making on the part of Comunn na Feinne's governing committee. The purchase of the building which became Comunn na Feinne's 'home' came, later, to be regarded as a means of bringing in a steady source of income by renting it out. This desire to squeeze every last penny out of the renting out of its Hall went as far as the Society, in 1933, tossing its own pipe band out of the Hall where it conducted its teaching and where it practiced, in order that the Society could hire out the space to rent-paying clients! In fact, the Society was so short of available cash that it had to hold a concert and biograph performance at the Mechanics' Institute on 16th October, reported the following day in the *Advertiser*, in order to raise funds, "towards defraying the expenses" of their own Pipe Band which was shortly to compete at South Street,

Ballarat.

Another sign of the economic problems, later to dominate the Society, was an appeal made by the directors directly to members at the annual general meeting of 6th October 1914, and reported in the *Advertiser* the next day, to double the amount of their subscriptions and if they did so the amount would be sufficient, "to wipe out the deficit existing on the Hall." Although the balance sheet, presented to the 1914 general meeting, showed an income for the year from all sources of £2,443/15/4, the expenditure had also been heavy and amounted to £2,440/9/11, "which left a credit balance of £3/5/5." The largest drain was, of course, related to the Hall debt, but the period of the First World War, necessarily disrupted many of the events in which Comunn na Feinne had engaged and which had brought in funds. The loss of so many members and supporters through enlistment meant that Pipe Band competitions, and events reliant upon male participation, could not be continued as before, and this was to the detriment of incoming funds.

The end of WW1 in 1918 did little to restore financial stability to the Society. Its annual meeting on 29th October, 1925, sounded an ominous warning regarding the persistence of the Hall debt which had been increased when the Society decided to purchase additional land from St Andrew's Church, to extend the Hall. Despite, on several occasions, appealing to Society members and supporters to make it their pledge to clear this debt, social and economic circumstances limited additional donations and the debt remained looming over the Society. What was also clear was that, unlike the earlier years of the Society, there were now few wealthy patrons to step in and 'save the day'. The Ladies' Committee, which had worked hard at reducing the debt, had recently held a successful Scottish Fair, and again received thanks from the annual meeting for the work they did on behalf of the Society.

All of this contributed, it seems, to the decision late in 1929 that there would not be the annual Highland Gathering on 1st January 1930, and no date was given when it might be revived.

From the announcements made throughout 1929 by the President of the Society, Charles A. Smith, it was clear that Comunn na Feinne was set to pursue a policy of holding social events as regularly as once a month. These nights had proved to be popular with the public and had also been a means of raising funds in order to keep the Society afloat. Furthermore, the lettings for the Hall were proving to be a 'money spinner' for the Society and, with the relinquishing of the annual Musical Competitions (the Eisteddfod), the Society could now expect an extra two months, or more, for which it could let the Hall at a profit. Rental from the use of its Hall was already bringing in a reasonable income for the Society and it foresaw that the Hall lettings were an effortless way to raise revenue. This mind-set, no doubt, had a large influence upon the Society's decision to relinquish its annual Eisteddfod.

The slow recovery of Comunn na Feinne after the war has already been noted, and the effects of the world-wide depression of the late 1920's made debt reduction a difficult task for the Society. The annual Highland Gathering, whose overall financial history had been one of just breaking even or of suffering a financial loss, as well as being very labour intensive, was dropped. The announcement of the 'postponement' of the New Year's Day Highland Gathering for January 1930 had, by the end of that year, come to mean that it was cancelled for good, despite some insincere commitments that it would be revived, 'sometime in the future' or 'maybe' or 'perhaps' or 'when the time is right.' The President's announcement of the cancellation of the 1930 Gathering, made on the last day of the year, was inexcusable, for the Games had long been the Society's signature event and such a late cancellation unfairly affected a large number of athletes. It seems likely that the President, Charles A. Smith, was working to another agenda regarding the Society's future direction.

The Directors' Meeting on 2nd September, 1930, continued the familiar theme of looking at ways and means of generating income and, significantly, also demonstrated the dependence there was upon rental from the Hall in keeping them 'afloat'. The financial report showed that the Society's overdraft had been reduced by £150 and that its Hall continued to be in demand for letting. The *Advertiser*'s report, the following day, said that the Society considered this as being, "a satisfactory position". At the Annual Meeting, on 16th September, 1930, reported in the *Advertiser* the next day, the Financial Statement, discussed at the 2nd September Meeting, was submitted for approval. Ominous signs were the considerable writing down of the Society's assets, "in compliance with the financial depression everywhere", and the bank's response to the size of the Society's overdraft. But, in spite of all this, the balance sheet was considered the best submitted for years! This was due to the close attention which had been paid to the finances, and, in part, "from letting the Hall, which continued to be in exceptional demand." The treasurer's report also singled out the Ladies' Committee efforts in fund-raising.

> The year commenced with an overdraft at the bank of £548/8/8, which has now been reduced to £442/0/0. This result has mainly been brought about by the splendid efforts of the Ladies' Committee, and the increased revenue from the Hall. The arrangements made for an additional overdraft at the bank last year up to £550/0/0 has now been withdrawn and the overdraft is now £400, which must not be exceeded. You will also note that the excess of assets over liabilities has been further increased notwithstanding the further writing down of assets.

The restrictions, imposed by the bank, on the level of overdraft the Society was allowed, suggest that the obliging bank was showing not a little nervousness! The Hall rental had shown a remarkable increase from £98/0/0 in 1928 to £213/0/0 in 1929 and, in the current financial year, 1930, to £322/11/9. It was obvious to the Comunn na Feinne executive, if the Society was to survive financially, that the outside use and rental of its Hall would have a large bearing upon this survival. The Pipe Band (despite having been put out of the Comunn na Feinne Hall), was coping, and it hoped to be in another 'home' before long. The President, Charles A. Smith, somewhat hypocritically, said, "We all recognize that the band is a 'great asset' to the Society and we congratulate them on their valuable work." Not "great" enough, however, to maintain their space at the Hall!

The Ladies' Committee was again given the recognition due to their hard work. Such praise makes the dismissal of the Ladies' Committee in a re-organization of the Society a few years later, hard to understand. As well as holding dances, fetes and stalls, the Ladies also catered for other organizations whose meetings were now being held at the Hall.

> We have to again express our thanks to the Ladies' Committee for the excellent work carried out both from the financial and social point of view. A special effort was made by holding a fair and a Queen Carnival competition which raised, altogether, the sum £184/13/7 which, with other amounts handed in, makes a total of £195/2/7. The Directors place on record their appreciation of the efforts of the Ladies Committee.

As a further fund-raiser, the Society decided to re-instate the "old time" annual Haggis Supper nights. These had always been a popular feature and a date for 27th November 1930 was set for this entertainment. However, in the midst of the cheering there were the bare statistics which showed membership at very low levels with their fees amounting only to £27/11/0. The report stated the obvious.

> This is far from satisfactory, and to the incoming [office-bearers] a director should be appointed whose sole duties would be to attend to member subscriptions and keep a proper list of same. The report added that, the social functions during the year had been "fairly well attended.

The leadership seemed unable, or unwilling, perhaps, to connect these falling numbers with the absence of the traditional annual New Year's Day Highland Gathering. Despite this, however, the Society continued to trust that rental from the Hall would save it. The question that was not asked was, "saving it for what?" While the Society's overdraft of £548/8/8 had been reduced to £442/0/0 by the end of 1930, largely as a result of Hall lettings and the outstanding revenue raising efforts by the Ladies, what was not factored into the treasurer's report was the outstanding interest payments due to the debenture holders. Some of this debt dated back to the purchase of the Hall in 1912 and most of the creditors were, or had been, Society members! Debenture debt was an item which was kept separate from the financial sheet and it was to cause some extra headaches later on when the debenture holders, not unreasonably, were apparently demanding their payments.

The annual New Year's Day Highland Games was cancelled for the second successive year, but the Scottish Concert on New Year's evening, in 1931, was held as usual, and at this some vague reference was made to the possibility of there being a Sports gathering at Easter, 1931. Whether this was to be a Highland Games or just a general sporting activity was not spelled out and, in any case, it did not eventuate. The *Geelong Advertiser* found the concert a far cry from the standard which used to fill the night with song, piping, dancing and humorous artistes. Apart from an exhibition of Highland Dancing, xylophone playing and mouth organ music, and some help from humorists from Melbourne, the concert was described as very lack-lustre. Financial constraints seemed to be reducing the former emphasis which had once been laid on excellence. The social calendar for the year, however, was quite full, with events such as a Robert Burns' night on 29th January, 1931 and another social night, Comunn na Feinne's Highland Ball, to be held on 7th May, 1931.

A Directors' meeting on 4th September, 1931, prepared the agenda which was to be taken forward to the Annual Meeting due to take place 22nd September, 1931. The financial position, as reported at the Annual Meeting by J. Angus Laird, the financial secretary, offered some encouraging news. It was suggested that a Haggis Supper be held 30th September, 1931, to which representatives of all kindred societies, as well as prominent citizens of Geelong, would be invited. Part of this reaching out to 'kindred societies' was an indication of attempts to establish friendly relations with the Geelong Caledonian Society and the Geelong Scottish Thistle Club. As we will see, the call for unity between these Societies (perhaps even for their amalgamation), made on many future occasions, was thought to be necessary for the survival of each and for the well-being of Geelong!

Reports from the social secretary indicated the emphasis that was being placed on fund-raising activities. As well as the usual New Year's Day evening Concert and the

Robert Burns anniversary event on 26th January 1931, Peter York, the social secretary, reported that the monthly social events were growing in popularity. The Highland and Thistle Balls were reported to have been financially successful and it was considered that they could be held yearly. The Ladies' Committee was heavily involved with the catering at such events and it was obvious that the Society had come to realize that it could save on costs when dispensing with the need to hire professional caterers. It was also agreed to hold an annual Haggis Supper. The Hall Committee reported that £84 had been spent on improvements to the Hall, especially to the kitchen, although roof repairs would have to wait until the coming year. The Pipe Band committee was able to report that the Band had secured the Drill Hall in Myers Street, "at a low rental", for its practice on Thursday nights. There was little doubt that the Society looked to the Hall as its financial 'golden goose'. The treasurer reported that there had been a slight recovery in membership numbers with the total now standing at 81. However, the improvement in the financial position was, the treasurer reported, "mainly due to the popularity of the Hall which is largely sought over." To all intents and purposes, the Society was now not much more than a dealer in the rental business!

Despite the optimistic tone of the various reports, the 'shaky' financial position continued to dominate Comunn na Feinne's concerns. It had good reason to be worried as the overall financial state of the Society continued to worsen and it was announced that the Trustees, under instructions, had sold part of the Society's property (land on the corner of Yarra and McKillop Streets). The treasurer reported that this had, "reduced the liability on the mortgage of £700. The Trustees on your behalf have undertaken to pay off the balance of the money, £200, by yearly instalments of £40, the first instalment to be paid on 1st July 1932. By disposing of this land, the total saving of interest [on the mortage] would be £45." This arrangement meant that the Society would be committed to repaying this debt at least until 1937!

The sale of part of its property seemed a drastic action, given the Society's view that it was the property which formed its main asset in borrowing negotiations and that, from at least of part of it, valuable revenue was received through Hall rentals. Comunn na Feinne regarded its property as bringing about its financial salvation, but there appears, possibly, to have been pressure from the Bank re the Society's liability with a suggestion, perhaps, that it do something to lower that liability. There was also another general appeal to the membership to cooperate (or, as some members were to see it, to accept changes without question), with what the Society was doing, and to help restore the Society to a sound financial position. The various reports presented at the meeting seemed to indicate that Comunn na Feinne had managed to stabilize itself and halt further membership erosion, but these encouraging signs had not yet translated into any substantial debt reduction or to the restoration of what had been its main drawcard every New Year's Day, the Highland Gathering!

A reduction of £9/5/0 in its overdraft, enthusiastically announced at the 1932 annual meeting, was hardly something worth shouting about from the housetops, and the Financial Secretary, J. Angus Laird, reported that the financial situation of the Society had not really improved from that of the previous year. However, despite the wider State, and national, economic conditions, which also affected the local Geelong population, there did not seem to be any immediate financial threat to the Society. The value of Comunn na Feinne's assets hugely dwarfed the mortgage still owing on the building. Hall-letting was bringing in a steady income, with the Hall being fully utilized by community groups, and regular payments were being made to reduce the mortgage, which should have kept the bank happy. Charity and volunteer communal services were, by now, not major features of the annual reports nor a concern, it seems, of the Society's hierarchy.

Comunn na Feinne's next Annual Meeting for 1933, held on 26th September, had a smaller attendance than the previous year, but it was reported that 27 new members had been signed up. The continuing failure to attract members in large numbers was still a concern for the Society and it again raised the matter of reducing membership fees. It was stated that many Scots and descendants of Scots in Geelong would be pleased to join the Society but could not afford to do so. J. Angus Laird, reported that not much had changed in the Society's financial state over the past year. There was, however, some better news when it was reported that a more harmonious relationship had been established with the Geelong Caledonian Society. The year thus ended with some encouraging news to the effect that the situation had not worsened, although with no real indication that the Society was fully out of its financial difficulties. The need to sell part of its property the previous year did reduce the bank debt and save on interest payments, although divesting itself of part of its asset holding suggests an act of desperation and an indication that full recovery was not yet on the horizon. There was also the issue of outstanding debentures, and the debt accruing on these, about which no action had yet been taken.

In the early years of the 1930s there seemed no immediate, or threatening, fiscal Sword of Damocles yet perceived as hanging over the life of the Society. Very shortly, however, it became necessary to consider that steps be taken to re-arrange the responsibility of the debt away from individual trustees and onto the property itself. The foregoing 'optimism' regarding this as a possible solution to the Society's troubles would suggest that factors, other than financial ones, might also be operating to bring about the collapse of the Society. In fact, it was to become increasingly clear that the President, at least, probably saw this financial maneuvering as a necessary step towards a total shutdown of the Society. There were, however, other realities, such as are presented in the following section, which point to practical reasons for the Society's demise which are unrelated to what may (or may not) have been the President's own desires to see "an end o' it".

2. Burden of Multi-Activities

For much of its life, Comunn na Feinne operated, basically, as a 'not for profit' organization which spent all of its spare income in doing a wide variety of 'good works', as well as paying its bills of course. It undoubtedly had stretched itself almost to the breaking point. It had relied, for its first 60 years, almost entirely upon membership fees, gate-takings and commissions from booth holders, registration fees from competitors and private donations from sponsors, as its main sources of income. The total of its prize monies more often than not exceeded what was taken at the gate. While many of its prizes, by way of trophies, were gifted by benefactors, the monetary prizes, which were small by comparison to what was offered by other Caledonian Societies, still had to be increased each year to attract enough serious contestants.

Its income from other sources, such as the holding of concerts, socials and dances, once expenses were met, was supposedly ear-marked for charitable purposes. The Society had, over three decades earlier, endowed a Hospital bed which still had to be financially supported, and it also acted as a 'welfare agency' for sick and out of work members. Its role in providing for Aboriginals, although by the 1880s no longer a great expense, its educational programme and its night school project, along with support for the town's Orphanages, constantly added demands on its purse, and its manpower. While some of these responsibilities were removed in the face of State intervention in such areas as education and pensions for the elderly and for invalids, the Society embraced more and more activities and introduced more and more events at its Gatherings, all of which also added a strain on the funds. It also placed a strain on manpower. All of these events had to be organized, supervised and judged by members and volunteers. Many of its members were also involved with other Volunteer movements in Geelong and this put further strain on manpower.

As we look at the history of Comunn na Feinne, it becomes obvious that its activities continued to widen as the decades went by. It sought always to have a certain sense of novelty with its New Year's Day Highland Games and thus there was an ever-growing number of events included in the programme. Some of these 'bombed' and, after one appearance, were never seen again. The Grand Tournament "à la Eglinton" was a good example of this, as was the Maypole Dancing event; but many others were added to the programme and remained, at least for several years, if not permanently. The increase in the number of events meant, of course, the greater need for manpower to organize and run them. This role was carried out by some of the office-bearers, members and volunteers along with some help from other organizations. But it was also the case that as more professional associations arose to govern and regulate an increasing number of the Society's sporting, musical and dancing activities, so too was there the increasing requirement to use professional judges and handicappers as well as for acceptable tracks for athletics and bicycle races. However, it was not only the foregoing needs which Comunn na Feinne was facing. For example, a report covering the bicycle races at the 1922 Gathering suggested that some bicyclists themselves were aiming to give future Comunn na Feinne Gatherings a miss on account of the poor cycle track which they had encountered. Some bicycle contestants from Werribee, as reported in the *Werribee Shire Banner* on 5th January, 1922, expressed this threat following the 1922 Comunn na Feinne Gathering.

> Mr J. Abbs secured a nasty fall in the two-mile bicycle race, when making his sprint, which he looked like winning. Accidents were frequent in the cycling events and many of the riders stated their intention of giving the oval a wide berth in future, unless something is done to improve the tracks.

These stresses and strains, under which the Society was labouring, were brought very much to a climax by the ever-growing demands which some of the Regulatory Bodies were placing on it. As the growing membership of athletes, musicians and dancers took place within the relevant regulatory bodies, so more and more 'controls' were put into place which organizations such as Comunn na Feinne were 'forced' to accept. These included the provision of regulated Athletic tracks and Cycle tracks as well as the payment of judges and handicappers. Athletic and cycling tracks, which had to conform to the rules of the new professional associations, had to be laid, all adding extra expense to the Society. If this sort of action was not undertaken by Comunn na Feinne, then the relevant regulatory bodies failed to recognise the competitors' results and could even ban the contests from taking place. If anyone doubted the resolve of the Victorian Amateur Athletics Association (V.A.A.A.) in these matters the example of its suspension of amateur athletes who, without seeking permission from the V.A.A.A., took part in a charity event at the Police Carnival in November, 1928, would have removed such doubts. These athletes from "the Melbourne University Athletic club and other clubs" were banned and then, following suitable attitudes of contrition, were reinstated at a meeting of the V.A.A.A. on 21st December, 1928. It was a chastened Melbourne University Athletic Club, therefore, which meekly applied to the V.A.A.A. "for permission to conduct a series of relay races ... at the University Oval on March 2nd 1929."

Societies such as Comunn na Feinne quickly had to fall into line, too, or risk the non-appearance of athletes or musicians or other contestants or judges or handicappers, at their sporting or musical contests. This was made clear in a blanket warning issued by the Victorian Amateur Athletic Association regarding Comunn na Feinne's New Year's Day sports in January 1929, as recorded in the *Australasian* 29th December, 1928, and served as a 'threat' to sporting organizations generally, and to intending athletes. "Members of the V.A.A.A. clubs are advised that the amateur events advertised to take place at the Comunn na Feinne sports at Geelong on New Year's Day have not been sanctioned." In other words, compete at your own peril!

Even traditional Scottish events such as tossing the Caber, throwing the hammer and putting the stone became subject to regulation. Comunn na Feinne would not have forgotten, either, that several of its post WW1 attempts at staging large scale Brass Band Competitions, which would have made the New Year's Gatherings a focus for Brass Band events and, eventually, for the Australian Brass Band Championships, had been wrecked by Brass Band Association rulings relating to the participation of certain Brass Bands. Compulsory membership of regulatory organizations, which meant membership fees were necessary both for athlete and musician, as well as for the Comunn na Feinne organisation itself, was another cost to the Society.

With the emergence of Pipe Bands, and the formation of the Pipe Band Association of Victoria (P.B.A.V.) in 1924, standards were laid down as to dress and music and judging and who could or could not compete. For example, the Pipe Band Association flexed its muscles in 1925 when it refused to recognize female Pipe Bands or female solo pipers, or allow them to compete or to join, "all male piping associations", a situation which continued in Victoria until the late 1940s. This Association, as already noted, refused to grant recognition and support of the world tour, undertaken in 1926, by such a group of young women calling themselves the Australian Ladies' Pipe Band. Despite its triumphs overseas the P.B.A.V. mean-spiritedly refused to sanction a welcome home rally when they arrived back in Melbourne full of overseas honours. The P.B.A.V. also advised the Melbourne City Council, and the State government, not to give recognition to the Ladies' Pipe Band tour abroad or to give it an official street parade to welcome the ladies home after the band's successful series of performances in Scotland. The Band's triumphs included successfully competing at such contests as the famous Cowal Games at Dunoon and performing before the King and Queen at Braemar, as well as popular performances in other countries. Despite such triumphs as they had experienced, the Band, it would seem, was largely ignored and denigrated by P.B.A.V., and quickly disappeared.

The growing professionalism required to operate Athletic, Cycling, Pipe and Brass Band competitions, as determined by their respective Associations, was soon to spread to the Society's other competitions such as those carried out at its annual Eisteddfod. Comunn na Feinne held its Directors' Meeting on 26th January, 1928, to discuss its forthcoming Eisteddfod and, as we have seen, it had been informed in 1928 that it would have to register with the Performing Rights Association in order that the Society's musical items "might be legalised." Furthermore, the Board of Health also set down several demands upon Comunn na Feinne regarding safety and health issues involving its Hall which involved it in expensive additions. As we have noted, demands such as these, from the various regulatory and local governmental bodies, had been increasing and their impingement on Comunn na Feinne's running of its annual Eisteddfod, and the extra financial burdens which this involved, was probably the last straw for the Society's executive.

The introduction, in 1912, of the Society's Elocution, Singing and Dance competitions (Eisteddfod), which grew "like topsy," was perhaps the most extreme example of how success outstripped the Society's ability, both financially and in terms of human resources, to handle the 'giant' which they had created. From its small beginnings in 1912, the Eisteddfod had grown by 1929 to be a large, costly and somewhat unwieldly *culture fest*. The number of contestants had grown to exceed two thousand and it became necessary to hold these events over a period of many weeks, and this continued to increase each year. The numbers for some events continued to grow to the extent that Comunn na Feinne's Hall, although already increased in size, could not handle them, and the Society had to hire the Mechanics' Institute Hall to accommodate the overflow. This enlarging of its own Hall and the need to hire overflow accommodation, and the increasing prize monies, continually added more costs to the Society's already over-stretched budget, and enormous pressure on its volunteer 'workers'.

Although there was an entry fee for the audience, and a registration fee for the performers, these were quite small and did not come close to covering the overall costs to the Society. In short, the whole affair had come to be seen by some of the Society hierarchy as being burdensome. While some local businesses were donating monetary prizes and giving trophies, the income the competitions was generating, from entry fees, performance tickets and revenue from concert nights, nowhere near covered the costs incurred. Matters were not helped by the failure of the Geelong town council to render support, despite the increased business brought to Geelong by the competitors and their families. In cultural terms the Eisteddfodau were very successful, launching the careers of several internationally-acclaimed singers,* for example, but strains emerged within the Society concerning the cost and complexity of the annual event.
*[See for examples in Appendix 14 (a)]

With, or without full executive backing of the Society, the President, Charles A. Smith, finally announced in January, 1929, that it would be relinquishing the running of its annual Eisteddfod, as it was felt that, "the Society could no longer accept the financial responsibility of managing the burdens with respect to these Competitions."

From that time, Comunn na Feinne relinquished 'ownership'.

Clearly there were members who placed the artistic value of the Eisteddfod above its financial cost, and two leading Comunn na Feinne officials (its Chieftain and its Secretary), immediately helped a new group to re-launch the Eisteddfod under a new name. The Society's secretary, James Galbraith, felt so strongly about the matter that, after 30 years of service to Comunn na Feinne, he resigned and set about helping the new musical committee. Although the Chief, Senator Plain, also felt strongly about the matter and, although he also gave his services to the new musical society, he remained as Chief of Comunn na Feinne.

So far, we have noted that the financial problems of the Society, the continued growth in its social responsibilities, as well as in its other activities, were factors contributing to its demise. The various ways by which its Executive went about trying to solve these foregoing problems had consequences that affected the harmony within Comunn na Feinne itself. It is to the consequences of these tensions, as they undermined the unity of the Society, to which we will now turn as the third of the main factors which led to the decline and end of the Society.

3. Internal Tensions

It would be incorrect to assume that the decline of Comunn na Feinne, and its ending, lay solely with financial or even manpower shortage problems. It would appear that other frictions within the Society were also fairly long-standing. The visit of the Duke of Edinburgh to Geelong in 1867 had, without doubt, been responsible for the Society being unable to stage the January, 1868 Gathering, but it was no royal visit which led the Society to cede its 1870 Gathering to the Geelong Volunteer Fire Brigade. Some of its founders had left Geelong, and rumours abounded suggesting that the Society was about to disband altogether. In January 1870, for example, the *Advertiser* noted that some ex-members of the Society had informed it that they were unsure whether or not the Society still existed.

Thus, references to 'trouble in the camp,' which had surfaced as early as 1870, suggested that there was an instability in the Society which had little to do with finances. Comunn na Feinne, weakened by the death of some of its 'old guard' (no fewer than six senior members of the Society died in 1870 alone), and by the departure of others from the district, had been staggering on its feet for a period in the years leading up to the new century. The death of Robert de Bruce Johnstone, the Society's Chief, in 1881, was undoubtedly a serious blow to Comunn na Feinne which found itself faced with having to find a replacement for a very remarkable leader who had served the Society in a variety of roles since its inception.

The new Chief (Hon. Francis Ormond MLC), was a prominent businessman and politician and was very much to prove an absentee leader for his short time in office (1881-1889). The President (1876-1895), was Robert Shirra, the only founding member still active as a senior office-bearer in the Society, but he was no longer a young man. It had been he, along with Robert de Bruce Johnstone and Archibald Douglas, who provided much of the moral heart of Comunn na Feinne. They were the champions of such causes as improving education, caring for the Aborigines, supporting the hospital and the two orphanages and of establishing a working boys' night school. There were few, immediately, who emerged with the energy and the purposeful vision able to take their place. It was, perhaps, the loss of those who set the 'philosophy' of Comunn na Feinne at its formation, which also brought a loss, in part, of its 'noble' purpose as spelled out in the earlier chapters. This found the Society, in its later years especially, with only a weak grasp of what it stood for and where it should be going. Following Shirra's long tenure, two other Presidents came and went in quick succession before there was a measure of stability in the form of Dr John Small, elected President in 1902.

When hints of internal dissension filtered into the newspaper in the 1890s, the immediate future of the annual Gatherings did not look promising. For example, there were no planning sessions held in 1893 for the 1894 Highland Games. These meetings generally were for the purpose of 'fine tuning' the New Year's Day programme and promoting the Gathering through newspaper advertisements. The Society's continued silence on the issue led the *Advertiser* to draw its own conclusion, announcing on 30th December, 1893, that there was not going to be a Gathering on New Year's Day, 1894, as the Society had, "allowed [it] to lapse." The *Advertiser* further reported, on 2nd January, 1894, that the reaction of disappointment to the Games' cancellation was not limited only to the public but was also apparent within the membership of the Society itself, even among the executive! It was an obvious hint that things were not right within the Society.

Despite some public murmuring, the Society managed to keep a tight lid on any internal disharmony and the public had to wait for almost a full year before it got a hint of what was to happen regarding the 1895 Highland Games. The *Advertiser* reported on 3rd November, 1894, that a special meeting of the Society had been held on the previous evening to discuss "important business," and it was obvious that there appeared to have been some disruption within the Society which, according to the newspaper's sources, had been disbanded and then re-formed. The *Advertiser*'s report thus spoke of a "resurrected Comunn na Feinne" suggesting that the old one had died. Captain John Percy Chirnside, MLA, of the Manor, Werribee, was now Chief and it was anticipated that the New Year's Day Gathering would take place on 1st January, 1895. However, there was no explanation of what had happened to the previous Chief, Sir James Munro, or the President, Robert Shirra, or the secretary, Robert J. McDonald. Did they resign or was there a *coup d'etat* within the Society itself?

After a period of executive instability, it was not until the coming together of four remarkable and able men that Comunn na Feinne righted itself. Phillip Russell (Chief, 1896-1923), Dr John Small (president, 1902-1916) and James Galbraith (Secretary, 1900-1929), together with George R. King as occasional Treasurer, brought back to the Society its sense of purpose. This 'golden period', although bright, was to be relatively short and different challenges emerged with which the Society had to contend.

Once public transport became more efficient (especially train services from the 1860s), attractions such as the beaches and other sporting events, including international cricket and horse racing, did pose a measure of competition. But this was certainly not enough fatally to weaken the Society. There was still a large amount of local goodwill and support for the Society, but the days of attracting crowds of 10,000, or even 6,000, had long since past.

From the early decades of the twentieth century other challenges in the form of new Scottish organizations such as the Home Rule Movement, the Thistle Club and the Caledonian Society, appeared in Geelong and engaged in competition with Comunn na Feinne for members, supporters and funds. This was at a time when Comunn na Feinne itself was desperately seeking new members and trying to stem the loss of existing ones, and to become financially secure. The new Caledonian Society, for instance, attracted almost two hundred members within a week or so of its formation. That this was affecting attendance numbers at the Society's Games, as well as at its other events and, as a consequence, reduced its gate-takings, is alluded to in its annual reports.

The *Advertiser's* view that the popularity of Scottish organisations was waning is hardly supported by the evidence cited, for example, in Alec Chisolm's book on the history of the Caledonian Society of Melbourne (see above). The large number of similar groups which had sprung up in the country areas (such as Shelford, Buninyong, Ballarat, Colac, Bendigo, Maryborough), and the number of other kinds of Scottish societies (e.g. Caledonian Society, Thistle Club, St Andrew's Society and the Home Rule movement) which emerged in Geelong, and the virtual explosion of Scottish organizations all over Victoria in the early decades of the new century, would seem to undermine the *Advertiser*'s analysis.

The new century actually saw a genuine revival in the fortunes of the Comunn na Feinne at Geelong although WW1 (1914-18) was to curtail its activities and competitions somewhat. A large part of this revival, as detailed elsewhere, can be attributed to the trio of Phillip Russell, Dr John Small and Mr James Galbraith as well as the occasional support of Mr G.R. King. Under the leadership, and example, of these men, the Society was re-set on a sure track and rediscovered its moral purpose. The role played by James Galbraith, the long-term secretary of Comunn na Feinne, also deserves mention. No one worked harder, or with more efficiency and dedication than did he, and his long tenure in office provided a continuing link with what motivated the 'golden age'. As we have seen, these men mentioned above guided the Society through some of its darkest times. Unfortunately, Dr Small died in harness in 1916, but his example as President and his military service as Major-Surgeon from 1914 to his death in 1916, demonstrated his qualities of service and his adherence to the principles of justice and fair play.

Similarly, Phillip Russell, Chief of the Society 1896-1923, who was a most generous benefactor, also gave his services to the war effort. His long-term illnesses, which eventually led to his resignation in 1923, did not hinder his work during the war or his contribution, especially with financial help, as Chief of Comunn na Feinne.

An element of tension which, later in September 1929, came out into the open, and which adversely affected Comunn na Feinne, lay in its relations with other Scottish Societies in Geelong. We have already noted that guests at the inaugural meeting of the Caledonian Society included Comunn na Feinne's President, Charles A. Smith, and two Comunn na Feinne identities, John Kidd and Donald McDonald, who were announced as the new Caledonian Society's honorary pipers. Initially, therefore, there appeared the utmost cordiality between the new Societies, especially between the Caledonian Society and Comunn na Feinne. However, it became obvious that some disagreements at the time had been suppressed and, despite this initial show of sociability, relations with the new Caledonian Society quickly cooled. Tension between the two groups was soon to break out into the open when the Caledonian Society sought affiliation with the Victorian Scottish Union.

As we have seen, the Victorian Scottish Union, formed in 1904, was the umbrella organization for all Scottish societies in Victoria. Any Scottish Society wishing to affiliate with the Victorian Scottish Union (VSU) had to submit its application to that

Body for discussion and decision by all of the member associations. The Geelong Caledonian Society's application for membership with the VSU came before that body's 1929 Conference, on 18th September, at Daylesford. The case 'for' was led by Comunn na Feinne's Chief, Senator William Plain. Opposing the application was James Galbraith, the long term, and highly respected, Secretary of Comunn na Feinne. Interestingly, these men had held office together at Comunn na Feinne, and they had worked together to continue the Eisteddfod movement in Geelong after the Society abandoned it. But, standing before the V.S.U. members in September, 1929, at Daylesford, they were opponents. This episode provided a glimpse of some of the tensions which existed within the Society itself as well as between it and the Geelong Caledonian Society.

William Plain said he saw no reason for denying the Caledonian Society in Geelong the affiliation it sought. He believed Geelong was large enough to support two such organizations as long as they were run properly.

James Galbraith argued the opposite and opposed the affiliation. There is a hint in his case of residual grievances created by the apparent disruption of the Society of some years earlier. Galbraith, and probably others in the Comunn na Feinne would have agreed with him, saw the new Caledonian Society at Geelong as, "clearly a breakaway [group] from his own Society or, rather, the result of some members having been expelled from Comunn na Feinne." He also pointed out the practical fact that, given the problems of the world-wide Economic Depression which was affecting their community, Geelong could not sustain two major Scottish societies. He thus strongly opposed the granting of affiliation to the new Society.

In reply, William Plain pointed out that Geelong had a population of 50,000 and that the Geelong Caledonian Society would be operating not from Geelong itself but from one of its suburbs, Geelong West, and that there need not be any overlapping of roles or competition for members between the two societies. He, therefore, saw no practical reason for denying the Caledonian Society's application.

James Galbraith again "begged to differ" from his own Chief's position. The Geelong West argument was irrelevant, he said. The truth of the matter was, he reiterated, that this new society was nothing more than a disaffected group who had been expelled from Comunn na Feinne and who had now formed a rival body. He strenuously opposed the granting of affiliation to the new society, and would tell the Conference without hesitation that the plain fact was that the new Scottish arrivals in Geelong, as well as the local Scots, "were not joining up with either society or manifesting much interest in the Scottish movement at all."

Burt Stewart, President of the Victorian Scottish Union, "considered it necessary for the Union to always have the power of exercising its discretion in the matter, because there would be occasions when the formation of a second society would tend towards disunion instead of union, which was their aim in all Scottish matters." John Stewart, another speaker, considered that when an application for affiliation came in from a second society in the same district, the Union should get in touch with the existing society before admitting the new one to find out what was the exact position. Eventually an amendment to the motion was moved by W.D. Leckie (Royal Caledonian Society, Melbourne), to the effect, "that the constitution and attitude of the Union in regard to affiliation of new societies remain as it is." Thus, the VSU's constitutional position, as stated by John Stewart, regarding new societies applying for membership, was upheld. The vote of the VSU, therefore, was for maintaining the *status quo ante* at Geelong, and the Geelong Caledonian Society's application for membership was refused. The strained relations between the various Scottish societies was to continue until the very end, although the Caledonian Society may have had the last laugh outliving, as it did, Comunn na Feinne by some sixty years!

The three main factors for the decline of Comunn na Feinne, elaborated in this chapter, eventually came to a head with two momentous announcements made by the President, Charles A. Smith, in 1929. The first of these was the relinquishing of the annual Eisteddfod starting from that year! This decision revealed some of the existing internal tensions within the Society, showing that the move did not have unanimous support among the executive. For example, as we have seen, James Galbraith, the indefatigable long-time Secretary of Comunn na Feinne, who had shouldered much of the burden of organizing these Eisteddfodau, as well as his Comunn na Feinne duties, demonstrated his disagreement with the foregoing decision by resigning his position as Secretary of the Society. In place of Comunn na Feinne, a "Committee of prominent townsmen ... with James Galbraith as secretary," had been set up to conduct the Eisteddfodau. This tension, arising from the above-mentioned decision, as also noted above, can be seen in the example of Senator Plain, Chief of the Society, taking up the position of Chairman of the new body formed to take over the running of the annual Geelong Eisteddfod (now renamed the Geelong Competitions). Although he obviously did not support the decision of the Society to relinquish the Eisteddfod, Senator Plain did continue in his role as Chief of Comunn na Feinne seeing this as not conflicting with his new position within the new Geelong Musical organization.

How much of this resolution by the Society, to give up its annual Eisteddfod, originated with ordinary members and how much it came from the President and Treasurer alone is difficult to judge, given the absence of the official Minute Books. However, the decisions made by Galbraith and Plain to be office-bearers in the new Musical organization, would seem to suggest that the resolution had less than unanimous support, at least from the office-bearers. Furthermore, the reference by the President, Charles A. Smith, that a Committee "of prominent townsmen, quite apart from Comunn na Feinne" had already been formed to take over the Society's role as organizer and conductor of these Competitions, sounds a little too convenient. This would strongly suggest that a fair bit of secret pre-planning had already taken place behind closed doors, between Smith and what was to constitute the new musical organization, now known as the Geelong Competitions. The President's decision could, presumably, thus have been formulated without any discussion with the whole executive or with the members at all; the new Board of Directors being called upon merely to ratify a decision which they may have had no part in deciding. This was then presented to the members as a *fait accompli*. It would appear that the President, Charles A. Smith, might well have been working according to his own plan for the Society.

The whole affair was then justified when Smith argued that it was to the Society's financial advantage to free up its Hall for commercial letting. The recommendation to the Board of Directors was accepted by that Board at its March 1929 meeting. Given that the Musical Competitions were due to be opened later that month, on 19th March, 1929, and knowing that Geelong had possibly only one other suitable building for staging these annual Musical Competitions (the Mechanics' Institute Hall), which had its limitations, Smith quickly took advantage of the new Competition's need for a suitable venue by renting to it the Comunn na Feinne's Hall for the purpose of staging the competitions. These were opened by Hon. H.I. Cohen, MLA., KC., Minister for Education, on 19th March, 1929.

The severe decline in gate-takings from the last of the annual New Year's Day Gatherings was undoubtedly serious although the Games had rarely returned much, if anything, of a profit over the years. Some of this loss of revenue from spectators could be attributed to the economic depression with its concomitant unemployment and decrease in disposable income available to households to be spent on entertainment. This fall in numbers, therefore, need not be taken as a sign solely, in itself, of decreasing interest in the Games. It may be, therefore, that we have to look closer and ask, "what, if anything, was changing within Comunn na Feinne itself" which would help explain its retreat from what the public would have regarded as its 'flagship' event, its New Year's Day Highland Gathering.

The Society held a Directors' meeting on 7th May, 1929, at the Hall where Charles A. Smith, the President, chaired the meeting before a good attendance. The financial state of the Society was discussed and some optimism was voiced as to its financial position. A Highland Ball was also being proposed for some later date in the year. The meeting also indicated what direction the Society would now be taking in terms of its social events with a concentration on less expensive and less demanding activities, but ones which were designed to return a profit. Monthly socials had already been announced and, following some discussion, a Highland Ball was proposed. It was clear that dependence upon the Hall to generate finances was increasing – it was already permanently booked four nights of the week - and this had become Smith's driving passion.

The Society's annual meeting was set for 11th September, 1929. Elections for office-bearers would be held at that meeting and it was anticipated that a keen contest for positions would ensue. Perhaps some of the tensions were dissipating as only the new secretary, James R. McDonald, was elected in place of James Galbraith who had resigned; all other positions being unchallenged. It was pointed out that applications for Hall rental were solid and that revenue from these rentals was expected to increase.

The largest attendance for some years was present at this Annual Meeting, and the mood was one of confidence. The financial position was said to be "much improved", receipts from Hall rental being "more than double those of previous years." The members, greatly encouraged by this, unanimously adopted the report. A social evening followed and it was announced that such social evenings were to be held regularly. The policy of 'bread and circuses' was, apparently, not dead!

The mood present at the annual meeting was, however, to change somewhat when the eleventh-hour cancellation of the 1930 Highland Gathering caused ripples within the Society, and outside it! Not only had Charles A. Smith, President, not given any reason for this, the fact that it was announced on the last day of the year meant that it would be too late to do anything about it. It would seem to some that this late announcement was deliberate on the part of the President. The *Advertiser*, on the 31st December, 1929, voiced what it claimed was the general disappointment of the people of Geelong and said that other groups, had they been told, would have been prepared to take over the running of the Gathering.

> Men who take a prominent part in bicycle racing stated on Monday that if they had known in time they would have been pleased to have undertaken the responsibility of carrying on the sports.

The timing of President Smith's cancellation announcement had, of course, precluded any such action as the foregoing. Was this a cynical decision taken by someone who, although President of the Society, was not a 'true believer'? The last of the original founders and organizers of Comunn na Feinne had long since died, although there were still a number of members and office-bearers whose time with Comunn na Feinne had overlapped that of some of the founders. They very much held the line of what Comunn na Feinne was all about and may be called 'traditionalists' in this regard. There also were, especially among reasonably recent members and supporters, some who viewed the Society as somewhat dated, an organization whose original 'charter' no longer represented 'modern' views of society or of appropriate social entertainment. These might be seen as 'reformists' within Comunn na Feinne and, probably, counted the President, Charles A. Smith, as their leading spokesman.

As the period of the 1930s unfolds we can see the position of each of these two groups becoming more pronounced and challenging. This difference becomes apparent in what might be seen as the focus of Comunn na Feinne activity. For example, as the *Advertiser* of 2nd January, 1930 noted, although the New Year's Day annual Highland Gathering had been cancelled, the New Year's Day evening concert was held as usual with the intention, again stated, that this would be just the first of such social evenings which would be held more frequently throughout the year. A new decade, a new 'vision' – and "de'il tak' the hindmost"

The 1st of January, 1930 thus began without the customary Highland Games, but the programme of events for the year sought to reassure supporters that Comunn na Feinne was still 'open for business'. However, it became increasingly apparent that the 'business' Comunn na Feinne would now be engaged in was that, principally, of money-making. It might be argued that this was hardly new as the Society had always sought the finances with which to maintain a wide range of charitable commitments as well as its public events. This new 'money-making' initiative by Comunn na Feinne, however, had less to do with supporting social concerns and more to do with simply financing its property debts. The Comunn na Feinne year of 1930 thus consisted of a series of events designed to provide entertainment producing a steady source of income with little overheads! One of these events consisted of a "Queen Contest" whereby each of the Scottish societies at Geelong would hold a competition to choose a "Queen" to represent them at the Highland Ball where the 'crowning' would take place. Altogether six Queens were to be chosen in this manner and out of these the Queen of the Scottish Societies would be chosen. The respective Queens representing designated groups were:

Queen of Comunn na Feinne	Queen of Scots
Queen of Heather	Queen of Caledonia
Queen of Thistle	Queen of Pipers

From some of the foregoing 'Queen' titles it would seem that a measure of peace had been made between Comunn na Feinne and the two rival Scottish groups in Geelong – the Caledonian Society and the Thistle Club. The departure of James Galbraith as the Society's secretary may have some bearing on this as it was Galbraith who had led the opposition to the Caledonian Society being recognised by the VSU. (Ironically, after resigning his secretary-ship, Galbraith's seeming cultural conservatism must have received a fillip when he received a letter, addressed to him as Secretary, from Marjorie Lawrence, an Eisteddfod protégé now singing on the concert stage in Paris.

Without too much to cheer them up, the Society eagerly accepted the good news of Miss Marjorie Lawrence's successful debut, as a 'pick-me-up'. Marjorie Lawrence had risen through the Comunn na Feinne annual Eisteddfod competitions to win many awards. With the aid of Comunn na Feinne, and other local sponsors, she had gone overseas to pursue an operatic career and, after some setbacks, it was announced that she had, at last, "made a successful first appearance on the concert platform in Paris. She was praised by her tutor, Madame Gilli, and M. Gaubet, the French conductor, paid her many compliments." This information, according to the *Argus* of 8th January, 1930, was contained in a letter received by James Galbraith, who had been secretary of the Comunn na Feinne Eisteddfodau. Galbraith was, of course, no longer secretary of Comunn na Feinne itself, although he retained his membership, but his organizational abilities were still valuable to it and he still, willingly, offered his services. He demonstrated this continued willingness to assist the Society, for instance, when he organized its concert on 7th October, 1930, "at which leading Scottish artistes would assist." His was a talent too valuable to the Society to lose and was one, ironically, in view of the new hierarchy's loss of 'vision', which came out of a sense of service!

The next two New Year days passed without any indication that the Highland Gathering would be restored, and it is clear from the annual programmes that 'for profit' social events were assuming greater prominence. A Burns' Night was held on 26th January, 1932, with much of the evening being engaged in 'talking up' Geelong, and hearing its leading local, state and federal politicians, who had been invited, mutually praising each other. It was largely left to William Plain, the Society's Chief, to remind the gathering of Burns' true worth and philosophy, and that Comunn na Feinne was founded to work towards fulfilling this humanitarian 'vision'. As the *Advertiser* reported the next day:

> Senator William Plain, in his toast proposing 'Scotland Land o' Cakes,' dwelt on the character of the Scotsman. Wherever Scots settled they were, he said, able to meet and handle the circumstances in which they found themselves. The spirit which Burns espoused was universal in its application and it was the Scots' responsibility to ensure this were passed on wherever they had settled.

It is clear from a cross section of Comunn na Feinne's programme for the rest of the year that revenue raising events, including the following, were taking precedence over any other activity.

Robert Burns' Night	26th January 1932
Highland Ball	7th July 1932
Thistle Ball	8th September 1932
Sir Walter Scott - centenary of his death	12th September, 1932
Kilties Ball	5th October 1932
Haggis Supper	30th September 1932

Continuing concern over the direction of the Society, and its on-going failure to attract members in any significant number, led the executive, in 1932, to consider further ways and mean, according to the executive's blueprint, of making Comunn na Feinne more relevant to the times and to the tastes of the public. A sub-committee was thus set up to look at the constitution and the whole structure of the Society itself. The 'reformist' Comunn na Feinne Directors met on 3rd September, 1932, when decisions were taken to reform the board. Efforts were made, in fact, to bring what the 'reformists' regarded as necessary structural changes to the Society to re-form it into a body suitable, in their minds, for modern times. This was never clearly explained, but it did become clear that business-style efficiencies were the broad aims, thus changing Comunn na Feinne from a service organization to that of a fully commercial entity. It was decided to reduce the number of members on the Board which consisted of 16 directors and 11 other office-bearers. This, it was claimed, made it too unwieldy to make sharp and quick decisions especially with there being some overlapping responsibilities between some office-bearers. The proposal was to reduce these numbers to make the organization leaner and more adaptable.

Significantly, the Directorate, which was to be reduced from 16 to 6 directors, would absorb the finance and social committees and was to be given "complete power." The Board was to include the Directors, the Chief, the President, the two vice-Presidents, the Treasurer and the Secretary (this latter position absorbing the social and financial positions). Weekly meetings of this body would be held with a monthly general meeting of members to keep them informed of the state of affairs.

Thus, a totally new 'lean' Board was to emerge from the 'wreckage' of the old. What seemed sinister to some members was the centralization of all power and all activities within the new reduced directorate. In an incomprehensible move, it was also decided to axe the Ladies' Committee. Given the regular praise directed towards this body, especially for its fund-raising abilities, it seemed decidedly odd that the executive should then turn around and abolish it! Again, there is the suspicion that the reformers did not want any 'independent' group within the Society which might be a focus of loyalty and dissent. Thus, the roles of the Hall Committee, the Pipe Band Committee and the Ladies' Committee were to be carried out by the new Board. A fresh election for the positions was to be held to bring the new structure into being with members having a free vote.

However, it was pointed out by the *Geelong Advertiser* that this election had the potential to raise the question of self-interest on the part of the electors when it came to voting. "An interesting situation may arise if some of the members on the board with the longest service, and who are the Society's financial guarantors, are not re-elected." In other words, if these men were not re-elected, who then would step forward as the new "financial guarantors?" Could the burden fall, perhaps, on the shoulders of the whole membership? Would the guarantors, if voted out of office, still carry the same fiscal responsibility? Such questions could influence the members, out of self-interest, into voting for those ex-directors who were the present "financial guarantors." At this point the *Advertiser* began to display significant insight into what was going on within the Society and its reports on the 're-structuring' meetings become fuller and more analytical. Following these announcements, it was further made clear that the new committee, "had taken charge of the Saturday night dances, and hoped in the near future to have them running as of old. The Pipe Band, it claimed, was now up to full strength and showed great improvement."

The changes to the structure of the Society did not meet with the approval of all members at the meeting. There were undoubtedly tensions within the Society, and the moves to reduce the number of directors, to amalgamate several responsibilities and to abolish some committees altogether, caused some members to have an uneasy feeling about what was really taking place. Overall, the process seemed, to some within the Society, very much like a grasp for 'power' by a small group within the executive. Such a suspicion that the executive was positioning itself as the only authority within the Society and, therefore, to become unchallengeable, and holding all the main functions of the Society under its control, was soon given voice.

Although the changes, both public and rumoured, had caused some muttering among the members, there was no outright dissent voiced at the Annual Meeting held on 13th September, 1932, when the foregoing changes were submitted for ratification. The proposal to reduce the board of directors did not meet with much opposition and the recommendations as to the reduced size of the Executive were carried. The meeting drew between 40 and 50 members and, perhaps due to its importance, it constituted the largest number at a meeting for some years. A special general meeting was to be held where it would be moved that the changes be given legal effect. When such changes then became constitutional, a new Board would be elected.

The President, Charles A. Smith, had sought to hold off any outbreak of dissent regarding the changes, explaining, "that it was in the interests of the members that the sub-committee had acted, and it was for members to decide whether the alteration should be made." Dissent was clearly not welcome, but it came anyway. Mr A. Campbell voiced concern about the centralization of power and, "suggested that the directorate was riding rough-shod over the rights of the members." William J. McLauchlan, however, made a spirited defence of the proposal suggesting that the reasons for the decline in the Society's fortunes lay in the administration and the apathy some within it had shown over the years. This charge hit a raw nerve with some longstanding members. Robert A. Henderson protested that he had been a member for 40 years and had never resorted to McLachlan's type of "destructive criticism".

The President, trying at all costs to avoid an open competition in verbal insults, sought assurances from those present that they would refrain from personal attacks and that all should work with each other to forward the interests of Comunn na

Feinne. Any chance of unanimity among those attending the meeting was soon disturbed by other angry voices. It was obvious that the dissenters had been in touch with James Galbraith, the ex-secretary of the Society. Galbraith, who was unavoidably absent from the meeting, serving as the Society's delegate to the VSU Conference at Maryborough, would no doubt have placed himself in the 'traditionalist' camp, and had obviously been giving the dissenters some advice.

Robert Henderson, for example, representing the 'traditionalist' position, pointed out that it was necessary when any proposed amendment to the constitution was made that a period of seven clear days' notice had to be given. In support of his point, Henderson quoted from a letter from Galbraith that, "all rules may be amended or added to at any special meeting of the Society, subject to specific notice of proposed alterations be given seven clear days before such meeting." As this had not been done, the proposed amendments could not be passed by their present meeting. William Miller replied that, of course, there was no intention of forcing such a change on the members.

The logic of the 'traditionalists' case was then obscured by an example of political 'double-speak' on the part of the 'reformers'. When the secretary, James R. McDonald, put Galbraith's constitutional point to J. Angus Laird, he, in turn, moved a resolution (seconded by James Black) that if the present meeting agreed to the changes then such changes would form part of a resolution in a more legal form at the next meeting of directors, and this would go forward to a general meeting which, at that time, could, if it wished, vote the measure down. This was agreed to, "without a dissentient voice." Some, no doubt scratching their heads as to what they had just agreed!

However, there were other decisions which were clear enough to elicit the voice of 'outrage', especially at the summary dismissal of the Ladies' Committee. Mr A. Campbell, for example, was shocked that one of the main, and one of the most hard-working bodies within the Society, providing a steady revenue towards reducing the Hall debt, the Ladies' Committee, had been abolished and no reference made to their achievements or to the reasons for such a draconian decision. With a moribund social committee, it was, he stated, the Ladies' Committee which had actually shouldered the hard work.

But then there was the voice of 'retreat' or, more probably, of sarcasm! William Campbell, one of the critics of the new powers, hastened to say that he did not for one minute believe that the directors were not acting out of the best interests of Comunn na Feinne. The President again appealed for calm and for the avoidance of any rift in the movement. And that was the end of 'revolt' – for the moment!

The meeting then went on to consider falling membership numbers. Given the economic impact of the Depression, it was reasoned that a reduction in subscription fees would result in increased membership. Robert Henderson moved a motion (seconded by William Miller) to this effect which was carried.

It is important to see how the *Geelong Advertiser*'s report sheds more light on this meeting. Although there had been no "active opposition" from a unified group opposing the proposals, the newspaper reported that the "opposition" actually had abstained from voting. The image of unanimity, therefore, was not an accurate picture of the situation which was far from clear. When the import of what the reduced directorate would mean, the opposition became more unified, more open and, more vocal. The social committee had felt itself constrained by a section of the directorate, presumably representing the 'traditionalists', in its ability to introduce changes affecting the original purpose of Comunn na Feinne. Its argument was that the Social Committee (comprising eight members) did the bulk of the work but could find implementation of their decisions, "hampered by the fact that the sanction of the full meeting of directors each month had to be obtained before any final action could be taken." What the Social Committee wanted, therefore, was to have a free hand. This would be delivered by reducing the Directorate from sixteen directors to a total of six. However, the true purpose of this reduction was only made clear when it became apparent that, "the social and finance committees" were to be merged into this new Directorate which would have total authority.

Further financial problems began to loom when it was reported that revenue from letting the Hall was falling. This demonstrated the obvious risk that lay in over reliance on one main source of revenue, namely Hall lettings. Obviously, the economic Depression was affecting this source of income upon which the Society had pinned its hopes of paying off its debt. The Treasurer's report showed that, after receipts and expenses, the Society still had a bank overdraft of £400/8/2, as well as an undisclosed debt involving interest payments to debenture holders.* However, it was optimistically stated, again, that the value of its assets over its liabilities, meant that the Society was in no imminent danger of financial collapse and that its foundations were secure.

*[This liability was, apparently, reaching dangerously high levels, but as it was not included in the Society's yearly annual financial statements, it remained largely unknown to members. The yearly balance sheet, therefore, never revealed the true extent of the Society's indebtedness!]

It was reported that, in the past year, activities had been run in the hope of increasing member interest, "but for some reason not understandable, the attendance [of members] had been far from satisfactory." It seems odd that obvious elements such as membership hostility, as well as apathy, were not considered as possible reasons for these poor attendances. Renewed efforts were to be made in the next 12 months to, "organize entertainments which would be more interesting and attractive to members." The 'reformers' also seemed to be looking in the wrong place for the answers to their other problems. It did not seem to occur to the new breed of office-bearer that the direction which Comunn na Feinne had been taking for some years under the Presidency of Charles A. Smith may have had something to do with this falling off of membership and interest. Indeed, there seemed to be no discussion at all of the impact of having jettisoned its New Year's Day Highland Gathering and its movement away from its foundational aims. Highland Gatherings, as can be seen from the flourishing Games at Ballarat, Castlemaine, Bendigo, and at other centres in Victoria, were not a thing of the past, and there had been no absolutely compelling argument for the abandoning of these at Geelong.

The General Meeting, promised by J. Angus Laird at the September meeting, was held on 11th October, 1932, with about 40 members attending. This was to decide on the outcome of the changes to the Constitution which had been proposed. The necessary election of office-bearers, including directors, was also to take place, and the number of directors elected would depend on whether the constitutional changes were ratified. It was reported that the position of Chief and that of President were not being challenged, and that Senator William Plain and Charles A. Smith, would, respectively, retain these positions. The other office-bearers' positions, once nominations had been received, were to be decided through voting by the whole membership present. Charles A. Smith, the President, advised the members that the Society was not going as well as it should, and this he attributed, for the umpteenth time, to the Depression. He said that improving the Society's situation lay behind the changes which had been proposed at the September general meeting. As promised at that meeting, the constitutional changes which, he believed, were in the interests of the well-being of the Society, were now to be put and voted upon. He appealed to the members to agree to them. The President, briefly, in a summary of the details, told the meeting what the changes proposed would mean for the running of the Society. The directors would have to meet weekly and the whole membership was invited to attend these meetings and to offer suggestions to improve the Society. However, the meeting would have no power to over-rule the new directorate's decisions!

The President then called upon J. Angus Laird formally to move, in accordance with the notice previously given, the adoption of the recommendations brought forward from the special meeting. Laird reported that alterations of Rules 8, 9, 10, and 13 would be necessary to affect the changes in numbers of office-bearers. The directors would be brought down to number only six. The other office-bearers would consist of Chief, President, two vice-presidents, honorary treasurer, general secretary, honorary Piper and immediate past President. The only nomination for the position of Hon. Piper was Archibald McLean. The proposal to reduce the number of directors from 16 to 6, as well as the other constitutional changes, were then put forward by

Laird as a motion and this was seconded, apparently by pre-planning, by James Black.

The President, Charles A. Smith, in an effort to allay the fears of some members regarding what these changes might mean, said that any alterations made by the meeting need only be in force for the next twelve months when it could be changed by the members if they so desired. This statement, whether deliberately or inadvertently misleading, was patently untrue. It was correct, that at the next general meeting, in 1933, members could change those who had been elected to their positions through the normal annual election. However, to change the Constitution again to what had previously existed, would require more than simply changing the office-bearers. However, with the President's assurance, and probably with some misunderstanding of what he meant regarding the term changing back, the meeting unanimously agreed to the changes to the Constitution.

Even if some members had not understood what was involved, the *Geelong Advertiser* had grasped the enormity of the changes that were being proposed. It also identified that the 'reformist' movement had been in existence for some time and had a deliberate objective of changing the Society, and that this latest achievement had been part of its goal all along. As we have seen, the alterations to the Constitution would result in a greatly reduced directorate which, merged with the social and finance committees, would hand to the 'reformists' "complete power". Controlling a small body would be easier than trying to control 16 directors whose sanction would be required before any changes could be made. What seemed to surprise the *Advertiser*, having reported some recent dissension within Comunn na Feinne, was the fact that there had been a unanimous vote for the changes!

The election, by ballot, for the vacant positions was then undertaken. The positions of two vice-presidents attracted nominations from William Stewart, James Black and James Galbraith. For the position of Secretary, the candidates were J.F. Ingram and Peter York, and for that of Treasurer, J. Angus Laird, Thomas H. Hiddleston and Robert Dawson. There were fourteen nominations for the six positions of director.

Alex McDonald	Arthur U. Shirra	William Drew
Thomas H, Hiddleston	James Black	David Sutherland
Victor G. McLean	James Galbraith	David Dawson
Peter York	Fred S. Marshall	L.S.D. Gordon
William McLaughlan	William Miller	

There seemed, on the part of the 'reformists', to have been some tactical withdrawals both for the directors' positions and for that of treasurer, in an attempt not to split the vote between so many candidates.

> Messrs William E. Drew, William Miller and Donald Sutherland had withdrawn their nominations for the directors' posts before the election. The three remaining nominees who were defeated were, James Galbraith, Peter York, and Fred G. Marshall … Before the election of the Treasurer, Thomas H. Hiddleston withdrew his nomination, leaving Robert Dawson unopposed.

The election for the vacant positions of Senior Vice-President and Vice-President was then undertaken. William Stewart was elected Senior Vice-President, but for the other position, James Galbraith and James Black tied in the number of votes received. These two names were submitted again to the ballot and James Black won by a small margin.

The general spirit of amity, which seemingly had characterized the meeting so far, started to crumble when the Secretary's position came up for ballot, revealing some of the cracks which existed within the body of the Society. A. McDonald objected to the candidacy of Mr J. Ingram for the position of secretary on the grounds that he was not a member of the Society. This then brought the previously disgruntled A. Campbell to his feet again, and once on his feet, he would not sit down! "A. Campbell rose to speak, and was referring to the excellent, but unremunerated service of the former secretary, when the chairman told him he was out of order, and asked him to sit down." Mr Campbell continued to speak, remarking that he did not see why there should be any objection to either of the nominees. He believed the two should go to the poll, and, "let the members decide."

The Chairman again tried for order and said to Campbell, "Will you kindly take the hint and sit down." Mr Campbell, not one to take obvious 'hints', reacted with, "I don't want any hints from you or anyone else. You are always giving hints." Then there was support for Mr A. McDonald's constitutional point questioning the candidate Mr J. Ingram's eligibility to stand for office. "Thomas Hiddleston said his opinion was that Mr J. Ingram was not eligible for the position."

> William J. McLauchlan then moved in accordance with his earlier suggestion that the Society should advertise, calling for applications for the position of secretary. The motion was seconded by Robert Dawson, and agreed to by a large majority, and it was further agreed that the President and the present secretary, James R. McDonald, should carry on until such time as a new secretary is appointed.

James Galbraith, the long-time and hard-working secretary of Comunn na Feinne, was defeated in his attempt to become a Vice-President and also in his effort to be elected a Director. It was noticeable, too, that a life membership had been handed out to Mr J. R. McDonald for his "valuable" service as secretary for four years, yet James Galbraith, who had served the Society for thirty years as secretary, and who had long been the undoubted 'engine room' of Comunn na Feinne, apparently received no such honour! It also seemed that long-standing office-bearers were being eased out of positions on the Comunn na Feinne Board, in a move to replace the 'traditionalist' section of the Society.

The ex-secretary, James Galbraith, had, of course, opposed the application of the Geelong Caledonian Society for membership of the VSU. He was undoubtedly seen as a 'traditionalist' and someone who would obstruct any 'modernisation' of the Society's activities such as the abolition of the Highland Gathering. He was also wary about having close relations with other Scottish groups in Geelong especially the Caledonian Society which, he had charged, was formed from expelled and disgruntled members of Comunn na Feinne. It appears, therefore, that part of the tension within Comunn na Society undoubtedly lay in the friction between the 'traditionalists' and the 'modernizers'. Having won the first round, the 'reformists' sought to chance their arm with further reforms.

The next proposed action of the modernizing faction, therefore, was totally to revise the Constitution of the Society, even to the extent of changing its name. These changes, were they to be accepted, would effectively mean that an altogether 'new' society was being proposed. This is clear from J. Angus Laird's proposal to the effect that the new Board seek to change, "the whole of the rules of the Society." Any dissent against this suggestion was tactically avoided by closing discussion of these matters and leaving it to the next Board of Directors (now of course greatly reduced!) to bring forward concrete proposals at the next general annual meeting sometime in 1933.

The new year again passed by without any mention of a Highland Gathering. It was obvious now that the Society had no intention of reviving the Games and any mention of them was dropped altogether from announcements by the Society. The New Year was ushered in on 1st January, 1933 with Comunn na Feinne celebrating in its own Hall while the Caledonian Society, according to the *Advertiser*'s report on 3rd January, held its celebrations at the Red Mill Hotel in Ryrie Street. It is significant that these two Societies held separate events. While Comunn na Feinne held a dance in its Hall, upstairs at the Red Mill Hotel, Ryrie Street, Hogmanay was celebrated in real Scottish fashion. "A very large attendance of old and new members and friends spent a most enjoyable evening." Piping, Scottish Dancing and Scottish songs were the main ingredients of the Caledonian Society's night at the Red Mill Hotel. The report on Comunn na Feinne's celebration, held in its own Hall in Yarra Street, was much more subdued with members dancing to the "delightful music of Harry Ritz's Orchestra" although, upstairs, there was something of a more traditional affair on 'auld year's nicht' for those who observed such things.

The Society held its first Directors' meeting on 4th January, 1933, where a programme of social events for the year was drawn up. A Burns' night, always a popular function, was to start off the year's activities.

> They discussed the upcoming Burns' Night, the speakers and the musical entertainments which would form the evening. At the close of the meeting the President, Charles A. Smith, extended to his fellow members of the Board the compliments of the season expressing the hope that the society's position

would show a great improvement during the coming year.

A. U. Shirra* reciprocated on behalf of the fellow directors.

*[This was the son of one of the Society's founders – Robert Shirra]

The Society celebrated Burns' anniversary on 26th January, 1933, at their Hall, but absent from the line-up of guests was any representative from the Caledonian Society. This would suggest that there still was not quite a harmonious relationship between the Scottish Societies at Geelong. Alexander U. Shirra, a member of the Comunn na Feinne Board of Directors, acted as toastmaster.

Perhaps as a sop to those disgruntled members within the Society who were nostalgic for the past, it was reported in the *Advertiser* on 29th January, 1933, that a list of past champions of the Heavy events at the Highland Gatherings was being prepared.

> At the request of George Worland of Winchelsea, and Cr. Alexander McLennan of Barwon Downs, James Galbraith is preparing a list of the men who, in his time, held the championship honours for the Stone, Hammer and Caber events at the Comunn na Feinne Highland Gatherings of past years. George Worland was the last to hold the title and McLennan's father was the former champion. The list, which James Galbraith is preparing, dates from 1856 to 1928. The first Champion was James Smith of Ballarat, but the Title was later wrested from him by John McLennan. Later came Peter Fleming of Newtown, who was the holder when the Highland Gatherings were discontinued in [1929] He retained the title for some twelve or fifteen years and is the only one of the four Champions who is still alive. A photograph of the four, taken when they were all together at one of the Society's Gatherings is to be enlarged and the President and Directors of Comunn na Feinne will be asked to accept it and hang it in their Hall among the many other pictorial records of the Society's activities.

The four ex-champions of the heavy events.
G.H. Worland, P. Fleming, J. Mc Lennan, J.H. Smith

The issue of divisions, not only within Comunn na Feinne itself, but also between the various Scottish Societies in Geelong, was again brought to the fore by yet another appeal for harmony between them. It was in the form of an appeal, reported in the *Advertiser* of 16th February, 1933, by Cr E.A. McDonald, Mayor of Geelong, that the various Scottish Societies should come together and that he would be willing to officiate at a meeting of all Scotsmen in Geelong to try and broker a situation of harmony between, "the various factions at present evident in Geelong and District." The Melbourne newspaper, the *Age* of 16th February, appeared somewhat more optimistic, regarding this meeting when it reported that, "Comunn na Feinne, the oldest Scottish society in the district, will consider a motion that the amalgamation move should be persevered with." However, despite this optimism, nothing seems to have been concluded.

Comunn na Feinne continued with its programme of social events throughout the year and held its Annual Highland Ball 24th June 1933. The Hall was suitably and magnificently decorated and the Ladies provided a "sumptuous supper." The Ball was just another event in the Society's calendar of social entertainments used as a means of raising funds to keep the Society afloat. The zeal which inspired a collective social conscience among the members of Comunn na Feinne seems now almost to have disappeared. It is also interesting that, despite having had their Committee dismissed by the Society's hierarchy, it was the Ladies who catered for the event!!!

Although Comunn na Feinne no longer conducted its annual Eisteddfod, which had produced so many talented men and women, it did continue to hold its programme of Pleasant Sunday Afternoon events at which it collected funds for its charities, and this seems to be one of the few references to the Society continuing with some community work. The guest speaker for one of the sessions in its 1933 programme was the President of Comunn na Feinne, Charles A. Smith. His subject was 'The Early History of Comunn na Feinne'. It was announced with the preface that the subject matter would be "of special interest to those who remember the old pioneers." Charles A. Smith's talk was due to be given on 31st July 1933, but it had to be postponed due to "inclement weather". It was also announced, in conjunction with this event, that a full set of minute and membership books were still held by the Society and would be used by the President to illustrate his talk.

Comunn na Feinne's annual Thistle Ball produced a 'Snow Scene' at Comunn na Feinne's Hall on 24th August, 1933. A "snowman" and "a veritable storm of snow descending", were just some of the features of the event reported in the *Geelong Advertiser* the following day. A vote of gratitude was given to the Ladies for organizing and catering for the Ball. "After supper, dancing was resumed amidst 'falling snow', the effect being most novel and entrancing."

The annual general meeting, held 22nd November, 1933, produced changes to its Board. The secretary, Thomas Goodall, who had only held office for less than the year, resigned and Peter G. Burns was appointed in his place. It is interesting to note that less than a year after the Society had reduced the number of Directors from 16 to 6, it did an about face and doubled the number of Directors to 12. This alteration to the

Constitution had taken place at an earlier meeting over which the President presided. The election for the sitting six positions, together with the additional six positions, was to take place on 12th December 1933 and nominations were thus called for. The Directors also discussed arrangements with the Women's Auxiliary* for a "Christmas Treat to be given to the children of members on Friday night the 22nd December, 1933, in the Comunn na Feinne Hall."

*[It would appear, too, that Comunn na Feinne realized the worth of the Ladies' input after all, and thus a Women's Auxiliary had been formed since the 1932 annual general meeting. This is witnessed to by the many references to the ladies having been responsible for, "organizing and catering" these social gatherings held at the Hall.]

The year had been full of changes for Comunn na Feinne especially with regard to the composition of its office-bearers and the alterations to its Constitution. There had been a reasonable programme of social events, but the Society seemed no closer to reaching a state of stability regarding its finances or its office-bearers or with the other Scottish societies in Geelong. The following period, until the outbreak of the second world war, is marked with little activity but with a sense of Comunn na Feinne merely marking time as it waited for the end.

Act 2 "Not with a bang" – 1934-1939

The period 1934 to the outbreak of the second world war in 1939 is sketchy, to say the least, as far as Comunn na Feinne activity and records are concerned. The *Advertiser* itself was unsure whether the Society still existed and was uncertain how to refer to it, whether in the present or past tense! However, the occasional references to activities suggest that some sort of temporary organization was still operating if for no other reason than to present an entity which was able to deal with legal and financial matters.

A calendar of events for 1934 was drawn up but it is unclear whether all of the social evenings listed actually took place as there seems not to have been a report on each of these in the *Geelong Advertiser* or in the *Carmichael Notes*.

25th January, 1934	Burns' Supper
12th June, 1934	Society's Annual Highland Ball.
26th September, 1934	Annual Thistle Ball.

The Society held its annual Burns' Night on 25th January, 1934, and about seventy attended, including a number of guests and visitors. After the welcome by the President of Comunn na Feinne (Charles A. Smith) the Haggis was piped in and around the room. The Women's Auxiliary catered for the night. Reflecting rising international concerns, Sir Thomas Maltby, addressing this Burns' Supper, regretted the "sad condition" in matters of defence existing for their district. Echoing some earlier Comunn na Feinne concerns of the previous century, he suggested the formation of a Scottish company which would help correct this neglect and appealed for someone of means who could cooperate with the government in providing uniforms for such a militia if it were formed. But for Comunn na Feinne, there was no longer a John Bell or a Phillip Russell willing to extend a financial hand.

Appropriately, at a Burns' Supper, there was an emphasis from several speakers on the necessity of the Scottish societies in Geelong to come together. This seems to indicate that the unity referred to at the 1933 annual meeting of Comunn na Feinne, where it was noted that there was, "harmonious relations existing" between Comunn na Feinne and the other Geelong Scottish Societies, had again been short-lived. However, in response to the Toast to 'the Visitors', it was John Sadler, President of the Geelong Caledonian Society, who responded, so there were at least some civilities being observed between those two bodies.

In their usual display of harmonious relationships with the Irish, the Geelong Hibernian Club was represented at this Burns Supper by its President, R.W. Dobson. It seems odd, as has been noted several times, that Comunn na Feinne should have had such a close and sustaining relationship with the Geelong Irish from its beginning yet, in these latter years, could not seem to maintain such a relationship with fellow Geelong Scottish Bodies! Pressing home this desire for unity, Cr E.A. McDonald, "said that he was looking forward to the day when Geelong Scottish Societies would join under one banner, "an' brithers be for a' that." He felt sure that such a day was fast approaching, and he hoped to see the union effected during the Centenary year.* He spoke of the work of the pioneers of Victoria, remarking that there was cause to be particularly proud of the womenfolk, and also referred to, "the part played by Comunn na Feinne in the history of Geelong."

*[This was the Centenary of the founding of the colony, Port Phillip, in 1834 (named Victoria, from 1851).]

The *Geelong Advertiser*, on 10th April, 1934, carried a report of a Directors' meeting under the banner 'Back to the Comunn na Feinne'. The Society had been established in December 1856, therefore the anniversary of its founding fell in that month. It was planned that the Society would hold a 'birthday bash' to celebrate that December anniversary. There was a hint of a possible "big sports meeting" being held in conjunction with this event, but there was no definite commitment to this. A Committee was formed to make all the necessary arrangements and this was to begin with the holding of a social gathering for members on 26th April, 1934.

However, the month of December came and went, without the great reunion sports day, referred to earlier, actually taking place. In fact, Comunn na Feinne does not appear even to have held its traditional Hogmanay concert nor the annual New Year's Day evening Scottish Concert. There is evidence, however, that Comunn na Feinne did hold a Highland Ball in 1934.*

* [In Mr Carmichael's miscellania there is an invitation card from Comunn na Feinne to Mr Ronald H. Carmichael requesting the pleasure of his company at the Grand Annual Highland Ball to be held at C.N.F. Hall on Tuesday 12th 1934. It is signed by the Hon. Sec. P.G. Burns 64 High Street, Belmont.]

There were some less than joyous occasions, too, in 1934. This year witnessed the death of two notable Comunn na Feinne members. The Society sadly announced the death of Piper John Kidd, the 'hero of Dargai'. Kidd had given the Society years of loyal and selfless service in his capacity as Piper at the Dancing Competitions, at the New Year's Day Gatherings, and as the tutor of the Society's Pipe Band. Members of

Comunn na Feinne attended the memorial service as did representatives of the Limbless Soldiers' Association and the British Ex-Services Legion. The service was held at the Belmont Presbyterian Church on 3rd June, 1934. The death of yet another Comunn na Feinne stalwart, James Robert McDonald, was reported as having taken place on 5th November, 1934. He had been secretary and a long-time member of Comunn na Feinne and Mayor of Geelong West.

Piper John Kidd

The Hall Debt

From what follows, it would seem that something drastic had taken place as far as the Society was concerned and its functioning was somewhat sporadic; for example, Charles A. Smith is described as "acting President". (*Carmichael Notes*). It is also clear that the financial difficulties of the Society were again paramount. Once more the call was for George R. King, principal of Gordon Institute, and thrice financial rescuer of Comunn na Feinne, to assist the Society. (*Carmichael Notes*) At a meeting of Comunn na Feinne members and life members, on 5th February, 1935, a discussion took place regarding the financing of the debt still owing on the Hall. According to the *Advertiser* on 6th February 1935, the meeting established a committee, to be chaired by George R. King, and consisting of Senator William Plain, George Raymond King and Cr Alexander McLennan, the latter in an advisory position, to, "investigate the general situation in regard to Comunn na Feinne, such committee to report to a further meeting."

The annual meeting of the Society was to have been held on 5th February, 1935, but had been adjourned to give time for this aforementioned committee to prepare a report. Amalgamation of all the Scottish Societies in Geelong still seemed to be an option for the Society. Charles A. Smith, the "acting President" of the "reconstituted" Comunn na Feinne, had called a meeting to seek a solution to the Society's problems in which he referred to previous attempts to unify all of the Scottish organizations of Geelong - none of which had succeeded. Perhaps this is not to be wondered at given the Comunn na Feinne's financial straits! The other Societies would have thought twice about an amalgamation which would, perhaps, have had them sharing Comunn na Feinne's debt. However, Smith tried once more, arguing that the survival of Comunn na Feinne might lie with the unity of all the Scottish organizations. Given that the various Scottish societies of Geelong had not yet even met to discuss the situation, it seemed unrealistically optimistic for Smith to report that, "he confidently expected, that at an early date, proposals will be submitted with a view to bring the various bodies into unity." (*Carmichael Notes*)

Before the meeting had adjourned, there appears to have been a renewed effort on the part of the 'traditionalists' to return the Society to its roots, at least as far as its Scottish sporting, dancing and piping events were concerned. For example, the *Geelong Advertiser*'s 6th February revelation that moves were afoot, "regarding the negotiations for re-constituting the Society", drew some comments from older members. Cr Alexander McLennan, a member of the special committee, recalled the fact that his late father, John McLennan, was outstanding as a competitor in the hammer, stone and Caber events. These trials of strength and skill, he said, were still popular in the country, and it was felt that, together with pipe music and dancing, they should form the nucleus of an attractive programme, and that the managers, "should seriously consider the resumption of the annual Highland Gathering." A further report appeared in the *Advertiser* on 8th April, 1935, suggesting that talks were being held, "with the possibility of reviving interest in the affairs of Comunn na Feinne."

While the Society had engaged in many other worthwhile activities it was, nevertheless, its annual New Year's Day Highland Gathering which had given it its identity and which was one of the main focal points of the year for Geelong out-door entertainment. This suggestion, to restore the annual Gathering, seemed an obvious move for the Society to have taken, albeit having to offset marginal profitability against raised public profile. It is difficult to see why it did not grasp this, other than the fact that the President and the 'reformists' within the Society were committed to a solution which lay, almost totally, with the rental of their property. Re-introducing the Highland Games, it was suggested, could possibly give the moribund Society a 'kick' in the right direction. One of the problems of the 'reformers' within the Society, and especially some of those holding office, was not that of ignoring necessary reforms, but in believing that everything about the Society needed reform! A clear case of, 'throwing out the baby with the bathwater.'

The *Geelong Advertiser* seemed suspiciously well-informed about the special committee and its inner workings and it was, obviously, being kept 'in the know'. This probably arose from the need to prevent any false rumours about the future of the Society getting out of control. The newspaper reported that the special committee had met initially to conduct a basic survey of the condition of the Society and the main problems facing it. Having considered its immediate state, the committee proceeded to draw up an "outline" plan, "not only for re-constitution, but also for the bringing in of various interests."

It was clear that the main obstacle was the debt which still hung over the Society, and it was proposed that steps be taken, "to provide for incorporation whereby the property itself would carry the liability." The *Advertiser*, on 23rd February, 1935, reported that if this could be achieved it would largely remove the main hurdle in the way of solving the Society's problems.

The matter of the re-arrangement of liabilities was officially brought to notice at a meeting on Saturday 6th April, 1935, at which the Trustees, together with the committee set up to investigate the situation, were present. The matters discussed were then, on the evening of 8th April, 1935, brought before a full Comunn na Feinne Board meeting. The special committee reported that it considered, "the aggregation of liabilities, debentures and otherwise, was a serious block to the general development of Comunn na Feinne, and considered it desirable that immediate attention should be given to finance."

The sub-committee identified two major financial problems. The first of these related to the burgeoning debt, especially that owed to debenture holders. This had never appeared in the annual financial reports of the Society and to members, and some of the executive, therefore, the extent of the Society's financial liabilities was never taken into account when the various reports were delivered at successive annual general meetings.

The second major problem, now revealed, related to the fact that the interest guaranteed to those who had loaned money to the Society had, apparently, not been regularly paid. The total was now so great that the amount owing to these debenture holders exceeded the assets which the Society had to cover their liabilities in this direction. The sub-committee's recommendations included that representation should be made to the Government seeking wider powers over the Society's estate to change this financial situation, including shifting the liabilities onto the property itself.

The sub-committee then met again with, "trustees of the Society, J. Angus Laird (Chairman), Charles A. Smith and James Galbraith, on Saturday afternoon, 13th April, 1935, to discuss the report. The *Advertiser* carried the discussions in its Monday edition, revealing that the outstanding liabilities "showed an extended (sic) debenture list." This was the first time that such a fact, and such a list, had been made public!!!

Reading between the lines, it seems as though some debenture holders may have been getting a bit 'nervous' about what they were due and becoming less confident in the Society's capacity to pay them and were, perhaps, demanding what was owed to them. The property had not been mortgaged but had been partially financed by an overdraft from the bank together with the aforementioned individual 'loans' from members. It was these two sources of debt, said King, which had to be tackled. The debentures had been issued without any assets and in the opinion of the sub-committee, the property itself should carry all liabilities, "rather than individual members of the Society." The sub-committee felt that it was this, "individual responsibility" which, to a certain degree, had impeded recent development of the Society.

> The sub-committee therefore recommended that the Government be asked to consider proposals which would give effect to this opinion." The *Advertiser* reported that, after discussion, the proposal was considered satisfactory by the Trustees, "who unanimously agreed to the recommendation and who [would] support the proposal" to be submitted at the general meeting to be held that night. References were made at the meeting to the valuable work rendered by J. Angus Laird and, "a resolution was carried appreciative of these.

The *Advertiser*'s report of the actual meeting, which appeared in its issue the day following, shows how accurate its information was as to the findings of the special committee. Although the report was described by George R. King as an interim one only:

> It was agreed … to recommend that representations should be made to the Government, whereby extended powers governing the control of the property should be sought to enable a loan to be effected on the property, the value of which affords a very substantial margin [and] Mr King added that should the recommendations contained in the report be adopted, the committee and trustees should then cooperate and approach the Minister for Lands. If permission to put the recommendations into effect was not forthcoming from this source, then other means would be sought. However, he considered that if all members cooperated in the matter, legislative assent was likely to be obtained. Contingent upon Government support for such a proposal, it was agreed that the society should be reconstituted.

In fact, responsibility for the Society's debts remained with the Trustees until 1946 when the property was finally sold. Although the aim was for the Society to divest itself of the responsibility for the property, it was also intended that the Society be "reconstituted" and, therefore, kept alive. In 'business as usual' fashion, social fund-raising events continued to be held. The Comunn na Feinne Ladies' Auxiliary held a Derby Whist evening at the Hall on 24th May, 1935, with another being planned for the following month. In addition, the Society's social committee had also begun a series of Euchre Parties on 11th June, 1935, with the enticement that, "seventy-five percent of the takings would be paid out in winnings. Admission price was 1/-." What the 'unco guid' of earlier days would have thought about the Society's descent into 'soft-core' gambling is not difficult to imagine!

The Geelong Pipe Band*, doing its bit for the cause, held its third annual Kiltie Ball on 17th July, 1935.

*[The Comunn na Feinne Pipe Band officially underwent a name change in 1935 when it was renamed the Geelong Highland Pipe Band, which continues to this day.]

After what seemed like a long period of silence regarding the Society and its activities, it appeared that some sort of 'temporary' organization was still operating in 1936, as can be seen from invitation cards sent out regarding social evenings. It was clear from the wording of these cards that financial matters still dominated Society discussions and that there would be a dish of 'reality' served up along with the entertainments.

> Mr and Mrs James Galbraith request the pleasure of Mr and Mrs Carmichael to an evening on Saturday September 19th, in the Comunn na Feinne Hall at 8pm.

However, as can be seen from the programme, the event was not all, 'on pleasure bent.'*

> ***At 8pm. - A short business meeting concerning the future of the C.N.F.**
> At 9pm - Songs etc., by old and young members of the directorate, Ladies' Committee & Pipe Band. Please bring your songs and have a happy evening.
> At 9.30pm - Dances old and new.

Signs of activity are few and far between in 1937, and events seem to be in the hands of other than any member of the official social committee. For example, James Galbraith, since giving up the position of Secretary of Comunn na Feinne, and failing to get elected to any of the other positions during the reconstitution of the Society, had no official role with Comunn na Feinne, other than as a member. However, he continued to be involved, apparently in a private capacity, in organizing events held at the Comunn na Feinne Hall. For example, although the Society had a social secretary, it was James Galbraith, according to the *Argus* of 24th December, 1937, who had organized the Burns anniversary supper for 1938.

> Mr James Galbraith is making arrangements for the celebration of the Robert Burns anniversary on January 25, 1938, and it is expected that a large gathering will be present at the Comunn na Feinne Hall.

This event did take place, according to the *Argus*, albeit on a later date in January to suit the convenience of the main speaker.

> Invitations are being issued by the Geelong Comunn na Feinne for a Burns night to be celebrated at the Comunn na Feinne Hall on January 27th 1938. The function was postponed from the actual birthday of the poet Robert Burns to allow the Rev. A. Boyd Scott, of Scots Church, Melbourne, to be present. It will be Mr Scott's first visit to Geelong.

The last social activity for which there is physical evidence seems to have been a Kilties' Ball held at the Society's Hall on 5th October, 1938. However, what seems, in retrospect, a 'last hurrah' for the Society's engagement with its own Hall, took place in July, 1939. Miss Marjorie Lawrence, who was set on her way to an international career as an opera singer by the Comunn na Feinne Eisteddfod, had given her farewell concert at Geelong on 18th October, 1928, after which she travelled to Europe for further training. Having achieved an international reputation, she returned home for one of her regular family visits and for a holiday. Comunn na Feinne was obviously still active in some form as it was able to muster a stirring 'welcome home' for Miss Lawrence. Her visit to Geelong in 1939 included giving a concert at the Comunn na Feinne Hall. Despite being crippled with polio, and being confined to a wheel-chair, she had continued her operatic career - although her roles were greatly restricted. Her incapacity, however, did not prevent her entertaining troops during the 1939-45 World War, both in Europe and in the Pacific, nor did it curtail her role as a Red Cross emissary. On one such engagement of the latter, she was again able to visit Australia, including Geelong where, reported the *Argus* on 12th July, 1944, she was, as always, enthusiastically received.

Marjorie Lawrence's 1939 return coincided with Mr Robert Menzies' visit to Geelong where he was giving a talk at the Society's Hall. The opportunity proved too good to pass up by the satirical column, 'The Passing Show'* by 'Oriel,' which appeared each Saturday in the Melbourne newspaper, the *Argus*. The issue of 29th July, 1939, carried the following humourous verse for the occasion.

> You can tell a Scot when he opens his mouth they say, but when Bob Menzies and Marg (sic) Lawrence were both on the bill at the Comunn na Feinne we wonder if the Geelong Scots were canny enough to tell which was a Scot, if either? Here is what we think and as we fall short of being a Scot, we are not taking any chances on pronouncing Comunn and the rest.
>
> The Lowlander Scots at Geelong
> Want rather a lot for a diner (sic),
> And you must be a star to get very far
> At the Comunn na Feinne.
>
> Though Menzies cracked hearty as ever
> They greeted his wit with disdain.
> For he spoke like a weed from south of the Tweed
> At the Comunn na Feinne.
>
> But they put down their haggis and listened
> When Marjorie sang them a line,
> And they shouted "Encore, she's bonnie, she's braw,"
> At the Comunn na Feinne.
>
> For she sang with a true Hieland burr
> Which could hardly have been any plainer
> If she had been a Scot (which of course she was not),
> At the Comunn na Feinne.

*[This was a column in the *Argus* newspaper started by John Sandes (1863-1938),

when, along with two other journalists on the Melbourne *Argus*, E. T. Fricker and D. Symmons, he began a column called 'The Passing Show', in 1891 under the pseudonym of 'Oriel'. Sandes wrote it from 1891 until 1903 when, presumably, one of the other founders took it over. It was, "a popular and durable Saturday feature which brought together topical gossip and whimsy, conservative social and political comment, solemn ethical speculation, and light and serious verse."]

Act 3 Final Curtain 1940-1946 – "Not with a bang but a whimper."

The second world war broke out on 1st September, 1939 and it appears that Comunn na Feinne suspended most of its activities between 1939-1945. Its doors were never opened again as Comunn na Feinne but, ironically, in a piece of circular history, the buildings reverted to being a 'House of Prayer' when the Lutheran Church purchased the property in 1946, and so it remains, today, 'a witness to the Light'.

The absence of Society records for the years between 1939-45 make a re-construction of this period in the life of Comunn na Feinne very difficult. Even the *Carmichael Notes* are silent for most of these years. Unlike the WW1 period, the Society apparently did not operate during WW2 but, according the *Argus* on 19th December, 1941, it allowed its Hall to be used for various war-time support agencies.

> The City of Geelong first aid post is now on a war footing. The post has been extended. In the Comunn na Feinne Hall on Thursday night it was announced by Dr Arthur Moreton that the post was now ready for 24-hour service.

If anything decisively presaged the end of Comunn na Feinne it was, surely, the death, in 1945, of its long-time secretary - the veritable 'engine-room' of the Society for three decades, Mr James Galbraith.*

> On the 25th July, 1945, at his home 165 Myers Street, Geelong, James beloved husband of the late Marjorie Marie Galbraith, and devoted father of Alfred (sic) V. Galbraith, Walter J. Galbraith, Ettie (Mrs W.H. Orchard), James C. Galbraith (deceased), Janet (Mrs E.E. Coleman) and Doreen F. Galbraith, aged 79.

It is comforting, perhaps, that he did not live to see the sad end of the Society nor the sale of the Comunn na Feinne building in May, 1946.

*[James Galbraith's full obituary can be found in Appendix 3 (b) Short Biographies.]

Following the 1939-45 war, it seemed that no attempt was made to revive Comunn na Feinne or its annual Highland Gathering although at least two Caledonian Sports events were held at Ocean Grove in the later 1940s. Unfortunately, in the newspaper reports, there is no mention of who had sponsored these Games.

Whether or not Comunn na Feinne was active in an attempt to revive Highland Gatherings following the end of the 1939-1945 War, there is incontrovertible evidence that it was active in the sale of its property. As noted above, the Society reached an agreement to sell its land and buildings to the Lutheran Church at Geelong. To solve the debt crisis, it was decided that the Society's Property in Yarra Street would have to be sold. However, an unknown complication arose to provide a slight, but expensive, hitch in the process. It was discovered that Comunn na Feinne did not, in fact, hold title to the whole of the land on which the Hall stood and which had been purchased from St Andrew's Presbyterian Church in 1912. The Society was advised that the Hall also occupied a small piece of government land. Thus, it was required of the Society, reported the *Argus* on 7th March, 1946, that it first obtain title to that small piece of ground before it could proceed with its sale of the whole property.

> The Society's Hall in Yarra Street is built on a small portion of Crown Lands as well as on freehold land adjoining. Title in the Crown Land will be issued to the Society on payment of £900 to the State Treasurer.

The *Argus* added that the necessary parliamentary legislation was prepared for submission to the Victorian parliament.

> A bill which will enable trustees of the Comunn na Feinne Society, Geelong, to dispose of their property was introduced by Mr Galvin, Minister for Lands, in the Legislative Assembly yesterday... The Second reading debate was adjourned for a week.

*[This information regarding the Title not covering the whole of the Land purchased from St Andrew's Presbyterian Church did not surface in 1912 when Comunn na Feinne, in good faith, originally purchased the land and the buildings etc., from that

Church.]

The *Argus* reported a week later that the parliamentary process had given effect to the sale of that piece of crown land to the Society, thus allowing for the disposal of the total Comunn na Feinne land and buildings.

> The bill was sent on to the Legislative Council, Entitled, 'The Geelong Land Bill': The Legislative Assembly yesterday passed a measure to revoke the reservation of an area of land in Yarra Street, Geelong, on which is erected the Comunn na Feinne Hall.

Subsequently, an advertisement appeared in the Real Estate section of the *Geelong Advertiser* in March, 1946 inviting offers for the Sale of the Comunn na Feinne land and buildings.

"Comunn na Feinne – Sale of The Comunn na Feinne Hall"

> Comunn na Feinne Hall.
> Freehold property situated in Yarra Street, Geelong.
>
> Tenders are invited by the Trustees for the purchase of freehold property known as the Comunn na Feinne Hall situated in Yarra Street, Geelong. The land has a frontage of 98 feet 6 inches to Yarra Street, Geelong by a depth of 150 feet 7 inches. Full particulars and conditions of tender are available at the office of William M. Reid Pty., Ltd., of Malop Street, Geelong.
>
> The highest or any tender not necessarily accepted.
> Tenders close Wednesday First of May, 1946 at Noon.
> Harwood and Pincott, Solicitors for the Trustees.

On the 2nd May, 1946, Comunn na Feinne's property was bought by the Lutheran Church, Geelong.

> The successful tenderer for the building … the Comunn na Feinne Hall … was St John's Lutheran Church, the pastor of which is Rev. F.H. Schulze. An official of the Church said yesterday that as soon as conditions allowed, the existing building would be taken down and a modern building erected. In the meantime, services would be held in the present building.

On 11th May, 1946, a church official reported on the plans of the Lutheran Church.

The ecclesiastical architecture of Yarra Street will be added to when the congregation of St John's Lutheran Church, has completed its building programme on the site of the Comunn na Feinne Hall, for the purchase of which they were recently the successful tenderer. This will be the first Lutheran Church building to be established in the city area. For £3,150, which is subject to Treasury approval, the congregation has secured one of the best sites that could have been acquired for such a purpose. It will, of course, be impossible for the building programme to be put in hand for some time. When conditions permit, a complete transformation of the site will be made. The present building will be demolished and in its place, will be erected a Church, a Parsonage and a Church Hall*; until that happens the present building will be utilized to the maximum in connection with all church activities. Divine service will be conducted in the main hall, and the other smaller rooms will be used by the various societies associated with the Church. The upstairs portion in the front of the building will be devoted particularly to the use of the Young People's Society. It also is proposed to close in the stage and thus make another big room available for social work.

* [The Lutherans, as noted above, planned to demolish the buildings and erect a brand-new Church and Hall. However, as the following recent photograph shows, the structure remains today much as it was when the Lutheran Church purchased it, now over seventy-years ago.]

Conclusion

It is now seventy years since Comunn na Feinne officially closed and sold its home in Yarra Street. It is even longer since the last Annual New Year's Day Highland Gathering and the last Annual Eisteddfod were held. The name Comunn na Feinne, as far as Geelong folk in general are concerned, if it has any meaning at all, would probably only conjure up the hotel in their town which bears that title – albeit incorrectly spelled!!!

It is possible to find the names of past Presidents and past Chiefs from information held by the Geelong Historical Society and, if an enquirer is prepared to spend enormous amounts of time trolling through the *Geelong Advertiser* for the years 1856 to 1946, that enquiry will yield a good harvest of information – not to mention considerable eye-strain!

Bare facts, however, will do little justice to the Society or lay bare its many activities apart, perhaps, from its annual flagship events - the Highland Gathering and the annual Eisteddfod. Comunn na Feinne stretched itself across a wide range of community groups, and there were few voluntary organizations in Geelong which were untouched by it. Many of these activities are dealt with in Appendix 14 and, when taken together, broaden the picture of the extent of the Society's contributions and what it was hoping to achieve.

In keeping with part of its original goals, Comunn na Feinne had always striven, in whatever it did, to embrace the whole community and to have a positive effect upon it. This can be witnessed in its extensive School examination competitions and its annual Eisteddfod, as well as its multifarious charitable activities and work with volunteer organizations throughout Geelong and district. The Society's 'vision' of a unified and harmonious society was, of course, understood as requiring certain pre-requisites not the least of which included equal access to a full formal education irrespective of one's economic or social circumstances.

But equal access to education did not mean equal results from it. It was inevitable that Comunn na Feinne's system, although open to all, would produce some individuals who would outshine their contemporaries in whatever field was involved. Comunn na Feinne's commitment was not to producing men and women of an equal level of achievement in terms of abilities or aptitudes. It was proud of those outstanding individuals, from whatever field, who had succeeded. The Society's definition of 'Education' was, as we have seen, a very broad one. This was completely in line with its overall philosophy which was encapsulated in its Gaelic Mottoes and in its Charter. These contained commitments to a sense of equality, fair play and justice which would contribute to creating and maintaining a harmonious society where everyone would use their talents to the well-being of the whole community - local or national.

Thus, although outstanding individuals would emerge, the Society's 'vision' was that such people would use their special gifts for the good of the whole community. We have seen that its vision was of an education which would equip an individual to improve not only himself or herself, but the whole of the community. This meant, therefore, viewing 'education' as extending far beyond that which was understood, at the time, by the term the '3Rs'.

Appendix 14 reveals some of the talent which emerged from the Society's various educational endeavours including its Eisteddfod, with some of these individuals also included in Appendix 3 - Short Biographies. These categories of achievement ranged from the arts to medicine and from engineering to politics and from business to education. While Comunn na Feinne did not take credit for discovering the talent of the long list of individuals who had succeeded in their chosen field in the arts, sciences, medicine, law, engineering and education, it could reasonably and proudly claim, "that [it] had played a very important part in the shaping of that talent" through its wide educational activities, as well as by its monetary support.

Many of the roles originally filled with volunteers in the community, and inspired by the 'vision' of Comunn na Feinne, are now fulfilled by the work of fully professional utilities and paid individuals within the civil service or other official organizations. However, the 'spirit' of volunteerism, as promoted by Comunn na Feinne, is still very much alive in the many service organizations which continue to provide necessary help where needed. Whether it is through Rotary or Lions or Breakfast Club volunteers at schools or through countless other groups which exist across the community, the founders of Comunn na Feinne would be pleased to know that the 'vision' which motivated its activities from its beginning, continues to inspire present day individuals who, knowingly or not, are honouring the goals of the Society and are remembering, as did Comunn na Feinne members and supporters, "the fame of their fathers."

Appendices

All appendices and tables referenced in this work can be found online at
https://comunnnafeinne.wordpress.com/

ABOUT THE AUTHORS

Two of the authors, now retired, met while working at Deakin University - Kerry Cardell in Humanities and Cliff Cummin in Social Sciences.

They share an interest in migrant cultures, specifically looking at how such cultures respond when faced with the challenging circumstances of colonial life and its competing nationalities.

They have researched and written extensively on this subject and only rarely have they engaged in duelling!

Robert Bakker is many things; proof reader, tour guide, book reviewer, thespian, flautist, Cajon Box Drummist, lead-lighting artiste and tin snippist extraordinaire, to mention just a few. Being a co-author adds another string to a very well-strung bow and another arrow in an already overcrowded quiver.

www.ingramcontent.com/pod-product-compliance
Lightning Source LLC
Chambersburg PA
CBHW060417010526
44118CB00017B/2253